A Handbook on Drug and Alcohol Abuse

A Handbook on Drug and Alcohol Abuse

The Biomedical Aspects

SECOND EDITION

FREDERICK G. HOFMANN

*Professor of Pharmacology and
Associate Dean, Columbia University
College of Physicians and Surgeons*

New York   Oxford
OXFORD UNIVERSITY PRESS
1983

Copyright © 1975, 1983 by Oxford University Press, Inc.

Library of Congress Cataloging in Publication Data

Hofmann, Frederick G.
A handbook on drug and alcohol abuse.

Bibliography: p.
Includes index.
1. Drug abuse—Handbooks, manuals, etc.
2. Alcoholism—Handbooks, manuals, etc.   I. Title.
RC564.H63   1983   616.86   82-18930
ISBN 0-19-503056-7
ISBN 0-19-503057-5 (pbk.)

Printing (last digit):   9 8 7 6 5 4 3 2 1

Printed in the United States of America

PREFACE TO THE SECOND EDITION

The public reception of the original version of this work has been highly gratifying to me and to my publisher. As time has gone by, however, it has become evident that a revised edition of the work has become increasingly necessary. This edition is an attempt to meet that need; the first two attempts were aborted by personal illness.

I regret that Dr. Adele D. Hofmann, the collaborator on the original study, was unable to play such a role in the current one. Her contributions to the first study are indicated in the preface to it. It is clearly noted in the current edition where it was not possible to retain a contribution of hers intact.

And now it remains only to acknowledge once again the appreciable support and assistance of my editor, Mr. Jeffrey House. And so, once again, Jeffrey, thank you so much.

Columbia University   F. G. H.
February 1983

PREFACE TO THE FIRST EDITION

Persistent myths and unanswerable questions are among the most vexing problems met today in the study of drug abuse. The myths deceive both drug users and nonusers. Users have a regard for heroin and cocaine as unique drugs, for example, that is not warranted by the facts. Laymen and physicians alike have said that many heroin addicts use this drug not for the pleasure it brings but primarily from fear of the withdrawal syndrome; if so, we wonder why the numerous periods of abstention from heroin that usually characterize the life histories of chronic addicts are followed so shortly by resumption of heroin usage in most cases. The terrors of the narcotic withdrawal syndrome are mythologized by addicts. They describe withdrawal to one another as an unexampled period of pain and anguish, a view reinforced by lurid (and often substantially inaccurate) simulations of it in films and on television. Apart from emotional distress, which varies considerably from one person to another, the heroin withdrawal syndrome nowadays rarely exceeds the symptoms one has on the first day or so of a heavy cold; this is so because the grossly diluted heroin sold today is incapable of inducing anything more than a mild degree of physical dependence.

There are many unanswerable questions on the adverse effects of drugs, particularly the long-term consequences of drug abuse. Few people appreciate, however, how difficult and how costly it will be to answer them. To be able to answer questions about the causal role of drug abuse in the genesis, for instance, of chronic psychotic states or "drop-outs" from the mainstream of society, complex investigations will be needed which will require years for completion. Maintaining contact with the subjects of these studies over so long a span of time will alone be a formidable chore. If such a study of amphetamine usage were started today, a study adequate in scope and with satisfactory financial support, within ten to twenty years we should be able to say with some confidence what role the use of amphetamine plays, for example, in the development of psychotic states that last for months or years in some "speed freaks."

It would be appropriate also to anticipate that answers to some of the questions will be unobtainable by means of clinical research because the requisite experiments would not protect satisfactorily the welfare and rights of the subjects of such studies. With reference to the problem cited in the preceding paragraph, we clearly cannot assemble a group of subjects, obtain as complete a psychiatric evaluation of them as possible, and then administer amphetamine until each develops a toxic psychosis. Though such a study would permit us to relate prior psychiatric status to the resultant instances of persistent psychotic states and to settle thereby one of the fundamental unanswered questions pertaining to drug abuse, the design of such an experiment is morally repugnant. The clinical studies cited in this book date from approximately 1950 to the present. During that span of time, there have been pronounced changes in our views about acceptable forms of human investigation. There is no question whatsoever that some of the clinical studies described in the following pages could not be performed today because they would be regarded as ethically unacceptable.

Perhaps the most commonly voiced question that we cannot answer is, "Why do people start using drugs in the first place?" To which we would add, "And why do some abstain from drugs or abandon them after preliminary experimentation?" When the answers come, they will be given by psychiatrists, aided by sociologists in some instances. If it is agreed that drug abuse is characterized by the nonmedical use of drugs for the purposes of altering the user's mood, producing novel experiences, changing his perception of himself and the world around him, and/or enhancing his ability to function in settings such as social or sexual ones, it is evident that the mind of the user must be the primary investigative focus. We have touched on psychiatric matters in this book only to the minimal extent that we regarded as essential, for we are not psychiatrists. We are skeptical about the validity of "one-factor" explanations given so glibly by both physicians and laymen to account for the origin of drug abuse. Such factors as life styles in urban ghettoes, broken homes, turmoil over racism, and a foreign war have no doubt contributed to the spread of drug abuse—but to what extent? Why do some children raised in the grinding poverty of the slums escape drug abuse? Why do some from affluent middle-class homes where the family unit seems intact and loving succumb nonetheless to drugs? Studies of drug abuse should be broadened so that greater attention is given to understanding the individuals who escape.

Our goal in this book has been to present salient information about the biomedical aspects of the most common patterns of drug abuse in America today. We have emphasized what we regard as important similarities and differences among these patterns. We indicated the areas in which we regard the evidential support as satisfactory, areas where judgment should probably be suspended for want of conclusive data, and areas where we feel prevalent views are in error. We have urged the abandonment of stereotypes and have indicated repeatedly how diverse drug experiences can be and how widely the consequences of drug usage can vary. In place of simple generalizations that ignore inconvenient facts for the sake of a telling impact, we have tried to demonstrate the relationship of drug abuse with other biological phenomena, which resist discrete categorization and exhibit rather a continuous spectrum of characteristics, responses, and consequences.

The title of our book contains the words "drug" and "alcohol" because of the widely held belief that alcoholism and drug abuse are fundamentally different; they are not. Although there are significant differences in general social attitudes toward "drinking" and toward "drug" usage, the salient biomedical features of the misuse of alcohol and of "drugs" are strikingly similar. Pharmacologically, alcohol is a member of a group of solid substances, gases, and liquids known as generalized depressants of the central nervous system; barbiturates are considered members of this group, as are non-barbiturate "sleeping pills," such as glutethimide (Doriden), the general anesthetic agents, such as ether, and the agents sometimes called "minor tranquilizers," such as diazepam (Valium). For this reason we have not devoted a separate chapter to alcoholism; our principal discussion of this problem will be found in Chapter 4, which deals with the misuse of generalized depressants. We have described in Chapter 10 the technique for the medically supervised withdrawal of individuals physically dependent on generalized depressants and have discussed there also the role of such substances as Antabuse in rehabilitative programs for alcoholics.

In writing this book, we have had a number of people in mind. Primarily, we have written it for physicians who want to learn more about the biomedical aspects of drug abuse. In addition to compiling information now distributed among a large number of journals and monographs, we have attempted to provide them with a critical evaluation of this material. We are aware that many workers in allied health professions have frequent contact with drug users and accordingly want to learn more about this general phenomenon. We are aware too that interest in drug abuse on collegiate campuses has been expressed in the form of courses for undergraduate students on this subject. Chapters 1 and 2 have been written in a way that we believe that an interested layman can profit from reading them. Much of the rest of the book can, with occasional resort to a medical dictionary, be understood by those without a medical education.

We have imposed certain limitations on ourselves in the preparation of this book. Virtually all of the evidence cited was obtained in clinical studies. Because drug abuse is characterized so prominently by drug effects on the mind and by the psychological responses of the user, we feel that findings from animal studies have an inherently limited value. There was no attempt to enumerate every substance that has been subjected to abuse; we have omitted, however, only those agents that have had brief and faddish use, such as sunflower seeds, or repeated use by relatively few people, such as antihistamine drugs. Judicious use of the bibliographies should enable readers to find out what is known about these drugs.

The number of articles about drug abuse published annually in scientific and medical journals as well as monographs and books has increased enormously in the past decade, and this presented a serious bibliographic problem for us. To keep our bibliographies within manageable limits, we have accorded first priority to the citation of review articles and monographs. We apologize to the many investigators whose studies, as a result of our bibliographic restrictions, have been cited only indirectly.

This book has been the collaborative effort of a pharmacologist (F.G.H.) and a pediatrician who specializes in the medical problems of the adolescent and deals with a patient population derived largely from the Lower East Side of Manhattan (A.D.H.). In addition to writing Chapters 5 and 9, plus the sections on babies born of addicted mothers and methadone detoxification and maintenance in Chapter 10, A.D.H. has reviewed the other chapters. We hope that the considerable differences in our previous training, our attitudes, and our specific interests in the various topics are reflected in the breadth of our coverage of drug abuse. It has been a mutually educational experience for us. In the course of reading critically the other's contributions, in innumerable discussions and in the resolution of differences, we have each learned much. We now have, moreover, a much deeper and broader appreciation professionally of one another.

We cannot resist mention of one last question, which in one form or another has been put to us frequently: What can be done about drug abuse? Do we need stricter laws, or is legalization of some or all forms of drug abuse the solution? Though we have no ready answers to these questions, any successful solution will have to take into account the following aspects of the general problem. Man has been using psychoactive substances from at least the start of recorded history. His use of these substances has waxed and waned with time for reasons unknown but has never disappeared entirely. At any one time, the prevalence of drug abuse has been very much a function of societies and cultures, being conspicuous in some and rare in others. America from colonial times onward has been conspicuously a drug-using society, with alcohol and tobacco as the staple items of use. With the advent of sedative drugs and, subsequently, of tranquilizers and "psychic energizers," physicians have been able to offer a medically regulated and in many respects a psychologically equivalent substitute for drug abuse. The fact that one of these agents, diazepam (Valium), is the drug most frequently named on new prescriptions in America today indicates the magnitude of the need for psychoactive substances, at least as physicians perceive it.

The evident need or willingness of many Americans to take psychoactive drugs, under medical auspices or illegally, is a factor to be reckoned with in evaluating any proposal for the regulation of drug abuse. A rigidly enforced ban on the non-medical use of psychoactive drugs with harsh penalties for offenders can succeed only if we are willing to turn America into a true police state. Alternatively, the mere legalization of drug abuse with no provisions for rehabilitation is a callous solution, though it is often called a realistic one. It may promise resolution of a troubling problem but the cost—abandoning the user in his drug-dependent state and strengthening that dependency by facilitating repeated drug abuse—is unconscionable. Rehabilitative programs, of which legal provision of drugs may be a feature, seem to be the best of the solutions

now available. The optimal solution would undoubtedly be the prevention of drug abuse. We do not feel that this goal will be achieved within
the foreseeable future because the etiology of drug abuse is so poorly
understood at this time.

To anyone seeking a model of patience, we commend our editor, Mr.
Jeffrey House. When inescapable academic responsibilities diverted us
repeatedly from the prompt completion of this book, he bore up under
these many taxes on his patience with amazing good grace. For your
forbearance and for docking our prolixities, thank you, Jeffrey.

Columbia University   F. G. H.
October 1974

CONTENTS

A Handbook on Drug
and Alcohol Abuse

Chapter 1

INTRODUCTION

THE MISUSE OF DRUGS: INTRODUCTORY COMMENTS

Patterns of drug abuse

Drug abuse refers to the nonmedical use of drugs and other substances*
typically self-administered for one or more of the following purposes:
to change the user's mood, to alter his perception of himself and the
world around him, to produce novel sensations and experiences, and
to enhance his ability to function in certain settings, such as social or
sexual ones. These are the goals of drug users as we perceive them.
The intensely subjective character of the drug experience limits the
ability of the observer to analyze the nature of the experience. Knowledge comes mostly from users' reports and from inferences drawn from
changes in the users' patterns of behavior. The foundation of knowledge
obtained these ways is clearly weak. We say this, recognizing that essentially no other means for obtaining significant information exist.

Because of the often lurid publicity that drug abuse has received, some
people believe that, when a drug is misused, the pattern of abuse will
usually, if not invariably, be extreme; that most drug users, for example,
regularly take large doses of drugs at short intervals. This is a simplistic
view, encompassing only one possible pattern of drug abuse, whereas

---

* These include substances such as LSD and mescaline, which have no generally
accepted medicinal value, crude plant preparations such as marihuana, the volatile
constituents of commercial preparations such as certain glues, nail polish removers, and gasoline, and the propellant gases of aerosol preparations.

3

numerous patterns exist. The pattern of abuse exhibited by an individual at any point in time is probably determined to varying degrees by a number of factors: the emotional needs of the individual, the nature of the effects exerted by a given drug or group of drugs, the drug or drugs currently being used by associates of the individual or by those whom he wishes to emulate, and the availability of the drug, by which we mean not only whether it can be readily purchased, but also its price and quality.

To determine an individual's pattern of drug abuse, certain information is required. Obviously, one must know what drug or drugs the individual uses. The answer may be simple or quite complex. Some users employ, in the course of their lives, just one drug, such as alcohol or marihuana. Some users employ one drug primarily but often try to supplement it with another, such as the heroin user who likes to take heroin in conjunction with a barbiturate or an amphetamine. And some users commonly employ several drugs in sequence; after a prolonged and eventually exhausting or frightening "high" produced by repeated doses of a stimulant, they purposely employ a depressant like a barbiturate. Scarcity of supply may force a user to employ some other drug in lieu of the one he prefers; when heroin is temporarily unavailable, the addict may take large quantities of barbiturates in a usually vain attempt to alleviate the symptoms of withdrawal. Some exhibit a preference for variety, using drugs like LSD, amphetamine, and marihuana plus whatever drug mixtures they may be offered; they may, in time, develop a preference for a given drug or mixture and thereafter use it predominantly or exclusively. Over a period of years, some users follow different patterns of abuse. As a quite young person, ten years of age, for example, a user may begin "glue sniffing," in time he may smoke marihuana, and, perhaps, by the age of fifteen, he may take heroin by intravenous injection. This type of pattern has often been described, but it is worth emphasizing that such a sequence of events is far from inevitable. By "sniffing glue," no young person is inexorably impelled toward a more detrimental form of drug abuse. The smoking of marihuana does not make the abuse of more powerful drugs an inescapable sequel. The explanation as to why some drug users exhibit such a changing pattern of drug abuse with age, whereas others do not, will not come from a study of the pharmacological attributes of the drugs involved. Rather, one surmises that the answer will come primarily from an understanding of the motivation for the abuse of drugs. As a last item in the present catalogue, mention must be made of the situation in which the identity of the drug, or drugs, being used cannot be determined. This is hardly a rare occurrence in a time when so many drug mixtures of unknown composition are being offered for sale. Some mixtures are offered as single drugs, though actually they contain two or more drugs. Other mixtures are truthfully represented to be mixtures; their composition is rarely revealed. The seller indeed may not know what he is selling, and it appears that buyers do not often inquire.

Determination of a pattern of drug abuse also requires knowledge about the schedule of usage; this phrase encompasses size of dose, frequency of use, and route of administration. Assuming that a user provides the pertinent information, an accurate measure of the size of the dose may be quite easy to establish or virtually impossible. Most alcoholics, for example, ordinarily consume commercially available beverages. Because their alcoholic content is specified within narrow limits by law, the user's daily intake of alcohol can be readily calculated. Dosage can likewise be computed accurately when the drug in question was originally manufactured for use by the medical profession but subsequently was diverted to illegal sale; this statement would apply, for example, to some of the barbiturates used by drug-dependent individuals. Dosage calculations, however, can rarely be anything but rough approximations when a drug has been obtained from illegal sources. Analyses of a large number of heroin samples obtained in various sections of an urban area may enable one to know, for example, just how much heroin an addict will get in a typical or an average sample, but wide variations in the extent to which heroin is diluted have been observed, and the concentration of heroin in the strongest sample may be more than seventy times greater than that in the weakest. The best one can usually do here to compute drug intake, is, from a knowledge of how many "bags" of heroin are being used daily, to calculate that the addict is probably using an average of so many milligrams per day, in the long run. It is known, too, that a number of factors can influence the pharmacological potency of marihuana cigarettes. Variations in content of active compounds have been demonstrated objectively by chemical analyses and have been reported, in an approximate way and according to subjective criteria, by marihuana users. Thus, for example, the smoking of one "strong" cigarette may expose the user to more active drug than the smoking of five "weak" ones. And, to belabor the obvious, when drug mixtures of unknown composition are being used, one can abandon all thought of calculating dosage.

The use of a drug at regular, and usually quite short, intervals is most likely to be encountered in instances of drug addiction; in a number of cases this is so because the addict anticipates or begins to experience withdrawal symptoms that are precipitated by inadequate dosage or abstinence. In drug habituation, the frequency of use can vary widely. It may entail the use of small-to-moderate amounts of marihuana at long intervals, a pattern of use that some might contend hardly merits the designation habituation. It may entail the use of a drug like cocaine, again at irregular intervals, but on those occasions in large, and even toxic, quantities. Small quantities of drugs like marihuana or amphetamine may be used quite regularly, even on a daily basis. In more severe patterns of frequent use of habituating drugs, the intake of drug on an almost daily basis may, for some period of time, such as a week or more, be very great.

The route by which a drug is administered can be a factor of considerable significance. If a drug, for example, can be taken by mouth or by injection, one may expect that more intense effects will usually be produced by injection. This factor will be considered in greater detail in the next chapter.

Great variability does exist in patterns of drug abuse, and this fact should make one realize how uninformative simple statements about drug abuse can be. If a newspaper article declares that one-third of the students at a given high school "have used marihuana," what can this statement mean? At most, we can imagine that each of the students involved smokes a large number of marihuana cigarettes each day. At best, we can imagine that each of the students has experimentally smoked one marihuana cigarette but no more. Most probably there are some students in each of these categories and a number whose pattern of use lies somewhere in between. We may hear it said of a person, "He takes heroin." Does this mean that the person in question is a confirmed heroin addict, using the drug intravenously at short, regular intervals? Possibly, but not necessarily. In regard to heroin, some individuals can "take it or leave it"; they may take heroin only at irregular and infrequent intervals possibly interspersed with the use of one or more other drugs.

We are told that drug abuse currently poses a threat to our society and, particularly, to the welfare of our young people. If we ask how great a threat, we are likely to receive answers supposedly illustrative of the magnitude of the problem, such as the finding that one-third of the students at a given high school "have used marihuana," which really does not tell us very much. Reports about the use of drugs in a given area rarely contain the type of information required to determine even the prevalent patterns of drug abuse in that area. Some such reports are confined to the abuse of a particular drug, whereas others just mention those drugs of current concern to the community. Typical doses are sometimes reported. Frequency and method of use, if described at all, usually are cited only in illustrative examples of extreme patterns of abuse. The type of information really required to determine the individual patterns of abuse in a population of drug users is almost never provided. In all fairness, it must be noted that the required information frequently is not easy to obtain. Adolescent drug users, in particular, often actively or passively resist attempts at interrogation by "Members of the Establishment." The requisite information may be secured if a physician, or another concerned individual, can obtain the user's confidence, but this often requires much time and patience. And, throughout it all, unless the physician's approach is genuinely one of concerned interest, free of censure, it is probable that little will be learned. Some physicians have neither the time for nor the interest in the general problem of drug abuse. Other physicians, because of their personal feelings about drug abuse and those who participate in it, are unable to adopt an attitude that is free of reproach. Thus, for a variety of reasons, available information on individual patterns of drug abuse tends to consist largely of illustrative examples and unverified anecdotes. Those who wish to determine the magnitude of the problem and the threat it poses to drug users and to society must necessarily make their assessments on the basis of possibly indicative, but also possibly misleading, criteria. How much marihuana has been seized recently? Has the school dropout rate increased? What is the hospital admission rate for illnesses probably resulting from drug abuse? What about the crime rate? Has the rate of arrests for drug possession increased in the past year? The answers to these questions will reflect, in part, the magnitude of the problem, and some of its consequences, but no one can say how accurately they reflect it. Adolescents drop out of school for a variety of reasons. Burglaries may or may not be committed to obtain money for drugs. The amounts of illegal drugs seized depend, in part, on the fluctuating investments in time and men made by law enforcement agencies in regard to control of drug abuse. Whether a psychosis was drug-induced can be determined on only some occasions; whether a case of hepatitis was, in fact, the result of the communal use of a needle can be determined in only some cases.

When an "authority" on drug abuse offers an assessment of the scope and peril of the problem, that assessment often appears to derive from the following: his personal experience with drug users (which is necessarily limited in regard to numbers and locale), his knowledge of the personal experience of his colleagues (subject to the same limitations), the few pieces of rather specific information publicly known (such as the number of heroin addicts identified by law enforcement agencies because of repeated arrests), and his personal interpretation of the extent of drug abuse of the type cited above, such as the quantity of illicit drugs that has been seized recently. We are not reproaching authorities for making assessments of this type; many of these men conscientiously make the best informed guess possible on the basis of the scanty information available. Rather, we wish to point out that accurate assessments of the problem cannot be made until we possess considerably more information than we now have on the relative incidence of the various possible patterns of drug abuse.

Even if we had all the information we might desire on individual patterns of abuse in a population of drug users, we still could not predict with a satisfactory degree of certainty what the consequences of that abuse would be. We would know what each user was exposing himself to in the way of drugs, but we could not often foretell precisely how he would respond. No one can, for example, assure a user of LSD that his next "trip" will be an enjoyable experience. Though we know that many users of large doses of amphetamine will experience paranoia, we cannot predict which user will translate these feelings of persecution into the reality of a physical assault upon another person. The interaction of effects and the user's current psychological makeup chiefly determines many of the consequences of drug abuse. We know little about how the drugs exert their effects and perhaps even less about the emotional factors that influence the exact form of the evoked response to the drugs. As a consequence, our ability to predict how much harm will come to an individual and to society from a given pattern of drug abuse is almost nonexistent. Today we can enumerate the possible harmful effects; in time we may be able to predict, statistically the probability of harm occurring in a given situation.

Any accurate estimate of the social and medical harm resulting from drug abuse will have to be based on much more information than we now have about the relative incidence of differing patterns of drug abuse and the probable consequences, both acute and chronic, of each pattern of abuse. This information will be difficult to obtain. For the present, we should respect the limitations that ignorance imposes. We cannot supply answers for many of the questions being asked. In all too many instances, we cannot support either the impassioned declarations of the essential harmlessness of some forms of drug abuse or the dire prophecies of mental and physical disability in regard to others. We can only suspend judgment until more facts become available.

The nature of the drug experience

The nature of individual drug experiences, which can vary greatly, is probably largely determined by the drug (including dose and route of administration), the user's response to the drug's effects, and the environment in which the drug is taken. It is a perplexing task, however, to determine just how each of these factors influences the ultimate nature of the drug experience.

Drugs commonly subject to abuse may act to disrupt the normal organization of the mind, perhaps in a fashion unique to each particular type of drug. As a result, a variety of psychological impairments develop. These may be relatively minor, such as a loss of ability to estimate the rate of passage of time, which is a typical consequence of smoking marihuana. There may be some loss of the ability to interpret and evaluate reality; relatively trivial changes in the user's environment may evoke great pleasure or profound sadness. The reaction to sensory stimuli may become so distorted that the drug user reports being able to "see" sounds and "smell" colors, events that sometimes occur after the use of LSD. Perception of self as well as the outside world may be disturbed; users of amphetamine, for example, often develop a sense of physical and mental omnipotence, whereas alcoholics may be dominated by a deep feeling of personal unworthiness. Thoughts that ordinarily trouble a drug user, such as a sense of personal inadequacy, may be regarded, under the influence of a narcotic, with complete indifference.

It seems evident that drugs can impair and distort, in various ways, the user's perception of reality—his perception of himself, the world around him, and the interaction between the two. Indeed it is often said that drugs are abused for one of two reasons: to suppress or distort a reality the user finds disagreeable or to create a new and more pleasurable "reality." The sleep (or state of unconsciousness) that develops upon the use of very large quantities of barbiturates, and the drug-induced psychoses in which contact with reality no longer exists, seem to be extreme expressions of such desires. Most disturbing to physicians are the drug users who, consciously or unconsciously, seem to seek death through the abuse of drugs.

In addition to producing "psychological" effects, the drugs subject to abuse also exert "physiological" or "physical" effects. Some of these effects are so minor, such as small changes in systemic blood pressure, that the user may well be unaware of them; others are so prominent that they cannot easily be ignored. Nausea and vomiting, headaches, tremors, and pupillary dilation producing exquisite photosensitivity are examples of the more intrusive physiological effects. We do not know how or to what extent the physiological effects of drugs influence the nature of the drug experience; because the response of the user to these effects will determine, in large part, the magnitude of their impact on the drug experience, we must assume that they are determinants of variable significance.

The intensity of a drug's effects is determined, to an important degree, by the dose used. Drugs subject to abuse that also have legitimate therapeutic uses are commonly employed by drug-dependent individuals in quantities considerably larger than the conventional doses prescribed by physicians. An addict's daily intake of pentobarbital (Nembutal), for example, might well be twenty to thirty times greater than the dose of this drug ordinarily prescribed as an aid to sleep. For those drugs to whose effects appreciable refractoriness (tolerance) develops, the user must eventually increase the dose if he wishes to obtain the original intensity of effect. The narcotic addict, in particular, continually faces this problem: the development of tolerance requires a larger dose, the larger dose produces, in time, more tolerance, which means the dose must be increased again, and so on. Even in patterns of drug abuse that are free of the problem of tolerance, drug users often deliberately increase their intake to intensify the drug experience.

The intensity of a drug's effects also depends in part on the route of administration. The effects of a drug are likely to be more intense, but of briefer duration, when a drug is injected than when it is taken by mouth, and in most cases the effects will appear more rapidly. Users of heroin have known for some time that the most pleasurable experience with heroin is obtained by intravenous injection of the drug, and many users of amphetamine have come to the same conclusion.

If we assume that the effects produced by a drug are approximately the same on each occasion of use, we must then attempt to account for the great variability known to exist in the nature of the drug experience.

Why are some alcoholics effusive and convivial, whereas others are abusive and belligerent? Why do only some users of amphetamine become sexually aroused while under the influence of the drug? Why are some LSD "trips" good and others bad? No truly satisfactory answer can be given to this type of question. We believe that the nature of a drug experience is influenced by the user's response to the drug's effects. The user's response we believe is determined, in turn, by his general personality structure and his particular emotional state at the time the drug is taken. This is a complex matter, and it is poorly understood, for there is much that is unknown about the development and structure of personality and the determinants of various emotional states.

The relationship between drug abuse and sexual behavior seems to be a fairly frequent topic for public discussion. It is often alleged that drugs promote sexual activity by causing arousal of sexual passions or loss of inhibitions. It is true that some individuals, while under the influence of drugs, do exhibit sexual behavior; a few have committed rape. None of the drugs subject to abuse is, however, a reliable aphrodisiac. For a number of reasons, the incidence of sexual activity among some categories of drug users is probably less than it is among non-users.

The typical heroin addict happily feels free of all wants, including those of a sexual nature. Ingestion of sufficient quantities of certain stupefying drugs, such as alcohol, can make sexual intercourse a virtual impossibility. The effects of some hallucinogens, such as LSD, may permit erotic thoughts to emerge, but they also often make the user quite introspective, too concerned with himself and his own fantasies to bother with others. Public discussion of this topic has received additional impetus from fanciful stories of "hundreds of orgasms" related by advocates of LSD use. If such stories have any foundation in fact, one assumes they are the products of mental distortion produced by LSD in which perhaps the reality of an actual sexual experience is perceived in the same bizarre, exaggerated, and unreal fashion as are other experiences perceived under the influence of this drug (1, p. 145).

Stimulants, such as amphetamine, do seem to give some individuals, a number of whom may be uncertain of their sexual prowess or dissatisfied with their performance, enough confidence so that, under the drug's influence, they actively seek sexual experiences. In fact, a few may become sexually insatiable (1, p. 82). Some heavy users of stimulants report that these drugs greatly enhance their sexual vigor so that they can have intercourse repeatedly and at short intervals. Others, perhaps with less strongly developed or more stringently inhibited drives, may exhibit no increase in sexual activity or even a decrease under the influence of a stimulant.

People, of course, experience and act upon sexual thoughts and desires, to varying degrees. The fact that they may continue to have such thoughts and desires while under the influence of some drugs and that they sometimes satisfy these desires hardly seems surprising. In sum, drug abuse, in company with a number of poorly understood social phenomena, has been endowed, in the public mind, with an aura of sexuality that is largely unwarranted.

The extent to which the user's environment can influence the nature of a drug experience is probably a factor of variable significance, depending upon the personality of the user and the type of drug taken. A common effect of heroin is to "insulate" the addict against unpleasant reality, both within and outside himself; he becomes indifferent to his environment, and it probably often has little effect on his response to the drug. When a drug enhances emotional lability, as does LSD, then relatively commonplace changes in the user's environment, such as the sun going behind a cloud, may evoke profound changes in mood (2). Feelings of guilt or anxiety that could influence a user's response about drug abuse are often attenuated, and the user's pleasure is increased if the drug is taken in the company of friends who are also "turning on." In some eastern Mediterranean countries, marihuana and hashish is used predominantly in a group setting at certain cafés; here they have become, in a sense, "social" drugs.

People frequently ask what happens to a person when he takes a certain drug. Only a qualified answer can ever be given, for we cannot predict what the user's mood or behavior will be under the influence of the drug. We cannot even predict that, if a drug experience is unpleasant, the user will thereafter refrain from further use of the drug in question. After a disagreeable experience with a particular drug, many individuals do stop taking that drug and do, in fact, abandon the use of drugs altogether; others do not. Some users of LSD have been known to continue using the drug even after experiencing one or more distinctly bad "trips." Heroin addicts not uncommonly report that their initial experiences with the drug were most disagreeable: they vomited and felt uneasy, anxious, and apprehensive. Other addicts had to encourage them to continue the use of heroin. In a number of cases, the experience gradually becomes, for unknown reasons, most pleasurable; that addict might continue to vomit from time to time but can now view his vomiting with indifference.

The role of the drug itself in determining the nature of the drug experience can be inferred to be an important, but limited, one. In our view, the effect of a drug is to partially disrupt the normal organization of the mind in a fashion that is determined by the type of drug used and to a degree that is determined by the dose and the route of administration. The nature of the drug experience thereafter is determined, we believe, by the response of the user. We do not believe that a drug can create wholly new and previously nonexistent patterns of thought, reaction, and behavior in a user. (The English author and user of opium, Thomas DeQuincey, said, in effect, that if one had not dreamed beautiful dreams before taking opium one would not do so under its influence.) We do not believe that the effects of a drug can compel a person, for example, to become a criminal "against his will." Only some users of stimulants, when they have taken psychotoxic quantities, physically assault others, though thoughts of persecution and other forms of paranoid ideation commonly develop when large doses of these drugs are taken. (We naturally exclude from consideration here crimes committed by drug users to obtain money with which to buy drugs; such crimes stem from economic necessity and not from drug effects. They do represent, however, one of the major adverse concomitants of drug abuse.)

The above simplified portrait of the role of the drug in determining the nature of the drug experience is based only on interpretation of the available evidence; it has not been clearly demonstrated to be true. It most probably does not apply to situations in which enormous doses of drugs have been taken; on these occasions, the user has little option in responding because the function of the "response" system—comprised principally of the neurons of the central nervous system—is so disturbed that the general type of response is usually quite predictable. Thus, very large doses of barbiturates will produce unconsciousness, and very large doses of potent hallucinogens will cause even well-adjusted individuals to lose, at least temporarily, substantial contact with reality.

THE NAMES USED FOR DRUGS

Each "legal" drug ordinarily has several names that serve in various ways to identify it. It has a name that describes its chemical structure, if it is known; this name is seldom used because it often is cumbersome. It also has a generic name, which has an official, or quasi-official, status; it is the name that is commonly used by pharmacologists and some physicians. And finally, each drug has one or more "trade names," each of which is the copyrighted property of a drug manufacturer; drugs that are popular and unpatented may have five or more trade names.

Within the world of drug abuse, names are given to drugs for quite different reasons. Drugs are rarely referred to by names known, at least initially, to the public or even to the medical profession. This practice reflects, in part, the necessarily conspiratorial atmosphere that envelops the sale and possession of illegal drugs, in which drug names are, in reality, code words. It also brings pleasure to many drug users; to be able to understand the code implies membership in a special fraternity, and to use the words is a relished means of excluding and baffling the "squares." For some teenagers, it is one manifestation of rebellion against and rejection of the adults' world; their use of "street" names for drugs (and, of course, the use of the drugs themselves) is, among other things, an expression of defiance against authority. (These feelings are most bluntly exemplified by a drug preparation that was given the name FUK.) Then, too, names must be devised for the various drug mixtures that have been concocted by "basement" chemists for sale to drug users; in this instance, there is no question of substitution for an official name, for such mixtures exist only for the purpose of drug abuse.

Street names for drugs can understandably baffle the non-user and they are intended to do so; sometimes they baffle and mislead the user also. For one thing, a name may not gain general acceptance. The currently prevalent street name for a marihuana cigarette in one city may be quite different from that used in another city; even within a large urban area, the name in current use may vary from one neighborhood to another. Street names tend also to be short-lived, for once the "code has been broken," and a name becomes generally known to the public through its use in newspapers, magazines, and the like, a new name must be used. Marihuana is a notable example of a drug that has had numerous names, the use of some being only local and the period of use of many being relatively short. There are names for marihuana in general (*pot, grass, tea*), names that purport to denote marihuana of high potency (*Acapulco gold, gold-leaf special*), names that refer to the quantity of the drug offered for sale or the price of a stipulated quantity (*ki* or *kilo, dime bag*), and names that refer to cigarettes containing marihuana (*joint, reefer*). Some of the examples cited are names still in use, whereas others, though once popular, are no longer used.

Because the number of drug users now is relatively large, and because the profits to be realized on drug sales can be enormous, the number of drug vendors has increased. At times when a drug supply is large, competition for sales is keen, and special promotional techniques are used. Manufacturers of LSD, for example, may prepare the drug in a unique shape and color and give it a "brand" name, such as *Blue Dot* or *Purple Flat* (2). At these times of intense competition, a popular drug may be offered for sale under fifteen or more brand names. Because illegal drug manufacturers rarely have the facilities required for production of drugs in large batches, the original supply, if popular, is soon exhausted. If a subsequent batch is made, both the potency of the drug and its brand name may change. Changes in even popular brand names are sometimes necessary because, if a certain brand gains wide acceptance, competitors often quickly prepare imitations. Some of the imitations will have the necessary appearance but will contain no drug; an initially popular brand name can thereby come into eventual disrepute.

A given street name may also be used to refer to more than one drug. The name "speed," for example, has been used variously to refer to amphetamine, to methamphetamine, and, in a generic sense, to any stimulant drug of the amphetamine type, a fair number of which exist.

Because street names often have short lives, and because some of them vary from one geographic area to another, we have decided not to provide a glossary of such names. We can discern little sense of order in the entire phenomenon of street names; no rules or conventions are generally observed, and any such expectation is probably unrealistic in so loosely organized and disparate a group as drug users. Street names do not invariably disappear, for example, following public exposure; the term *acid,* though now generally known as a synonym for LSD, appears still to be used fairly widely at this time by those who take the drug.

We regard the matter of street names for drugs as a colorful, but minor, aspect of the problem of drug abuse. The principal significance of street names for non-users is largely obfuscatory. These names can obstruct possible identification of a drug subject to abuse. In addition, their use by well-meaning, but inexperienced, members of the health professions is potentially self-defeating. Many adolescents have repeatedly proclaimed their hostility toward adults and their belief in natural and honest behavior. Those who seek to help adolescent drug users are aware of this hostility and may attempt to bridge the "generation gap" by the use of words peculiar to the adolescents' vocabulary, such as the street names

for drugs. Because these names are not a part of the normal working vocabulary of most adults, some teenagers will regard their use by adults as
only further evidence of hypocrisy and dishonesty on the part of the older
generation (3).

THE CLASSIFICATION OF DRUGS

For purposes of classification, each therapeutically useful drug is assigned membership in a specific group. The groups are devised on the
basis of various criteria: the principal anatomical site of action of the
drugs (e.g., drugs acting on the central nervous system), the type of
effect they produce (e.g., skeletal muscle relaxants), the therapeutic indication for their use (e.g., drugs used in deficiency anemias), their
mechanism of action (e.g., carbonic anhydrase inhibitors), and, occasionally, their chemical structure (e.g., drugs containing heavy metals).
Such a classification of drugs facilitates communication among the informed, as a great deal of information about the general nature of a drug
can be conveyed simply by designating the group to which it belongs.

In the study of drug abuse, a knowledge of drug groups can be of
value because it often enhances understanding and confers predictive
ability. The salient pharmacological aspects of abuse are usually similar
for all drugs within a given group. Likewise, if an individual has developed tolerance to the effects of one drug within a group, one can expect
that he will exhibit some degree of tolerance to the effects of all drugs
within that group; he will not, however, be tolerant to the effects of drugs
belonging to any other group. If an individual has developed physical dependence upon the effects of one drug within a group, he will also be
physically dependent upon all other drugs in that group, but upon no
other drugs; this particular manifestation of group interrelationship
means that a withdrawal (or an abstinence) syndrome can be prevented
or stopped by an appropriate dose of any drug belonging to the group
and not just by the specific drug the addict has been using.

We know too little, unfortunately, about the pharmacology of some
drugs commonly subject to abuse to be able to place them meaningfully
into groups. Such drugs as LSD, marihuana, and mescaline are sometimes classified as "hallucinogens" because of the "visions" that their use
can elicit. This is largely a nominal grouping, however, as indicated by
the fact that a knowledge of the pharmacological properties of one of
these drugs enables us to predict essentially nothing about the pharmacological attributes of other members of this "group."

At this point, we would like to characterize briefly the groups of drugs that will be discussed in subsequent chapters.

Narcotics

The principal therapeutic use of these drugs is to produce analgesia (relief of pain); they are also used to reduce the frequency of coughing and to stop diarrhea. Upon prolonged use, great tolerance to the effects of narcotics develops, and, if the schedule of usage is regular, physical dependence upon their effects develops. The narcotic withdrawal syndrome, given the degree of addiction most commonly developed at this time, is distressing to the addict but rarely threatens his life.

Narcotics can be divided into three groups on the basis of their origin; the important pharmacological attributes of the drugs in all three subgroups are, with but a few exceptions, nearly identical.

1. Naturally occurring narcotics: opium and the two narcotics that it contains—morphine and codeine.

2. Semi-synthetic narcotics (derivatives of morphine or codeine chemically prepared): heroin, dihydromorphinone, oxymorphone, metopon, dihydrocodeinone, hydrocodone, and oxycodone, among others.

3. Wholly synthetic narcotics: (a) meperidine and such chemically similar compounds as anileridine and alphaprodine; (b) methadone and such chemically similar compounds as dextromoramide; (c) the morphinan compounds, such as levorphanol; and (d) the most recently introduced synthetic narcotics, benzomorphan compounds, such as phenazocine.

Many of the prominent effects that are characteristically produced by all narcotics can be abolished or substantially reduced in intensity by a group of drugs known as "narcotic antagonists." Intravenous injection of such a narcotic antagonist as nalorphine (Nalline) into a narcotic addict can produce a fully developed withdrawal syndrome within approximately 30 minutes.

Generalized depressants of the central nervous system

These drugs appear to be able to depress activity in all parts of the central nervous system and, in sufficient doses, to cause death from respiratory depression. With regular use, physical dependence upon their effects develops but only if the daily intake of the drug exceeds a "threshold" dose, the size of which appears to be peculiar to each drug. A relatively small degree of tolerance to the effects of these drugs develops upon repeated use. The withdrawal syndrome associated with addiction to this type of drug can be horrendous and occasionally ends in death; it commonly begins with a period characterized by an increasing degree of hyperactivity of the central nervous system, which may culminate in one or more grand mal convulsions and is followed by several days of psychotic agitation. The withdrawal syndrome usually lasts from 5 to 10 days.

This group appears to be heterogenous; certainly, the drugs do not all exhibit identical patterns of pharmacological activity. From a therapeutic standpoint, however, they all produce much the same type of effect in patients; in addition, the important pharmacological aspects of the abuse of these agents are quite similar for all drugs within the group.

SEDATIVE AND HYPNOTIC DRUGS The principal therapeutic uses of these drugs are to calm patients and, in larger doses, to enable them to obtain satisfactory amounts of sleep. The barbiturates are the most widely used group of drugs in this category; phenobarbital, secobarbital (Seconal), and pentobarbital (Nembutal) are representative examples. Also included in this category are such relatively old, "non-barbiturate" drugs as chloral hydrate and such relatively new agents as glutethimide (Doriden) and ethchlorvynol (Placidyl).

ANTI-ANXIETY AGENTS ("MINOR TRANQUILIZERS") The manufacturers of these drugs recommend them for the management of milder forms of certain types of emotional disturbance; some physicians believe they are no more valuable for this purpose than are the conventional sedative and hypnotic drugs. Representative drugs in this category are meprobamate (Miltown) and diazepam (Valium).

ETHANOL (ETHYL ALCOHOL) Though ethanol (often just called "alcohol") has no generally recognized therapeutic use, its pharmacological effects closely mimic those of the other generalized depressants. In regard to drug abuse, it is, by a wide margin, the most popular agent in the group; indeed, the number of alcoholics may exceed the number of users of any other drug subject to abuse.

GENERAL ANESTHETIC AGENTS These drugs are usually gases or volatile liquids that, upon inhalation, can produce unconsciousness and the profound muscular relaxation required for many types of surgical procedures. Only rarely are these drugs abused; the volatile components of some preparations, such as nail polish remover and certain types of glue, however, do produce effects similar to general anesthetics, and these preparations are subject to abuse. Inhalation of their fumes usually produces a state of intoxication that resembles the early stages of anesthesia seen with the use of certain slowly acting anesthetics. Users of these preparations, however, rarely achieve a depth of depression of the central nervous system comparable to that necessary for surgery.

It is of general pharmacological interest that the drugs in this group and the narcotics, whose effects on the central nervous system are predominantly depressant, are the only ones which have proved to be addicting and subject to abuse. Notably, and inexplicably, such "major" tranquilizers as chlorpromazine (Thorazine) have not figured prominently in the phenomenon of drug abuse. No physical dependence upon their effects develops, regardless of the amount of drug taken daily or the length of the period of use. Only occasionally have they been used by drug-dependent individuals, and the demand for them on the illegal drug market has been minimal to date.

Stimulants of the central nervous system

This general designation has been applied to a large number of drugs that are used for a variety of therapeutic purposes. Among the "recognized" uses of central nervous system stimulants are the treatment of emotional depression, suppression of appetite in the management of obesity, and antagonism of the effects of depressant drugs. Included in the group are such powerful convulsant drugs as strychnine and pentylenetetrazol (Metrazol); such antidepressants (used specifically for alleviation of psychic depression) as imipramine (Tofranil) and tranylcypromine (Parnate); and such less potent stimulants as amphetamine and caffeine. Tolerance to certain effects of some of these drugs develops upon regular use. Again, we note with interest that several types of drugs belonging to this group have not been widely subject to abuse, though they might be regarded as likely candidates. Such antidepressant drugs (also called "mood-elevating" agents and "psychic energizers") as imipramine (Tofranil) represent a type of drug one might suppose would be quite prone to abuse. They can "stimulate" an apathetic and withdrawn individual so that his mood improves and his activity increases. An important deterrent to their popularity among drug users may be the fact that the effects of these drugs often develop slowly, some requiring several weeks to become fully effective.

Amphetamine and several compounds similar to it in chemical structure and pharmacological activity, such as methamphetamine (Methedrine), have been the stimulants most commonly subject to abuse. They may be less potent than other stimulants, but this criterion refers only to the size of the effective dose. The ready availability of drugs of the amphetamine type on the illegal market makes possible the use of very large doses, which fully compensate for any relative lack of potency. Upon regular use, the development of tolerance to the desired psychic effects of amphetamine has been reported by drug users, and some users have eventually come to take extraordinarily large quantities of the drug each day. The potential toxicity of this type of drug has been enhanced not only by the fact that very large doses are being employed but also by the fact that now they are often injected intravenously, rather than taken by mouth, which was the previous custom. Physical dependence upon these drugs probably does not develop, regardless of the quantity of drug taken daily or the frequency of use.

COCAINE   Cocaine is a natural component of the leaves of the coca plant. For some years it was the only effective local anesthetic drug possessed by physicians. The search for synthetic substitutes for cocaine was prompted, in part, by this drug's ability to cause excitation of the central nervous system; this property of cocaine, regarded as an untoward effect by physicians, constitutes its principal attraction for drug-dependent individuals. Because the effects of cocaine and amphetamine, when subject to abuse, are similar in so many respects, cocaine will be discussed in detail in the chapter devoted to stimulant drugs. Synthetic local anesthetic drugs, of which procaine (Novocain) and lidocaine (Xylocaine) are examples, have almost wholly supplanted cocaine for medical purposes; the central nervous system excitatory effects of the synthetic drugs are relatively weak, and they have rarely figured in patterns of drug abuse.

Hallucinogenic (psychotogenic, psychotomimetic,
psychedelic) drugs

This category of drugs is both ill-named and ill-defined, largely out of ignorance. We speak of these drugs as "hallucinogens," though they appear to elicit true hallucinations only infrequently; they do induce sensory perceptions that are not based on external reality, but, throughout such experiences, critical self-judgment often is retained, which is not typical of a hallucination. We speak of them as "psychotogenic" or "psychotomimetic," as if they were capable of producing a state identical with or substantially similar to a psychosis—more specifically, schizophrenia. Again, the terms are applicable but only with substantive qualification. These drugs can produce a state that resembles an acute schizophrenic reaction in some respects, but other characteristics of the drug-induced state are not typical features of schizophrenia. (Perhaps the most accurate term would be "semi-psychotomimetic.") These drugs have also been called "psychedelic" or mind-manifesting. As a person's mind is "manifested" under the influence of these drugs, proponents of their use maintain that new insights into one's self may be gained, horizons of thought expanded, and great truths unveiled. As little objective evidence to support these claims exists, we feel that the term "psychedelic" too is inapt. Recognizing the limitations, and for want of a more accurate term, we shall refer to these drugs as hallucinogens.

The group is ill-defined, in part, because all drugs subject to abuse that do not fit comfortably into any other group are placed into this one. On the other hand, it does not encompass all of the drugs that may cause delusions and perceptual distortions that resemble hallucinations; by such criteria, cocaine and amphetamine should be members of the group. In point of fact, we do not yet know enough about the pharmacology of these drugs to permit meaningful classification of them. These drugs differ widely in their chemical structures and, to the extent of our limited knowledge, in their pharmacological effects.

Commonly included in this group are substances of plant origin, including marihuana, mescaline, psilocybin, and harmine, and synthetic compounds, including lysergic acid diethylamide (LSD; LSD-25), phencylidine (PCP), and dimethyltryptamine (DMT). No physical dependence upon the effects of these drugs is known, but considerable tolerance to the effects of some of the hallucinogens does develop upon regular and frequent use.

TERMINOLOGY: CONFUSION AND PROLIFERATION

Drug addiction, habituation, dependence, and abuse

The various terms that refer to the illicit use of drugs were originally coined and defined by physicians and pharmacologists, who have managed subsequently to use them in most confusing ways. The broad legal, social, and psychological ramifications of the "drug problem" have commanded the attention of representatives of paramedical disciplines, the executive and legislative branches of government, and the community at large. Members of each of these groups have used the various terms according to their own interpretation of the problem and, often, in ways to promote their own special purposes.

Though terminology is not an inherently exciting topic for discussion, we are aware of the widespread confusion over the meanings of common terms referring to drug abuse and the resulting semantic disputes, to which, in our opinion, inordinate amounts of time have been devoted. We will, therefore, discuss briefly the origins of this confusion and indicate what terminology will be used in this book.

In the early decades of this century, the term drug addiction was felt to satisfactorily denote the illicit use of drugs, though it also erroneously promoted a contemporary belief that only individuals "deficient in moral fiber" succumbed to drug addiction and that they, while under the influence of drugs, committed vicious criminal acts. As the characteristics of drug abuse became better understood, differing patterns of illicit use became more clearly delineated. Not only were the effects produced by heroin and cocaine, for example, different, but the problems faced by the users of these two drugs were, in certain respects, quite dissimilar. It became possible to classify differing patterns of illicit drug usage on the basis of their pharmacological characteristics and, thus, the process of terminological proliferation began.

An early and notable attempt to use pharmacological criteria to designate differing patterns of drug misuse was made in 1931 by Tatum and Seevers (4) with their definitions of the terms *drug addiction* and *drug habituation*. An addicting drug was distinguished from a habituating drug principally on the basis that, in drug addiction, physical dependence on the effects of the drug developed; this meant that an involuntary physiological illness (the withdrawal or abstinence syndrome) would be precipitated if the intake of the drug was markedly reduced or stopped altogether. By way of contrast, withdrawal from a habituating drug might provoke emotional distress, but no physiological upset. This is more than an academic distinction. Most narcotic addicts and alcoholics have experienced at least the early stages of withdrawal and so have learned the critical importance of a reasonably regular schedule of drug intake. As a result, their lives are commonly dominated by drugs, and they usually devote a considerable part of each day to procuring drugs (and the money with which to buy them). The user of a habituating drug is nominally free to select the occasions of drug use; he need not necessarily fear the time when the drug, or the money, is in short supply. He may be decidedly unhappy on these occasions, but he does not face the threat of an impending and inexorable physiological illness.

In the years following 1931, the distinction between addicting and habituating drugs proposed by Tatum and Seevers was respected by some and disregarded by many. The connotative power of the word addiction is clearly greater than that of habituation. Thoughts of practices detrimental to the drug user and to society come readily to mind when "addiction" is employed, whereas, "habituation" seems often to imply the use of relatively weak drugs on a casual and intermittent basis—hardly the type of problem worthy of serious attention. As a result, those wishing to suppress the use of habituating drugs, as for example, marihuana, often referred to such drugs as addicting drugs, in part to enlist public support more readily for restrictive legislation. When we consider the truly grave effects produced by toxic doses of such habituating drugs as cocaine and amphetamine, it seems hardly appropriate to refer to such patterns of use as habituation, and so again the term drug addiction was not uncommonly used. Confusion arose in the minds of physicians and laity alike because some authorities referred to most forms of drug abuse as drug addiction, whereas others scrupulously observed the distinction proposed by Tatum and Seevers. Then, too, the word addiction had entered the lay vocabulary, where it was employed in the context of situations not involving drugs, usage exemplified by expressions like "I'm addicted to hot fudge sundaes," or "He's a jazz addict." Some physicians have even referred to an intense relationship between an individual and an aspect of his environment as an addiction; one finds, for example, that patients with disorders caused by the daily ingestion of very large quantities of coffee may be characterized as "caffeine addicts."

As the problem of drug abuse grew and took on new forms in the decades following World War II, a need developed for terms that would aptly and succinctly describe the new manifestations of the problem. Continued use of the phrase "drug addiction" seemed profitless in the absence of general agreement about which of the many drugs subject to abuse should be designated addicting. It likewise seemed impossible to devise a definition of drug habituation that would encompass the characteristics of the misuse of all drugs upon whose effects no physical dependence developed. It was decided that the best way out of the semantic muddle would be to coin a new phrase, *drug dependence;* this term was advocated not so much because it further clarified the nature of the phenomenon but because it offered a means of avoiding the confusion attendant upon the use of the older terms.

The above sequence of events is well illustrated by the series of definitions pertaining to illicit drug usage issued by Expert Committees of the World Health Organization in the period 1950 through 1964. The Expert Committee on Drugs Liable to Produce Addiction offered the following definition of *drug addiction* in 1950: "Drug addiction is a state of periodic or chronic intoxication, detrimental to the individual and society, produced by the repeated consumption of a drug (natural or synthetic). Its characteristics include: 1. An overpowering desire or need (compulsion) to continue taking the drug and to obtain it by any means; 2. A tendency to increase the dose; 3. A psychic (psychological) and sometimes a physical dependence on the effects of the drug." *Drug habituation* was defined in the following way: "A habit-forming drug is one which is or may be taken repeatedly without the production of all of the characteristics outlined in the definition of addiction and which is not generally considered to be detrimental to the individual and to society." These definitions appear to classify all of the medically and socially significant patterns of drug abuse under the heading of addiction; habit-forming drugs seem not worthy of concern, as their use, according to the definition, harms no one.

One may assume that, in time, the essential inadequacy of the definition of habituating drugs was appreciated, for, in 1957, the Expert Committee on Addiction-Producing Drugs issued the following new definition of drug habituation: "Drug habituation (or habit) is a condition resulting from the repeated consumption of a drug. Its characteristics include: 1. A desire (but not a compulsion) to continue taking the drug for the sense of improved well-being which it engenders; 2. Little or no tendency to increase the dose; 3. Some degree of psychic dependence on the effect of the drug, but absence of physical dependence and hence of an abstinence syndrome; 4. Detrimental effects, if any, primarily on the individual." The definition of drug addiction remained essentially unchanged; the phrase "physical dependence," however, preceded by the word "sometimes" in the definition of 1950, was, in 1957, preceded by the word "generally." Again, the definition of habituation was, by and large, unsatisfactory. Some users of LSD are known to continue use of this drug, despite the experience of one or more distinctly unpleasant "bad trips"; such an episode cannot be described as a "sense of improved well-being." Many users of amphetamine markedly increase their daily drug intake in the course of time. The assaults on others, resulting from paranoid delusions induced by toxic quantities of stimulant drugs, hardly exemplify detrimental effects confined to the drug user. The definition seemed applicable only to some users of some habituating drugs on some occasions.

The semantic difficulties could have been overcome by expanding the definition of drug habituation so that it encompassed salient aspects of the varied patterns of use of habituating drugs and by reserving the term addiction for the use of those drugs upon whose effects physical dependence developed. This solution, however, would have resulted in a definition of drug habituation, that, if truly accurate, would have been so lengthy and complex as to constitute a short monograph. To many it seemed undesirable also to continue to use so pejorative a term as addiction; the growing concept of the drug user as an emotionally disturbed individual who required medical attention was not in accord with the traditional popular view of a "drug addict" as a spineless, hedonistic criminal who should be jailed as quickly and for as long as possible. The Expert Committee on Addiction-Producing Drugs, therefore, recommended in 1964 that the term, *drug dependence,* be used in place of addiction and habituation. The new term was preliminarily defined in the most general way: "a state arising from repeated administration of a drug on a periodic or continuous basis." Recognizing some of the shortcomings of previous definitions, the committee then went on to say: "Its characteristics will vary with the agent involved and this must be made clear by designating the particular type of drug dependence in each specific case—for example, drug dependence of morphine type, of cocaine type, of cannabis type, of barbiturate type," and so on.

Though the new term, drug dependence, seemed largely free of the connotative liabilities of its predecessors, by the same token it seemed too benign a term to some for so grave a problem. In the mid-1960's, and particularly in the United States, one increasingly encountered the term, *drug abuse.* Usually used without being defined, abuse is a more comprehensive, a more graphic, and, in the view of some, a more censorious word than dependence. For perhaps just these reasons, an American reader may expect to meet the term, drug abuse, considerably more often than drug dependence. From the context of its usage, one can infer that a definition of drug abuse would entail reference to all forms of the illicit use of drugs. It is used to refer not only to well-established patterns of drug usage, as does drug dependence, but also to any instance of the illicit use of drugs, which would include, for example, even an adolescent experimenting with his first marihuana cigarette.

The proliferation of terms has not resolved the confusion over terminology. No term has been devised that clearly and specifically denotes the particular type of drug misuse we are presently considering. Problems in communication arise from the fact that drugs can be misused in various ways. Consider, for example, the physician who prescribes a drug, which has the capacity for causing serious toxic effects, when no acceptable therapeutic indication for its use exists; this can and has been described as an example of drug abuse. In point of fact, one sometimes cannot use the term "drug abuse" in medical circles without specifying the type of abuse. Consider also the individual who believes that he requires large doses of aspirin daily for optimal function and so induces in himself salicylate intoxication. Within the literal meanings of the words, this situation exhibits elements of drug habituation, dependence, and abuse: the drug is used habitually, dependence upon its effects, real or imagined, has developed, and, judging by the resultant toxicity, the drug is being abused. Though consideration of such forms of drug misuse lies outside the scope of this book, it should not be inferred, thereby, that we consider them to be of only minor importance. Serious consequences, including death, can result from the types of practices just described.

None of the terms proposed has gained general acceptance. The use of the various terms in the medical literature appears to reflect the influences of tradition, uncertainty, and personal preference. The *British Medical Journal,* for example, published articles in the issues of 24 and 31 October, 1964, in which the definition of the then new term, drug dependence, was reported, in the series, and the recommended terminology was used (dependence of morphine type, dependence of cocaine type, and so on). The series was entitled "Drugs of Addiction"! The pertinent chapter in the most recent edition of a popular pharmacological text, published in 1980, bears the title, "Drug Addiction and Drug Abuse"; there is less overlap in terminology, however, than the title suggests, for the author of the chapter provides a rather unique definition of addiction, which stresses "the degree to which drug use pervades the total life activity of the user" (5). This definition has not enjoyed wide acceptance, possibly because, in the words of the author, "In most instances it will not be possible to state with precision at which point compulsive use should be considered addiction." In the November 4, 1968 issue of the *Journal of the American Medical Association,* a series of papers presented at a "Conference on Drug Abuse" was published. The titles of the various papers contain the words *drug dependence, drug abuse,* and, in several, *drugs;* the last surely represents the ultimate in economy of terminology. Authors who appear to prefer the newer terms, drug abuse or drug dependence, and use them predominantly in their publications, not infrequently fail to use them exclusively; particularly when the gravity of a problem is to be emphasized, the word addiction appears.

Difficulties have been encountered in the use of the new terms as adjectives. Perhaps from long usage, the phrases "addicting drugs" and "habituating drugs" have an acceptable ring to them, but the phrases "dependent drugs" and "abusive drugs" may appear awkward and even faintly ludicrous.

The terms to be used in this book

The terminology one uses is really a matter of minor importance, so long as the reader or listener fully understands what is and what is not known about the phenomenon under consideration. Given this information, terminology then becomes merely a convenient means of communicative shorthand. Unless one enjoys them as exercises in disputation, semantic quarrels should not be joined, in our opinion, unless terminology is being used for purposes of distortion: to deny an established fact, to assert to be factual that which remains conjectural, or to affirm the existence of that which has been satisfactorily demonstrated to be nonexistent. Such distortions occur with distressing frequency in testimony given at legislative hearings preceding the formulation of laws pertaining to drug abuse; on these occasions, words like "addiction" and "narcotic" seem to be used more for their emotional impact than for conveying factual information.

In the succeeding chapters, our goal will be to relate what is and what is not known about the pharmacological and medical aspects of certain types of drug abuse. We will use most of the terms mentioned in the preceding section, but we will, however, observe certain conventions that reflect our personal preferences. A drug will be described as *addicting* only if it is known that physical dependence upon its effects can develop. A drug will be described as *habituating* only if no physical dependence upon its effects has ever been satisfactorily demonstrated, regardless of the schedule of use. *Drug abuse* and *drug dependence* will refer only to the abuse of or dependence on the drugs specifically considered in subsequent chapters. No other significance should be imputed to our usage of terms; no term will be used to imply that a given form of drug abuse is more or less detrimental to the user or to society than another.

REFERENCES

1. Louria, D. B., *The Drug Scene*. New York: McGraw-Hill, 1968
2. Smith, D. E., Use of LSD in the Haight-Ashbury. *Calif Med* 110:472, 1969
3. Solursh, L. P. and W. R. Clement, Hallucinogenic drug abuse: Manifestations and management. *Canad Med Assoc J* 98:407, 1968
4. Tatum, A. L. and M. H. Seevers, Theories of drug addiction. *Physiol Rev* 11:107, 1931
5. Jaffe, J. H., Drug addiction and drug abuse. In: Gilman, A. G., L. Goodman and A. Gilman, eds., *The Pharmacological Basis of Therapeutics*, ed. 6. New York: Macmillan, 1980

Chapter 2

SOME GENERAL ASPECTS
OF DRUG ABUSE

BUYING DRUGS ILLEGALLY

In buying drugs illegally, the buyer not only takes into his possession substances that make him liable to arrest, but he usually does not know just what he has bought and may not know until he has used it. Through experience, the user has come to anticipate that he will receive from the vendor a typical quantity of active drug. He knows that sometimes he will be cheated and will receive an unusually small quantity of drug or perhaps none at all and that he also runs the risk of receiving an unexpectedly large quantity of drug, which may cost him his life. He may come to learn too that a product represented to be a single drug may, in fact, be a mixture of drugs.

Notoriously unscrupulous, the typical "pusher" sells drugs primarily to make money. Most will vend any preparation, whether it be wholly inert or a potentially catastrophic mixture of very powerful drugs; only a few seem to have pretenses of being ethical businessmen and of dealing fairly with the user. To this conventional picture of the supply, distribution, and sale of drugs for abuse, some new aspects have been added in the recent past. In regard to supply, one must reckon now with the amateur pharmaceutical chemist who specializes in the synthesis of hallucinogens and stimulants and in the concoction of mixtures of these types of drugs. He sometimes claims great social significance for his work: he is providing the drugs that will enable users to achieve fuller and happier lives. Relatively new to the scene too are the numerous adolescents who now sell drugs (and who often use them personally). In the typical suburban setting, they deal most often in marihuana, LSD, and amphetamine-type drugs; only rarely do they sell narcotics. Though apparently not averse to the profits to be made on drug sales, they too often extol the social value of their activities. The fact that they must also defy the law and risk arrest may, for some, make these activities seem all the more appealing and "righteous." Much of the illegal drug market today is supported by adolescents who actively seek novel and exciting experiences. Their unhesitating willingness to use any preparation offered that promises such experiences is one of the graver aspects of the present situation.

With this general introduction, we would like now to consider in greater detail some of the aspects of illegal drug sales.

Variable potency

Ordinarily, the only drugs of constant potency available for sale illegally are compounds that were originally made by reputable manufacturers for prescription by the medical profession but that were subsequently diverted to the illegal market. In this category would be most of the generalized central nervous system depressants that are subject to abuse, including barbiturates and some of the amphetamine-like compounds, which are diverted from legal channels by unethical drug wholesalers and pharmacists in this country, a process facilitated by inadequate law enforcement. Diversion also occurs by means of drug sales to apparently legitimate outlets in such foreign countries as Mexico, with resale to those who smuggle the drugs back into this country. The extent of drug diversion can be enormous: the Food and Drug Administration estimates that, of the approximately eight billion conventional doses of amphetamine manufactured legally in this country in 1967, about one-half were eventually sold illegally.

The problem of variable potency arises almost always in connection with drugs that are always illegal, such as marihuana and heroin. Before World War II, when heroin addiction was a problem of relatively modest proportions, the heroin available for sale was reputedly either practically pure or only slightly diluted. After the war, certain criminal groups recognized the profits to be made in the sale of heroin and organized channels of supply and distribution. Though their product was illegal, they adopted many of the practices derived from legitimate business. The ancient practice of "short-weighting" the customer is scrupulously observed. To increase profits, the vendor dilutes the pure heroin he receives with various substances, so that the drug itself typically comprises only a very small percentage of the total weight of the material purchased by the user. The use of heroin so grossly diluted has resulted, however, in degrees of narcotic addiction much less intense than the addiction encountered when relatively pure narcotics were available.

Diluted heroin makes an addict's existence uncertain and precarious largely because the degree of dilution and the nature of the diluents vary so greatly. Analyses of packets of "heroin" seized by the police indicate that their relative content of narcotic can vary from none at all to 77%; in many samples, the relative heroin content ranges from 1 to 5%. Numerous explanations have been offered to account for such variability: demand remains steady while supply fluctuates, which means that, within limits, degree of dilution varies inversely with size of supply; fearing imminent arrest, a supplier may sell his heroin as quickly as possible and so lack time to dilute it to the customary extent; the independent entrepreneur who imports heroin at irregular intervals may dilute it in an unpredictable fashion; and so on. Addicts had come to anticipate in the mid- to late-1960's that the heroin "caps" or "bags" they bought would contain approximately 5% heroin, and they administered their dose accordingly. If the relative heroin content fell below 3%, the addict formerly rejected such material as "junk," for its effects were too weak. Today, much of the "heroin" being sold is only 2 to 3% heroin and the remainder diluent. If the relative content of heroin exceeds 20%, the user is then in danger of administering a fatal overdose (1), which is one of the principal causes of death among addicts; it is an omnipresent threat particularly to those who inject the drug intravenously.

The problem of variable potency in regard to marihuana is considerably more complex. The pharmacologically active compounds present in marihuana occur in a resin found on the flowering tops and adjacent leaves of the hemp plant; some strains of hemp plant are known to produce resin that has a higher content of these compounds than others. The warmer the climate in which the plant is grown, the more resin it forms. When harvested, the inclusion of such non-resin-bearing parts of the plant as the stems serves to reduce the potency per unit volume of a marihuana preparation, as would, for example, addition of ordinary tobacco. The resin contains a number of compounds, a few pharmacologically active, others inert. Some of these compounds are not chemically stable and, after harvest, may be converted spontaneously to other compounds under appropriate conditions; a rise in temperature is known to effect such conversions, to yield compounds with enhanced or reduced pharmacological activity (2).

Chemical analysis of marihuana to ascertain its content of active drug supplies an objective measure of the great variability in the intensity of the effects produced by different batches. Three different batches of "good" marihuana, supplied and analyzed by governmental representatives, were utilized in two clinical studies on the effects of the drug (3, 4); the most potent batch contained more than four times as much active drug by weight than did the least potent batch.

The problem of variable potency in regard to LSD stems largely from the fact that no one dose has been accepted as standard. As all LSD is of illicit origin, each chemist who synthesizes it is free to determine the quantity of drug present in each dose he prepares. The selling price of LSD is usually so high in comparison to the expense of preparation that cost ordinarily is not a primary determinant of dosage size. Thus, the user of LSD, unless he prepares the dose himself, does not really know how much drug he is taking; not infrequently, the quantity of drug is less than the seller's claim (5). The user has come to anticipate receiving a typical dose, which ranges from 50 to 300 μg. If the dose is unusually large, the chance that a "bad" trip will result is increased.

The sale of phony drugs occurs from time to time under various circumstances. We have already noted that some packets of "heroin" have been found to contain no heroin at all and that imitations of a popular brand of LSD may have the requisite tablet shape and color but contain no LSD. Pharmacologically inert imitations of virtually all of the drugs subject to abuse have been marketed at one time or another. The suburban adolescent, who wishes to experiment with drugs and who has not yet learned to mistrust others as has his counterpart raised in the urban ghetto, is one type of victim sought by the seller of phony drugs. To such teenagers, aspirin tablets have successfully been represented as amphetamine and cigarettes containing various dried and shredded plant preparations as marihuana. Typifying one of many ways in which the gullible can be hoaxed was a teenage girl who confidently told a high school psychologist that she had no fear of the consequences of sexual intercourse because she was taking "birth control" pills; her pills contained, in fact, a mixture of drugs designed to bring relief from mild degrees of pain.

The defrauded participant in an illegal transaction has little opportunity for redress of grievances, though drug dealers have been assaulted by outraged users and occasionally killed. It seems probable that variable drug potency, in one form or another, will always be a part of the phenomenon of drug abuse. A proposed solution for this problem is governmental provision of pure drug for users. This proposal would, in our opinion, provide few benefits. The illegal market in drugs probably would not disappear because it seems to us highly unlikely that any governmental agency would agree to supply all of the drugs and drug mixtures now in popular demand. The British have supplied pure heroin to addicts, but the incidence of deaths attributed to heroin in that country does not appear to be significantly lower than that in the United States.

Drug diluents

The dilution of pure drug with presumably inert substances is a matter of medical significance primarily in the instance of intravenous usage. The process of dilution commonly appears to occur under unsterile conditions and entails the use of whatever substance the dealer chooses to regard as appropriate. His choice of a diluent may be a matter of no small consequence because heroin is so often injected, particularly by vein.

To prepare his drug for injection, the heroin addict frequently puts it into a spoon and adds a small quantity of water, usually tap water. To speed the process, the mixture is heated, often by holding the spoon over a candle or several matches. A piece of cotton gauze is added, and the solution is drawn up through a needle into a syringe or eye dropper; the gauze serves as a filter to trap larger pieces of particulate matter, an important precaution if the diluent happens to be, for example, highly insoluble magnesium silicate (talc).

One of the commonest diluents encountered is lactose, or milk sugar, an essentially innocuous substance; less frequently used carbohydrates are sucrose, starch, and mannitol. Another commonly used diluent is the antimalarial drug, quinine, which is added for a very specific purpose. Heroin is an alkaloid and has the characteristic bitter taste of this group of compounds. As a rough measure of potency, an addict may ask to taste the "heroin" prior to purchase; because quinine is also an alkaloid, it provides the requisite bitter taste. (It seems reasonable to assume that many experienced addicts know that the bitter taste of "heroin" may stem as much from quinine as from the narcotic, but there is really very little they can do about it.) Other diluents known to have been used are baking soda, procaine (Novocain), and an Italian laxative preparation, Mannite (1).

There has been much speculation about the possible adverse effects of the diluents of drugs, but little sure knowledge exists. It is a difficult situation in which to determine cause and effect for, even in the course of a single day, an addict may be exposed to several different diluents. The incidence of infectious diseases among heroin addicts, for example, is probably higher than that of the general population. It is possible that some diluents may contain pathogenic microorganisms, inadvertently introduced in the processes of dilution and packaging; on the other hand, the addict's typical methods of dissolving the drug and injecting it are hardly sanitary. (In moments of desperation, the water needed to dissolve the drug may be obtained from a public toilet bowl.) Thus, it is usually difficult to trace the source of an infection.

Some diluents cause tissue injury and may thereby facilitate the development of certain infectious diseases. This statement applies particularly to such diluents as quinine, which is so irritating that tissue necrosis is often produced at the site of injection. Those addicts who inject heroin just beneath the skin ("skin poppers") typically display numerous skin abscesses, both recent and chronic. These necrotic skin lesions are usually deep and yield little pus, the latter observation suggesting their chemical origin. Such lesions are regarded by microbiologists as most favorable sites for the growth of the bacterium responsible for tetanus, *Clostridium tetani;* this disease is a possible, and frequently fatal, sequel of heroin addiction (1, 6). Often present at or near the site where heroin containing a histotoxic adulterant has been injected are signs of inflammation and localized infections caused by a variety of other pathogenic bacteria that commonly invade open wounds.

Sudden deaths among heroin addicts (so sudden sometimes that the needle may still be in a vein) are classified by some as the consequence of an overdose. Others believe that death comes too quickly to be attributed to heroin and feel that some of these deaths might be attributed to the presence of "colloidal, particulate, or partially soluble materials" in the injected solution; they note that the intravenous injection of solutions containing such materials have been known to cause sudden, severe drops in blood pressure and death (6). The incompletely dissolved substances in these instances would presumably be the insoluble, or poorly soluble, diluents. In numerous reports, inexplicable illness and death in heroin users have been tentatively attributed to unidentified diluents. But even if a diluent is thought to have played a causative role, identifying it can be a formidable chore.

Mixtures of unknown composition

Drug users, particularly adolescents, who will take almost any drug mixture of unspecified composition so long as it is sold with the promise of providing a novel and intensely gratifying experience, provide the market for the products of the amateur pharmaceutical chemist, of whom we have spoken previously. In concocting drug mixtures, these chemists ordinarily do not wish to defraud the user—quite the contrary. They often sympathize with the goals of the drug user and wish to prepare a "mind blower" that will produce an unparalleled "trip." To say that some of these chemists have achieved their goal would be to understate the case considerably.

A drug user cannot be certain that when he buys what is represented to be a single drug he will not, in fact, receive a mixture of drugs. Even the most potent of the hallucinogens, LSD, seems no longer a satisfactory product for some amateur pharmaceutical chemists. In addition to LSD, they may synthesize methamphetamine, a potent stimulant related in chemical structure to amphetamine. Mixtures of LSD and methamphetamine have been sold to users as pure LSD. To a mind already disorganized by LSD, such effects of methamphetamine as muscular tremors and a sense of anxiety may readily evoke a reaction of severe panic, which some drug users describe as a "death trip" (5).

The original STP is an excellent example of the "success" that the amateur chemists have attained. The initial word-of-mouth advertising for STP was highly enthusiastic; the testimonials of those who had taken it portrayed the product as capable of creating an unprecedented "high." Users avidly sought STP, and imitations of it quickly appeared. Within only a few weeks, the tenor of the testimonials changed drastically; now reports of psychotic episodes lasting for 4 days or more began to circulate. A number of users voluntarily surrendered their supplies of STP to physicians, and STP rapidly waned in general popularity; it had proved to be too potent for all but most ardent devotees of hallucinogens.

Samples of what was purported to be the original STP were subjected to chemical analysis, and a new hallucinogenic compound was isolated: 2, 5-dimethoxy-4-methyl-amphetamine (DOM). In its chemical structure, DOM resembles both amphetamine and mescaline; in human beings, DOM was found to be a considerably more potent hallucinogen than either of the two related drugs. Clinical investigation of DOM, however, failed to reproduce all of the signs and symptoms of STP, in particular, those which were typical of an atropine type of drug (7). Moreover, attempts at treatment of users of STP with the tranquilizer, chlorpromazine (Thorazine), had produced cardiovascular shock in a number of cases and had possibly caused some deaths (8), but subjects who received pure DOM in the clinical trials were essentially unaffected by concurrent administration of this tranquilizer. Furthermore, the psychotic state induced by pure DOM, even with the largest doses used, rarely persisted beyond the day of the trial, whereas the psychic effects of STP had been reputed to last as long as a week (8). The clinical investigators of DOM speculated that these prolonged psychotic episodes may have been caused by "STP" that contained, in addition to DOM or possibly in lieu of it, an atropinic drug (7), for large quantities of such a drug could produce the reported reactions, which would persist for a number of days.

And what of the imitations of STP, offered for sale soon after it became popular? Some were found to contain atropine and mescaline and some atropine and methamphetamine (9); others were never analyzed chemically. It seems clear that "STP" was neither a single drug nor a drug mixture of standard composition but a name given to a variety of preparations, most of which probably contained two or more drugs.

The story of STP has been reported in some detail because it illustrates so well the fact that illicit drug mixtures are a frustrating problem for pharmacologist and physician alike. In many instances, we are not able to discover what a mixture contained. Often, by the time we are aware that a new product on the illegal market has become quite popular and is possibly proving also to be dangerous, imitations of it are already being sold. Samples obtained for analysis may be the original product or an imitation. The imitations may be pharmacologically inert or may contain effective quantities of one or more drugs that will have a more pronounced, though different, impact on the user than the original product had. Because physicians commonly cannot find out what a drug mixture contains means, among other things, that rational treatment cannot be provided for any adverse effects that may develop. And treatment based on guesswork may well be ineffective or even harmful.

ROUTES OF DRUG ADMINISTRATION

Historical records indicate that early man not unexpectedly utilized the most readily available orifices of the body, the mouth and the nose, to take drugs. These drugs were, of course, crude plant preparations, whose physical nature influenced the route of administration. There is much evidence to indicate that many centuries before the Christian era man had already become a keenly observant and quite ingenious user of drugs. If the active substance was contained in seeds that were found to pass through the gastrointestinal tract unchanged, then the seeds were ground prior to ingestion. If the drug appeared in the urine in an active form, then the drug effect was prolonged by the individual drinking his own urine or that of a fellow user. Man learned to roast certain types of beans and, with the aid of a hollow tube made of bamboo or bone, to blow the ground residue of the bean into the nostrils. Dried hemp plants were burned as a form of incense, and the fumes were inhaled during religious ceremonies. The identification and use of hallucinogenic drugs of plant origin have been discovered in societies, both ancient and still extant, that range in structure from the primitive to the more highly developed (10).

Until approximately the middle of the 19th century, drugs of abuse were taken by mouth, inhaled in the form of vapors or fumes, or placed into the nostrils as snuff would be; it was at this time that the hypodermic syringe came into general use in the world of medicine. Its impact on narcotic addiction was striking, and its use contributed greatly to the rapid rise in the incidence of this form of drug abuse in America during the latter half of the century. When morphine is taken by mouth, its effects develop rather slowly; the intensity of its effects, whether for relief of pain or for pleasure, is less than that maximally possible. By injection, however, the effects of morphine develop more rapidly, and by vein, they are maximal. During the Civil War, the physicians of the time, many of them poorly trained and most of them ignorant of the dangers of drug addiction, freely prescribed morphine for the many battlefield casualties, even providing some patients with a personal supply of morphine and a syringe. The problem of "morphinism" among soldiers and discharged veterans grew to such proportions that narcotic addiction was commonly called the "army disease."

Drugs subject to abuse cannot exert their characteristic effects until effective quantities of them have been conveyed, via the bloodstream, to their principal site of action, the central nervous system. The rate of onset of their effects and, to a lesser degree, the intensity of their effects are determined largely by the rapidity of this process. The route of administration determines, in turn, how rapidly a drug gains access to the blood. (Once in the blood, however, a number of things can happen to drug molecules, other than being borne to their principal site of action: they may be carried to the liver and there metabolically inactivated, they may be carried to the kidney and there excreted, they may be carried to cells of such "indifferent" tissues as skeletal muscle or depot fat, where they exert no observable effect, or they may be temporarily immobilized by being bound to plasma proteins.) How rapidly the effects of a drug become evident is determined also by the relative ease with which a drug enters cells or gains access to the "receptor" sites within or on the surface of a cell.

Drugs that exert effects on other tissues in addition to the central nervous system often exert observable effects first on this system because, relatively speaking, it has an unusually rich blood supply. Thus, when a drug is injected intravenously, the brain, because of the many blood vessels that enter it, is more quickly exposed to greater quantities of the drug than are other organs of the body having fewer blood vessels. Seconds after the intravenous injection of heroin a user begins to feel the effects of the drug and obtains the most intense narcotic effect possible. Many addicts once they have experienced the impact of intravenously injected heroin will thereafter countenance no other route of administration.

When a drug is injected directly beneath the skin, it is injected into an area that has a relatively sparse supply of blood vessels. The opportunities for a given drug molecule to enter the bloodstream are accordingly reduced, and it will take at least 30 minutes after subcutaneous injection of heroin, for example, for its maximal effects to be experienced. If a drug is injected intramuscularly, the rate of onset and degree of intensity of drug effect are intermediate between the subcutaneous and intravenous routes. By this route, the drug is placed into a region relatively well endowed with blood vessels, which explains why its entrance into the bloodstream is more rapid than in the case of subcutaneous injection.

Inhalation is a possible route of administration in those instances where a drug exists physically as a true gas or, upon heating, volatilizes to produce a drug-containing vapor, smoke, or fume. For many drugs, inhalation provides a rapidity of onset of effect exceeded only by intravenous injection. This is so because anything inhaled is, within seconds, exposed to the large alveolar surface of the lung. Once a molecule has diffused across the alveolar surface, it enters the bloodstream immediately. The amount of drug transferred across the alveolar membrane and into the blood per inhalation is, in part, a function of time. This fact is recognized by experienced users of marihuana who attempt to retain each inhalation within their lungs as long as possible.

Inhalation of drug-laden smoke from such plant preparations as opium or marihuana naturally can occur only after the preparation has been heated, or combusted, as within a pipe or cigarette. Pharmacologists have wondered what effect the heating process has on the potency of the preparation. One answer to this question was provided by the following experiment: cigarettes containing hashish were "smoked" by a machine of the type used to determine the tar and nicotine content of cigarettes. The smoke was collected and its components, other than true gases, were electrostatically precipitated; the precipitate was put into solution and injected into mice to test its toxicity. The toxicity of an amount of un-smoked hashish equal to that contained in the cigarettes was also determined. The results indicated that the smoking of hashish reduced its toxicity by approximately 75% (11). Insofar as we can extrapolate from the toxic effects of hashish in mice to its effects in human beings, these findings suggest that the smoke of hashish lacks an appreciable portion of its initial content of active drug.

If a drug, in solution or crystalline form, is placed into the nostril as snuff would be, the onset of the drug's effects will be reasonably rapid, for the interior of the nose has quite a rich supply of blood vessels. This route of administration does not provide as rapid an onset of drug effect as does inhalation, but it has been employed for decades by users of heroin and cocaine. Chronic use of this route has been associated with perforation of the septum that separates the nostrils. In the case of cocaine, this occurrence may be attributed to the intense construction of blood vessels this drug produces, with tissue damage resulting from a relative lack of oxygen and other substances supplied by the blood.

When taken by mouth, an appreciable portion of the dose of most drugs appears to enter the blood through the walls of the upper portion of the small intestine; this means that the rate of drug absorption is substantially dependent on how rapidly the drug moves from the stomach to the small intestine. If a drug is taken directly after a meal, it will be diluted by gastric juices and dispersed among the gastric contents; under these conditions, several hours may elapse before all of the drug enters the small intestine. If the meal has been unusually rich in fat or has contained such irritating substances as strong spices, the stomach may empty even more slowly. A drug, particularly if in liquid form, traverses the stomach quite rapidly when it is empty; solid substances, unless they quickly break down into finely divided particles, leave the stomach more slowly. Taking a drug by mouth provides the slowest rate of onset of effect, and, in terms of reproducibility of effect, it can be one of the least reliable routes of drug administration. Though the extent of absorption of pure drugs is probably much the same for a given individual from one occasion to another, if the stomach is empty, variable absorption can be a significant problem with crude plant preparation and particularly with those that can induce vomiting, such as peyote.

The sublingual route of administration entails placing a drug tablet in the mouth, under the tongue, and allowing it to remain there until it has fully dissolved. Drug absorption occurs through the richly vascularized mucous membranes of the oral cavity. It provides a faster onset of drug effect than would ingestion of the tablet and is currently being utilized by some users of LSD.

Few drugs will penetrate intact skin when applied to it, and topical application of drugs is an administration route essentially never used in drug abuse. There are a few recorded instances, however, of addicts, desperate for want of a needle or unable to find an accessible vein that had not been already occluded by a previous injection, who have abraded their skin and rubbed the drug into the wound in the hope of speeding its entrance into their blood (12).

Most drug users appear to have a narrow choice of routes of administration, in part because of the physical nature of the drug as they receive it and in part because of tradition. Alcoholics, almost without exception, take ethanol by mouth, though it could be heated and the vapors inhaled; by this route its effects would certainly develop more quickly. The oral or sublingual routes seem to predominate, also, in the use of LSD; the tablets of LSD supplied by drug vendors could be pulverized, and the resulting powder put into solution for injection, but again this appears to be an uncommon practice. Those who have attempted to inject intravenously pulverized forms of commercially manufactured pills intended for oral administration have encountered serious difficulties, since these pills contain such inert binders and fillers as talc. The general problem encountered in this type of situation is well illustrated by the experiences of those using the preparation known as "Blue Velvet."

To prepare Blue Velvet, the user first boiled paregoric until virtually all the alcohol it contained had been evaporated; the resulting "sludge" contained opium, camphor, and anise oil. To this sludge was added pulverized tablets of an antihistamine drug, tripelennamine (Pyribenzamine), which are blue. The resulting mixture was injected intravenously. Not all the users of Blue Velvet survived the experience. Those who died were found at autopsy to have numerous small arteries plugged with thromboses that pathologists felt had originated from the talc (magnesium silicate) filler used in the antihistamine tablets (13). Word of these deaths spread among drug users, and, happily, the popularity of Blue Velvet was short lived.

The narcotic addict probably has the widest choice of routes of administration, though injection appears to be the predominant form of usage. Inhalation of narcotics usually means the smoking of opium or of heroin; this practice is commonly associated with a relatively mild degree of addiction and is infrequently utilized today by the American addict. The inhalation of powdered heroin into the nostrils is a practice that seems to wax and wane in popularity; its efficacy would be compromised at those times when an addict suffered from pronounced nasal congestion, as during a common cold, for mucus within the nose would surely slow the rate of drug absorption. Ingestion of narcotics usually entails the use of paregoric, which contains opium, or codeine-containing cough medicines. For the injection of heroin, more timid users may begin with subcutaneous or intramuscular routes. Many, encouraged by other addicts, eventually progress to "main-lining" (intravenous injection), by which route the greatest intensity of effect can be obtained.

MEDICAL PROBLEMS OF DRUG USERS
NOT CAUSED BY DRUGS

This type of problem typically arises from the irritant properties of substances, other than the drug, present in the preparation used or from infectious diseases that appear to result from unsterile injection procedures.

We have already described the abscesses that develop as a consequence of the subcutaneous injection of heroin diluted with quinine or other irritating adulterants. Multiple abscesses and scars are found also on the skin of that minority of barbiturate users who inject the drug; these wounds have been ascribed to the effects of the high molecular weight alcohols in which the barbiturates are dissolved (12). When such scars occur in muscle, permanent muscular contractions can result, so that fingers, or even an arm (depending on the site of the scar), become "frozen" in one particular position. These contractures can usually be relieved by surgical excision of the scar.

Local and systemic infectious diseases developing in conjunction with the injection of drugs are relatively common and may result in death. They arise because drug users, with what one is almost tempted to call suicidal intent, ignore sterile precautions during the injection of drugs. The site is never cleaned before injection, the needle is frequently licked or rubbed on the scalp so that it will penetrate the skin more easily, the drug is dissolved in any water available, and syringes are freely shared with other users and probably not cleaned until clotted blood impedes their operation. As a result, a variety of infectious diseases is encountered among drug users. Formerly, the problem of infectious disease existed primarily among narcotics addicts, but, more recently, it has appeared among users of amphetamine-type drugs because of their increasing use of the intravenous route of administration.

HEPATITIS   Serum hepatitis is a viral disease transmitted by the intravenous injection of infected blood. Transmission of the disease in drug abuse occurs when a person who has the hepatitis virus present in his blood uses a syringe for an intravenous injection and then permits others to use the same syringe (contaminated by blood from the original user) for intravenous injection. The resulting infectious inflammation of the liver can be anything from a relatively mild disease to a fatal one.

The relative incidence of hepatitis among heroin addicts is quite high; it is the opinion of one group of physicians experienced in the treatment of addicts that "it is safe to assume that any confirmed addict has had hepatitis" (12). If an addict requires hospitalization for an infectious disease, it will most commonly be for hepatitis (1, 6). In such a large urban hospital as Bellevue Hospital in New York City, a majority of all patients hospitalized for hepatitis will probably be found to be heroin users (1).

The relative incidence of death from hepatitis among drug users is not known. It is known that evidence of chronic liver dysfunction can be detected in a very high percentage of heroin users. It is doubtful that all of these cases can be classified as "chronic viral hepatitis," nor is there any satisfactory evidence to suggest that chronic exposure to heroin impairs liver function (1, 6, 14). It has been suggested that some of the cases of chronic dysfunction may be caused by a diluent of heroin or may represent some form of allergic manifestation (1).

ENDOCARDITIS   This infectious disease, characterized by inflammation of the inner lining of the heart, is more commonly fatal when it arises as a sequel of drug injection than when it does not; in one study of users who were suffering from this disease, only 31% survived (1). This finding appears to be principally due to the fact that the disease in addicts is often caused by bacteria and fungi that are resistant to available antibiotics. Among non-users, the causative bacterium is likely to be a species of *Streptococcus*. Among drug users, however, streptococcal endocarditis is encountered in only a minority of the cases (1, 15); most commonly it is a staphylococcal infection. Causally implicated also are Gram-negative enteric bacteria, such as *Escherichia coli* and *Pseudomonas aeruginosa*, enterococci, and various species of the fungus *Candida* (1, 15); for some of these organisms, in addition to possibly antibiotic-resistant staphylococci, no generally effective means of treatment is available. The unsanitary conditions associated with drug injection may offer an explanation for the atypical spectrum of causative organisms, for many of them are commonly found in dirt and excreta, as well as being present on the skin and, particularly the fungus, *Candida*, in the vagina. Endocarditis of fungal origin develops with greatest frequency in users with a history of previous heart disease (1). One characteristic of endocarditis is the presence of nodules formed by clumps of bacteria, fibrin, and cells (fibroblasts) on the edges of the valves of the heart, notably the aortic and mitral valves (15); as a result, the valves may become scarred and incompetent, so that fatal congestive heart failure can develop. A commoner cause of death in this disease is the formation of blood clots; emboli may lodge in the heart itself, the brain, the lungs (15), the spleen, or the kidneys (1).

PULMONARY COMPLICATIONS   As we have just mentioned, emboli, some of them infected, may form as a consequence of endocarditis; these may lodge in the lungs and there give rise to embolic pneumonia. This disease may also be caused by emboli originating in infected injection sites (1). It is commonly severe and sometimes fatal.

Bacterial pneumonia also occurs among addicts. As yet, it has not been clearly demonstrated that any causal relationship exists between heroin addiction and this type of pneumonia. The available evidence has been interpreted to indicate that addicts are unusually susceptible and that susceptibility increases the longer the duration of the addiction (1, 14).

Some reduction in the ability of gases to diffuse across the alveolar surface of the lungs has been measured in individuals who have been heroin addicts for many years and who had not, at the time of the measurement, recently suffered the effects of an "overdose," which produces pulmonary congestion. The etiology of this mild form of chronic lung disease has no easy explanation, though a mechanism involving deposits of heroin diluents within the lungs has been considered (16).

TETANUS   The association of tetanus with narcotic addiction was first observed almost 100 years ago. We have already noted that the numerous deep abscesses at injection sites, which have been attributed to irritant diluents of heroin, are believed to provide ideal conditions for the growth of *Clostridium tetani*. We also noted that a high percentage of addicts who develop tetanus inject heroin subcutaneously. Most of them have been addicted for many years and have sclerosed or obstructed all easily accessible veins by previous intravenous injections. More women than men resort to "skin popping," for, typically, women have fewer superficial veins accessible to injection, which is a consequence of a greater abundance of subcutaneous fat. Thus, the majority of addicts developing tetanus are women. Though the incidence of tetanus among addicts is not great, when it does develop, the resulting death rate may be as high as 90% (1, 6). Survival of one attack of tetanus does not confer immunity against subsequent attacks (1).

MISCELLANEOUS PROBLEMS   The unsterile injection technique of the addict frequently results in the development of bacterial infections at the injection site, which evoke cellulitis or an inflammatory response in the neighboring tissues; emboli may gain access to the general circulation from such sites, as we have already mentioned. Bacteria may enter the bloodstream directly as a consequence of unsterile intravenous injections and produce septicemia. Injections also result in a high incidence of thrombophlebitis among addicts. Malaria was at one time a significant hazard for narcotic addicts; just 30 to 40 years ago, there were hundreds of cases of malaria among addicts. Today, addicts rarely contract malaria (1, 6). The current absence of this disease from the addiction scene is a reflection of the fact that it has been almost entirely eradicated in this country.

Though some addicts have tuberculosis, and a few die as a result of it, the disease is not believed to be causally related to drug usage but rather to the user's typical environment and way of life. The incidence of tuberculosis is high among those who live in crowded marginal housing and whose dietary intake is nutritionally inadequate.

FACTORS INFLUENCING RESPONSES TO DRUGS

The placebo effect

A placebo may be defined as an inert substance represented to be an active drug. Under appropriate circumstances, and particularly when anticipation is great, the administration of placebos can produce quite striking effects. It has been repeatedly demonstrated in clinical experiments, for example, that among patients who are most probably in pain, such as those recovering from major surgery, one-third will report appreciable relief from pain following injection of a placebo.

Trust and anticipation appear to be the keystones of the placebo effect: trust in the enthusiastic recommendations of others about a certain preparation and, based on this trust, anticipation so powerful that an effect is produced despite the fact that the pharmacological activity of the preparation is negligible. It is the adolescent, early in the course of experimentation with drug abuse, who is most likely to respond to a placebo or near-placebo. The veteran user, through experience, is able to critically appraise the quality of drug he receives; sometimes he can detect rather small reductions in potency, and it is unlikely that he would experience any effect from a preparation nearly or totally pharmacologically inactive.

The recent, but short-lived, vogue for the smoking of dried banana skins appears to have been essentially a testimonial to the power of the placebo effect. Early converts to this practice praised the sensations produced. Pharmacologists were delighted that the vogue had developed, for they doubted that banana skins could produce anything but a rather innocuous, though perhaps mildly disagreeable smoke. A skeptical majority of users were unimpressed with the effect produced, and the practice died out.

One may also say that a form of the placebo effect is operative in those situations in which a user's response is disproportionately great relative to the amount of drug taken. A person who unconsciously or consciously wishes to become a drunk may feel quite intoxicated after only one or two drinks. We suspect but cannot provide that some of the effects reported by users of marihuana, particularly by adolescents following their first or second exposure to the drug, belong largely in the category of a placebo response. Much of the marihuana of domestic origin, particularly that grown in our northern states, is weak. Experienced users contemptuously reject marihuana of this quality; some naive users, however, report that it produces a pleasant "high."

Dose of drug

One naturally expects that the larger the dose of drug the more intense its effects, and this is usually the case. We have already noted that many drug-dependent individuals find the more intense effects of some drugs highly pleasurable, as evidenced by the fact that they actively seek the most potent preparations available or increase their daily intake with time. We are considering dosage again to make the additional point that a few types of responses to drugs are not, strictly speaking, dose-related phenomena.

The dose of LSD taken, for example, does not always determine whether a trip will be good or bad. In the words of a physician working in the Haight-Ashbury area, "Susceptibility to 'bad trips' is not absolutely dose-related, but depends upon the experience, maturity and personality of the user, as well as upon the external environment in which the trip is taking place" (5). For the inexperienced user, a small or conventional dose of LSD may evoke a severe state of panic as he undergoes the drug-induced perceptual distortions. Extreme anxiety may develop in the regular user if a typical dose of LSD is taken in an environment that he regards as hostile, whereas, under optimal conditions, "A panic reaction in the more experienced user can often be credited to the high dosage he has taken" (17).

Experience with drug abuse

In some categories of drug abuse, experience and guidance are necessary before the drug experience becomes gratifying. The naive user hardly knows what to expect, and the actual drug effect may differ considerably from what is anticipated. The novice heroin user frequently needs encouragement from veteran addicts to ignore such unpleasant effects of the narcotic as nausea and dizziness and to concentrate on those effects that can be pleasurable. Some initiates to LSD, and even regular users, on occasion, may have a "guide" with them while under the drug's influence. The guide, commonly a user familiar with the effects of LSD, serves as a link with reality and as one who may be able to abort an impending bad trip by "talking down" the user. The talking-down technique, employed by guides and physicians alike, essentially entails reassurance: the user's present state is drug induced, he is not losing his mind, the experience will end, and so on.

The importance of experience with drug abuse was clearly demonstrated in a recent study on the effects of marihuana in man (3). The subjects were chronic users of marihuana and a "naive" group that had neither used the drug before nor seen anyone else use it. Both groups were supplied with marihuana cigarettes of demonstrated potency, as well as placebo cigarettes containing material from pharmacologically inactive portions of the hemp plant. The naive subjects were taught the proper technique for smoking marihuana (a procedure mastered by street users only through guidance and experience). By subjective and objective criteria, all of the chronic users became "high." Under the same circumstances, only one of the nine naive subjects evinced a typical psychic reaction to marihuana. (This subject alone before the experiment, had proclaimed a desire to get "high" because the sensation had been so enthusiastically recommended to him. This may be an example of a form of the placebo response, or the influence of trust and anticipation, on the nature of the drug experience.) Most of the naive subjects could distinguish placebo cigarettes from those containing marihuana but had greater difficulty in distinguishing between the two types of marihuana cigarettes provided, which had a fourfold difference in their content of drug.

The authors of this study note that their findings with naive subjects agreed with "the reports of chronic users that many, if not most, people do not become high on their first exposure to marihuana even if they smoke it correctly" (3). The novice usually must be taught to notice the psychic effects of this drug, which may be subtle when produced by the marihuana cigarettes typically available for sale in this country.

Guidance and experience play a dual role in influencing the response to drugs: they can enhance pleasure and they can minimize the incidence of undesirable psychic reactions. Through guidance, the user learns to administer his drug most efficiently and to direct his attention toward those aspects of the drug's effects that can be pleasurable and away from the effects that may distress or frighten him or even make him panic. Upon repeated exposure to the drug, the user becomes accustomed to the drug's effects, and, if he is psychologically susceptible to drug dependence, he appears to gradually lose whatever anxiety he may have felt initially about drug abuse. His inhibitions, which may have originally dampened the full emergence of the drug experience, gradually disappear. With time, he learns to relax and "let it happen." He comes to relish, and not be frightened by, the mind-distorting effects of hallucinogens. As experience enables the user to gain greater pleasure from drugs, his craving for drugs is reinforced.

Experience affords the user only limited aid and protection, however, and this is particularly true for those dependent upon hallucinogens. The user of LSD, for example, becomes accustomed to the effects produced by the typical doses of this drug offered for sale. Should he, by chance, receive an unusually large dose, or a mixture of LSD and one or more other drugs, such as methamphetamine (Methedrine), the effects produced can be of a magnitude foreign to his experience and result in acute panic or the onset of such psychotic symptoms as paranoia. The relatively high risk of inadvertently purchasing such potentially catastrophic drug mixtures in some areas has been one factor that has induced many users of LSD to discontinue this form of drug abuse (17).

Social setting

Most people get more pleasure dining in the company of friends than in eating alone, and this same reaction is observed in some forms of drug abuse. Many users of marihuana regard it principally as a "social" drug, to be smoked in the presence of friends. This is especially true of adolescents, for whom the social use of marihuana may alleviate problems arising from a sense of low self-esteem, the need for acceptance by one's peers, and the difficulty in forming relationships with others (18). The group setting seems to still qualms, quiet anxiety, and express united defiance against "hypocritical" and unjust laws. This atmosphere of social acceptance and moral righteousness enhances the pleasures of marihuana for many users.

As we have already noted briefly, social setting can also be important in determining the type of drug response experienced by a user of LSD. Since this drug produces marked emotional lability and enhanced suggestibility, with faulty cognition, impaired judgment, and, possibly paranoia, the social setting or environment in which LSD is taken can be a prime determinant of the nature of the drug experience. Taken in the company of friends, the experience can be most pleasurable; so much so, in fact, that a user may not mind, for example, if others bite his face so badly that plastic surgery is subsequently required (19, p. 151). On the other hand, if LSD is taken in an environment in which the user feels uncomfortable, or if he regards it as hostile, as in the company of relative strangers or on the street, he may become agitated and panic-stricken. He wants to be out of the situation immediately and may dash across a busy street disregarding traffic. Alternatively, he may become quite suspicious of those around him and attack them verbally or physically (17).

Drugs that can reduce a user's contact with his environment and make him quite indifferent to it, as the narcotics can, are agents whose effectiveness probably is relatively independent of social setting. Early in the course of use, the user typically falls into a state of light sleep shortly after the injection of heroin; since this can be a time of pleasurable reveries, he dislikes being disturbed. The user commonly becomes so engrossed with his inner feeling of contentment that little attention is given to his environment; since he can view his social setting with indifference, it probably neither substantively enhances nor detracts from his response to the drug.

If an individual is given a sleep-inducing dose of a barbiturate at the end of the day and goes to bed in a darkened, quiet room, he probably will fall asleep; given the same dose on some other day early in the morning and placed in a setting of noise and bustle, he probably will remain awake but will appear to be somewhat intoxicated. The doses taken by barbiturate addicts are usually larger than the conventional hypnotic doses, and addicts often continue to function in social situations where repeated stimuli may keep them more or less awake. They function now, however, as mildly to grossly intoxicated individuals; whether the drug experience will be pleasurable or not will depend greatly on the addict's personality and the types of situations he encounters.

The influence of social setting or environment on the response to drugs is, by and large, inconstant and unpredictable. People ordinarily vary in the extent to which they are sensitive to their environment, that is, in the degree to which it may influence their mood and behavior. Though the population of drug users appears to contain an unusually high percentage of suggestible people, it seems likely that here, too, variations in environmental sensitivity exist.

Psychological Susceptibility to Drug Abuse
In the previous chapter, we expressed our belief that the nature of the drug experience is determined, to an important degree, by the user's response to the effects produced by the drug. In this section, we will con-

sider some of the psychological factors that we believe may, in turn, influence the character of the response.

Initial drug experiences, it appears, are not always pleasurable; it is often through something akin to a learning process that the naive user evolves into a regular user who will gain gratification from drug abuse. The process of evolution is accomplished by guidance and encouragement from others, confidence and discrimination gained through experience, and appropriate psychological susceptibility to drug abuse. Many novices never complete the process of evolution. They progress no further than the initial stage of an experimenter; it is commonly assumed that they lack the requisite psychological susceptibility to or motivation toward drug abuse. Though many attempts have been made to characterize more specifically the terms "susceptibility" and "motivation," as used in the context of etiological factors in drug abuse, it is our opinion that they have not yet been described in a way that makes drug abuse the inexorable result of a given type of personality or a given constellation of psychological and social circumstances. From the reports of psychologists and psychiatrists who have studied drug users, it appears that no one clearly distinctive type of personality is encountered among users; moreover, the constellation of psychological and social circumstances associated with drug users may also be found in non-users. We interpret such findings to mean that, though it is possible to identify certain facets of an individual's personality that might make him particularly receptive to drug effects or impel him to resort to drug abuse, these same personality attributes might be present in another individual who adjusts to his problems or meets his needs without the aid of drugs.

Some psychiatrists feel that certain prepsychotic individuals have been able, by resort to certain forms of drug abuse, to delay or prevent the onset of the active form of a psychosis. Drugs do represent the principal means of treating many forms of emotional disorders today, though this type of therapy, in contrast to drug abuse, occurs under the supervision of a physician and routinely entails the use of drugs other than those commonly subject to abuse. We definitely do not advocate drug abuse as a treatment for the emotionally disturbed; we simply wish to record the impression that, on occasion, it may serve that purpose. (We do not refer here to the lay use of stimulants and hallucinogens, for, as we have already noted, the risk is great that their effects will serve to disrupt the prepsychotic user's last ties with reality.)

Though some users do report their first drug experience as pleasurable, for many others this event has been unimpressive, disgusting, or frightening. We have noted that, at this stage, regular users often encourage and instruct the novice. But why do some beginners respond favorably to guidance and "benefit" from experience, whereas others, under apparently the same circumstances, become "dropouts" from the drug scene? Here one might invoke personality as an explanation: a psychological susceptibility, perhaps a "drive," that permits the heroin experience to evolve from an initial reaction of dysphoria and disgust to one of a highly satisfying euphoria; that enables the reaction of the user of LSD to change from one of initial fright to eventual pleasure and motivates the user of hallucinogens to continue use of these drugs despite the experience of one or more bad trips; and that perhaps is instrumental in influencing the decision of some marihuana users to turn to a stronger drug.

The nature and the degree of the susceptibility to drug abuse seem to vary from one individual to another. In recognition of these probable differences, we have qualified many of our statements for, whenever possible, we want to avoid stereotypes. The use of stereotypes in thinking about the many aspects of drug abuse is an oversimplification of the matter and serves to limit one's understanding of the general phenomenon. It is axiomatic in medicine that one does not often encounter patients who are classical or "textbook" examples of a particular disease; we feel much the same about drug users. One may describe a "typical" case of drug abuse, but, in reality, one can detect in each user a unique blend of the many facets of drug abuse. Not only are patterns of drug abuse likely to be highly individualistic, but the various factors that can influence the nature of the drug experience seem to vary in importance from one user to another and, in an individual user, from one time to another.

Though psychological susceptibility to drug abuse no doubt varies greatly among individuals, it is probably one of the most important causative factors in both the onset and the continuation of the practice of drug abuse. It has long been maintained by many psychiatrists that the use of drugs is not a discrete disease but a symptom of an underlying emotional disturbance; and in the absence of strong motivation for drug usage, the problem of drug abuse would essentially disappear. The effects of drugs are not inherently irresistible for an emotionally healthy individual; on the contrary, he may find many drug effects most unappealing. Not everyone can be "caught in the toils" of drug abuse. Over a period of more than 100 years, millions of patients have been exposed, for example, to the effects of morphine; initially suffering, they have been able to experience the euphoria and the sense of indifference to pain and worry that morphine can produce. And yet only a minuscule fraction of them have subsequently become narcotic addicts. Clearly something was present in this tiny group that the vast majority lacked.

In addition to psychological susceptibility, other causative factors appear to be operative in instances of drug abuse in urban ghettoes. Feelings of being trapped and of hopelessness are pervasive in these areas, and they serve to intensify the appeal of a new and exciting "reality" to be gained through the use of drugs. Furthermore, the incidence of various forms of drug abuse, and narcotic addiction in particular, is extraordinarily high in the slums. Children are aware of drug abuse at a very early age, and many resort to some form of it before the age of 10. Peer-group pressure to use drugs can be intense and drug usage, as a means of coping with both personal and environmental problems, becomes an accepted fact of everyday life.

In this particular setting, we feel that probably both psychological and sociological factors operate in the spread of drug abuse. Not all ghetto residents misuse drugs, however, and, in all, we still feel that pre-eminence must be accorded psychological susceptibility as a causative factor; until more is learned about the nature of this susceptibility, however, a full understanding of the phenomenon of drug abuse cannot be achieved, nor can any truly rational plans of treatment be devised. This state of relative ignorance about underlying psychological factors is not uniquely confined to drug abuse, among the vexing medical problems of the day; a comparable degree of ignorance impedes our full understanding of criminal behavior, compulsive overeating, and homosexuality, to name but a few.

PSYCHOLOGICAL DEPENDENCE

The only condition common to all forms of chronic drug abuse is psychological or psychic dependence, which are synonymous terms used to describe the user's attitude toward the taking of drugs and the effects they produce. This attitude is such that "the effects produced by a drug, or the conditions associated with its use, are necessary to maintain an optimal state of well-being" (20). The degree of psychological dependence developed varies widely. In its mildest form it may be manifested as an intermittent, not particularly strong desire to experience the effects of a drug, such as the occasional smoker of marihuana would evince. In its most severe form, drug abuse becomes an obsession; the individual's life is virtually dominated by thoughts of and compulsive behavior directed to the procurement and the use of drugs. Such an intense degree of psychological dependence makes the user completely amoral; he will do anything to get the money needed for drugs. Money and salable items are stolen with a catholic lack of regard to source. He seems not to want to cause personal harm to others in the course of his search for money but will do so should it prove necessary. Women frequently turn to prostitution to obtain money for drugs, and users, similarly, have been known to permit their children to be exploited sexually in return for money.

The degree or intensity of psychological dependence present in an individual user cannot be measured precisely and is usually described by such words as mild, moderate, or marked. Most users of addicting drugs eventually develop marked psychological dependence, whereas dependence may vary from extremely mild to marked among users of nonaddicting drugs.

With drug addiction, the compulsive use of drugs may stem, in part, from fear of the withdrawal syndrome. This fear has been designated "secondary psychological dependence" (21), for primary psychological dependence, it is postulated, is associated with the reward of the drug experience. Some narcotic addicts have claimed that, after being addicted for a number of years, the pleasure they obtained from heroin diminished greatly, and thereafter they remained addicts largely through fear of the withdrawal syndrome. Such statements probably are not wholly truthful, for they fail to explain why many such addicts do not seek treatment or why repeated relapses are so common after treatment (20).

In the view of some workers, psychological dependence develops as a result of the "rewards" the user obtains from the drug experience: "If the first drug trial is a rewarding experience, a few more rewarding trials follow until drug-taking becomes a conditioned pattern of behavior" (21). Each additional pleasurable experience provides "continued positive reinforcement." Though we believe that such a concept may apply to some instances of drug abuse, we feel that it fails to account fully for the development of much drug abuse. First drug trials, as we have already noted, are often not "rewarding," and regular users do not always obtain "continued positive reinforcement"; they may experience bad trips, but they persist in drug abuse nonetheless. Psychologists and psychiatrists have attempted to define the many personal and social factors that prompt adolescents and young adults to experiment with drugs (21, 22, 23). Their findings suggest that, psychologically, drug abuse can serve many purposes. If "reward" is defined strictly in terms of a normally pleasurable experience, then, as a motive for drug abuse and as the principal contributor to the establishment and maintenance of psychological dependence, it seems to be an unsatisfactory explanation for all instances of drug abuse. Reward can have general significance, in our opinion, only if it is defined in terms of the gratification afforded the user by the act of taking drugs as well as the resulting drug experience. Individuals differ widely in what they regard as reward, gratification, or "an optimal state of well-being." Older accounts of drug abuse have, we think, unduly stressed such pleasurable drug experiences as the sense of euphoria that can be produced by heroin, which probably would be enjoyed by most anyone, as a factor in the development of psychological dependence. The bizarre world into which one can be plunged by LSD, however, does not represent a universally pleasurable experience; it gratifies the psychological needs of only some people. For many, the effects produced by LSD, even on a good trip, would hardly be an inducement to continue use of the drug.

Much of the evidence in support of the view that psychological dependence develops as a result of the repeated rewards of irresistibly pleasurable drug experiences has been obtained in experiments with animals. We feel, however, that it is virtually impossible to simulate in animal experiments all of the factors that appear to be operative in the human situation. One can readily demonstrate that, once monkeys have been given cocaine and are allowed thereafter, by means of appropriate equipment, to administer the drug to themselves on a schedule of their own choosing, the animals, in time, will elect to use cocaine with increasing frequency, even to the point of death. One might conclude from such experiments that it was a growing and continually reinforced desire in the animals to recreate the cocaine experience that impelled them to use the drug at an accelerated pace and that such an experiment demonstrates how psychological dependence develops. This view is in accord with the classical psychological concept that repeated rewards can foster growth of a behavior pattern.

It seems reasonable to assume however that, before the experiments, the animals had no knowledge about the nature of the reward and therefore could anticipate nothing, nor had they formed any opinion about the desirability of utilizing drugs as a means of coping with whatever problems might exist in their lives. Human beings do not usually begin the practice of drug abuse so naively. They know before they start, for example, that drug abuse is forbidden by the mores and laws of society in general; this awareness, it seems to us, probably influences both their attitude toward drug usage and their response to the drug, at least initially. Moreover, they have heard or read accounts of drug experiences, which to variable degrees have made them anticipate that experience. And, as a result of their decision to try drugs and in accord with the nature and intensity of the motives that favored this decision, some degree of commitment is tentatively made to the concept that drugs should be employed to meet their needs.

The development of psychological dependence during adolescence, in any but the mildest form, is regarded as particularly harmful, for this is a period during which the final stages of maturation, both physical and psychological, occur. Psychological dependence upon drugs provides the adolescent with an artificial and harmful crutch, which helps him to "cop out" from reality. Unpleasant decisions and responsibilities can be evaded; the development of self-reliance and the enhancement of self-confidence are stunted. The drug can supply an unreal sense of confidence and a quite false self-image. For seriously disturbed adolescents, drugs can provide an escape from an external reality that seems inimical and an obliteration of "severe, deep-seated intrapsychic misery" (23).

Though psychological dependence on drugs is viewed as a state that can hinder emotional maturation in adolescents and as a cause of "arrested psychosocial development" (26), it should be recognized that immaturity and poor social adjustment antedate the onset of drug abuse in some adolescents and may lead them to experiment with drugs. In such individuals, the subsequent use of drugs and the development of psychological dependence often exacerbates an already abnormal situation.

PHYSICAL DEPENDENCE

When certain drugs are taken on a regular schedule in appropriate quantities, the state known as physical dependence develops. The drugs known to produce physical dependence are the narcotics and the generalized central nervous system depressants, which include such sedative and hypnotic drugs as the barbiturates and alcohol and such "minor tranquilizers" as meprobamate (Miltown). We have elected to designate such drugs as addicting and to reserve this designation for them; thus, when a drug is called addicting, the reader will know immediately that its abuse potentially entails the development of physical dependence.

Physical dependence develops only if the intake of an addicting drug conforms to a regular schedule; that is, the interval between doses is so short that the effects of the drug never wear off completely. This means that one can take an addicting drug on so irregular a schedule that physical dependence will never develop, as exemplified by the person who takes heroin on an occasional or intermittent basis. Such a schedule does not meet the needs of a typical addict, however, for his degree of psychological dependence on the effects of an addicting drug is ordinarily so great that he attempts to be continuously under the influence of that drug.

Physical dependence upon drugs is occult in that, so long as drug intake remains adequate, its existence can in no way be detected either by the addict or by an observer. The presence of physical dependence can be determined only if the intake of drug is stopped abruptly or markedly reduced, for then an involuntary physiological illness develops. This is called the withdrawal or abstinence syndrome.

Physical dependence usually develops quite rapidly once regular use of a narcotic drug is begun. By the use of special techniques, it is possible to demonstrate that a small degree of physical dependence has developed within 48 to 72 hours in human beings who have received therapeutic doses of narcotic drugs four times a day; this dosage schedule is what many physicians would prescribe for patients in pain. Within very broad limits, the degree of physical dependence developed is directly proportional to the amount of drug used daily. This fact has been ascertained, however, only with the aid of hindsight, for the degree of physical dependence is usually judged by the severity of the withdrawal syndrome.

Narcotic drugs traverse the placenta. This means that if a female addict becomes pregnant, the fetus will be exposed to the drug and will develop physical dependence. Therefore, shortly after birth the infant will begin to show signs of the narcotic withdrawal syndrome.

The severity of a withdrawal syndrome as judged by the intensity of the various signs and symptoms is dependent upon several factors. It is directly proportional to the quantity of drug taken daily. This appears to be true without qualification in regard to the generalized central nervous system depressants. In the case of narcotics, however, the severity of the withdrawal syndrome is proportional to the daily intake of drug only until the intake reaches the equivalent of 500 mg of morphine/day (very approximately equivalent to 125 to 250 mg of heroin/day); beyond this point increments in daily narcotic intake produce no further enhancement of the severity of the withdrawal syndrome. (This "ceiling" has little significance for today's addicts receiving grossly diluted heroin, for attaining such a high intake would be financially prohibitive.)

The more rapidly the withdrawal syndrome develops, the more severe it will be. More severe withdrawal syndromes are likely to be associated with drugs having a relatively short duration of action, for, it is felt, as their effects wear off rather quickly, the withdrawal syndrome is permitted to develop or emerge quite rapidly. Physical dependence has often been characterized as a state of "latent hyperexcitability." Theoretically, if equieffective (i.e., equianalgesic) doses of two addicting drugs are taken, they will produce an equal degree of physical dependence or latent hyperexcitability. If one of the drugs has a short duration of action, then, as its effects wear off relatively quickly, the latent hyperexcitability is permitted to be manifested in a rapid and rather explosive fashion (20). If the other drug has a relatively long duration of action, its effects will wane less rapidly; thus, manifestations of the latent hyperexcitability will develop more gradually. Slowly developing physiological disturbances, whether they be an instance of glandular insufficiency or a withdrawal syndrome, are commonly tolerated better, possibly because sufficient time is allowed for body stabilizing mechanisms to become operative and thereby minimize the magnitude of the disturbance.

In the case of narcotic addiction, it is possible to precipitate a fully developed withdrawal syndrome extremely rapidly by the use of drugs known as narcotic antagonists, of which nalorphine (Nalline) is an example; these drugs are able to abolish virtually all of the effects of any narcotic drug. Whereas a spontaneously developing withdrawal syndrome in a heroin addict might require 48 hours following abstinence to achieve maximal intensity, the equivalent point in the syndrome can be reached within 30 to 60 minutes after intravenous injection of nalorphine. Because it develops so rapidly, the nalorphine-induced withdrawal syndrome is typically severe.

Once physical dependence has developed, a marked withdrawal syndrome will occur only if the intake of drug is abruptly stopped or is reduced so greatly that the dose taken is too small to prevent manifestation of the latent hyperexcitability. If, however, the quantity of drug used daily is gradually reduced over a period of days or weeks (the time required depends very much on the particular drug being used and the amount that has been taken daily), then the signs and symptoms of withdrawal will be very mild indeed. This is the technique employed by physicians in helping addicts rid themselves of physical dependence. (Most experienced addicts eventually come to know that physical dependence upon drugs can be lost in only one of two ways: by submitting to medically supervised gradual reduction of drug intake or by subjecting themselves to the technique of "cold turkey," i.e., by voluntarily stopping drug intake abruptly and thereby precipitating a withdrawal syndrome.) When the process of gradual reduction has been completed and drug intake stopped altogether or when the withdrawal syndrome has run its course, the addict will have lost all of his physical dependence.

The term, "cross-dependence," refers to the fact that once physical dependence upon the effects of any one drug within a group has been established, dependence will then extend to all members of the group. A person who has developed physical dependence upon the effects of one generalized depressant, for example, has some degree of physical dependence on all generalized depressants. This means that a barbiturate addict who was unable to obtain his drug and felt the early symptoms of an impending withdrawal syndrome, could prevent its appearance by taking sufficient quantities of another generalized depressant, such as alcohol. No drug from any other group, however, would be effective. Heroin addicts, unaware of the limitations of cross-dependence, have been known to attempt to alleviate the narcotic withdrawal syndrome by taking barbiturates; short of taking sufficient barbiturate to produce unconsciousness, such attempts will fail.

Cross-dependence is of little practical significance to the typical addict, for he is unaware of its existence. Physicians do rely on cross-dependence, however, in programs of gradual drug withdrawal to effect loss of physical dependence. For purposes of gradual withdrawal, heroin addicts are commonly given methadone, which is a narcotic drug having a relatively long duration of effect. The daily dose of methadone is gradually reduced, so that by the end of 10 days at the most narcotic intake can be stopped completely, and all physical dependence on narcotics will have been lost. Alcoholics are usually placed on a generalized depressant having a longer duration of action than alcohol, such as a barbiturate. Barbiturate addicts are usually kept on barbiturates, with the daily intake being gradually reduced. It is becoming increasingly less rare today to encounter a drug user who has developed concurrently physical dependence on two different types of drugs, such as heroin and a barbiturate.

Gradual withdrawal can be accomplished in such cases in one of two ways: simultaneous withdrawal programs for both drugs or sequential withdrawal, in which the daily dose of one of the drugs is gradually reduced while the daily dose of the other is kept high, until withdrawal from the first drug has been effected.

The cellular mechanisms that underlie physical dependence are not understood. The fact that a withdrawal syndrome is characterized generally, though not entirely, by events directly opposite in character to the effects of addicting drugs has attracted much attention. Barbiturates, for example, can prevent or stop grand mal convulsions; the barbiturate withdrawal syndrome is often characterized by the appearance of such convulsions. Narcotics constrict pupils; pupillary dilation occurs during the withdrawal syndrome. As a result, the withdrawal syndrome is often spoken of as a "rebound" phenomenon, as if the depression of the central nervous system by addicting drugs is rather violently reversed when the restraining influence of the drug is no longer present. We agree with those who feel that this general view of the nature of physical dependence and the origin of the withdrawal syndrome is oversimplified and inadequate. More attractive theories have been advanced (20), but their status is still largely conjectural. The true nature of physical dependence and of the origin of the withdrawal syndrome remains essentially unknown.

It is worth emphasizing that physical dependence and psychological dependence are largely independent and unrelated entities. Physical dependence develops as an inevitable and involuntary consequence of the regular usage of appropriate doses of addicting drugs. Any dose of a narcotic given regularly will produce some degree of physical dependence. Patients in pain who are given narcotics regularly by their physicians do develop physical dependence on these drugs; as their pain subsides and the physician gradually reduces their narcotic intake, they will eventually lose their physical dependence, and virtually none of them will be aware that this state had ever developed within them. In the case of generalized depressants, physical dependence develops only when the total daily intake of drug exceeds a certain "threshold" quantity; in those instances where the threshold value is known, it definitely exceeds the quantity of drug that would be normally prescribed by a physician. This means that patients can, for example, take barbiturates daily for years for sedative purposes or as an aid to sleep without developing physical dependence. When the threshold value is exceeded, it is usually through an individual's deliberate resort to drug abuse. This individual, however, may well not know that he will develop physical dependence. Though physical dependence on narcotics and the resulting withdrawal syndrome have received considerable, and often unrealistically lurid publicity, there is no comparable degree of public awareness of the situation in regard to the abuse of generalized central nervous system depressants. This limited knowledge is indicated by the fact that many laymen tend to think of these drugs as merely "habit-forming."

The loss of physical dependence upon the effects of an addicting drug, whether by abrupt abstinence or gradual withdrawal, can have a variable effect on an individual's subsequent psychological dependence on that drug. A particularly traumatic withdrawal syndrome, such as that which follows abrupt withdrawal from alcohol or barbiturates, may on occasion sufficiently alarm an addict so that psychological dependence on the drug in question is decreased. The personalities of many drug users are such, however, that they may then turn to the use of another drug, unless rehabilitative measures after withdrawal have successfully reduced the individual's susceptibility to drug abuse. In the case of narcotic addicts, it is a common experience that loss of physical dependence either has no effect on or may appear to intensify psychological dependence on these drugs. Many narcotic addicts resume use of these drugs shortly after withdrawal is completed, some within 24 hours.

TOLERANCE

When a given dose of a drug is administered repeatedly over a period of days or weeks, and its effects gradually decrease in intensity, it is a sign that tolerance has developed to the effects of the drug. Tolerance can be overcome either by increasing the size of the dose administered or by abstaining from the use of the drug for a matter of days until tolerance abates.

Tolerance develops not only to the effects of some of the drugs subject to abuse but to other compounds as well. Patients who take nitrites or organic nitrates chronically to prevent attacks of angina pectoris are commonly troubled by the development of tolerance to the effects of these drugs, as are severe asthmatics who resort frequently to the use of epinephrine (Adrenalin) for relief of respiratory distress.

As with physical dependence, tolerance develops most readily when a drug is taken regularly, so that the body is exposed to its effects almost continuously. Under these conditions, an appreciable degree of tolerance can develop very rapidly—within only 3 or 4 days in the case of LSD. Clinical investigations have demonstrated that within 10 days human beings can become tolerant to the effects of 500 mg of morphine/day, which is a quantity roughly five times greater than the ordinary lethal dose of this narcotic.

It is rare for the same degree of tolerance to be developed toward all of the effects of a given drug; this phenomenon is called "incomplete tolerance." In the case of heroin, maximal tolerance is developed to its ability to produce euphoria, analgesia, sedation, and depression of respiration. Only a moderate degree of tolerance (partial tolerance) is developed in regard to heroin-induced constriction of the pupils, and virtually no tolerance develops to the constipating effect of this drug. Though physicians ordinarily can detect no development of tolerance to the sleep-antagonizing effects of amphetamine when it is used chronically in the treatment of narcolepsy, those habituated to amphetamine report that its euphoric effects gradually weaken with time. They increase their daily intake as a result and have been known to take quantities of amphetamine twenty or more times greater than the maximal amount a physician would prescribe for therapeutic purposes. Because no objective criterion exists by which tolerance to the euphoric effects of any drug can be measured, the user's reports must be accepted tentatively, for it is possible that two factors are operative in the situation. It is possible that tolerance does develop to those effects of amphetamine or heroin, for example, that users find pleasurable; its occurrence would hardly be surprising. The other factor could be a change in the user's emotional status with time, such that larger quantities of the drug are required to produce the desired effect. An increase in the user's "emotional requirements" would be the practical equivalent of, though it would not be identical with, the development of tolerance, pharmacologically.

The phenomenon of cross-tolerance has much the same general characteristics as cross-dependence. When tolerance has developed to the effects of one drug within a group, tolerance will be exhibited to the effects of all drugs within that group but not to the effects of any other drugs. Cross-tolerance can be a frustrating impediment for physician and drug user alike. In the treatment of chronically painful diseases with narcotic analgesic drugs, the steadily increasing degree of tolerance to the drug's effects obliges the physician to continually increase the dose administered as time passes; in a matter of months, enormous doses are required to bring relief from pain. Until recently, the existence of cross-tolerance prevented the physician from overcoming this problem by switching to another narcotic drug. Fortunately, fairly effective non-narcotic analgesic drugs are now available, toward whose analgesic actions relatively no cross-tolerance with narcotic drugs exists.

In the case of the narcotic addict, the inexorable increase in degree of tolerance with time requires the addict, if he wishes to recapture the initial intensity of euphoria, to steadily increase the quantity of heroin he uses daily. A point is eventually reached when the addict literally cannot steal enough each day to support his addiction. At this juncture, the experienced addict is likely to do one of two things. He usually knows that once the withdrawal syndrome has occurred all tolerance to, as well as physical dependence on, the effects of narcotics will be lost, and so he may subject himself to abrupt abstinence. Alternatively, but with the same end in view, he may present himself to a physician as one seeking a cure for addiction, in order to experience a relatively painless, medically supervised withdrawal program and immediately thereafter to return to his previous environment, where, at least temporarily, he can once again afford his addiction. Some addicts have been known to utilize this second procedure twenty or more times.

Addicts to generalized central nervous system depressants appear to develop only a low degree of tolerance. It is not possible at this time to characterize this degree of tolerance more precisely. It is known that users addicted to this type of drug do not usually increase their daily intake with time, nor is the lethal dose of these drugs appreciably different for addicted and non-addicted individuals. (In contrast, the lethal dose of narcotic for an addict may be markedly greater than that for a non-addicted person.) Evidence of cross-tolerance exists, as exemplified by the finding that unusually large quantities of anesthetic drugs are required to induce surgical anesthesia in alcoholics.

The biochemical changes that occur as tolerance develops are only partially understood. The term, metabolic tolerance, refers to an enhanced ability of the body to inactivate a drug as a consequence of repeated exposure to it. It has been demonstrated that following prolonged administration of barbiturates the liver's content of enzymes responsible for the metabolic inactivation of these drugs is increased somewhat. This observation represents the most clearly delineated example of what is meant by metabolic tolerance available thus far. The terms, pharmacological, tissue, or pharmacodynamic tolerance, refer to the concept that through repeated exposure to a drug the responding cells of a tissue somehow accommodate to the drug's continued presence in such a way that the drug elicits a progressively weaker cellular response. This process of cellular accommodation or adaptation, it has been speculated, might be characterized by the development of an immune response to the drug or by an enhanced degree of immobilization of the drug through binding to intracellular proteins. This concept has been advanced, in large part, to explain numerous instances of tolerance in which no accelerated disposition or inactivation of the drug can be detected; to date, little direct evidence has been obtained to support the view that such an adaptive process does, in fact, occur, though it remains an attractive theory.

The similar courses of the development of tolerance and physical dependence and, in particular, the fact that both arise concurrently with regular use of narcotics have led some to conclude that an interrelationship exists between the two phenomena. The bulk of the evidence indicates that this is not so. Tolerance to many drugs develops in the total absence of any physical dependence upon their effects. And, in the case of addiction to generalized depressants, a very high degree of physical dependence can develop, as illustrated by the extremely severe withdrawal syndromes that may occur following abstinence, while only a low grade of tolerance is present. The two phenomena appear to be independent and unrelated.

CONSEQUENCES OF PROLONGED DRUG ABUSE

One of the commoner questions asked today is whether any permanent damage to mind or body develops as a result of prolonged drug abuse. We will consider this subject in a general fashion in this section; a more detailed presentation of the evidence of such damage will be found in subsequent chapters concerned with specific groups of drugs.

A variety of medical and psychiatric disorders have been diagnosed in drug users; the exact nature of the relationship between these disorders and the use of drugs is, however, frequently difficult to ascertain. In a few instances, a cause-and-effect relationship can be readily demonstrated; a user who persistently "sniffs" a solvent containing benzene may subsequently become anemic, since benzene has long been known as an agent capable of damaging those cells in the bone marrow responsible for producing red blood cells. The more typical complexity of the problem is well exemplified by the current dispute over the relationship between alcoholism and cirrhosis of the liver. For decades it was believed that this disorder is caused by excessive consumption of alcohol and develops only in alcoholics. In point of fact, cirrhosis of the liver occurs in only a minority of alcoholics (approximately 10%) and, in addition, in non-alcoholics as well (25). Alcohol somehow predisposes an individual to the development of cirrhosis of the liver. The principal determinant of hepatic damage may well be the nutritional deficiencies in an alcoholic's diet. For a variety of reasons, the diet of many alcoholics is inadequate, and it has been found that some of the medical disorders associated with alcoholism can be partially or wholly reversed by a nutritionally adequate diet, if they are detected before extensive permanent damage has occurred.

Certain of the drugs subject to abuse can produce the type of psychiatric disorder known as a toxic psychosis; it can be caused by an external agent and is distinguished from psychoses that develop spontaneously. A drug-induced toxic psychosis is usually characterized by the finding that, as the causative drug is metabolically inactivated or excreted, the signs and symptoms of the psychotic state gradually abate, and the patient typically returns to an essentially normal state of mental health. A number of investigators have observed, however, that approximately 5 to 15% of the patients experiencing an amphetamine-induced toxic psychosis do not recover completely; they continue to display schizophrenia-like symptoms and may do so for 5 years or more thereafter (26). This finding has been interpreted in two ways. First, it has been argued that those displaying a persistent psychiatric illness probably were schizophrenic before exposure to the drug. This view cannot always be supported by retrospective studies of those patients who recover completely and those who do not; the psychiatric histories of patients in these two categories sometimes appear to be "qualitatively similar, so much so that the two were nearly indistinguishable from this point of view" (26). The validity of such evidence clearly depends on the reliability of the past histories; if the patients involved had not previously sought professional assistance, it is unlikely that any competent evaluation of their prior psychiatric status would exist. Attempts to assess their prior status by retrospective study may yield an incomplete or a partially incorrect history. Moreover, classification of "borderline" cases is difficult enough when confronted with the patient, without the additional burden of having to sift and interpret bits of historical evidence.

The second interpretation is that the drug is causally implicated in the production of the lasting mental illness. Advocates of this view cite the fact that an amphetamine psychosis bears a markedly close resemblance to paranoid schizophrenia and the finding that long-term studies of chronic amphetamine users, not initially considered to be schizophrenic, have revealed that some eventually developed this psychosis. These findings, in our opinion, do not satisfactorily demonstrate that the persisting psychoses are wholly drug induced and that all other possible causative factors can be excluded from consideration. Even if toxic doses of amphetamine can produce a state closely simulating paranoid schizophrenia, the available evidence indicates that in 85 to 95% of patients so afflicted the psychotic state is apparently completely reversible. At present we lack sufficient evidence to determine if toxic doses of amphetamine can produce a persisting psychosis or if this state arises only in those with a pre-existing psychiatric illness. It may well turn out that the truth lies somewhere between these two positions.

Similar difficulties arise in the evaluation of findings of arrested psychosocial development or of "personality deterioration" in individuals with a history of chronic drug abuse. It is often difficult, if not impossible, to determine which came first. Did an immature person with, and possibly because of, arrested psychosocial development turn to the use of drugs or was psychic maturation, proceeding normally until drug usage started, impeded or stopped by the effects of the drug? Was it a matter of an individual, initially maladjusted, whose psychic status deteriorated further during the period of drug abuse? If so, did the individual have a form of spontaneously progressive mental disease, in which further deterioration would inevitably have occurred whether or not drugs were used, or did the drugs directly and significantly influence the pace and/or the extent of the deterioration? In general, we cannot answer these questions completely and confidently.

As a remedy for our ignorance, a very large and lengthy study of drug users and non-users alike would have to be instituted. The group of users would have to be sufficiently large and heterogeneous so that the possible influence of the following factors could be determined: differing patterns of abuse of various drugs, differing states of mental health prior to drug usage, age at the time of onset of drug abuse, duration of the period of drug abuse, and differing social environments. We might, as a result, be able to predict with a fair degree of success the psychiatric consequences of a particular pattern of drug abuse in an individual beginning the use of drugs in a given state of mental health. The enormity of the type of study described above would seem to make it unlikely that the study would ever be conducted, yet it is not unduly large or expensive relative to the magnitude of the problem of drug abuse today and its possible consequences.

We do not believe that the long-term psychic consequences of drug abuse will be known in the near future. Disentangling the threads of possibly spontaneous psychic changes from the poorly understood impact of different patterns of drug abuse on individuals in varying states of mental health is today an impossible task. We are slowly committing more of our national resources to studies of psychic development and the phenomenon of drug abuse. This is an encouraging and needed development; considering our present ignorance, however, and the enormity and complexity of these problems, it seems reasonable to anticipate a long wait for reliable data and meaningful answers.

REFERENCES

1. Louria, D. B., T. Hensle, and J. Rose, The major medical complications of heroin addiction. *Ann Int Med* 67:1, 1967
2. Grlic, L., Recent advances in the chemical research of cannabis. *Bull Narcotics* 16:29, 1964
3. Weil, A. T., N. E. Zinberg, and J. M. Nelson, Clinical and psychological effects of marihuana in man. *Science* 162:1234, 1968
4. Crancer, A., J. M. Dille, J. C. Delay, J. E. Wallace, and M. D. Haykin, Comparison of the effects of marihuana on simulated driving performance. *Science* 164:851, 1969
5. Smith, D. E., Use of LSD in the Haight-Ashbury. *Calif Med* 110:472, 1969
6. Cherubin, C. E., The medical sequelae of narcotic addiction. *Ann Int Med* 67:23, 1967
7. Snyder, S. H., L. Faillace, and L. Hollister, 2,5-Dimethoxy-4-methyl-amphetamine (STP): A new hallucinogenic drug. *Science* 158:669, 1967
8. Solursh, L. P. and W. R. Clement, Hallucinogenic drug abuse: Manifestations and management. *Canad Med Assoc J* 98:407, 1968
9. *Non-medical use of drugs, with particular reference to youth.* Report of the Special Committee on Drug Misuse, Council on Community Health Care, Canadian Medical Association. *Canad Med Assoc J* 101:804, 1969
10. Schultes, R. E., Hallucinogens of plant origin. *Science* 163:245, 1969
11. Joachimoglu, G., Natural and smoked hashish. In: Wolstenholme, G. E. W. and J. Knight, eds., *Hashish: Its Chemistry and Pharmacology.* Boston: Little, Brown, 1965, p. 2

12. Eiseman, B., R. C. Lam, and B. Rush, Surgery on the narcotic addict. *Ann Surg* 159:748, 1964

13. Wendt, V. E., H. E. Puro, J. Shapiro, W. Mathews, and P. L. Wolf, Angiothrombotic pulmonary hypertension in addicts. "Blue velvet" addiction. *J Amer Med Assoc* 188:755, 1964

14. Louria, D. B., Medical complications of pleasure-giving drugs. *Arch Int Med* 123:82, 1969

15. Cherubin, C. E., M. Baden, F. Kavaler, S. Lerner, and W. Cline, Infective endocarditis in narcotic addicts. *Ann Int Med* 69:1091, 1968

16. Karliner, J. S., A. D. Steinberg, and M. H. Williams, Jr., Lung function after pulmonary edema associated with heroin overdose. *Arch Int Med* 124:349, 1969

17. Smith, D. E. and A. J. Rose, The use and abuse of LSD in Haight-Ashbury. *Clin Pediat* 7:317, 1968

18. The UCLA Interdepartmental Conference, Drug dependency. Investigations of stimulants and depressants. *Ann Int Med* 70:591, 1969

19. Louria, D. B., *The Drug Scene.* New York: McGraw-Hill, 1968

20. Jaffe, J. H., Drug addiction and drug abuse. In: Gilman, A. G., L. Goodman, and A. Gilman, eds., *The Pharmacological Basis of Therapeutics,* ed. 6. New York: Macmillan, 1980, p. 276

21. Seevers, M. H., Psychopharmacological elements of drug dependence. *J Amer Med Assoc* 206:1263, 1968

22. Cameron, D. C., Youth and drugs. *J Amer Med Assoc* 206:1267, 1968

23. Solomon, P., Medical management of drug dependence. *J Amer Med Assoc* 206:1521, 1968

24. Wilmer, H. A., Drugs, hippies and doctors. *J Amer Med Assoc* 206:1272, 1968

25. *Manual on Alcoholism.* American Medical Association (No city or date of publication given)

26. Angrist, B. M., J. Schweitzer, A. J. Friedhoff, S. Gershon, L. J. Hekimian, and A. Floyd, The clinical symptomatology of amphetamine psychosis and its relationship to amphetamine levels in urine. *Int Pharmacopsychiat* 2:125, 1969

Chapter 3

NARCOTIC DRUGS

A narcotic drug, by pharmacological definition, is one that brings relief from suffering caused by pain and produces sleep. Of Greek origin, the combining form *narco-* meant originally to benumb or to deaden; its subsequent use in the formulation of medical terms has had the effect of amending the meaning somewhat to put greater emphasis on the presence of sleep or a stuporous state, as in narcolepsy and narcosis.

The pharmacological properties of morphine, the prototype of all narcotic drugs, are described well by both the original and amended meanings of *narco-*. Minimally effective doses of this drug often bring relief from pain (benumb) and sedate the patient. Somewhat larger therapeutic doses usually produce sleep. (The name *morphine* was derived from *Morph*eus, an ancient Greek god of sleep and dreams, plus the conventional pharmacological suffix for an alkaloid, *-ine*.)

The word *narcotic* has also acquired, in time, an additional popular meaning, i.e., any agent used by "drug addicts." This usage has been promoted by those who, either from complete ignorance of drug abuse or for purposes of swaying the uninformed, choose to refer to all drug users as narcotic addicts and to all drugs subject to abuse as narcotics. (There are probably no words used in connection with drug abuse that have a greater emotional impact on the average person than the words *addict* and *narcotic,* assuming we exclude the slang term *dope* from consideration.) As a result, not only have a great variety of drugs been mislabeled publicly as narcotics but, in the laws of some states, certain non-narcotic drugs, such as marihuana, have been legally designated narcotics. Though words can and have changed their meaning with time, we think that the promiscuous application of the term, narcotic, has not effectively changed its meaning but rather has created confusion and disseminated misinformation. To designate as narcotics only those drugs whose effects are similar to those of opium and its derivatives serves a valuable communicative purpose, for it enables succinct reference to be made to a specific and pharmacologically unique type of drug. But to categorize the misuse of heroin and of marihuana, for example, as forms of "narcotic addiction" is not only, in most respects, pharmacologically and medically absurd, but serves also to obscure or remove important qualitative and quantitative differences among various drugs subject to abuse that have been established after years of study. The more important consideration in this situation is not that the use of both heroin and marihuana is illegal and may harm the user and society but that the salient pharmacological and medical aspects of the abuse of heroin differ markedly from those of the abuse of marihuana. The appropriate use of the term, narcotic, is one means of indicating these differences.

SOURCES OF NARCOTIC DRUGS

Narcotic drugs can be divided into three groups, as noted in Chapter 1, on the basis of their origin. Only two drugs are naturally occurring: morphine and codeine, as constituents of the crude plant preparation, opium. The semisynthetic agents are chemical derivatives of morphine and codeine; of these, none even closely approach heroin in the extent of their abuse. The wholly synthetic drugs are only episodically available to the average user; abuse of these drugs occurs most significantly among members of the health professions.

Opium is obtained from the poppy, *Papaver somniferum,* a close relative of such common garden plants as the Oriental poppy (*Papaver orientale*) and the corn poppy (*Papaver rhoeas*). Only the "opium poppy," however, yields narcotic drugs. It is an annual plant, 3 to 5 feet in height, that appears to have originated in Asia Minor. It has subsequently been grown illegally in many parts of the world, including the United States, but, to this day, countries of Asia Minor, Turkey in particular, and of the Far East remain the primary and constant source of both legal and illegal opiates. (Cheap labor is one important prerequisite for successful commercial cultivation of the opium poppy; it has been estimated that the collection of 1 kg of opium requires approximately 280 hours of labor.)

Maximal yields of the highest quality opium are obtained only by ex-perienced growers. In the Near East, certain strains of the poppy, known to yield opium with a high narcotic content, are cultivated. As with many plants that produce drugs, the time of harvest is critical. Several days after the poppy's petals fall, a greenish seed pod (2 inches long and 2 inches wide) forms on the plant; while it is still unripe, and at a time dictated by experience, a cut is made in the pod so shallow that it does not puncture it. A milky juice is exuded through the cut, which coagu-lates upon exposure to air. The coagulated exudate (opium) is brownish in color and has a musty odor; its content of morphine can range, in sam-ples of good quality, from 9 to 20% and of codeine from 0.5 to 2.5%. Opium contains, in addition, approximately twenty other alkaloids, only a few of which, papaverine, for example, have ever been regarded as having medicinal value. Purchasers of opium in the form of masses of gummy exudate sometimes find that drug dilution begins at this stage, for rocks and other foreign material designed to increase the weight of these masses have been found embedded within them. Opium of USP quality consists of thoroughly dried and subsequently ground material which has had its relative content of morphine adjusted to 10%.

Heroin, the most widely abused semisynthetic narcotic drug, was first synthesized from morphine in 1874; the chemical transformation is quite a simple one, entailing only acetylation of the two hydroxyl groups on morphine. Because it is a relatively simple and fairly rapid reaction, which provides a high yield of the desired product, it is well suited to the conditions obtaining in the illicit drug trade: little laboratory equipment is required, and, if police activities result in a rapid turnover of personnel, new "chemists" can be readily trained. Most of the heroin that reached America originated from "laboratories" in southern France; today's sources include the Far East and Colombia. A number of other deriva-tives of morphine and codeine have also been prepared. A few of them—particularly dihydromorphinone (hydromorphone, Dilaudid), oxy-morphone (dihydrohydroxymorphinone, Numorphan), and metopon (methyldihydromorphinone)—have an analgesic potency (as judged by the size of the effective dose) equal to or slightly greater than that of heroin, yet only rarely are narcotic addicts encountered who use these drugs. They are, by and large, unavailable for illicit purchase and certainly lack the high reputation accorded heroin by most addicts.

The first wholly synthetic narcotic drug, meperidine (pethidine, Demerol, etc.), was introduced in 1939, and the second, methadone, was discovered in 1945 to have been synthesized by German chemists during World War II. Since that period, chemists have prepared numerous structural variants of these two compounds. Though all of these compounds have chemical structures only faintly resembling that of morphine, their pharmacological actions are qualitatively quite similar to those of morphine. (Meperidine and its congeners are, in a few respects, appreciably dissimilar, and we will discuss these differences later.) Addiction to synthetic drugs, as we noted above, is particularly prevalent among members of the health professions, for they alone have ready access to these drugs. This situation stems, in part, from the tragic error of introducing meperidine initially as a "non-addicting" narcotic drug.

NATURALLY OCCURRING AND SEMISYNTHETIC DRUGS: HEROIN AND MORPHINE

It is not difficult to obtain satisfactory pharmacological evidence to account for the typical addict's preference for heroin over morphine. It is true that today's addicts rarely are offered a choice of the two drugs, and we would not be surprised to learn that a number of addicts had never heard of morphine. For decades, however, American narcotic addicts have maintained that the pleasurable effects produced by heroin are definitely superior to those produced by morphine, and the findings of some investigators have appeared to support this view. It has been said anecdotally that, in double-blind trials, addicts can distinguish between the effects of heroin and morphine; this may be so because the effects of heroin develop more rapidly, a difference veteran addicts should be able to detect. It is also true that it is quite difficult to obtain an accurate measure of the narcotic effects that addicts seem to prize, such as euphoria. Nonetheless, the conclusions drawn from seemingly the most critical comparative studies of the effects of heroin and morphine suggest that the two drugs do not differ significantly in their "addiction potential" (1). Though we are instinctively uneasy about evaluating evidence that, among other things, attempts quantification of "euphoria," we are inclined at this time to agree with those who hold that there are no significant differences between the psychic effects of heroin and morphine; we suspect that the supposed differences derive from folklore rather than fact. It is of interest that the preference of narcotic addicts for heroin is not universal; in such places as Singapore, the Philippines (22), and Afghanistan, morphine is used predominantly.

There is general agreement that certain pharmacological differences between morphine and heroin do exist. (1) The analgesic potency of heroin, on a weight basis, is two to four times greater than that of morphine. (2) When these drugs are injected, especially intravenously, the effects of heroin are perceptible more quickly than those of morphine. (3) The effects of morphine ordinarily persist for 4 to 5 hours, those of heroin for 3 to 4 hours (31). It seems unlikely that any of these differences could account wholly for an addict's preference for heroin over morphine. Because American addicts do use heroin almost exclusively today, it will be the primary subject of discussion in this section. The important features of heroin and of morphine addiction are so similar, however, that, unless otherwise noted, statements about heroin apply equally to morphine, and indeed to other semisynthetic narcotic drugs that are occasionally abused, such as dihydromorphinone.

Patterns of use

Since much of the important information about this topic has been presented in the first two chapters, this section will largely be a brief recapitulation. Pure heroin is a white, crystalline material, with the characteristic bitter taste of an alkaloid. The appearance of heroin purchased illicitly will be determined largely by the diluents it contains, for pure heroin typically makes up only 2 to 5% of the weight of such samples. (The commoner diluents are, however, also white and crystalline.)

Heroin is virtually never taken by mouth for its effects are essentially imperceptible after ingestion. The cautious novice may begin the use of heroin by inhaling ("snorting") it; perforation of the nasal septum sometimes results from chronic utilization of the inhalation route. American users of heroin rarely smoke it, though this practice is popular in certain Mid- and Far-Eastern countries (2). The majority of heroin users appear to adopt, sooner or later, the practice of injecting the drug. Both newcomers to heroin abuse and veteran addicts inject the drug subcutaneously, though for different reasons: the newcomer from timidity and the veteran for want of accessible veins not scarified by previous injections. The resulting dermatological damage and infectious sequelae have been described in Chapter 2. If a faster onset of drug effect is desired, then the drug is injected intramuscularly or, much more commonly, intravenously.

The reasons for the enormous popularity of the intravenous injection of heroin can be readily understood. Only by this route are the effects of heroin felt almost instantaneously and with maximal intensity. Only by this route may the user experience a profound abdominal sensation, which has been likened to a sexual orgasm displaced to the abdomen from the pelvic region. And only by utilization of this route will an individual be regarded as being among the elite of heroin users. There are numerous reports of peer-group pressure being exerted in one form or another on individuals to adopt the intravenous route of injection, even to the point that experienced users inject those too faint-hearted to inject themselves.

Because heroin is an addicting drug, it is possible that the majority of users employ it on a fairly regular schedule, which means, given the duration of action of heroin, that the interval between injections probably will not be longer than 6 to 8 hours at the very most. The conditions obtaining in the life of an individual addict may not, of course, permit such a schedule of usage to be observed at all times; in addition, the effects of the last dose taken by an addict before retiring usually do not persist throughout the period of sleep so that upon awakening the addict commonly experiences the early stages of the withdrawal syndrome. To cope with the problem, many addicts try to save a supply of heroin (a "wake up") for use at this time. It is worth repeating that not all users of heroin employ it on so regular a schedule that they develop physical dependence upon its effects. Because the pertinent evidence is so scanty, we can offer only our guess that such individuals constitute a large proportion of all heroin users; some of them do gradually increase their frequency of drug use to the point where they exhibit strong psychological and physical dependence and become heroin addicts. We have arbitrarily elected to use the term "addict" to designate those individuals who take heroin on so regular a basis that, to some degree, physical dependence on and tolerance to the effects of the drug develop. Those who take heroin on an irregular and intermittent schedule will be designated "users." When the need arises to refer to addicts and to users, the latter term will be employed.

How much heroin does a typical addict take each day? Though this is a most important and pertinent question, it is difficult to answer precisely. The average "bag" of heroin contains about 300 mg of particulate material (4); assuming a relative heroin content of 5%, each bag yields 15 mg of drug. Another estimate places the heroin content of each bag at from 3.75 to 7.50 mg (5). The finding that withdrawal of many addicts (even those injecting the drug four to eight times a day) can be accomplished successfully without resort to gradual withdrawal from methadone, supports the view that the smaller estimates are probably more accurate (6). The fact that the relative heroin content per bag can vary from none at all to more than 75% (5) and the fact that there is as much as an eight-fold difference in the estimates of authorities about the actual heroin content of a "typical" bag (4, 5) make the problem of calculating the probable daily drug intake of an addict most difficult. If one knows how many bags of heroin a particular addict uses each day, a *very approximate* estimate of his total daily intake can be made by assuming that each bag contains 5 to 10 mg of drug. We are hesitant to offer even so qualified an answer, for what seems a reasonable guess early in 1974 may be invalid at some later date.

THE EFFECTS OF HEROIN   The intensity of the effects of heroin on any given occasion is determined by a number of factors: (1) the quantity of heroin taken; (2) the route of administration; (3) the interval between doses, which, when considered with the size of the doses, determines the maximal heroin concentration in blood; (4) the degree of tolerance of the user to the effects of heroin. The nature of the response of the user to the drug effects, however, cannot be predicted; in particular, whether he experiences euphoria or dysphoria, as we emphasized in Chapters 1 and 2, appears to be determined by psychological factors that have not yet been identified. The following discussion will be concerned primarily with the effects experienced by an addict who injects the drug intravenously and who has developed only minimal tolerance to its effects.

Among the first sensations experienced after intravenous injection of heroin is that in the abdomen, which, as we have said, has been likened to a sexual orgasm. Referred to variously as a *thrill, kick,* or *flash,* it has been characterized as a "turning in the stomach," accompanied by a tingling sensation and a pervasive sense of warmth, which may be felt most intensely in the epigastric region. To varying degrees, users of heroin prize this sensation as one of the rewards of intravenous injection. Release of histamine occurs rather promptly, too, and is manifested in several ways: a sense of itching, which may be body-wide and quite disconcerting to the naive user, a reddening of the eyes, and a fall in blood pressure. The fall in blood pressure may cause dizziness in some and frank orthostatic hypotension in others; when very large doses have been taken, a small degree of hypotension may be present even in recumbent individuals (6). The fall in blood pressure probably cannot be attributed wholly to histamine; for one thing, it is only partially prevented or reversed by antihistamine drugs. In addition to the histaminic effects, narcotic drugs appear to produce a very mild degree of hypotension themselves, which may be caused by a central or a direct vasodilatory action. By and large, however, direct narcotic effects on blood pressure tend to be minimal, even in the range of toxic doses.

The central nervous system depressant effects of heroin also appear rapidly after intravenous injection. Until tolerance to this effect develops, users of heroin become quite heavily sedated. Mental clouding develops, visual acuity is decreased, the extremities feel "heavy," and there is little inclination toward physical activity. During this "foggy" period, the user may experience frequent periods of light sleep, during which vivid dreams may be prominent. The euphoria produced by heroin is commonly present at this time, also, and has been characterized as a feeling of sublime contentment. Anxiety and worry are absent as are sexual desire and, usually, appetite. The whole body is suffused with a feeling of warmth, and sweating may be profuse. Euphoria, as we have previously noted, is hardly a universal experience among naive users of heroin; not rarely, the first few doses may produce dysphoria, which is the typical response of a person, who is not in pain, to a narcotic drug. How some users eventually achieve euphoria after initial dysphoric experiences is still largely a matter for conjecture.

The effects of narcotic drugs on the central nervous system are often described as mixed: predominantly depressant but, in a few respects, stimulatory. The vomiting that heroin can cause most clearly exemplifies its mixed effects. Initially, heroin stimulates the "chemoceptive trigger zone" in the area postrema of the medulla. Many users of heroin experience nausea after its injection, and a relatively small percentage of them subsequently vomit. The incidence of vomiting is greater among those who remain ambulatory after injection than among those who are recumbent, suggesting that vestibular stimuli at this time initiate vomiting. It has also been observed that certain people vomit frequently after receiving narcotic drugs, whereas others almost never vomit. If heroin-induced euphoria is present at the time vomiting occurs, the user commonly regards the event with great indifference. More slowly thereafter, heroin directly depresses the vomiting center itself; when this depression has been established, typical emetic stimuli are ineffective.

By reducing the sensitivity of medullary respiratory neurons to carbon dioxide (CO_2), heroin depresses pulmonary ventilation to a degree that is very much dose related. The extent of respiratory depression produced by the typical quantities of heroin employed today is ordinarily physiologically insignificant, unless some pulmonary abnormality is also present such as pneumonia or an asthmatic episode. Larger doses of heroin, in the absence of tolerance, will depress respiration to the point where the resultant hypercarbia will produce sufficient cerebral vasodilation to cause a significant increase in cerebrospinal fluid pressure.

One of the most widely advertised effects of heroin is its ability to produce miosis, so that even many laymen know the possible diagnostic significance of "pinpoint" pupils. Despite rather intensive investigation of this phenomenon, the site of drug action remains undetermined. It has been discovered that direct application of heroin to the eye does not change pupillary size, that heroin-induced miosis can be antagonized by atropine, and that the miosis persists to some degree in total darkness. The findings in regard to the effects of narcotic drugs on the eyes of animals have hardly facilitated study of this problem; in some animals these drugs produce mydriasis, and this is so both in animals that are sedated by morphine, such as monkeys, and in those that are excited, such as cats.

The effect of heroin on the smooth muscle of hollow organs is predominantly spasmogenic. We say predominantly for, in the case of the gastrointestinal tract, the effects are diverse. Increased muscular tone, which may periodically achieve the intensity of a spasm, is most evident in the antral portion of the stomach, the upper portion of the duodenum, and virtually all of the large bowel; periods of spasm may be succeeded transiently by periods of relative atony. Gastric motility is decreased but rhythmic, and nonpropulsive contractions in all portions of the intestines are commonly enchanced. Propulsive intestinal contractions, however, are markedly inhibited and may briefly be absent altogether. The tone of both the ileocecal valve and the anal sphincter is increased. Digestion is delayed in part because of the mechanical factors just mentioned and in part because some reduction also occurs in the secretion of gastric acid and in pancreatic and biliary secretions. The fact that the intestinal contents move at a subnormal rate allows them to become abnormally desiccated, which, in turn, further slows their progress. Neither ganglionic blockade nor severance of the extrinsic innervation of the bowel has any influence on these effects of narcotic drugs; atropine partially antagonizes their spasmogenic actions, but depression of propulsive activity remains unaffected. Though heroin is constipating, the typical addict is commonly unable to use it on so regular a schedule as to be constipated; he is troubled only by labored defecation. The more typical schedule of usage results in periodic waxing and waning of narcotic effects on the gut, and his pattern of bowel habits is often one of alternating periods of constipation and diarrhea.

Even therapeutic doses of narcotic drugs can produce striking increases in biliary tract pressure of the order of ten- to fifteen-fold. A most clearly defined aspect of the biliary spasm roentgenographically is a sharp constriction in the vicinity of the sphincter of Oddi (7). Atropine and nitrites are both capable of partially relieving the heroin-induced spasm. The ability of atropine to partially antagonize some of the spasmogenic effects of narcotic drugs on smooth muscle suggest the possibility that these effects may, in part, be a consequence of activation of postganglionic parasympathetic fibers.

Therapeutic doses of narcotic drugs appear to have little effect on the human uterus at term; if such a uterus is made hyperactive by oxytocic drugs, however, opiates will reduce to normal levels the amplitude, frequency, and tone of uterine contractions. Though prolonged labor is associated with the use of narcotics, it seems unlikely that any direct myometrial effect of the drugs is responsible; it is thought rather that both involuntary ("bearing-down") contractions of the abdominal musculature and, as a result of the drug's central nervous system effects, voluntary cooperation by the woman are reduced in magnitude (6, 7).

Genitourinary difficulties arise as a consequence of several actions of narcotic drugs. They are able to enhance secretion of the antidiuretic hormone and increase the tone of the vesical sphincter. The tone of the detrusor muscle is also increased and may cause a sense of urinary urgency; difficulties in starting micturition, however, are not uncommon, and frank urinary retention occurs on occasion. The tone and amplitude of ureteral contractions are often increased initially, but, since the antidiuretic hormone slows urine flow, the ureters often become quiescent (7).

A true account of the sexual activities of a typical heroin addict would doubtlessly be a sore disappointment to the avid devotee of tabloid journalism. Then central nervous system effects of heroin are such that sexual desire is minimal or absent. In addition, though penile erection is possible, ejaculation is reputedly delayed or absent (6). The ability of heroin to interrupt the normal pattern of gonadotropin secretion is frequently manifested in women by either scanty menses or amenorrhea. The degree to which ovulatory activity is disturbed in female addicts is variable, however, and sterility is not inevitable, as evidenced by the not insignificant incidence of pregnancy in this group. In addition to impairing gonadotropin secretion, heroin is able to block some, though not all, of the pathways by which pituitary output of adrenocorticotropin is increased.

Since heroin has been most difficult to obtain, even for investigative purposes, upon passage of the Harrison Narcotic Act in 1914, many of the clinical observations reported above have necessarily been made in subjects who received morphine; as noted before, however, the pharmacological effects of these two drugs appear to be so similar that reference to such data is most probably wholly valid.

Distribution and metabolism of heroin

The most striking aspect of the pattern of distribution of narcotic drugs is that only a small portion of any dose enters the central nervous system; this is true at least in animals (8). Human data on this subject are not yet available. Radioautographic sections of the brains of animals receiving labeled morphine indicate that little drug is found in the vicinity of neuronal elements but rather is concentrated in more highly vascularized areas, such as the choroid plexus. Considering the tiny fraction of a dose of a narcotic drug that actually enters the central nervous system, and, since this quantity of drug is not preferentially situated in the vicinity of neurons, it must be concluded that the brain (in animals, at least) is exquisitely sensitive to the effects of this group of drugs.

Intravenously injected heroin disappears very rapidly from the blood of animals; its biological half-life is approximately 2.5 minutes (9). It is currently believed that the metabolism of heroin begins with the hydrolytic loss of one of its acetyl groups, transforming it to 6-monoacetylmorphine (6-MM); this metabolite is formed very rapidly after injection of heroin, and the transformation has been observed to occur *in vitro* in human blood, brain, liver, and kidney. Biologically, 6-MM appears to be equipotent with heroin in pharmacological activity. The second metabolic step occurs a bit more slowly: the second acetyl group is hydrolyzed, and 6-MM is converted to morphine. The morphine formed is thereafter metabolized and excreted in the conventional fashion. Heroin appears to be almost completely metabolized, for, after its administration to human beings, virtually no heroin appears in the urine. One finds mostly morphine, both free and "bound," and an occasional trace of 6-MM (8).

Because heroin is converted to 6-MM so rapidly, it has been postulated that only after intravenous injection of rather large doses of the drug does any heroin per se gain access to the central nervous system. The effects produced by much of the heroin injected intravenously and by all of the heroin administered by any other route, it is felt, are produced by its two principal metabolites, 6-MM and morphine. Studies in animals indicate that both heroin and 6-MM enter the brain more rapidly than morphine. Since heroin has a more rapid onset of action after injection than has morphine, it seems likely, given the rapid rate of conversion of heroin to 6-MM, that most of the initial effects attributed to heroin are in fact produced by 6-MM. And, since 6-MM is subsequently converted to morphine, most of the prolonged effects attributed to heroin probably are actually effects of morphine. These findings help to explain why it has been so difficult pharmacologically to detect significant differences, other than on a temporal basis, between the effects of heroin and of morphine (8). When equianalgesic doses of heroin and morphine are injected subcutaneously or intramuscularly, the effects of heroin persist for a shorter period of time, as noted above, than do those of morphine (3, 7). We believe this temporal difference can be explained in the following way: doses of heroin one-half to one-quarter the size of those of morphine are considered equianalgesic, the usual operative criterion being the intensity of analgesic effect, not its duration. The bulk of the heroin administered is probably converted fairly rapidly via 6-MM to morphine, yielding of course at most only one-half to one-quarter the amount of morphine contained in an equianalgesic dose of that drug. The morphine derived from heroin is excreted in an unchanged form or inactivated upon conjugation with glucuronic acid; and this relatively small quantity of morphine is more quickly reduced to clinically ineffective levels through metabolism and excretion than would the larger quantity of drug contained in an equianalgesic dose of morphine itself.

Tolerance to heroin

When heroin is used regularly, tolerance to many of its effects develops rapidly, though, as we mentioned previously, tolerance is always incomplete. Very little tolerance to its constipating effects develops and only partial tolerance to its miotic effects; though this partial tolerance is often characterized as mild, one should not expect to observe pinpoint pupils in all chronic heroin users who are under the influence of the drug. Maximal tolerance is developed to those effects of heroin viewed as manifestations of its depressant actions, such as sedation, analgesia, euphoria, and respiratory depression. The user becomes aware of the development of tolerance in large part because the effects of heroin gradually decrease both in intensity and duration; most noticeable to him will be the waning intensity of the "thrill" and the euphoria and the fact that he is becoming progressively less sedated and sleepy after administering the drug.

The degree to which heroin is diluted appears to have been increasing steadily in the past decade or so; as a result, one does not often encounter today heroin users exhibiting a marked degree of tolerance. Evidence about the potential degree of tolerance that can be attained derives largely from the period prior to enactment of the Harrison Narcotic Act in 1914. Accounts from this period tell of addicts taking as much as 5500 mg of morphine intravenously over a period of 16 hours without exhibiting marked respiratory depression or other signs of opiate overdosage. Even in the 1950's, one could read reports of addicts who had died shortly after undergoing withdrawal because they too quickly returned to a daily intake of heroin equivalent to that which they had been using just prior to withdrawal. In these instances, it was assumed that the addicts were unaware of, or chose to ignore, the facts that they had lost all tolerance upon withdrawal and that the degree of tolerance they possessed before withdrawal could not be regained in only a couple of days.

The mechanism by which tolerance to the effects of heroin or morphine develops is not known. No increase in the rate of inactivation or excretion of a narcotic drug can be demonstrated when tolerance is present, nor is distribution of the drug throughout the body altered. Many theories, some of them quite elaborate, have been offered as explanations for the mechanism of tolerance to narcotic drugs (8, 10); all of them suffer from a grievous lack of supporting evidence. It is of interest, however, that both tolerance to and physical dependence upon morphine can be prevented in mice by the concomitant administration of cycloheximide; the effects produced by this compound, which interferes with protein synthesis and may produce other metabolic disturbances as well, suggest the possibility that the development of tolerance and physical dependence is characterized by specific biochemical changes within the receptor cells of the central nervous system (11).

Physical dependence on heroin and the withdrawal syndrome
The belief that the typical heroin addict today develops only a mild degree of physical dependence stems in large part from the finding that "the addict admitted to a medical ward for withdrawal or a medical complication can usually be treated with mild sedation without resort to substitute narcotics such as methadone hydrochloride. This is true even if the amount of heroin taken daily costs the user $20 to $40 (four to eight in-

jections)" (12). This situation reflects, of course, the extreme degree to which heroin is being diluted currently; for an addict to develop a marked degree of physical dependence today, he would probably have to be able to amass $100 to $200 each day for the purchase of heroin.

A second, possibly pertinent, finding is that addicts are often encountered who take another drug, commonly a barbiturate or a stimulant of the amphetamine type, intravenously with heroin. Though we believe that this practice is most probably a reaction of addicts to the unsatisfactory effects of today's heroin, it may also be, in some cases, a reflection of the pronounced tendency of many current drug users to experiment with drug combinations in an attempt to produce novel experiences. When a barbiturate is the second drug, the addict should be followed very carefully during the period of withdrawal. Though some barbiturates sold illegally appear to have been made in "basement labs" and are therefore of unknown potency, most barbiturates have been diverted into the illicit market subsequent to manufacture by legitimate pharmaceutical companies; one may therefore encounter an addict having only mild physical dependence on heroin but marked dependence on barbiturates.

Less than 10 years ago, one could hear heroin addicts characterize their existence as a shifting among three states—*high, straight,* and *sick* (4). The addict is high just after he has injected heroin intravenously, a period when he would experience the euphoria most intensely, be sedated or sleepy, be highly self-absorbed, and be quite indifferent to his own problems and to the world around him. As the high gradually dissipates, the addict becomes straight, a period of "normal alertness and well-being" (4). Save for the needle marks and pupillary miosis, he would at this time be virtually indistinguishable from a non-user in terms of speech, behavior, ideation, and so on. An addict with moderate tolerance to the effects of heroin can often get no more than straight or perhaps just mildly high unless he is able to buy sufficient drug to increase his intake significantly. And those who use today's heroin, even when no tolerance has developed, often complain that one "bag" produces only a weak and brief high, if any high at all. As the straight wanes, the addict becomes sick, which is merely another designation for the onset of the withdrawal syndrome. Addicts are typically sick to some degree upon awakening, which is a consequence of the relatively short duration of action of heroin.

Manifestations of the withdrawal syndrome in heroin addicts first appear at about the time the next dose ordinarily would be taken, i.e., about

4 to 8 hours after the last dose. They slowly increase in intensity, reaching a peak at 36 to 72 hours; they subside gradually thereafter, and, depending on the severity of the withdrawal syndrome, gross disturbances are usually no longer evident at the end of 5 to 10 days. For decades, physicians could not agree whether the withdrawal syndrome was primarily organic or psychic in origin; it is generally agreed today that the syndrome contains both voluntary and involuntary elements. Some of the symptoms bespeak the addict's psychic distress at being deprived of the drug and represent also his attempts to get more drug. During medically supervised withdrawal, pleas, demands, complaints, and feigned symptoms arise in the hope that more drug will be given and the pace of withdrawal slowed or postponed altogether; when the addict is convinced that such behavior will have little influence on the quantity of methadone that he receives or the rate of withdrawal, these manifestations of withdrawal are usually minimal (13).

Though the psychogenic aspects of the syndrome of withdrawal from heroin can vary widely in their intensity from one addict to another, the intensity of the involuntary symptoms are, as we observed previously, a direct function of the degree of physical dependence. Because today's addicts are in fact taking relatively little heroin, the bodily distress occasioned by the withdrawal syndrome has often been likened to that occurring during a mild case of influenza. The first symptoms to appear are likely to be rhinorrhea, lacrimation, yawning, and sometimes perspiration. The addict may fall asleep some 10 to 15 hours after the last dose for several hours; this is characteristically a tossing sleep from which he awakens unrefreshed and miserable. He has no appetite, nausea usually being present, and vomiting and diarrhea commonly follow. The addict is restless and irritable; he feels chilly and has "gooseflesh," and these symptoms are succeeded periodically by episodes of flushing and profuse perspiration. The "rebound" excitability of the central nervous system is manifested by pupillary dilation, increases in heart rate, a rise in blood pressure, and involuntary twitching and kicking movements; spontaneous sexual orgasms may occur in both men and women. Tremors may be evident, and the addict often complains of pain from spasm in the intestinal region and in the muscles of the extremities and the back; he may feel pain in his bones as well. Leukocytosis often develops. Because no food and little, if any, fluid are taken during the intense period of withdrawal and because of the concurrent fluid loss from vomiting, perspiration, and diarrhea, the addict may lose 10 pounds in 24 hours and suffer as well from dehydration and disturbances in acid-base balance. At this point, though only rarely, cardiovascular collapse may occur. After 48 to 72 hours of abstinence, these symptoms gradually decrease in intensity. In the absence of serious organic disease, it is extremely rare for any addict's condition to deteriorate during withdrawal to the point where his life may be in danger.

The physiological travail to which an addict is subjected during medically supervised withdrawal is considerably less than that in the "cold turkey"-type of withdrawal described above; the latter type of withdrawal, it is worth noting, can be essentially completely reversed at any point in less than an hour by the injection of an appropriate dose of a narcotic drug. Any abnormalities in fluid and electrolyte balance will, of course, require separate and additional attention.

Though we conventionally regard withdrawal from narcotic drugs as being complete in 10 days, at the most, recent studies have indicated that certain mild physiological disturbances persist for 6 months or more thereafter; this latter period has been referred to as one of "protracted abstinence" (14). In these studies, addicts were observed for as long as 30 weeks after the start of withdrawal. Certain physiological disturbances, such as rises in blood pressure and increases in heart rate, body temperature, and respiratory rate, persisted to a significant degree, it was found, for 4 to 10 weeks after abstinence, though not so markedly as in the first week of this period. The "protracted" phase began between the 6th and 9th weeks and was characterized by mildly subnormal systolic blood pressure, body temperature, and pupillary diameter. It was found also that urinary epinephrine output, which rose markedly during the first week of abstinence, remained at a lower, though still significantly elevated, level for 16 weeks thereafter. Daily urine volume, when compared with pre-addiction values, remained significantly depressed for the first 7 weeks of abstinence (15). "Protracted abstinence" is not a consequence of abrupt withdrawal, since all of the subjects utilized in these studies had been withdrawn gradually.

Abrupt withdrawal from heroin, in summary, subjects the addict to physiological upsets, mild to moderate in intensity, and to an individually variable degree of emotional distress. Because today's addicts can usually afford only relatively small amounts of heroin, which is greatly diluted, the physiological aspects of withdrawal are typically mild. Nevertheless, all addicts should be carefully observed during withdrawal. Some can afford to buy sufficient heroin to induce a moderate degree of physical dependence and will require methadone; the technique of methadone withdrawal is discussed in Chapter 10. More importantly, the physician must be aware of the possibility of concurrent barbiturate addiction and must do what is necessary "to prevent the occasional death associated with abrupt barbiturate withdrawal in an individual severely dependent on this agent" (12).

Morbidity and mortality

The various medical disorders associated with heroin usage, which are mostly infectious in nature, have already been described in Chapter 2; as noted in that chapter, virtually all of these disorders are regarded as consequences of unsterile injection techniques or the dilution of heroin with tissue irritants. Thus far, numerous searches for possible functional or structural abnormalities resulting from the chronic use of heroin, which could be attributed to some effect of the drug itself, have proved fruitless; even when the drug has been used regularly for a number of years, no marked functional disturbances have been detected during life, and findings on autopsy have been essentially negative.

Nonetheless, the death rate among heroin users appears to be unusually high, particularly as a large proportion of the population of users appears to be less than 30 years of age; the average annual death rate in this segment of the total group has been calculated to be as high as 16.0 per thousand and, for users over the age of 30, 30.7 per thousand (16). (In marked contrast, the average annual death rate among non-users, aged 15 to 24, is 1.0 to 1.6 per thousand and for those 25 to 34 years of age, 1.3 to 2.3 per thousand.) Because the exact total number of users is unknown, these rates must be regarded as approximate; even if calculations are based on the most liberal estimates of the probable total number of users in the United States, however, it still appears that the death rate among users is abnormally high.

Some of the deaths are attributable to certain of the infectious diseases described in Chapter 2. Most of the deaths, perhaps as many as 87% of them (17), have been attributed to what has been variously described as "acute reaction to dosage or overdosage," "acute intravenous narcotism," or, more commonly today, merely as an "overdose." In New York City, the Office of the Chief Medical Examiner attributed more than 800 deaths to this cause in 1969, for example; of this number, more than 200 deaths occurred in individuals less than 21 years of age, with the youngest victim being 12 years old. Expressing these findings another way, it appears that 0.5 to 1.0% of the probable total population of American heroin users (100,000 to 200,000) dies of an "overdose" each year.

At first glance, the overdose phenomenon seems readily explicable: inadvertently, or with suicidal intent, the user takes a dose of heroin that substantially exceeds his tolerance for the drug; respiratory depression develops predictably, and death results from hypoxia. The principal findings on autopsy are pulmonary congestion and edema, which are similar to those described in individuals accidentally receiving an overdose of pure morphine (7). Cardiac dilation is frequently observed at autopsy (17, 18), though evidence of cardiomegaly during life is often absent (18). Other findings at autopsy, such as lymphocytic portal infiltration of the liver, seem not to be a necessary consequence of an overdose, for they are found in heroin users dying of other causes (17). The diagnosis of death from overdose is made largely on the basis of a fresh needle puncture (the significance of which can often be adduced by the fact that the victim was a known heroin user, his admission of heroin use before dying, or reports of others about the victim's use of heroin) and the characteristic pulmonary findings.

It is thought that a great many chronic heroin users have had the experience of an overdose at least once (5). On some occasions, the syndrome arises shortly after the addict has completed a prolonged jail sentence, during which period tolerance to heroin would be lost. In some cases, the user appears to have employed an unusually large dose (relative to his customary dose); in others, users maintain that they took only their customary dose (18). In a few cases, a user may take what he thinks is an overdose, but he becomes only mildly ill thereafter (19). The confusion about the quantity of heroin taken by the victims is an inevitable consequence of the unpredictable degree of dilution of the drug. It should be noted, too, that the term, acute intravenous narcotism, is not applicable in all instances, for the syndrome of the overdose has developed in those who merely inhaled, or "snorted," the drug. Also, it has been observed that the syndrome may develop upon the first exposure to heroin or following repeated use (18).

Study of the various reports about overdose leads one to the conclusion that this phenomenon cannot be easily explained. Some of the victims, for example, die so quickly that they are found with a needle still in their veins; death from hypoxia due to inadequate pulmonary ventilation could hardly occur so rapidly. One is put in mind rather of an anaphylactic reaction, possibly characterized by a massive release of histamine, and initiated by the presence in the heroin of some diluent to which the victim was hypersensitive. The concept that death may result from an allergic reaction is indirectly supported by the fact that, in a number of cases of death from "overdose," no detectable quantities of narcotic drug can be found in the tissue or body fluids of the victim (17, 18). It seems an unlikely explanation in all instances, however, for pulmonary edema in some cases does not develop until several hours after the "heroin" was taken.

It is sometimes said that victims of an overdose most typically either die rapidly or recover fully in a relatively short time, often within 48 hours (5); it has been found, however, that the manifestations and clinical course of an overdose can vary considerably (18). Most patients present with signs of respiratory disturbances, ranging from tachypnea to varying degrees of respiratory depression, including apnea; many are cyanotic; and coma is commonly present. Pulmonary rales may be present on admission or may develop subsequently. Some patients have no fever, others have transient febrile episodes, and in still others fever may persist for more than 48 hours. The initial white blood cell count can be highly variable, ranging from 1000 to 26,000 cells/mm^3; an increased incidence of immature forms is commonly observed. The electrocardiogram frequently shows the presence of a sinus tachycardia, though a recent report indicates that paroxysmal atrial fibrillation may be present in some cases (20).

The course of development and the extent of the pulmonary abnormalities can also vary considerably. Most of the victims are clearly ill on admission, and a tentative diagnosis can be made quickly; in some cases, however, the diagnosis can be made only with the aid of radiographic evidence. There is a curious difference in published accounts of the findings made in victims of an overdose: one group reports that radiographic evidence of pulmonary edema (specifically, a diffuse bilateral infiltrate) was observed in only a minority of their patients (5), whereas another group obtained such evidence in virtually all of their patients (18). There is general agreement that the great majority of these patients do develop pulmonary edema, which is often complicated by the aspiration of gastric contents and various secretions. Acute pulmonary congestion likewise develops in a great majority of patients; it may be present on admission, however, it may develop several hours after recovery from coma, or, on occasion, up to 24 hours may elapse after the heroin has been taken before congestion appears (18, 19). In some patients, the congestion and edema may gradually progress to an acute exudative lobular pneumonia. Unless the user dies almost immediately after the overdose, he typically recovers completely, given supportive therapy, within 2 to 5 days despite the fact that he may at times appear to be gravely, and even terminally, ill. The management of acute narcotic intoxication is described in Chapter 10.

In an attempt to determine the cause of the overdose phenomenon, several questions come to mind. First, is heroin the causative agent or is some diluent? The findings of acute pulmonary congestion and edema are typical of an opiate overdose and were first described (in 1880) before heroin was in general use (5, 17). The characteristic pathology is unlikely to be merely a result of hypoxia, secondary to heroin-induced respiratory depression. For one thing, pulmonary edema develops only rarely in cases of profound respiratory depression induced by overdoses of such other central nervous system depressant drugs as barbiturates. Further, coma and hypoventilation, which should produce hypoxia, often precede the development of pulmonary congestion and edema; by the same token, hypoxia probably cannot be said to be a consequence solely of pulmonary pathology. If heroin is the offender, then we must postulate that the pulmonary changes are a consequence of some effect of heroin heretofore unrecognized. Yet, if this is so, how are we to account for the victims who appear to die almost immediately following injection and in some of whom no trace of narcotic drug can be detected at autopsy? Likely guesses at the moment are that these deaths are anaphylactic in origin or the result of the use of heroin containing relatively insoluble diluents, so that, in effect, a suspension is injected which produces a "nitritoid" or "colloidoclastic" crisis (17). And yet, if this is the case, why is the same pulmonary pathology found at autopsy in these cases as in the cases of victims who die more slowly? The pathogenesis of the overdose syndrome is clearly a mystery, as is the probable cause of death when it occurs rapidly.

CODEINE

Medically, codeine is used principally as an analgesic and a cough suppressant. By a long tradition of uncertain origin, it is almost always given by mouth, which is probably, as in the case of morphine, a most ineffective route of administration. In point of fact, it is difficult to demonstrate clinically that codeine by mouth exerts any appreciably stronger analgesic effect than does aspirin (1). If a dose of 120 mg of codeine is injected, however, the degree of analgesia obtained closely approximates that obtained with 10 mg of morphine; under these conditions, codeine also produces the same spectrum of untoward effects as morphine.

The pharmacological effects of codeine when taken by mouth are identical to those of morphine, though much less intense. The degree of euphoria produced by codeine is mild; the experienced user of narcotic drugs typically finds it unsatisfactory, and it is extremely rare to find a user who employs codeine or a codeine derivative exclusively. Indeed, many discussions of drug abuse omit mention of codeine altogether. One can read of codeine addiction principally in accounts of the comparative handful of narcotic addicts that existed in Great Britain before 1960; most of these people were "therapeutic addicts" (i.e., introduced to narcotic drugs in the course of medical treatment), and some of them subsisted on relatively small doses of codeine daily.

There do appear to be two circumstances under which codeine, or congeners of it, are subject to abuse in this country today. The first involves the adolescent drug experimenter, who has learned that certain codeine-containing cough medicines may be obtained fairly easily. Periodically, vogues develop for the use of such preparations, particularly elixir of terpin hydrate with codeine. Commonly sold in 4-oz bottles, this mixture contains 2 mg of codeine/ml and has an alcoholic content equivalent to a 78- to 88-proof whiskey. Adolescents often consume the contents of one or more bottles as quickly as possible; the effect obtained is such that, for example, they are unsafe drivers. As a result of this abuse, the law in New York City was changed in 1973 to require a prescription for the dispensation of codeine-containing preparations.

The second circumstance involves the heroin user who is temporarily unable to obtain this drug. If he has sufficient information about narcotic drugs, he will sometimes attempt to obtain drugs pharmacologically related to heroin. If codeine or some of its popular derivatives such as hydrocodone (dihydrocodeinone, Hycodan, etc.), dihydrocodeine (Paracodin), and oxycodone (dihydrohydroxycodeinone, Percodan) are available at these times, he will use them until heroin again becomes available.

OPIUM

The incidence of opium abuse in the United States today, like that of codeine, appears to be very small. Even in such mid- and far-eastern areas as Iran, Thailand, India, Hong Kong, and the Philippines, where opium abuse is a traditional and often socially acceptable practice, it is being supplanted by heroin or morphine as the drug of choice among younger users; perhaps only in Singapore is the use of opium still pre-eminent (2).

For purposes of abuse, opium is almost always smoked or taken by mouth. We are not aware of any accurate surveys of the incidence of opium smoking in this country, past or present, or of any scientific studies reporting the approximate magnitude of the narcotic effect produced by this practice. Accounts of drug abuse dating from the first decades of this century commonly describe opium smoking as the least harmful form of dependence on narcotics; in the estimate of workers of that period, opium smokers displayed less psychological dependence on narcotics than did users who ingested or injected drugs of this group, and their lives appeared to be characterized to a lesser degree by behavior directed toward procurement and compulsive use of narcotics. We wonder, however, how meaningful this comparison is, for, during this period, all forms of narcotic drugs were readily available. It is possible that those who chose to smoke opium in preference to, for example, the injection of morphine, were less susceptible psychologically to the abuse of drugs. Because of their less intense emotional needs, they would find the possibly weaker narcotic effects produced by the smoking of opium quite satisfactory and, for the same reason, would be less likely to develop a strong degree of psychological dependence.

Though ingestion is a relatively inefficient route of administration for narcotic drugs, rather severe forms of addiction have resulted from this practice. Though opium is literally eaten in India to this day (2), most European and American devotees of this practice have utilized alcoholic solutions of opium. Tincture of opium (laudanum) is a potent preparation, which contains 10 mg of anhydrous morphine/ml. The English opium "eaters," of whom De Quincey wrote, used this preparation; De Quincey himself eventually developed such a degree of tolerance to narcotics that he could take daily by mouth an amount of opium that would yield about 4700 mg of morphine.

Because little laudanum is compounded today, American users of narcotic drugs do occasionally utilize the only readily available preparation, paregoric; it contains only 0.4 mg of morphine/ml, along with camphor, benzoic acid, and anise oil. Its alcoholic content is equivalent to that of a 86- to 92-proof whiskey. It offers, as do codeine-containing cough medicines, the opportunity to abuse two drugs simultaneously, and the (quite rare) paregoric addict may consume as much as a quart of this mixture daily. It is used also by heroin addicts as a temporary substitute for their drug of choice. In spite of its relatively small content of opium, paregoric cannot now be dispensed without a prescription.

SYNTHETIC NARCOTIC DRUGS

As noted in Chapter 1, these drugs can be divided into four groups on the basis of their chemical structures. The largest group is that of meperidine (pethidine, Demerol) and its congeners. The "addiction liability" of this group, as well as that of such substituted morphinans as levorphanol (Levo-Dromoran), is high. The abuse of methadone (Dolophine) is growing as significant quantities of it have become available from inadequately supervised detoxification and maintenance centers. This problem could disappear rapidly if such centers were supervised more vigilantly. The newest of the wholly synthetic narcotics, such benzomorphan compounds as pentazocine (Talwin), rarely produce euphoria, and little physical dependence develops upon regular usage unless the daily intake is very high; hence, their addiction liability is regarded as minimal.

The abuse of synthetic narcotic drugs (other than methadone at this time) contribute very little to the total incidence of the illegal use of narcotics. By and large, these drugs are unknown to most users and are not regularly offered for sale on the illicit market. Of these synthetic drugs, only meperidine has been abused appreciably. This reflects the fact that the bulk of meperidine addicts are either members of the health professions, who have reasonably easy access to the drug and who were told at one time that it was non-addicting, or lay people, who were initially introduced to this drug by their physicians in the course of treatment and upon whom they are dependent for a continuing supply of the drug.

Meperidine

This drug was introduced, most unfortunately, as a compound able to produce the same degree of analgesia as morphine, without many of morphine's shortcomings: little or no respiratory depression, a spasmolytic, rather than a spasmogenic, action, and virtually no addiction liability. In addition, meperidine, in contrast to morphine, can be effectively administered by mouth, though, by this route, it is not as effective as it is upon injection. As these claims were subjected to close scrutiny with the passage of time, some of them were shown to be substantially false.

There are several probable reasons why meperidine was initially characterized incorrectly. It is a common experience for the potency of a new analgesic drug to be overestimated at first; it was only when the effects of truly equianalgesic doses of meperidine (100 mg) and morphine (10 mg) were compared that one could observe, for example, that the two drugs produced an equal degree of respiratory depression. Then, too, some of the pharmacological effects of meperidine are unpredictable; only by accumulating a fairly large number of observations can some idea of the nature and approximate incidence of meperidine's effects be obtained. Meperidine can, for example, be fully as constipating as morphine and can produce the same intensity of biliary spasm, but the relative incidence of the occurrence of such effects is lower with meperidine than with morphine. In light of later findings, we must conclude that the preliminary investigations of the properties of meperidine were inadequate, particularly in regard to its addiction liability.

Users of meperidine must contend with two properties that ordinarily should reduce its attractiveness as a drug of abuse. First, it is a tissue irritant. Meperidine users who want a more rapid onset of effect than is possible by oral administration, commonly inject it subcutaneously or intramuscularly; the chronic injector of meperidine is thus easy to detect, for tissue indurations and skin ulcers are plentifully evident. Second, this drug has a relatively short duration of action and for a sustained effect probably should be used at intervals of no more than 3 hours. Meperidine's relatively short duration of effect has been invoked to explain why tolerance to its effects develop more slowly than in the case of heroin, for it is postulated that few users take it at short enough intervals to keep the drug at pharmacologically effective levels in the body. The short duration of action means also that if physical dependence is established, and the drug intake at some time thereafter is abruptly stopped, the withdrawal syndrome will develop rapidly but will be relatively brief. Manifestations of abstinence are usually first evident 4 to 5 hours after the last dose and reach maximal intensity at 7 to 12 hours. Abstinence from meperidine is qualitatively similar to that from heroin, though such autonomic disturbances as mydriasis and gastrointestinal upsets are commonly less intense. Conversely, restlessness, nervousness, and muscular twitching may be more pronounced (21).

The fact that meperidine was introduced as a non-addicting analgesic drug induced many people in the health professions—physicians, nurses, pharmacists, and so on—to feel that it could be taken with impunity to overcome fatigue or to alleviate manifestations of somatic or psychic disorders. Even those who now know that physical dependence on and tolerance to the effects of meperidine will develop with regular usage still appear to hold the mistaken idea that this drug is "less addicting" than other narcotics and, therefore, that addiction to it will be a relatively easy habit to break (13).

Tolerance to meperidine, like that to other narcotics, is incomplete and extends primarily to the depressant actions of the drug. Even an addict using 3000 to 4000 mg/day shows little tolerance to the stimulatory actions of the drug; in such addicts, very high doses of meperidine produce few signs of central nervous system depression, but mydriasis, tremors, involuntary muscular activity, mental confusion, and, rarely, grand mal convulsions may occur (13). In contrast, when non-tolerant individuals are given very large doses of this drug, respiratory depression is produced, which may be followed by coma and death.

It seems evident that meperidine has more marked central nervous system stimulatory effects than do most other narcotics. The stimulatory effects of meperidine can be attributed in part to its demethylation in the liver to form normeperidine, a metabolite that possesses greater central nervous system stimulatory activity than the parent compound. The stimulatory effects of meperidine (and normeperidine) are often masked by the drug's depressant effects, but the former can be unmasked under certain circumstances. If a very large dose of the drug is given parenterally, the rate of drug absorption probably exceeds the rate of conversion of meperidine to normeperidine, and the depressant effects of the parent drug will prevail. If nalorphine (Nalline) is given at this time, the depressant effects will be more effectively antagonized than the stimulatory effects; as a result, the stimulatory effects will become evident, so much so that barbiturates may be required to combat the ensuing convulsions. This situation mimics, in many respects, the consequences of administering a large dose of meperidine to an addict who has developed substantial tolerance to the depressant effects of this drug.

Though the pharmacological effects of meperidine differ somewhat from those of heroin, the consequences of addiction to the two drugs are substantially the same. It is true that the meperidine addict commonly does not have to worry about variable potency or possibly harmful diluents, and, because many addicts are members of the health professions, the injection technique is likely to be sterile. Yet problems stemming from psychological and physical dependence and from tolerance are much the same as in heroin addiction. Though lay addicts rarely hold jobs, many meperidine addicts in the health professions do attempt to carry on their professional duties; in this regard, it is noteworthy that some workers regard meperidine as capable of producing a greater impairment of working ability than morphine (13). The risk to patient care seems evident.

REFERENCES

1. Lasagna, L., The clinical evaluation of morphine and its substitutes as analgesics. *Pharmacol Rev* 16:47, 1964
2. Cameron, D. C., Youth and drugs. *J Amer Med Assoc* 206:1267, 1968
3. Dundee, J. W., R. S. J. Clarke, and W. B. Loan, Comparative toxicity of diamorphine, morphine and methadone. *Lancet* ii:221, 1967
4. Dole, V. P., M. Nyswander, and M. J. Kreek, Narcotic blockade. *Arch Int Med* 118:304, 1966
5. Louria, D. B., T. Hensle, and J. Rose, The major medical complications of heroin addiction. *Ann Int Med* 67:1, 1967
6. Murphree, H. B., Narcotic Analgesics. I. Opium Alkaloids. In: DiPalma, J. R., ed., *Drill's Pharmacology in Medicine,* ed. 3. New York: McGraw-Hill, 1965, p. 246
7. Jaffe, J. H. and W. R. Martin, Opioid Analgesics and Antagonists: In: Gilman, A. G., L. Goodman and A. Gilman, eds., *The Pharmacological Basis of Therapeutics,* ed. 6. New York: Macmillan, 1980, p. 494
8. Way, E. L. and T. K. Adler, The pharmacologic implications of the fate of morphine and its surrogates. *Pharmacol Rev* 12:383, 1960
9. Way, E. L., J. W. Kemp, J. M. Young, and D. R. Grassetti, The pharmacologic effects of heroin in relationship to its rate of biotransformation. *J Pharmacol* 129:144, 1960
10. Seevers, M. H. and G. A. Deneau, Physiological aspects of tolerance and physical dependence. In: Root, W. S. and F. G. Hofmann, eds., *Physiological Pharmacology,* vol. I. New York: Academic Press, 1963, p. 565
11. Way, E. L., H. H. Loh, and F. Shen, Morphine tolerance, physical dependence and synthesis of brain 5-hydroxytryptamine. *Science* 162:1290, 1968
12. Louria, D. B., Medical complications of pleasure-giving drugs. *Arch Int Med* 123:82, 1969
13. Jaffe, J. H., Drug addiction and drug abuse. In: Gilman, A. G., L. Goodman and A. Gilman, eds., *The Pharmacological Basis of Therapeutics,* ed. 6. New York: Macmillan, 1980, p. 535
14. Martin, W. R. and D. R. Jasinski, Physiological parameters of morphine dependence in man—tolerance, early abstinence, protracted abstinence. *J Psychiat Res* 7:9, 1969

15. Eisenman, A. J., J. W. Sloan, W. R. Martin, D. R. Jasinski, and J. W. Brooks, Catecholamine and 17-hydroxycorticoid excretion during a cycle of morphine dependence in man. *J Psychiat Res* 7:19, 1969
16. Duvall, H. J., B. Z. Locke, and L. Brill, Followup study of narcotic drug addicts five years after hospitalization. *Pub Hlth Rep* 78:185, 1963
17. Cherubin, C. E., The medical sequelae of narcotic addiction. *Ann Int Med* 67:23, 1967
18. Steinberg, A. D. and J. S. Karliner, The clinical spectrum of heroin pulmonary edema. *Arch Int Med* 122:121, 1968
19. Karliner, J. S., A. D. Steinberg, and M. H. Williams, Jr., Lung function after pulmonary edema associated with heroin overdose. *Arch Int Med* 124:349, 1969
20. Labi, M., Paroxysmal atrial fibrillation in heroin intoxication. *Ann Int Med* 71:951, 1969
21. Isbell, H. and W. M. White, Clinical characteristics of addictions. *Amer J Med* 14:558, 1953

Chapter 4

GENERALIZED DEPRESSANTS OF THE CENTRAL NERVOUS SYSTEM

ALCOHOL, BARBITURATES, AND OTHER DRUGS EXERTING SIMILAR EFFECTS

Alcohol, sedative and hypnotic drugs, and the so-called "minor tranquilizers" are a seemingly heterogeneous collection of compounds, and, indeed, they do not exhibit identical patterns of pharmacological activity, nor are they all of equal value for certain therapeutic purposes. Yet all of these drugs are capable of producing clinical effects, sedation and sleep, for example, that are strikingly similar; more significantly, for our present purposes, the most important pharmacological characteristics of the abuse of these drugs are qualitatively identical. The smallest therapeutic doses of these agents exert a calming (sedative) effect, and larger doses exert a sleep-inducing (hypnotic) effect. Though some individuals who have taken intoxicating quantities of generalized depressants may disregard the sensation of pain if it arises, these drugs usually are not reliable analgesics. If used alone in persons in severe pain, they may well produce a state of marked agitation and disorientation. Because they do not produce analgesia in a consistent and predictable fashion, generalized central nervous system depressant agents cannot be regarded as narcotic drugs according to the criteria recognized by pharmacologists, which are set forth at the beginning of Chapter 3.

In contrast to other forms of drug abuse, the following features are typical of generalized depressants: (1) They are potentially addicting compounds but, for physical dependence to develop, the daily intake of drug must exceed a certain threshold value, which appears to be peculiar to each agent; (2) the withdrawal syndrome can be so traumatic that death can result, even in healthy young adults; (3) only a low or moderate degree of tolerance to the effects of these drugs develops, regardless of the pattern of usage; (4) they may well be the most widely abused drugs in Western nations; (5) they have been implicated in what may be a greater incidence of drug-related deaths than any other group of drugs subject to abuse; (6) the fact that all of these drugs are potentially addicting has yet to receive widespread recognition by members of both the medical profession and the laity as a whole; and (7) of all the potentially addicting drugs, it is only the acquisition of alcohol that is not stringently regulated by law in the United States today.

Chronic use of large quantities of these drugs usually results in marked deteriorative changes in the user. Though a narcotic addict with a similar pattern of drug usage could still function as a useful and apparently normal member of society (though very few do), the persistently intoxicated state of the heavy user of generalized depressants leads to a neglect of personal appearance and hygiene. The marks of traumatic injuries incurred while intoxicated may be readily evident, as are abnormalities in speech, behavior, neuromuscular coordination, and dexterity. Though the individual who uses relatively small quantities of alcohol or a barbiturate on a regular or episodic basis may not be identified as a drug user, even by those having frequent and close contact with him, the heavy user is easily detected.

A full listing of the types of drugs classified as members of this group would include general anesthetic agents. Though these drugs are rarely subject to abuse, the volatile solvents contained in a number of household products, including certain glues, nail polish, and spot removers, exert effects similar to general anesthetics. The abuse of these products will be discussed in the next chapter.

ALCOHOL

Introduction

Alcohol (ethanol, ethyl alcohol, grain alcohol) probably was among the first substances to be misused by man. It has been postulated that alcoholic (i.e., ethanolic) beverages were first made in prehistoric times as a result of the (probably) accidental fermentation of honey, grain, or fruit juices, which would yield, respectively, mead, beer, or wine. Stronger alcoholic beverages became possible when the process of distillation was devised, a feat generally said to have been accomplished around A.D. 800 by Jabir ibn Hayyan (known as Geber in the Western world). Like the distillation process, the word *alcohol* is also of Arabian origin, the antecedent word usually being transliterated as "alkuhl" (1).

There are many alcohols in addition to ethanol, of which methanol (wood alcohol) is an example. Compared to ethanol, the other alcohols are less intoxicating and considerably more poisonous.

Social attitudes about alcohol differ markedly from those manifested toward other drugs of abuse. It is a familiar substance for many people, having been present at home from the time of their earliest memories. Because he is not an unaccustomed sight, the non-belligerent drunkard is, in many cultures, an object of genial tolerance. It is evident that less than a majority of Americans react to alcohol with the same mixture of emotions—revulsion, scorn, and fear—that is commonly elicited by the abuse of such drugs as heroin and LSD. Though satisfactory evidence has existed for approximately 20 years that alcohol can be an addicting substance (2), today, easy access to alcoholic beverages is generally denied by law only to the young and the grossly intoxicated. The tolerant attitude exhibited by many adults toward the use of alcohol does make them vulnerable to the charge of hypocrisy made by many young people on the grounds that adults use or sanction the use of alcohol while (often severely) proscribing the use of such other drugs as marihuana, that might be less harmful than alcohol.

Diagnosis and patterns of use

The many and varied patterns of alcohol consumption comprise a spectrum of such breadth and diversity that the determination of where essentially benign use ends and abuse begins is most difficult. Though dependence on alcohol has been studied more extensively than any other form of drug abuse, no generally accepted definition of alcoholism has been formulated. Disputes regarding definitions center principally about the degree of psychological dependence an individual must develop to be classified an alcoholic. Because "degree of psychological dependence" on the effects of any drug is little more than a subjective evaluation, impossible to measure precisely, universal agreement may never be obtained.

For these reasons, it seems a futile chore to present a sampling of the various definitions of alcoholism that have been proposed and to discuss the possible significance of the differences among them. And yet, in one sense, these differences inescapably intrude upon us. Each authority who estimates the prevalence of alcoholism must necessarily base his calculations on what he accepts as a definition of the disease; the discrepancies existing in estimates of the present incidence of alcoholism in the United States most probably stem, at least in part, from the lack of a commonly accepted definition (3).

To provide a basis for discussion, we have elected to use the definition of alcoholism provided by the American Medical Association in its *Manual on Alcoholism* (4): "Alcoholism is an illness characterized by preoccupation with alcohol and loss of control over its consumption such as to lead usually to intoxication if drinking is begun; by chronicity; by progression; and by tendency toward relapse. It is typically associated with physical disability and impaired emotional, occupational, and/or social adjustments as a direct consequence of persistent and excessive use of alcohol." The phrase in this definition descriptive of the degree of psychological dependence that an alcoholic develops is "loss of control over its consumption" and, indeed, the manual stresses that "control" is the keystone of the definition.

In company with others, the manual points out that alcoholism is not necessarily associated with certain characteristics that some laymen regard as pathognomonic of the disease. Not all alcoholics are solitary drinkers, nor do all of them begin each day with a drink. Many alcoholics drink on virtually a daily basis, whereas others are "spree" drinkers who become grossly intoxicated only on occasion and may even be virtually abstemious during the intervening periods. Thus, the total quantity of alcohol consumed per unit time (in the course of a month, for example) is not necessarily a useful diagnostic criterion. An individual whose schedule is heavy with business and social obligations entailing drinking might actually consume more alcohol per month than some spree alcoholics, yet such individuals can face the prospect of abstinence without undue psychic distress.

Likewise, and contrary to popular belief, a number of alcoholics never experience certain degenerative physical and sociological changes regarded as inevitable sequelae of severe alcoholism. Not all are affected with cirrhosis of the liver, for example; in fact, only some are. Not all severe alcoholics come eventually to live in a Skid Row-type of environment, and, conversely, not all "bums" are alcoholics; it has been estimated that of the approximately five to seven million alcoholics in the United States today, only 5% eventually reach the status of a derelict (5). Many affluent alcoholics in particular never exhibit these "requisite" stigmata of an alcoholic, for they represent not the consequences of alcoholism per se but secondary manifestations of this form of drug abuse. Specifically, and most importantly, they reflect a diet lacking such nutrients as vitamins and the essential fatty acids as well as the swift descent into poverty which the less affluent alcoholic can experience when his employability is compromised.

The uncertain validity of many popular criteria for the identification of an alcoholic serves to focus our attention on the view held by the great majority of authorities on alcoholism that the most important diagnostic criterion is the degree of psychological dependence on the effects of alcohol. This doubtlessly often makes the diagnosis of alcoholism an uncertain and highly individualistic matter, with the degree of variability from one physician to another being particularly high when the distinction must be made between a "heavy social drinker" and an alcoholic (3).

Abuse of alcohol is typically (though not invariably) characterized by progressively increasing dependence on the drug. One of the earliest signs of alcoholism may be the need to "fortify" oneself before a social event in order to enjoy it (4). In time, alcohol is increasingly turned to routinely as a means of dealing with stress and anxiety. The frequency of inebriation slowly increases, as do episodes of apparently unintentional incapaciting states of severe intoxication. Comments, inquiries, and expressions of concern from others about this changing pattern of alcohol intake are likely to evoke brusque denials that a problem exists. Despite these denials, at this stage, the alcoholic probably is already aware that he has a problem and that he feels some guilt about his drinking; though intoxication often becomes a regular event now, covert drinking may become a more significant facet of the pattern of usage. On the one hand, he may more openly acknowledge his alcoholism by offering excuses and "explanations" to justify his drinking, but, at the same time, if bluntly confronted with the problem, his defensive reactions may now be characterized by greater vehemence and even overt hostility.

The pattern of abuse, to this point, may not be one of uninterrupted progression but may be broken by one or more periods in which the alcoholic "swears off" or "goes on the wagon." Well-meaning physicians may attempt to help the alcoholic persist in abstinence by prescribing barbiturates, minor tranquilizers, amphetamine, and the like for "nervousness," depression, and insomnia; apparently this practice often introduces the alcoholic to patterns of multiple drug abuse. The periods of abstinence are typically not of long duration, and, for a number of alcoholics, when drinking resumes, the effects of alcohol are now supplemented with those of barbiturates, for example, and may be combatted on the "mornings after" by amphetamine.

Often the next serious development is the occurrence of amnesia ("blackouts") for varying portions of the time during which he has been intoxicated; reaction to the blackouts can range from mild annoyance to marked concern. With repeated intoxication, emotional lability is often increased, and patterns of irresponsible behavior may be exhibited. The alcoholic may range emotionally from periods of extreme euphoria during which plans for reformation may be formulated repeatedly, though they are rarely realized, to periods of pronounced depression, which appear to be provoked in part by feelings of guilt and by the censorious attitude of others toward him. The mornings after may be characterized more frequently now by the discovery of injuries (bruises, contusions, lacerations, skin burns from cigarettes, and the like) incurred while intoxicated.

When psychological dependence becomes maximal, severe intoxication, often to the point of stupor, increases in frequency. The schedule of daily activities is now arranged so that two primary goals can be met; a steady supply of alcohol and sufficient time to drink it in a setting of choice. Occupational, social, familial, and marital relationships may be severed or basically altered, often voluntarily by the alcoholic, to be replaced by more tolerable relationships with fellow drinkers. The chronic disorders associated with alcoholism (to be described below) now are often clearly evident, as are deteriorative changes in personality structure. The alcoholic finally reaches "bottom" in a state of marked incapacitation, psychologically and often physically.

The medical histories of all alcoholics will not correspond to the account presented above, for not all reach the nadir we have described, and some may follow different paths to the same end. A few may be diverted at some point to the primary abuse of other drugs. (It is not uncommon, for example, to encounter barbiturate addicts who have been alcoholics.) We have presented the foregoing account because it contains a number of features commonly present in the histories of many alcoholics (4).

The term, *alcohol addict,* refers to an alcoholic whose pattern of drinking is such that any marked alteration in the pattern will provoke the onset of a characteristic withdrawal syndrome. Despite the extensive investigation to which alcoholism has been subjected, there are largely inexplicable gaps in our knowledge, and we still cannot describe precisely the pattern of abuse requisite for addiction to alcohol. It seems reasonable to assume, however, that not all alcoholics should be classified as addicts. The risk of developing physical dependence on the effects of alcohol is greatest in the more severe forms of alcoholism, when daily consumption of large quantities of this substance is the typical pattern of use.

Effects of alcohol

Nineteenth-century pharmacologists regarded the effects of alcohol on the central nervous system as stimulatory in small doses and depressant in larger doses. In this century, alcohol has been regarded as a uniformly depressant drug, with its apparently stimulatory early effects on speech and behavior being attributed to an alcohol-induced depression or disruption of the mechanisms that normally regulate these activities. It is said that the reticular activating system in the brain stem is among the first areas of the central nervous system to be depressed by alcohol and that loss of the integrative control of the cortex by this system accounts for many of the subsequently observed effects (6). The concept that *small* doses of alcohol (2 to 4 oz of whiskey) may actually exert a stimulatory effect has been recently revived as a result of experiments in which very intelligent subjects were required to solve highly demanding intellectual problems as Boolean logic; it was found that their performance after taking small doses of whiskey was clearly superior to their performance when sober or following ingestion of 6 oz of whiskey. Similar, though far from invariable, findings have been made in other tests of the effects of alcohol on various forms of intellectual activity (7). Whether such experiments actually demonstrate a stimulatory effect of small doses of alcohol on cerebration or merely a release from some controls, perhaps of an emotional nature, that are normally present cannot be determined at this time.

The effects of moderate quantities of alcohol are familiar: ordinary restraints on speech and behavior are weakened ("release of inhibitions"), euphoria may develop, self-confidence is often increased, and there are reductions in neuromuscular coordination (manifested in speech, gait, and manual dexterity), visual acuity, and perception of pain and fatigue. In addition, reaction time is prolonged, memory, insight, and the ability to concentrate are impaired, and sexuality, as manifested in speech and purposive behavior, may become overt. It is difficult, however, to predict the degree of intoxication that any individual will exhibit at intermediate blood concentrations of alcohol. Individual susceptibility to intoxication, or at least to manifesting signs of it, varies considerably. At low blood alcohol concentrations (50 mg/100 ml or less), 10% of a population of drinkers appear intoxicated (as determined by trained observers utilizing such criteria as slurred speech, obvious loss of inhibitions, and locomotor difficulties). At levels regarded as significant both medically and legally (for example, 101 to 150 mg/100 ml), just 64% appear intoxicated. Only at levels exceeding 200 mg/100 ml do virtually all drinkers appear intoxicated (8).

If alcoholics are similarly evaluated, additional variables must be considered. Some degree of tolerance to the effects of alcohol develops in alcoholics as do patterns of behavior designed to minimize the outward manifestations of intoxication; as a result, alcoholics with blood concentrations as high as 300 mg/100 ml may appear only mildly intoxicated (9). Conversely, in the most severe stages of alcoholism, relatively small quantities of alcohol may produce marked intoxication, possibly because of degenerative changes in both the principal site of action of alcohol, the brain, and the organ largely responsible for its metabolic degradation, the liver (4).

It is difficult to predict what the predominant emotional mood of an intoxicated person will be or what he might do. Most moderately intoxicated people are convivial; a few become argumentative, some are even vicious in their speech and behavior; while others may be maudlin, full of self-pity, or suffer from psychic depression. During prolonged periods of high alcoholic intake (45 days or more), it has been observed experimentally that some of the subjects who were initially happy and gregarious gradually became morose and withdrawn as the period of chronic intoxication lengthened (10). In a similar type of study, other observers have reported that, as drinking progressed, anxiety increased as manifested by the subjects' reports of feelings of tension and apprehension and by their difficulties in sleeping; these observations, it was felt, might explain why, during prolonged bouts of drinking, frequency of alcoholic intake often increases with time. Paradoxically, the subjects in the latter study also reported that, as the period of chronic intoxication increased, they experienced a continually growing desire to stop drinking; this ambivalent attitude resulted in voluntary cessation of drinking in only one of four subjects, however (9).

When sufficient alcohol is consumed so that blood levels exceed 300 mg/100 ml, most drinkers will be markedly intoxicated, and some will be stuporous. As blood concentrations rise to 400 mg/100 ml and above, a state resembling surgical anesthesia develops, which can be succeeded by coma and death from respiratory paralysis. It is commonly said that death occurs at blood levels in excess of 550 to 600 mg/100 ml, but 350 mg/100 ml has been lethal on occasion, and, conversely, a few individuals have been reported to be still ambulatory with blood alcohol concentrations of 700 mg/100 ml (2).

The mechanism of the depressant action of alcohol on the central nervous system is unknown; this is also true of all other generalized central nervous system depressants. Investigations of their primary mode of action have succeeded principally in characterizing secondary consequences of that action. Individual neurons are less excitable, repolarize more slowly after excitation, and exhibit reduced spontaneous electrical activity. Synaptic transmission is impaired. Spinal reflexes are initially enhanced (probably a consequence of the loss of higher inhibitory influences), but, as intoxication increases, they too become depressed.

A second and often prominent site of action of alcohol is the gastro-intestinal tract. When alcohol is present at concentrations exceeding 15 to 20% (which would be the case if any beverage approximately 40 proof or greater were taken undiluted), gastrointestinal responses to its irritant effects can be observed. Gastric secretions and motility are depressed, pylorospasm may occur, and the musoca becomes hyperemic; the nausea that can occur after the use of alcohol probably stems from gastrointestinal inflammation. Vomiting is caused by both local irritant and central actions of alcohol (8). Diarrhea is thought to be provoked by the irritant properties of the various oils present in most alcoholic beverages. Prolonged, excessive use of alcohol leads minimally to gastritis, sometimes accompanied by edema and hyperemia of the tongue and buccal mucous membranes (6). More serious degrees of mucosal erosion can progress to frank ulceration and hemorrhage (4). Both motor and secretory activities of the entire gastrointestinal tract essentially cease during severe intoxication.

The cardiovascular effects of alcohol are minimal but, under certain circumstances, may hasten death. Alcohol causes cutaneous vasodilation, most probably by a central nervous system action, to produce a warm, flushed skin and an increase in the rate of heat loss from the body. Because the effects of alcohol prevent reflex cutaneous vasoconstriction in response to cold, the moderately intoxicated individual will succumb to a cold environment with abnormal rapidity. In addition, large quantities of alcohol directly prevent essentially all effective central nervous system regulation of body temperature, which, in turn, further speeds the onset of hypothermia. Alcohol is not a reliable coronary vasodilator, and it is thought that the relief from anginal pain it produces stems largely from its central nervous system effects. Even lethal quantities of alcohol do not significantly impair myocardial function; the heart usually continues to contract for some time after respiratory movements have stopped.

The offspring of alcoholic mothers may exhibit the *fetal alcohol syndrome,* which is characterized by slow growth, brain-related abnormalities such as a low IQ and microcephaly, characteristic facial anomalies such as a short nose, an underdeveloped upper lip, and short folds of the eyelids and a variety of other malformations (25). These teratogenic occurrences appear to reflect, in part, the ability of ethanol to depress directly the normal growth patterns of fetal tissues (26). "Ethanol seems to be the most frequent cause of teratogenically induced mental deficiency that is known in the Western world; even moderate drinking of alcohol is clearly contraindicated during pregnancy" (6).

Absorption, distribution, and metabolism
Though alcohol can be absorbed slowly into the body while in the stomach, the upper portion of the small intestine represents the principal site of its absorption. Here absorption is rapid and virtually complete so that the rest of the intestinal tract is ordinarily exposed to very little alcohol.

The critical determinant of the rate of absorption appears to be the emptying time of the stomach, which is subject to various influences. The presence of food slows gastric emptying as do high concentrations of alcohol, which can produce gastric irritation and pylorospasm. The crucial role of the stomach as a temporary impediment to absorption is graphically illustrated by findings made in patients who have undergone massive gastrectomies. These patients usually become intoxicated rapidly with relatively small quantities of alcohol because, when they drink, alcohol is delivered almost immediately to the site of its rapid absorption in the small intestine (6).

The partition coefficient for alcohol between water and fat is about 30:1 (8); consequently, the distribution of alcohol throughout the body at diffusion equilibrium very closely approximates that of water. The rate of entrance of alcohol into various tissues varies directly with the blood supply to the tissue; the concentration in the highly vascularized central nervous system, therefore, rapidly comes into equilibrium with that in the systemic arterial blood. Concentrations in more poorly perfused tissues, such as depot fat and resting skeletal muscle, increase more slowly; alcohol does increase hepatic fat mobilization (6). It may take 45 minutes or more before the alcohol concentrations in venous blood coming primarily from skeletal muscle approximates that in systemic arterial blood. Recognition of this situation has enabled investigators to explain several puzzling phenomena observed in subjects ingesting alcohol.

The first observation to be clarified was that of a person who takes a few drinks rapidly on an empty stomach, quickly becomes intoxicated, and, then, in the succeeding 30 minutes or so, gradually becomes more sober. The time involved is too short for metabolic degradation to contribute appreciably to the waning state of intoxication. It appears, rather, that the concentration of alcohol in the brain falls as the drug is redistributed slowly to other body tissues. Alcohol seems capable of entering and leaving most tissues, including the brain, by the process of passive diffusion, so that the net direction of movement, into or out of cells, is governed largely by the character of the concentration gradient across the cell membrane. Thus, as alcohol slowly enters the large mass of skeletal muscle, the blood level falls, and eventually the concentration gradient with respect to the brain becomes such that alcohol diffuses out of this organ.

A more puzzling observation has emerged from studies in which the blood alcohol concentration has been plotted as a function of time, and the degree of intoxication associated wtih various points on the curve has been determined. It has been repeatedly observed that the degree of intoxication present at a given point on the rising slope of the curve is greater than that associated with the equivalent point on the declining slope. The resolution of this discrepancy was achieved when it was recognized that the various points on such curves are commonly obtained by determining alcohol concentrations in forearm venous blood; as noted above, it may take 45 minutes after the ingestion of alcohol for levels in the veins of the forearm to equal the alcohol concentrations in the intracranial arteries (8). For this period of time, then, points on the rising slope of the curve, as determined by sampling blood in the forearm, would be spuriously low.

More than 90% of the alcohol absorbed into the body is metabolized, chiefly in the liver; the complete oxidation of alcohol to carbon dioxide and water yields 7 Cal/gm. The remainder of the alcohol is excreted largely unchanged in urine and in expired air. Small quantities may also be found in saliva, sweat, and tears. For mediocolegal purposes, a knowledge of the relationship between blood alcohol concentrations and those in readily obtained biological samples is critical. The concentration of alcohol in urine is about 1.25 times greater than that in blood, and the concentration in saliva 1.12 times greater, whereas the concentration in blood is about 2100 times greater than that in alveolar air. It is commonly said that there is a maximal rate at which alcohol can be metabolized (which is typical of enzymatic reactions), and the figure cited most often is 7 gm (9 ml) of alcohol/hour for a person weighing 70 kg. This should be regarded only as an average value to which individual variations as large as plus or minus 50% may be encountered. In an experimental simulation of severe chronic alcoholism, it has been found that rates of metabolism can in time become double the accepted average (8, Table 1); this study also indicated that the largest quantity of *alcohol* that an individual is capable of metabolizing in a 24-hour period is probably in the vicinity of 500 ml (roughly 1250 ml of 80-proof whiskey).

The first step in the metabolism of alcohol—its conversion to acetaldehyde—is the over-all rate-limiting step, and it is most difficult to accelerate the pace of this reaction. Of all the substances reputed to enhance the rate of this reaction, perhaps only fructose (0.8 to 1.2 gm/kg) can actually do so, and it has proved to be effective in only some people (8).

The second metabolic step entails the conversion of acetaldehyde to acetyl-coenzyme A or acetate, most of which is then oxidized to carbon dioxide. All of the steps in the metabolism of alcohol are catalyzed by enzymes requiring NAD (DPN). The diversion of NAD to the metabolism of alcohol and the consequent increased yields of NADH disturb a number of biochemical equilibria. It has been postulated that the prolonged imbalance in cofactor availability, as might occur in chronic alcoholism, coupled with dietary deficiencies and the possibly direct hepatotoxic action of alcohol all play roles in the etiology of cirrhosis of the liver (6).

Tolerance

Though it is commonly said that tolerance to the effects of generalized depressant drugs develops on prolonged usage of high doses, this phenomenon has never been systematically investigated. Anecdotal evidence abounds, but only a relatively small number of well-designed experiments have been conducted. No more than a very rough estimate of the magnitude of the tolerance developed is possible at this time; it appears to be a complex situation in which a number of causative factors must be considered in arriving at any tentative conclusion.

INNATE OR INHERENT "TOLERANCE"   We noted previously that there is considerable individual variation in the degree of intoxication displayed at a given blood concentration of alcohol or following consumption of a given quantity of alcohol. In the experimental study of simulated severe chronic alcoholism alluded to above (2), no good correlation was observed between the amount of alcohol consumed and the degree of drunkenness displayed by the various subjects, even in the early part of the experiment. One subject, who had not previously been an alcoholic, was able to consume an average of 450 ml of 95% alcohol daily for 79 consecutive days without appearing more than mildly intoxicated; he appeared markedly intoxicated only when his intake was increased to between 600 and 700 ml/day.

METABOLIC TOLERANCE   This form of tolerance is characterized by an enhanced rate of inactivation of a particular drug; in the present context, it implies that individuals have, through drinking, acquired an increased capacity to metabolize alcohol. Evidence supporting the concept of metabolic tolerance to alcohol was obtained by Isbell and his colleagues in their experimental simulation of chronic severe alcoholism (2). Certain subjects were given alcohol hourly from 6 A.M. to 11 P.M., plus triple doses at midnight and 3 A.M.; the size of each dose was gradually increased until blood alcohol concentrations between 150 and 250 mg/100 ml were obtained. At this point, the subjects were consuming in excess of 400 ml of 95% alcohol daily and were judged to be markedly intoxicated. Within 10 days, however, though intake was maintained, blood levels of alcohol gradually fell to nearly zero, and signs of intoxication disappeared. The subjects were metabolizing alcohol at this time at an estimated average rate of 455 ml/day, in comparison with a rate of 346 ml/day in the control period. This was apparently the maximal degree of metabolic tolerance that could be achieved, for, when total daily intake was increased by only 3 to 65 ml, and alcohol was supplied now every 2 hours from 6 A.M. to midnight, blood alcohol concentrations rose sharply, and signs of intoxication reappeared.

Other studies have indicated that metabolic tolerance to alcohol is rapidly lost when drinking stops. In one such study, isotopically labeled alcohol was administered to control subjects and to currently abstinent alcoholics; the rates of elimination of radioactive carbon dioxide in the 3 hours following ingestion of alcohol were essentially identical for the two groups (11). In one study, Mendelson concluded that metabolic tolerance developed by alcoholics is transitory and can be lost after just 3 weeks of abstinence, even in individuals who had previously been severe alcoholics for 5 years or more.

The development of metabolic tolerance to alcohol is often said to be the result of induction or accelerated biosynthesis of the enzyme responsible for the first step in its metabolism, alcohol dehydrogenase. The rate of the first step is not limited merely by the specific activity of this enzyme, however, but probably reflects such other factors as the rate at which hepatic tissue can regenerate the requisite oxidized form of NAD from its reduced form and, possibly, the rate at which acetyl-coenzyme A or acetate is converted to carbon dioxide.

PHARMACODYNAMIC OR TISSUE TOLERANCE   It has been postulated that, during prolonged exposure to a drug, the magnitude of the evoked response gradually diminishes as a result of adaptive changes in the responding cells. Many authorities on alcoholism regard this form of tolerance as the most important type operative in alcoholics, despite the fact that there is as yet little evidence to support the concept. One of the clearest expressions of what appears to be pharmacodynamic tolerance to the effects of alcohol was reported by Isbell and his colleagues (2) in their experimental simulation of severe alcoholism, which entailed average individual consumptions of 266 to 489 ml of 95% alcohol daily for periods of time as long as 87 days. After the first week of drinking, the EEG pattern became "slow" and showed an "increased occipital alpha percentage, a slowing of alpha frequency and an increase in percentage of waves of frequencies of 4 to 6 cycles per second." As the period of drinking increased, the slowing of the EEG pattern was appreciably less evident, even though blood alcohol concentrations during this time were 200 mg/100 ml or higher.

CROSS-TOLERANCE   The observation that alcoholics can be unusually resistant to the effects of sedative and hypnotic drugs and general anesthetic agents is commonly interpreted as a manifestation of cross-tolerance by alcoholics to other generalized depressant drugs; the nature of this tolerance is usually implied to be pharmacodynamic. It may, in part, be a reflection of metabolic tolerance, however, for a short study has indicated that alcohol can effect induction of hepatic microsomal drug-metabolizing enzymes in man of the type responsible for the degradation of barbiturates and other drugs (12). Such a mechanism, of course, could not explain tolerance to general anesthetic agents, for they are metabolized to a negligible extent. The demonstration of cross-tolerance to other generalized central nervous system depressant drugs by alcoholics provides presumptive and indirect evidence of their tolerance to the effects of alcohol.

PATTERN OF USE   The typical pattern of drug usage exhibited by narcotic addicts is one clear manifestation of the problem that ever-increasing tolerance poses for them. That alcoholics do not face a problem of comparable magnitude is demonstrated by the fact that some of them do keep their intake at a high, but quite stable level for considerable periods of time. Moreover, though the pattern of drug intake in alcoholism can superficially mimic that of narcotic addiction (i.e., a progressively greater intake with the passage of time), such a pattern usually has quite different pharmacological consequences in the two forms of drug abuse: it enables the narcotic addict to regain an intensity of drug effect similar to that felt at the start of addiction but usually produces progressively deeper degrees of intoxication in the alcoholic. The alcoholic does not appear to be on the same inexorable escalator in regard to dose that tolerance forces the narcotic addict onto.

LETHAL DOSE   One readily appreciated criterion of tolerance to the effects of drugs that can kill is whether the size of the lethal dose increases significantly with abuse of the drug; this is most definitely so in instances of narcotic addiction but appears not to be the case even in severe forms of alcoholism. It is a general finding that the size of the lethal dose for individuals dependent on any generalized depressant drug is probably not significantly larger than that for non-dependent individuals.

SUMMARY   Tolerance to the effects of alcohol may exist innately in some individuals and may be acquired by others to a variable degree, as a result of prolonged consumption of intoxicating quantities of this substance; in the latter case, it probably stems from the development of pharmacodynamic tolerance, metabolic tolerance, or both. The maximal degree of tolerance that can develop is limited, but the limit cannot be described precisely at this time. The lethal dose of alcohol is approximately the same for alcoholics and non-alcoholics alike. In contrast to the degree of tolerance developed by narcotic addicts, tolerance to generalized central nervous system depressant drugs is often characterized comparatively as *low* or *moderate.*

Physical dependence and the withdrawal syndrome

The literature on addiction to alcohol generally lacks both clarity and useful quantitative information. There is now at least fairly widespread agreement among pharmacologists that physical dependence on the effects of alcohol can develop and that, under certain circumstances, a withdrawal syndrome, which closely resembles the effects of abstinence from other generalized depressant drugs, can develop.

The pattern of usage of alcohol necessary for the development of physical dependence has not been clearly established and remains in dispute. In the view of some workers, physical dependence develops rapidly so that even a few hours of moderate intoxication may lead to withdrawal symptoms that form a part of the state commonly called a "hangover" (5). Others regard tremulousness as the mildest symptom of withdrawal that can be precipitated by abstinence after several consecutive days of marked intoxication (13). More traumatic manifestations of abstinence, such as a psychotic delirium, occurred in the study of Isbell *et al.* (2) only after 400 to 500 ml of alcohol/day had been consumed for 48 or more days. We do not know, however, if such a pattern of usage is the minimum required for the occurrence of a severe withdrawal syndrome. Compounding the confusion in this area are the differences in terminology used for the various phases of withdrawal and the fact that even severely addicted alcoholics undergoing withdrawal do not exhibit all of the same signs and symptoms (2). It may nevertheless be said that both the nature and the intensity of the alcohol withdrawal syndrome appear to depend usually on the degree and duration of chronic intoxication before abstinence or a sharp reduction in intake.

It is possible to divide the withdrawal syndrome into three chronological stages. Manifestations of the first stage usually appear within a few hours after drinking has been sharply reduced or stopped. Blood alcohol levels at this time may be 100 mg/100 ml or higher (2). Tremulousness (the "shakes"), weakness, and profuse perspiration are among the first signs to develop, and complaints from the patient of anxiety (the "jitters"), headache, anorexia, nausea, and abdominal cramps may accompany them. Retching and vomiting may follow. The patient has a flushed face and injected conjuntiva. He is restless, agitated, hyperreflexive, and startles easily, but he generally remains alert. Cravings for alcohol or a sedative drug may be voiced strongly and frequently. In time, the tremors become generalized and more marked. The EEG pattern at this time may be mildly dysrhythmic, with random spikes and brief episodes of high-voltage slow waves appearing; the degree of abnormality of the EEG pattern, however, does not appear to be a reliable prognostic sign of whether convulsions will subsequently occur (2). The patient may also begin to "see" or "hear" things (acute alcoholic hallucinosis), often at first only when his eyes are shut but later also when they are open. Insight is commonly retained initially, but may be subsequently lost, particularly during the third or delirious stage of withdrawal; indeed, we wonder if the disorder designated *acute alcoholic hallucinosis* may not merely be the early manifestations of delirium tremens. For the alcoholic who has developed only a mild degree of physical dependence, the withdrawal syndrome may consist merely of the signs and symptoms described above, which gradually disappear within a few days.

The second stage, alcoholic convulsive seizures ("rum fits"), appears to develop in only some alcoholics, but the true incidence of seizures during withdrawal has not yet been determined satisfactorily. In two studies in which a total of 272 alcoholics undergoing withdrawal were observed, the incidence of patients exhibiting one or more seizures was just 13% (2, 13). The seizures are typically of the grand mal type and may begin as early as 12 hours after abstinence (2) but appear perhaps more often during the 2nd or 3rd day. The number of seizures can range from just one to frank status epilepticus, which is one possible cause of death during withdrawal.

The third stage is one of an agitated delirium (delirium tremens, the "horrors"), in which auditory, visual, and tactile hallucinations occur, commonly with loss of insight. During this period (often 3 to 4 days in length), the patient sleeps little, if at all; he is severely agitated, often completely disoriented, restless, and almost continuously active. Fever, profuse perspiration (to the extent that marked dehydration is possible), and tachycardia can be observed at this time. The patient may describe quite bizarre delusions. It is typical of withdrawal from generalized central nervous system depressant drugs that the character of the delusions and hallucinations, though individual in nature, are virtually always terrifying to the patient. This is why the patient is continuously agitated and also why his behavior may become aggressive toward others or harmful to himself. Though manifestations of narcotic withdrawal can generally be reversed at any stage by an appropriate dose of a narcotic drug, once delirium tremens develops, it is extremely difficult to calm the patient by what would be regarded as a safe dose of any generalized depressant drug. Delirium tremens is a potentially fatal disturbance, with death usually being attributed to hyperthermia, peripheral vascular collapse, or a self-incurred injury (4). Estimates of the death rate range from 1 to 37% (8), but a mortality of approximately 10% is a commonly encountered value. The duration of the alcohol withdrawal syndrome seems to vary directly with the degree of physical dependence that has developed; it usually lasts from 5 to 7 days (5).

As traumatic as this syndrome can be, and regardless of whether convulsions develop or not, recovery is usually complete, and no persisting medical or psychological sequelae can be detected (2). A few patients, however, do not recover from the hallucinatory and delusional state and remain chronically incapacitated in a psychotic state closely resembling schizophrenia (4); whether this development is a direct consequence of the withdrawal syndrome, or merely an intensification of a pre-existing psychotic tendency, is not known.

Many problems in regard to alcohol addiction remain unsolved. Does delirium tremens occur, for example, only as a part of the withdrawal syndrome from alcohol? Some say it can be precipitated by injury, surgical procedure, or intercurrent infection (4), but we wonder, can an injured or infected alcoholic always maintain his intake of alcohol in an unchanged fashion? The following statement most emphatically dissociates delirium tremens from withdrawal: "In alcoholics who have abstained from alcohol for several months, delirium tremens may occur following operation, trauma or severe illness. During the attacks of delirium tremens the body may be alcohol-free" (8). This statement raises questions in our minds. Was the duration of abstinence established by evidence other than the alcoholics' own statements, which are notoriously unreliable? Did abuse of such generalized depressants as barbiturates occur during the abstinent period? Clearly, we must investigate further the concept that alcoholism can somehow predispose an individual to the development of delirium tremens, even though he may have been abstinent for a considerable period of time before the delirium began.

Morbidity and mortality

The medical problems associated with alcoholism can arise as a direct consequence of the effects of alcohol (e.g., gastrointestinal upsets), as an indirect consequence of being intoxicated (e.g., self-incurred traumatic injuries), and as a consequence principally of dietary deficiencies (e.g., alcohol amblyopia); there is a current impression that the incidence of dietary deficiencies in alcoholics is declining, possibly as a consequence of an increasing tendency to "fortify" foods nutritionally during the manufacturing process (4). These problems concern primarily the central nervous and digestive systems, and our discussion of them will be oriented accordingly, even though such a separation is at times artificial, as when disturbances in mental processes are caused by impaired hepatic function.

THE DIGESTIVE SYSTEM   Disturbances in this system are commonly attributed to the collective impact of the direct toxic effects of alcohol, dietary deficiencies, especially of vitamins, and the biochemical disequilibria occasioned by the continuing necessity for metabolism of large quantities of alcohol.

1. The gastrointestinal tract. Morning nausea and vomiting are common experiences for alcoholics. They may be early signs of abstinence, since they can usually be quelled by several drinks, and, since, in the early stages of alcoholism, gastroscopic evidence of gastritis is not consonant with the magnitude of these symptoms (4). Irritation of gastric mucosa caused by alcohol usually subsides quickly after intake ceases, but, in severe alcoholism, erosion develops to a more serious degree. Gastric or duodenal ulcers are not uncommon and can be sources of serious hemorrhage.

2. The pancreas. Various degrees of acute pancreatitis can develop after chronic use of large quantities of alcohol. The mildest form is diagnosable only on the basis of abnormal serum amylase concentrations; the most severe form is characterized by necrosis within and hemorrhage from the pancreas. Chronic relapsing pancreatitis also occurs in alcoholics; the presenting sign and symptoms are typical for this disorder, and its course can be benign if the patient abstains from alcohol (4).

3. The liver. None of the principal abnormalities in hepatic structure

and function associated with alcoholism occurs only in alcoholics. Fatty infiltration of the liver appears several days after heavy drinking is begun but usually subsides 2 weeks after the intake of alcohol is stopped. Cirrhosis, with all of its complications, is encountered in about 10% (4) of all alcoholics. Its etiology is unknown. Its occurrence in non-alcoholics mitigates against the view that it reflects only the hepatotoxic effects of alcohol. When cirrhosis occurs in alcoholics, it is typically in individuals who have been heavy drinkers for a number of years (4).

THE CENTRAL NERVOUS SYSTEM   Disturbances in this system have been attributed to dietary deficiencies, hepatic insufficiency, manifestations of the withdrawal syndrome, repeated traumatic injuries to the head, and anatomical changes of uncertain origin. It is not uncommon for several of these disorders to be present simultaneously, and, considering the numerous similarities among these disturbances, we wonder if indeed as many discrete disorders exist as have been described.

1. Alcoholic polyneuropathy. First and most severely affected in this disorder are the distal portions of the legs, where numbness and pain may develop. In some instances, however, these symptoms may be absent, and the diagnosis can be made on the basis of muscular wastage, calf tenderness, signs of impaired motor and sensory innervation, and reduced knee and ankle jerks (4). Progression of signs and symptoms to the upper extremities may occur in time, and contractures and paralyses may also develop. Even partial recovery may require years, and permanent changes are frequent. Though this syndrome is most likely the result of a vitamin deficiency (most probably thiamine), its etiology remains uncertain.

2. Alcohol amblyopia. A bilateral and symmetrical loss of visual acuity for both near and far objects, characterized by a painless blurring of vision, central scotomata, and papillitis (4). A relatively infrequent occurrence among alcoholics, it is believed to stem from nutritional inadequacies, particularly vitamins. Optic nerve degeneration may occur if treatment is inadequate.

3. Structural changes in the brain. Some of the changes in the brain and surrounding tissues, which may be permanent or temporary, including cerebral lacerations and subdural hematomas, are probably the result of traumatic injuries incurred while intoxicated. Others, diagnosed during life or found at autopsy, are of unknown origin. Representative of this latter group are alcohol cerebellar degeneration, cerebral atrophy, degeneration of the corpus callosum, and central pontine myelinolysis (4).

4. Wernicke's encephalopathy. An acute disorder characterized by ocular abnormalities, of which nystagmus is the most common, ataxia and mental confusion, often manifested as profound disorientation, inattention, apathy, and drowsiness. Commonly, this disorder occurs with alcoholic polyneuropathy. The risk of congestive heart failure is high in this disorder, and it should be regarded as a medical emergency (4). Thiamine deficiency appears to play a major etiological role in Wernicke's encephalopathy, and the ocular and ataxic difficulties usually can be reversed satisfactorily by prompt administration of thiamine. Indeed, the signs and symptoms of both alcoholic polyneuropathy and Wernicke's encephalopathy so closely resemble some symptoms of beriberi (both "wet" and "dry") that we wonder if these two disorders should not be subsumed under some such common designation as "Alcoholic neuropathies resulting primarily from thiamine deficiency."

5. Psychotic states. Various psychotic states arise in alcoholics (a) the usually transitory delusional-hallucinatory states, which characterize alcoholic hallucinosis and delirium tremens; (b) the dementia, resulting from advanced hepatic insufficiency; (c) a progressive endogenous disorder, such as schizophrenia, whose onset may antedate alcoholism and whose progress may be exacerbated or essentially unaffected by drinking; (d) a disorder termed "chronic alcoholic deterioration," characterized by such "typical" facial stigmata of alcoholism as dilation of facial capillaries and a "bloated" look, pronounced physical deterioration, and such mental abnormalities as diminution of will power, impairment of memory, and emotional lability (8) (we are not convinced that this syndrome merits the designation of a psychosis); and (e) Korsakoff's psychosis, an infrequent disorder in alcoholics, which is most notably characterized by severe impairment in memory and learning ability. Disorientation in space and time, apathy, and little insight about the memory defect occur also, as does confabulation occasionally. This disorder often develops gradually in patients with Wernicke's encephalopathy; the two disorders, therefore, are sometimes given the single designation of the Wernicke-Korsakoff syndrome.

MORTALITY About one-third of the deaths attributed to alcohol result from acute alcoholism when the fatal quantity that produces respiratory paralysis has been taken usually by individuals already quite intoxicated. The typical findings on autopsy are edema at the base of the brain and hyperemia of the gastric mucosa (8).

Alcohol is second only to carbon monoxide as the agent responsible for the most deaths attributed to poisons in the United States; each year these two compounds cause a greater total number of deaths than do all other poisons together (8). The prominent role of the intoxicated person in fatal automobile accidents, whether as driver or pedestrian, has been widely publicized.

It is commonly said that the life expectancy of a heavy drinker is less than that of a moderate drinker or an abstainer (6); this seems a reasonable statement and, in the foregoing paragraphs, we have indicated that there is no dearth of means by which an alcoholic may die. We doubt, however, that the precise decrement in life expectancy is known, for we doubt that the death rate due to alcoholism is accurately known. Because no systematic survey has been undertaken, we suspect that fewer death certificates implicate alcoholism as a contributory factor than would be warranted by the facts. Such certificates may indicate only the immediate cause of death, either from ignorance or to protect the sensibilities of the family. Last, when an alcoholic dies from ingestion of methanol (methyl alcohol, wood alcohol), his death can never be, as some believe, a wholly accidental affair. No methanol is produced by fermentation of grain, and so it cannot appear in "moonshine" whiskey as the result of some misadventure in the fermentation process; rather it must be deliberately added to such whiskey. Methanol is a relatively cheap, weakly intoxicating, very toxic compound. It occurs alone or in conjunction with ethyl alcohol in a number of relatively inexpensive preparations such as "rubbing" alcohol, paint thinners and removers, solid canned fuels, and antifreeze fluids that have occasionally proved to be irresistible lures to impoverished alcoholics (8).

BARBITURATES AND OTHER SEDATIVE AND HYPNOTIC DRUGS

The most commonly abused barbiturates are such short-acting agents as pentobarbital (Nembutal), secobarbital (Seconal), amobarbital (Amytal), and the secobarbital-amobarbital mixture known as Tuinal. Such longer-acting agents as phenobarbital are rarely subject to abuse. Because barbiturates are dispensed in distinctively colored capsules, users often refer to them by names derived from these colors, such as "red devils" or "yellow jackets"; they refer to barbiturates collectively as "goofballs" or "downers."

All sedative and hypnotic drugs must be regarded as potentially addicting, unless proof to the contrary is provided. Abuse of such older nonbarbiturate hypnotics as chloral hydrate and paraldehyde no longer poses a significant problem. As objects of abuse, they have been replaced today by the newer nonbarbiturate agents, including glutethimide (Doriden), ethinamate (Valmid), ethchlorvynol (Placidyl), and methaqualone (Quaalude, Ludes) (5). In common with other types of drugs (see CNS stimulants, in particular), users tend to attribute special effects or intensity of effect to specific drugs; methaqualone, for example, is said to exert a notable aphrodisiac effect by numerous users of it. Such claims are understandably difficult to substantiate, nor is one surprised to learn of such activity among adolescents and young adults. Increased sexuality is a common concomitant of aging among those fifteen to twenty-five years of age.

The abuse of all sedative and hypnotic drugs is characterized by similar patterns of abuse, pharmacological effect, degree of tolerance developed, nature of withdrawal syndrome, and morbidity and mortality. Among all of these drugs, barbiturates have been subject to abuse most frequently, and we have the most information about their abuse. The following discussion will therefore be concerned primarily with the barbiturates, though the information presented will be equally applicable to all sedative and hypnotic drugs unless otherwise noted.

Patterns of use

Many of the barbiturates taken by drug users are made by reputable manufacturers and are subsequently diverted to the illicit drug market, though the possibility of barbiturates being sold that have originated from "basement laboratories" cannot be discounted. The cost of these drugs to illicit users is typically high; capsules containing 100 to 200 mg of drug can range in price from 50¢ each to $5 or more.

The vast majority of barbiturate users take these drugs by mouth. Those who attempt subcutaneous injection of barbiturates face the same problem of cutaneous lesions as do narcotic "skin poppers." In the case of barbiturates, however, the lesions have been attributed to the histotoxic action of the high molecular weight alcohols in which the barbiturates are dissolved (15) or to the marked alkalinity of solutions of barbiturate salts. The intravenous administration of barbiturates by drug users has been reported; the solution injected may contain heroin as well (16).

Barbiturate abuse is characterized by the exclusive use of one of these drugs or by the use of a barbiturate in conjunction with one or more other drugs, either concurrently, in a purposive sequence, or as a substitute. Much barbiturate abuse is, unfortunately, iatrogenic. Individuals susceptible to the development of drug dependence, who often cannot be readily identified, are introduced to barbiturates or other "sleeping pills" by their physicians for relief of insomnia. Less defensible medically is the practice of freely prescribing these agents for patients known to be prone to drug dependence, such as the temporarily abstinent alcoholic troubled by nervousness and insomnia. The susceptible individual, in time, adopts a pattern of drug intake that produces intoxication rather than sedation or sleep. To meet his growing drug needs, the user may obtain prescriptions for barbiturates by consulting a number of physicians, he may discover an obliging pharmacist, or he may seek out barbiturate pushers who are reputedly abundant in all large cities.

If a pattern of barbiturate use progresses from one that is medically therapeutic to one of frank abuse, the user, if his drug supply permits, often rapidly increases his daily intake within a matter of weeks. He may not stop until the limit of his inherent tolerance has been reached (17), which can mean his total daily intake may ultimately range from 1500 to 3000 mg. Users who take more than 3000 mg daily are not often encountered. Other users may stop increasing dosage at a daily intake that produces a degree of intoxication pleasing to them. For some this may mean an intake of just 800 to 1000 mg/day; in time, a drug intake at this level may produce a degree of impairment so mild in the addict that many of those having prolonged daily contact with him may not suspect drug abuse. Those who use barbiturates primarily exhibit schedules of abuse similar to those of alcoholics: some take them daily, while others use the drugs only during sprees that may last from one night to several weeks (17).

Barbiturates may be used concurrently with other drugs, usually deliberately but occasionally unwittingly, when they are present in drug mixtures whose composition is unknown to the user. The typical role of the barbiturate in this situation is to potentiate the effects of the drug on which the user is primarily dependent, commonly heroin or alcohol. In the opinion of some opiate addicts, the effects produced by the grossly diluted heroin they often get today make for so unsatisfactory a "high" that a second drug must be used (18). Though "dual abuse" may appear to be a new phenomenon related to today's "weak" heroin, it has existed for decades, even during periods when presumably quite pure opiates could be purchased illegally (17). The barbiturate may be taken by mouth shortly before or at the time heroin is injected, or it may be injected intravenously along with the heroin. Though all generalized central nervous system depressants are presumed to exert similar effects, it is not uncommon to encounter alcoholics who use barbiturates concomitantly to enhance their degree of intoxication, and there is a recorded instance of simultaneous addiction to alcohol, barbiturates, and paraldehyde (17). As we cannot conceive of any pharmacological advantage to be derived from the concurrent use of two or more generalized depressant drugs, whose effects should be merely additive, we assume that this form of multiple drug abuse must gratify psychological needs peculiar to some drug-dependent individuals. Mixtures of pharmacological antagonists, such as a barbiturate plus an amphetamine, are also used and, in effect, represent one of the most popular medical remedies for mild psychic depressions.

Barbiturates are widely used as "downers"—drugs that can bring one down (i.e., depress or stultify) from a state of normal consciousness or from a state of abnormal excitation produced by stimulant drugs. Thus, they are taken when the user wants to sleep after a prolonged and exhausting "high" from amphetamine or cocaine or when he becomes disturbed by the motor manifestations that develop when repeated doses of stimulants are taken at short intervals. The spree alcoholic may use barbiturates when he stops drinking to quell such early signs of withdrawal as the jitters.

As noted before, when the narcotic addict, cannot obtain heroin and knows that the signs and symptoms of withdrawal are imminent, often uses barbiturates to dull his awareness of withdrawal. This is done even though the addict may openly admit that barbiturates are essentially ineffective for this purpose. He recognizes, too, that he is often more belligerent or even violent when taking barbiturates rather than heroin, and he may feel that he has lost "face" with other heroin addicts by using barbiturates (18).

Effects of sedative and hypnotic drugs

The effects of large doses of all generalized depressant drugs are so alike as to be essentially undistinguishable; only users of alcohol and of paraldehyde can be identified because of the unique odor of their breath. Large doses of all of these drugs produce a state of intoxication in which the degree of mental and motor impairment is, as a first approximation, a function of the quantity of drug taken. The description of alcoholic intoxication presented earlier in this chapter (see p. 101) is equally applicable to the state produced by large doses of sedative and hypnotic drugs, with the following exception: during alcoholic intoxication, the EEG pattern displays an increased incidence of delta waves (4 to 6 cps), but, during intoxication from sedative and hypnotic drugs, the incidence of beta waves (15 to 30 cps) is increased. Users of these drugs are not, of course, subject to the gastric irritation caused by alcohol.

Absorption, distribution, and metabolism

When taken with the stomach empty, most sedative and hypnotic drugs are rapidly absorbed into the body in the upper portion of the small intestine. Such longer-acting barbiturates as phenobarbital are absorbed more slowly than the more rapidly acting agents (secobarbital), which explains, in part, the addict's typical preference for the latter type of barbiturate. The rate of absorption of glutethimide (Doriden) is often erratic, probably because it is so poorly soluble in aqueous solutions.

The presence of food in the stomach, as one would expect, slows the absorption of these drugs. In a clinical experiment in which severe, chronic barbiturate addiction was simulated, with a total daily intake of 1300 to 1800 mg, fluctuating responses to 300-mg doses of secobarbital in the morning was found to be a matter of whether or not the subject had eaten. Doses that produced only mild intoxication when taken 90 minutes after a standard breakfast produced severe intoxication and even slight coma when taken before breakfast (19).

Of all sedative and hypnotic drugs, the distribution of the barbiturates in the body has been studied most intensively; our discussion of distribution will be confined to them and, specifically, to the short-acting barbiturates most commonly subject to abuse. In contrast to alcohol, about 30 to 40% of the barbiturate in blood is bound to plasma protein (probably albumin); thus, drug concentrations in such protein-poor fluids as cerebrospinal fluid are always less than in blood. The extent of intracellular protein binding of these drugs roughly approximates that of plasma binding. The water:lipid partition coefficients for these compounds are much lower than that for alcohol. This is of particular significance in a comparison of the various barbiturates, since the lower the partition coefficient of a barbiturate, the more rapid its action, the greater its extent of binding to plasma proteins, and the briefer its duration of effect. The last observation is explained by the fact that rapidly acting barbiturates readily enter a variety of tissues; though a high brain concentration is achieved initially, the distribution thereafter into skeletal muscle, depot fat, and the liver (where they are inactivated) lowers plasma drug concentrations continually so that sufficient drug eventually diffuses out of the brain to reduce concentrations in that organ below the level of clinical efficacy. Barbiturates also cross the placenta, and a diffusion equilibrium between maternal and fetal blood is established. Relatively large doses of barbiturates are required to produce even small drug concentrations in milk (20).

The intoxicating effects of the commonly abused barbiturates ordinarily last from 4 to 5 hours; this would hold true for the doses likely to be taken by an addict whose total daily intake approximated 2000 mg. To remain continuously intoxicated, therefore, addicts have to take three to four doses of short-acting barbiturates in the course of each day. Though the sensation of intoxication may wane within hours, it has been observed experimentally that cumulative effects develop upon such a schedule of administration; the severity of neurological disturbances, it was noted, was minimal in the morning, increased throughout the day, and became maximal in the late evening (19). It was also observed that doses of barbiturate, such as 300 mg of secobarbital, that exerted relatively little effect when given alone prior to addiction often produced severe intoxication when incorporated into the type of schedule described above.

The action of the commonly abused barbiturates is terminated principally by means of hepatic metabolism; essentially no unchanged barbiturate appears in the urine. If an hypnotic dose of secobarbital is given to a non-addicted individual, the drug, after reaching equilibrium, disappears from the plasma at a rate equivalent to approximately 2.5% of the dose per hour. Inactivation is accomplished principally by mixed-function oxidases located in the endoplasmic reticulum ("microsomes") of hepatic cells. The reaction typically entails oxidation of the larger of the two substituent groups attached to the barbituric acid nucleus at carbon 5; a polar alcohol, ketone, phenol, or carboxylic acid is produced, which appears in urine unchanged or as a glucuronide.

Tolerance

As with alcohol, evidence exists that tolerance can develop, but its magnitude can be described only in a broad and imprecise way. In contrast to narcotic addiction, the maximal degree of tolerance that can be acquired to any sedative and hypnotic drug is again termed moderate, largely because the lethal dose of this type of compound appears to be not markedly different for addicted and non-addicted individuals (17).

The development of tolerance to barbiturates can be manifested in various ways. Despite the fact that he may be taking the equivalent of 20 sleep-inducing doses of pentobarbital (2000 mg) daily, for example, the typical barbiturate addict sleeps only an hour or two more than an average person each day. One change in the EEG pattern (large, slow waves), which appears early in the course of addiction, disappears as addiction progresses (17); this finding, as in the case of the alcohol addict, appears to reflect the development of pharmacodynamic or tissue tolerance. In a clinical experiment, subjects were given gradually increasing doses of secobarbital (up to 1800 mg/day), pentobarbital (up to 1800 mg/day), or amobarbital (up to 3800 mg/day) for periods ranging from 92 to 144 days; 2 to 3 months after the end of the experiment, some of the subjects were given the highest dose of barbiturate that they had received during the experiment. They became more severely intoxicated at this time than they had at any time during the course of the experiment, indicating that some degree of tolerance had developed during the period of simulated addiction but that it did not persist long after withdrawal from barbiturates (19). The authors of this study concluded their description of this finding with the following statement: "In fact, it would have been dangerous to the lives of these subjects to continue administration of barbiturates àt the same dosage they had attained during chronic intoxication." Though the lethal dose may increase as a result of addiction, the degree of increase will probably not be large, and, as with alcohol, considerable individual variability exists. The probability that barbiturate addiction produces at most a relatively small increase in the size of the lethal dose is indicated by the finding that survival rates among barbiturate addicts following ingestion of a "large dose" is not significantly higher than it is among non-addicted individuals in similar circumstances (17, 21).

Metabolic (or "drug-disposition") tolerance to the effects of the barbiturates develops because barbiturates can induce, or accelerate, the biosynthesis of the hepatic microsomal enzymes responsible for their inactivation (22). Similar findings have been made after prolonged administration of gluethimide and meprobamate (Miltown) with respect to the rates of their metabolism. The fact that individuals addicted to these drugs develop no *marked* degree of tolerance delineates the limitations of enzyme induction as a mechanism for attaining tolerance.

The Committee on Alcoholism and Addiction of the American Medical Association has described an unusual development during barbiturate abuse in which "a paradoxical reaction of excitation . . . occurs after tolerance has developed because of prolonged abuse. The drug now stimulates rather than depresses and is taken to exhilarate and animate the person to so-called increased efficiency" (21). That a few individuals will consistently respond to barbiturates in an idiosyncratic fashion (i.e., become excited rather than sedated) has long been known; the mechanism underlying such responses is unknown, but they frequently occur in children and in the elderly, usually without barbiturate abuse. We can understand how tolerance to the depressant effects of meperidine can permit expression of its stimulant effects, for they are an inherent part of the pharmacological properties of that drug. Barbiturates, however, are widely regarded as exerting only depressant effects; tolerance to these effects should result merely in a diminution of them or in an absence of any effect of barbiturates on the central nervous system.

As with alcohol, some individuals exhibit subnormal susceptibility to the effects of barbiturates, which can be regarded as an inherent or innate form of tolerance. Such individuals can be most readily identified in clinical experiments in which barbiturate addiction is simulated in groups of subjects and in which the correlation between dose of drug being taken and degree of intoxication manifested by the subjects has been found to be poor (19).

In summary, tolerance to barbiturates closely resembles tolerance to alcohol. An appreciable, but moderate degree of tolerance develops in the course of addiction; the lethal dose of a barbiturate for an addict probably does not differ substantially from that for a non-addicted individual. Innate or inherent tolerance exists, and there is evidence to indicate that both pharmacodynamic and metabolic tolerance develop to variable degrees upon chronic use.

Physical dependence and the withdrawal syndrome

The first barbiturate (barbital) was made available for medical use in 1903, followed by a second (phenobarbital) in 1912. By 1914, the German literature already contained a description of the barbiturate withdrawal syndrome (17). For a long time, however, most American and

British physicians refused to believe that physical dependence upon the barbiturates could be established. This reluctance probably could be accounted for by the fact that the requirements for development of physical dependence on barbiturates and other sedative and hypnotic drugs differ in one critical respect from the analogous situation in regard to narcotics: a certain threshold quantity of generalized depressant drugs must be taken daily for physical dependence to develop. This fact was not well understood, nor were the sizes of the threshold doses known; thus, the prevailing view could be supported by instances in which barbiturate intake was abruptly stopped without untoward sequelae in patients in whom daily intake was high by medical standards (300 to 400 mg of pentobarbital daily) but still, we were to learn, below the threshold value for physical dependence.

The situation was not clarified until 1950 when Isbell and his colleagues reported the results of a clinical study in which severe barbiturate addiction had been simulated (19) by administration of approximately 1500 to 3000 mg of various barbiturates daily for periods ranging from 92 to 144 days. Under these conditions, abrupt cessation of barbiturate intake provoked a withdrawal syndrome highly reminiscent of the sequelae of abstinence in severe alcoholism. Judicious selection and management of patients made untenable such earlier explanations for barbiturate withdrawal symptoms as an antecedent epileptic or psychotic diathesis, concurrent addiction to opiates, marked malnutrition, and so on.

Despite the clear demonstration by Isbell's group of the existence of physical dependence upon the effects of barbiturates and the nature of the withdrawal syndrome, general recognition of these findings has not yet been achieved. This state of affairs is reflected by the fact that, in 1967, the *Lancet* felt it appropriate to publish a report that "withdrawal fits" can occur in barbiturate addicts (23). The only note of special interest to us in this report was the observation that a barbiturate addict, if hospitalized during the convulsive stage of withdrawal, may find himself, on discharge, in the happy state of being provided with a supply of barbiturates because he has been diagnosed as epileptic.

Since 1950, the necessary information to establish the size of the threshold dose required for development of physical dependence upon the effects of a number of sedative and hypnotic drugs and minor tranquilizers has been obtained. These values are reported in Table 1. (We re-

TABLE 1

Minimal (or threshold) doses of
generalized depressant drugs required
for establishment of physical dependence

Drug	Threshold Dose (mg/day)
Pentobarbital (Nembutal)	400
Secobarbital (Seconal)	400
Ethchlorvynol (Placidyl)	2,000*
Ethinamate (Valmid)	13,000*
Glutethimide (Doriden)	2,500*
Methyprylon (Noludar)	2,400*
Chlordiazepoxide (Librium)	300
Diazepam (Valium)	100
Meprobamate (Miltown, Equanil)	1,600–2,400

* The true threshold dose may be lower; the value given is merely the lowest reported thus far to have produced physical dependence (14, 24, 25).

gret that we have been unable to discover the minimal daily dosage of chloral hydrate or paraldehyde necessary for establishment of physical dependence. Some physicians today wrongly consider these drugs, which were once subject to considerable abuse, to be "safe" for treatment of insomnia in drug users or in those with a seeming propensity for drug dependence.) In general, a daily intake of drug at or slightly above the threshold value will result, upon abstinence, in a mild withdrawal syndrome. More severe signs and symptoms of withdrawal usually occur only when daily intake substantially exceeds the threshold value.

How rapidly physical dependence develops in the case of generalized depressant drugs is not known. Clinical studies designed to determine the size of the threshold dose for various drugs have entailed administration of the drug for a minimum of 1 month, but it is possible that physical dependence can be established within a shorter period of time.

Following abrupt withdrawal, barbiturate addicts exhibit some or all of the same disturbances observed in alcoholics upon withdrawal (see p. 110). The initial manifestations are tremulousness, followed by one or more grand mal convulsions, which are succeeded in time by a psychotic delirium that very closely resembles alcoholic delirium tremens. In one study of barbiturate withdrawal, convulsions occurred in 75% of the patients and delirium in 60% (10); it appears that both occur much more frequently in barbiturate withdrawal than alcohol withdrawal. This conclusion must be regarded as tentative, however, since the data are derived from relatively small samples. Withdrawal from non-barbiturate sedatives and hypnotics and minor tranquilizers qualitatively mimics withdrawal from barbiturates.

The rate of development of withdrawal signs and symptoms and the duration of the withdrawal syndrome are a function of a duration of action of the drug in question. Thus, convulsions ordinarily occur, for example, on the 2nd and 3rd day of withdrawal from short-acting barbiturates but may not occur until the 7th to 12th day of withdrawal from such longer-acting agents as phenobarbital and chlordiazepoxide (5, 25).

Morbidity and Mortality

Barbiturate addicts face many of the same problems encountered by alcoholics. Persistently or episodically intoxicated, their employability is minimal or nil. The incidence of traumatic injuries resulting from falls while intoxicated is high. Like alcoholics, their tendency to start fires by falling asleep while smoking is great. Unlike alcoholics, their state of nutrition is reasonably good on the average; because they are not obtaining hundreds to thousands of calories each day from the metabolism of alcohol, their intake of essential food substances is generally satisfactory.

If psychoses are discerned in barbiturate addicts, they represent most often an endogenous disorder, whose origin may have antedated the onset of drug abuse, or persistence of the hallucinatory-delusional state that develops during withdrawal. It is rare, however, for a psychotic state to develop during intoxication, provided drugs of other types are not being used concurrently.

Since "sleeping pills" have been very frequently utilized by would-be suicides for at least several decades, it seems unlikely that the true mortality associated with prolonged abuse of these drugs will ever be known. Undoubtedly, addicts to sedatives and hypnotics contribute, deliberately or not, to the large number of deaths attributed to overdoses of these drugs each year. The incidence of addicts' deaths can only be estimated. An addict's psychological dependence on these drugs can become so great that he will persistently demand additional quantities even when he is so intoxicated that he cannot walk (19); one can thus readily envision the possibility of acute fatal barbiturate intoxication being superimposed on chronic intoxication. There is frequent mention in the literature on barbiturate addiction of the development of psychic depression during intoxication so intense "that suicide is a distinct possibility" (19). Though we regard such statements as accurate, suicidal thoughts and behavior are hardly unique to barbiturate abuse; self-destructive tendencies are evident in virtually all patterns of severe drug abuse.

ANTIANXIETY AGENTS ("MINOR TRANQUILIZERS")

Though these drugs are often placed in a separate category, they do not merit it in our opinion. Their specific effects on the central nervous system may differ in a few respects from that of conventional sedative and hypnotic drugs, but the patterns of their abuse do not differ in any significant detail from those of other generalized depressant drugs. Abuse of minor tranquilizers occurs typically in individuals first introduced to these drugs by their physicians in the course of treatment; the demand for these compounds in the illegal drug market is not large at this time, and they are not routinely available.

The first minor tranquilizer, meprobamate (Miltown, Equanil), was introduced in the mid 1950's. It was represented at that time to be a pharmacologically unique entity, capable of relieving anxiety without undue sedation. It gained instant popularity as patients with anxiety, tension, and nervousness are legion, and some physicians prescribed it liberally. Reports about addiction to meprobamate and the nature of the withdrawal syndrome appeared as early as 1956 (14). In all respects, withdrawal from meprobamate was found to be qualitatively identical to withdrawal from barbiturates. The subsequently marketed chlordiazepoxide (Librium) and diazepam (Valium) were found in time to have similar patterns of addiction and withdrawal. The threshold doses for development of physical dependence on these three minor tranquilizers are reported in Table 1. To exert a lethal effect, these drugs must be taken in conjunction with adequate quantities of another generalized central depressant such as alcohol (15).

As the most frequently prescribed drugs in this country until recently diazepam and other benzodiazepines are currently misused to an appreciable extent (5).

REFERENCES

1. Roueché, B., Cultural factors and drinking patterns. *Ann NY Acad Sci* 133:846, 1966
2. Isbell, H., H. F. Fraser, A. Wilker, R. E. Belleville, and A. J. Eisenman, An experimental study of the etiology of "rum fits" and delirium tremens. *Quart J Stud Alcohol* 16:1, 1955
3. Criteria Committee, National Council on Alcoholism, Criteria for the diagnosis of alcoholism. *Ann Int Med* 77:249, 1972
4. *Manual on Alcoholism.* American Medical Association (No city or date of publication given)
5. Jaffe, J. H., Drug addiction and drug abuse. In: Gilman, A. G., L. Goodman and A. Gilman, eds., *The Pharmacological Basis of Therapeutics,* ed. 6. New York: Macmillan, 1980, p. 535
6. Ritchie, J. M., The aliphatic alcohols. In: Gilman, A. G., L. Goodman and A. Gilman, eds., *The Pharmacological Basis of Therapeutics,* ed. 6. New York: Macmillan, 1980, p. 376
7. Keller, M., Alcohol in health and disease. *Ann NY Acad Sci* 133:820, 1966
8. Harney, R. B. and R. N. Harger, The alcohols. In: DiPalma, J. R., ed., *Drill's Pharmacology in Medicine,* ed. 3. New York: McGraw-Hill, 1965, p. 210
9. Mendelson, J. H. and N. K. Mello, Experimental analysis of drinking behavior of chronic alcoholics. *Ann NY Acad Sci* 133:828, 1966
10. Essig, C. F., Newer sedative drugs that can cause states of intoxication and dependence of barbiturate type. *J Amer Med Assoc* 196:714, 1966
11. Mendelson, J. H., Ethanol-1-C^{14} metabolism in alcoholics and nonalcoholics. *Science* 159:319, 1968
12. Rubin, E. and C. S. Lieber, Hepatic microsomal enzymes in man and rat: Induction and inhibition by ethanol. *Science* 162:690, 1968
13. Victor, M. and R. D. Adams, The effect of alcohol on the nervous system. *Res Publ Ass Nerv Ment Dis* 32:526, 1953
14. Essig, C. F., Addiction to nonbarbiturate sedative and tranquilizing drugs. *Clin Pharmacol Therap* 5:334, 1964
15. Baldessarini, R. J., Drugs and the treatment of psychiatric disorders. In: Gilman, A. G., L. Goodman, and A. Gilman, eds. *The Pharmacological Basis of Therapeutics,* ed. 6. New York: Macmillan, 1980, p. 439
16. Eiseman, B., R. C. Lam, and B. Rush, Surgery on the narcotic addict. *Ann Surg* 159:748, 1964
17. Louria, D. B., Medical complications of pleasure-giving drugs. *Arch Int Med* 123:82, 1969
18. Isbell, H., Addiction to barbiturates and the barbiturate abstinence syndrome. *Ann Int Med* 33:108, 1950

19. Cumberlidge, M. C., The abuse of barbiturates by heroin addicts. *Canad Med Assoc J* 98:1045, 1968

20. Isbell, H., S. Altschul, C. H. Kornetsky, A. J. Eisenman, H. G. Flanary, and H. F. Fraser, Chronic barbiturate intoxication. *Arch Neurol Psychiat* 64:1, 1950

21. Stewart C. Harvey. Hypnotics and sedatives In: Gilman, A. G., L. Goodman and A. Gilman, eds., *The Pharmacological Basis of Therapeutics,* ed. 6. New York: Macmillan, 1980, p. 339

22. AMA Committee on Alcoholism and Addiction, Dependence on barbiturates and other sedative drugs. *J Amer Med Assoc* 193:673, 1965

23. Conney, A. H., Pharmacological implications of microsomal enzyme induction. *Pharmacol Rev* 19:317, 1967

24. Gardner, A. J., Withdrawal fits in barbiturate addicts. *Lancet* ii:337, 1967

25. Fraser, H. F., A Wikler, C. Essig, and H. Isbell, Degree of physical dependence induced by secobarbital or pentobarbital. *J Amer Med Assoc* 166:126, 1958

26. Clarren, S. K. and D. W. Smith, The fetal alcohol syndrome. *N Engl J Med* 298:1063, 1978

27. Brown, N. A., E. H. Goulding and S. Fabro, Ethanol embyrotoxicity: direct effects on mammalian embryos *in vitro. Science* 206:573, 1979

Chapter 5

GENERALIZED DEPRESSANTS OF THE CENTRAL NERVOUS SYSTEM

VOLATILE SOLVENT AND AEROSOL INHALATION ("GLUE SNIFFING")

In this chapter we will consider all types of voluntary, purposive solvent inhalation of which the sniffing of airplane glue or model cement has been the most common example in the United States. Though drug abuse via the route of alveolar absorption dates back to the nitrous oxide and ether "jags" commonly indulged in shortly after the discovery of the euphoric and hallucinogenic properties of these anesthetic agents, contemporary abuse of volatile substances was first recorded in the literature in 1951 with a description of gasoline sniffing in two boys (1). In subsequent years, increasing numbers of reports about many youths and some adults sniffing such fluids as model cements, lighter fluids, lacquer thinners, and cleaning solutions (2), and, more recently, the propellant gases of aerosol products (3) have appeared.

In the early 1960's, the problem became more acute, and a number of deaths were reported. The Hobby Industry Association of America and concerned industries gradually acted to remove the two most toxic solvents, benzene and carbon tetrachloride, from those commercially available products most apt to be sniffed or inadvertently inhaled in large amounts. Today few products (and none of those generally used by sniffers) contain either of these two compounds. As an added safeguard, the federal government has now banned the inclusion of carbon tetrachloride in any product sold to the public.

Approaching the problem of control from a different point of view, in

1969, the Testor Corporation, the nation's largest manufacturer of plastic cement (and of the single brand of glue most frequently subject to abuse in the United States), announced the addition of oil of mustard (allyl isothiocyanate) to its basic formula. This additive, when sniffed, produces severe nasal irritation similar to that of horseradish but does not affect the less intensely exposed model builder. Testor stated further that this new formula was available to any other manufacturer of products in corporating volatile solvents.

By 1966, some 26 cities and 6 states (California, Illinois, Maryland, New Jersey, New York, and Rhode Island) had enacted statutes designed to control solvent inhalation. Many cities now legally restrict glue sales to presumably bona-fide users of the product. In New York City, Detroit, San Antonio, and Minneapolis, for instance, no minor may purchase plastic cement unless a model kit is also bought. The effectiveness of such legislation in times of affluence is open to question, however. In some urban and suburban areas, trash cans near hobby stores have been noted to be filled with unused inexpensive model kits.

The problem of aerosol gas propellants has become increasingly more serious since 1967 with the introduction of cocktail glass chillers and the discovery by young people that the fluorinated hydrocarbons in this and a variety of other aerosol products produces an excellent and supposedly safe "high." Subsequent events, however, have shown that this form of sniffing bears a significant risk of death (*vide infra*). To meet this serious problem, concerned industries have formed the Inter-Industry Committee of Aerosol Use (Aerosol Education Bureau, 300 East 44th Street, New York, N.Y. 10017), which has developed an educational program to inform young people about the lethal hazards of aerosol sniffing. Currently there are no legislative restrictions on sales of aerosols, nor are contents required to be identified in most non-food products under existing packaging laws.

The full scope of intentional solvent intoxication in the United States remains undetermined. Reported cases are usually those of youths who have come to the attention of juvenile authorities because of delinquent behavior, with many others undoubtedly remaining undetected. Since solvent effects are usually of short duration, subsequent illnesses requiring medical attention are few, and the death rate is presumptively low. Data from other than law enforcement sources are essentially noncontributory toward estimating the magnitude of the problem. Though New York City's juvenile department reported only 1173 instances of "glue sniffing" in 1965, and similar sources revealed 507 and 651 cases in Chicago and Los Angeles, respectively (2), the true incidence in these cities cannot even be approximated.

Outside the United States the incidence of solvent abuse varies. Scandinavian countries have reported many instances of inhalation of toluene-containing lacquer thinner (2). One Canadian authority, while reporting brief epidemic use of nail polish remover, suggests the problem is not as widely endemic in Canada as it seems to be in the United States (4). This phenomenon appears not to be a serious problem in Great Britain.

PREPARATIONS USED

Today the range of products employed is extensive and includes gasoline, cleaning solutions, lighter fluid, and paint and lacquer thinners, as well as the more commonly used household and plastic model cements and glues. In the past several years cocktail glass "chillers," spray deodorants, foot powders, spot removers, furniture polish, "non-stick" frying pan sprays, and other aerosol products have been added to the list and perhaps will become increasingly popular as glues are rendered unpalatable.

All the aforementioned products contain one or more of a wide variety of volatile substances that have a generalized depressant effect upon the central nervous system similar to that of volatile general anesthetic agents. Indeed, one substance, trichloroethylene, has been employed as a surgical anesthetic agent as well as an industrial solvent. Though toluene (toluol) outdistances all other solvents in popularity because of its minimal irritant effects, not unpleasant odor, rapid vaporization, and supposedly "good high," also implicated, by fact or hearsay, have been some twenty-three other solvents in the following chemical categories: aliphatic hydrocarbons and gasoline, aromatic hydrocarbons, halogenated hydrocarbons, ketones, esters, alcohols, and glycols. Plastic model cements generally contain toluene, lighter fluids naphtha, cleaning solutions and aerosol products halogenated hydrocarbons, and nail polish remover acetone. Aerosols, however, may be propelled by carbon dioxide, nitrous oxide, or other relatively inert compressed gases as well as fluorocarbons. Information relating the type of propellant used or even other contents of the specific product in question is rarely printed on the container except in such categories as foods and insecticides where it is required by law. Table 2 lists the ingredients of commercial products commonly involved in volatile solvent sniffing.

TABLE 2
*Types of commercial products
commonly involved in volatile solvent sniffing*

Brand	Solvent
Glues:	
Black Magic adhesive	Naphtha
Bond's Rubber Cement	Petroleum distillates
Dupont "Duco" household cement	Ethyl acetate, methyl ethyl ketone
Dupont Plastic Cement	Toluol (toluene)
Testor's Plastic Cement	Toluol
Testor's Specific Formula Plastic Cement	Methyl isobutyl ketone, methyl cellosolve acetate
Laquer and Paint Removers:	
Baldwin's "Benzine"	Naphtha
Baldwin's Lacquer Thinner	Toluol
Bulldog Paint and Laquer Remover	Methylene chloride, methanol
Bulldog Paint Brush Cleaner	Toluol, acetone, methanol
Red Devil Paint and Varnish Remover	Benzol, acetone, methanol
Nail Polish Removers:	
Cutex	Acetone
Revlon	Acetone
Cleaning Fluids and Spot Removers:	
AFTA	Trichloroethylene, petroleum distillates
Carbona	Trichloroethylene, 1,1,1-trichloroethane
K2R	Perchloroethylene
Lighter Fluid:	
Ronsonol	Naphtha

PATTERNS OF USE

Most reported volatile solvent sniffers are boys between the ages of 10 and 15 years. Many offenders are as young as 7 or 8 years old, however, and many girls and some adults are also known to follow this form of drug abuse. Though boys outnumber girls 10 to 1 in published data, identification usually occurs, as noted earlier, as a result of delinquent acts, a form of behavior indulged in less frequently by girls than boys whether sniffers or not. In general, sniffing as a form of intoxication is given up by the mid-teens and is generally perceived by the older adolescents as an unacceptably childish way of getting one's "kicks" (2).

Though some youths undoubtedly replace inhalation with other forms of drug abuse, the use of these substances does not lead, per se, to the use of "harder" drugs; the whole framework of drug dependency in all of its social and psychiatric aspects determines for each individual subsequent forms of drug abuse, if any. The socially and emotionally healthy juvenile casually experimenting with solvent sniffing does not bear any greater potential for heroin addiction than had he not sniffed solvents. Conversely, the disturbed youth from a broken home, who is frequently exposed to pushers, probably bears the same high risk of ultimate narcotic abuse whether or not he sniffs glue. Regardless of surrounding circumstances, however, any significant resort to intoxicating substances in childhood should be carefully noted as a potential warning of a growing emotional disturbance or as a predictor of a future drug-dependent personality.

Solvent sniffing, as with other forms of drug abuse, has no particular social or geographic boundaries and occurs among the poor and the affluent in cities, suburbs, and rural areas alike. As a form of casual, experimental intoxication, it can be considered to have the same magnitude of psychological import as occasional marihuana smoking. At the other end of the spectrum, it offers another form of habitual escape for those unable to cope with reality. Solvent sniffing, particularly of halogenated hydrocarbons, however, does entail a significant risk of death (*vide infra*).

Sociological and psychological studies of juvenile chronic sniffers have been carried out in some depth by a number of observers (2, 5, 6). Though intellectual capacity, per se, is not believed to be a determining factor, nearly all the subjects studied were found to have poor school adjustment and scholastic performance. Truancy and other forms of delinquent behavior were also common. Generally these youths came from disorganized, multiproblem homes in which the father often was actually or effectively absent. Alcoholism in one or both parents was common.

METHODS OF ADMINISTRATION

Sniffers of such semi-liquid materials as glues and cements generally squeeze anywhere from one-third of a tube to five tubes of the preparation into the bottom of a paper or plastic bag. The opening of the bag is then held tightly over the mouth, and sometimes the nose as well, and the vapors are inhaled until the desired effect is produced or the solvent evaporates completely. Liquid materials may be either inhaled directly from the container or from saturated cloth, gauze, or cotton. The solvent-impregnated cloth may be held in the hands and placed over the mouth and nose; more often, it is placed in a bag and sniffed. Sometimes beer or wine is drunk to further potentiate the effect.

Most aerosol sniffers separate the propellant gas from the particulate contents. A variety of techniques has been employed to accomplish this; the can may be held in an inverted position, thus evacuating the gas only; the contents may be pre-filtered through a washcloth or rag, theoretically allowing passage of the gas only; or, as with glue sniffing, the aerosol may be sprayed directly onto the sides of a plastic or paper bag, with the gaseous contents alone being inhaled. Some have used balloons instead of bags. Other sniffers resort to spraying the contents of the can directly into the mouth, without pre-filtering.

Volatile solvents are often warmed by cupping the bag in the hands or even holding it over a radiator or hot plate to increase the solvent concentration. It has been estimated that this technique can result in vapor concentrations 50 times the maximum allowable industrial concentration (which for toluene is 200 parts per million). Up to 3.6 mg of toluene have been recovered from 100 ml of air from such a glue-containing paper bag (2).

The sniffer usually inhales from his own or, less often, a shared bag until the desired degree of euphoria is produced; this usually occurs within a few minutes. He may continue to sniff off and on perpetuating his state as long as the solvent supply lasts. Excessive, prolonged continuous sniffing of high vapor concentrations will ultimately result in unconsciousness. The user will then relax his grip, so the paper bag falls away from his mouth. Thus, unconsciousness can protect the user from deep respiratory depression, hypoxia, and death. This hazard, however, is greatly increased by the use of a plastic bag. Little ambient air enters the respiratory tract, since the plastic is non-porous, and the seal between the mouth and bag is tight. A partial vacuum may even result. Hypoxia develops rapidly and if, in his stuporous state, the abuser cannot or fails to remove the bag from his face, he may die. Indeed, in company with deaths attributable directly to the toxic effects of halogenated hydrocarbons in some aerosol propellants and cleaning solutions that produce cardiac arrest, plastic bag suffocation is a leading cause of death among volatile solvent sniffers.

Some youths gather for sniffing in groups of from three to ten persons of the same sex, whereas others may carry out their habit alone. Because of the pervasive tell-tale odor, group users, in particular, tend to seek out such areas as abandoned buildings and rooftops where they and their vapors will be undetected. Consequently, in northern cities, there may be a decline in glue sniffing in winter months when such areas are physically uncomfortable and evaporation of the solvent is slowed because of the cold. Basements, school lavatories, and locker rooms, as well as an individual's bedroom, are also common locations. The discovery of rags, handkerchiefs, balloons, or plastic or paper bags containing dried films of solvent-containing products should alert parents or teachers. Another significant finding is that of a white powdery ring that appears around the mouth of the forgetful novice glue sniffer, where the bag was held and glue contacted the skin. Also, vapors may be readily smelled on the breath from some distance away for an hour or so after a sniffing episode.

EFFECTS OF VOLATILE SOLVENTS

All materials used in sniffing contain volatile or gaseous substances, which are primarily generalized central nervous system depressants. A number of immediate and transient effects occur, ranging from a simple somnolence and dizziness to delusions of unusual strength or the ability to fly to outright visual and auditory hallucinations similar to those experienced with the ingestion of psychotomimetic agents. Slurred speech, ataxia, impaired judgment, and feelings of giddiness and drunkenness accompanied by a marked sense of euphoria are experienced by almost all users even at the time of their first episode of sniffing. These feelings are accompanied by a sense of reckless abandon and omnipotence, often leading to impulsive and destructive behavior. Others have described sensations of numbness, being "blank" or "dead," of floating or spinning in space. It is not unusual to experience distortions of space and visual perception with the walls closing in, the sky falling, or visible objects changing shape, size, or color. One youth reported that the tube of glue he held in his hand seemed to become an ice cream cone. Another saw a picket fence turn into a row of toy soldiers. The extent to which any of these feelings are experienced by a given user depends not only upon the dose received but also upon ill-defined aspects of psychic susceptibility. Visual and auditory hallucinations are not universal and appear to happen only in certain youths; such experiences may occur repeatedly in these persons on subsequent episodes of inhalation. Users not having such symptoms early in their habituation will rarely experience them, even after prolonged use. The only exception to this generalization occurs among gasoline sniffers who regularly report visual hallucinations. An unpleasant experience (a "bad trip") appears to be exceedingly rare.

It is during the stage of euphoria, with feelings of omnipotence that the intoxicated youth is of greatest danger to himself and others. There have been instances of young boys jumping off roof tops, often to their death, in an effort to fly, or sustaining severe lacerations on putting their hand through a glass window they perceived as open.

The symptoms of giddiness, dizziness, and lightheadedness and the sensations of floating and freedom from inhibition appear similar to those sometimes produced by alcohol ingestion. Users say, however, that the degree of euphoria and sense of omnipotence as well as distortions of perception are usually far more pronounced in solvent sniffing.

The immediate effects of euphoria, giddiness, ataxia, slurred speech, perceptual distortions, and so on usually last for the duration of active sniffing and for 15 to 45 minutes thereafter. The user may then experience 1 or 2 hours of drowsiness and stupor, with all of the depressant effects gradually wearing off, and then the subject returns to his usual state of consciousness. When sniffing is a group experience those youths experiencing exhilaration may indulge in "horseplay," roughhousing, fighting, or, occasionally, homosexual activities. Heterosexual activities occur only rarely, and sniffing is not known to have an aphrodisiac effect. Those experiencing more pronounced stuporous or hallucinatory symptoms may remain apart from the group, appearing to be asleep. These experiences may be prolonged by frequent intermittent sniffing over many hours. Indeed, some youths may devote as many waking hours as possible to continuous sniffing, periods of unconsciousness permitting (2, 7).

Following sniffing, amnesia, either total or partial, may exist for the period of intoxication. A number of unpleasant side effects are also experienced both during use and for variable periods thereafter; these include photophobia, irritation of the eyes, diplopia, tinnitus, sneezing, rhinitis, coughing, nausea, vomiting, diarrhea, chest pain, and vague muscle and joint pains. No cases of mucosal ulceration or nasal perforation have been reported. Anorexia occurs among users who sniff more frequently. All of these symptoms, however, as well as those attributable to central nervous system depression, appear to be fully reversible. Studies of cognitive functions have shown no impairment whatsoever after intoxication has waned (8). Electroencephalographic examinations have failed to reveal any abnormalities except for transitory ones consistent with the solvent-induced state of depression (6). Possible damage to other organs and serious hazards to health will be discussed below, but, with the exception of trichloroethylene, trichloroethane, and fluorinated hydrocarbons used as propellants in some aerosol products, the majority of commonly inhaled substances appear to bear minimal risk of permanent organic damage.

HABITUAL USE OF VOLATILE SOLVENTS

Psychological dependence

Habituation occurs quite regularly. Many users become psychologically dependent upon the effects achieved generally, preferring to sniff a particular product (and even brand) as their method of psychic escape. Alternative substances are readily substituted, however, when that of choice is not available. Compulsive, repeated sniffing has been reported in a number of studies. Indeed, one large-scale user is said to have inhaled up to 25 tubes of glue (21 cc each) daily (2).

Tolerance

Sniffers of all products abused for any length of time report the development of tolerance to the central nervous system effects. Only those exposing themselves to low vapor concentrations for brief periods of time appear to escape this phenomenon. How quickly tolerance develops is uncertain, but a report indicates that it was observed after 3 months of once-weekly usage of unspecified amounts of model cement in one user. Another individual was found to require 8 tubes of glue to achieve the same effects that had been obtained from 1 tube 3 years before (2). Tolerance to gasoline sniffing has not been noted in the literature, but, since gasoline sniffers usually sniff from the opening of a large container (tank, barrel, one-gallon tin, etc.), it is difficult to estimate whether an ever increasing dose is required to achieve the same effect or not.

There are no data concerning possible cross-tolerance among different solvents. The period of abstinence required for tolerance to disappear is unknown.

Physical dependence

There is little to suggest that the practice of volatile solvent inhalation is addicting. No substantial evidence of physiological dependence has been presented. Some individuals have reported fine tremors, irritability, anxiety, and insomnia on cessation of sniffing. Such symptoms can be as readily psychic in origin as physical (2). Other persons have reported that they felt "better" on cessation of their habit. Two patients have been noted to have symptoms of delirium tremens on withdrawal from toluene (9). One instance of transient tingling and cramps of hands and feet on cessation of glue sniffing has also been cited (10). These findings are so rare and variable that they cannot be considered conclusive. Therefore, if physical dependence exists at all it is very mild, occurs only rarely, and cannot be considered to be a significant part of the experience of the vast majority of sniffers.

TOXIC EFFECTS OF VOLATILE SOLVENTS

Potential toxicity of various solvents
Based upon industrial and laboratory studies and inadvertent poisonings, as well as upon available information from sniffers themselves, the following toxic potential can be considered to exist for the compounds discussed above (11, 12, 13).

ALIPHATIC HYDROCARBONS   Hexane, petroleum naphtha, and petroleum distillates have never been implicated in organic disease through either sniffing or industrial exposure.

AROMATIC HYDROCARBONS   Benzene is markedly toxic producing bone marrow aplasia, anemia, and necrosis or fatty degeneration of the heart, liver, and adrenal glands. Xylene has essentially no effect on bone marrow and is minimally toxic to other organs; because its vapors are highly irritating to mucous membranes it is an unlikely substance for significant abuse. Ball point pen ink, however, which frequently does contain xylene, has been reported to have been used in rare instances (14).

Toluene is also considerably less toxic than benzene. Some 25 years ago, commercial toluene was contaminated with as much as 20% benzene, thus accounting for early reports of marked toxicity among industrial workers (11). In the past 20 years, however, toluene has been much more highly purified and now contains less than 0.5% benzene. Little major toxicity can be ascribed to toluene itself. (Metabolically it is converted to benzoic acid, conjugated with glycine, and excreted as hippuric acid.) Some industrial workers have been found to have mildly enlarged livers, and others have an absolute lymphocytosis and slight changes in red blood cells with macrocytosis (15). Animal studies have revealed variable findings on prolonged exposure to high concentrations of toluene vapors (16). These include such scattered abnormalities in the brain and spinal cord as increased pigmentation, neuronal shrinkage, patchy loss of myelin, and decreased numbers of central nervous system Purkinje fibers. Additionally, investigations in animals have demonstrated a slight, reversible anemia with an initial leukocytosis or leukopenia, but in others no general changes in blood morphology were found (17). Liver or kidney damage has not been found.

HALOGENATED HYDROCARBONS   Trichloroethylene can produce cardiac arrhythmias. This is a well-known hazard when it is used as a surgical anesthetic, and it has moreover been responsible for several industrial deaths. Acute renal failure, myocarditis, and heart failure following inadvertent excessive exposure to trichloroethylene (as a tile cement solvent) have been described rarely. Hepatic cell dysfunction and hepatomegally have also been found through industrial exposure and, on occasion, among Carbona sniffers (18). (Carbona contains trichloroethylene and trichloroethane; accordingly, the hepatotoxic effects of the two agents both singly and in combination must be considered. No specific data are available, however, on the combined effects beyond isolated case reports.)

1,1,1-Trichloroethane has rarely been implicated per se in the production of organic damage. Exposure of animals to high vapor concentrations of this compound, even those sufficiently high to kill by respiratory depression, results only in minimal organ damage. Indeed its safety has been regarded as sufficiently great to permit its use as a carrier for medicinal ingredients in a Canadian anti-tussive aerosol spray (3).

Trichlorofluoromethane, dichlorodifluoromethane, cryofluorane, and other fluorocarbons are substances that have wide application singly or in combination with other hydrocarbons as pressurized refrigerants and propellants for aerosol spray can products. Until recently, they have been believed to possess exceedingly low toxicity in animal experiments.

Trichloroethane and the fluorinated hydrocarbons, nonetheless, have been implicated in a large number of recent deaths from cardiac arrest due to sniffing (see Mortality, below) and cannot continue to be regarded as essentially innocuous agents (3). Indeed, these agents have now been demonstrated to have a strong potential for toxic effects on the myocardium (27).

Carbon tetrachloride, chloroform, and ethylene dichloride are highly toxic, injuring all body cells; they can produce central nervous system edema with congestion and hemorrhage, edema of the lungs, heart, spleen, and kidneys, and fatty degeneration of the liver, as well as cardiac arrhythmias.

KETONES   Acetone, cyclohexanone, methyl ethyl ketone, and methyl isobutyl ketone are all highly irritating to the mucous membranes and rarely produce any systemic effects other than central nervous system depression. An attempt to produce a more rapidly setting synthetic "plaster" cast utilizing acetone as the solvent did, however, result in eight cases of poisoning from skin absorption with vomiting, dysuria, albuminuria, tachycardia, dysarthria, incoordination, torpor, and coma; fortunately, all of the patients recovered completely (7). There have been no reports of significant acetone toxicity resulting from either purposive or accidental inhalation of acetone.

ESTERS   Ethyl acetate is said to produce liver and kidney damage, but no chronic toxicity has been found following industrial exposure. Amyl acetate and butyl acetate are not known to produce liver, kidney, or hematological damage.

ALCOHOLS   Butyl, ethyl, methyl, and isopropyl alcohols are not as volatile as most solvents and therefore are not particularly rewarding compounds for sniffing. Oral ingestion is a much more effective route of administration. On inhalation, metabolism and toxicology are largely similar to that of ethyl alcohol. Isopropyl alcohol may cause central nervous system excitation as well as depression. Methyl alcohol must be assumed to be as capable of producing blindness by inhalation as by oral ingestion, but blindness has not been reported to occur from vapors. Liver, kidney, and blood abnormalities have not been reported from any form of alcohol inhalation.

GLYCOLS   All of these compounds are highly irritating to mucous membranes and are only rarely implicated in sniffing. Ethylene glycol, found in antifreeze soluitons, is metabolized to oxalic acid, which may, with prolonged exposure, give symptoms of oxalosis with impairment of liver and renal functions; it may produce permanent brain damage. A single episode of ingestion of this substance in a suicide attempt has been reported to have resulted in prolonged oliguria secondary to hydropic degeneration and crystal deposition in the kidney (19). Acute poisoning may also result in pulmonary edema. Urinalysis in those chronically exposed to ethylene glycol vapors have shown calcium oxalate crystals, albuminuria, hematuria, and casts. Crystals have never been found in the urine of sniffers, however.

Methyl cellosolve acetate, a solvent used in some liquid plastic cements, produces significant liver and kidney damage.

GASOLINE Acute excessive exposure to fumes of leaded gasoline has resulted in petechial and gross pulmonary hemorrhages, pneumonitis, and bronchitis in factory workers. Chronic industrial exposure may result in anemia, paresthesias, neuritis, and cranial nerve paralysis. Similar findings have not been found among gasoline sniffers. In considering its further toxic potential, one must also take into account possible plumbism, since one instance of toxic psychosis from lead encephalopathy has been reported in a gasoline sniffer (20).

MORBIDITY AND MORTALITY

Toluene

The literature on the toxic sequelae of sniffing products containing toluene is unclear. A number of studies of seemingly normal youths known to have abused toluene report some mild, reversible, and highly variable findings (2). Possible chronic neurological damage has been described in just a handful of subjects (8); and the few single case reports of dramatic and serious sequelae only add to the confusion (21-23). The minimal hazards incurred by workers exposed to low and non-intoxicating levels of toluene for periods of months to years (13) are difficult to compare with those of the sniffer and his intermittent, brief episodes of exposure to high concentrations. Interpretation of the more subtle pathological changes and their implications for potential serious damage has been, moreover, sometimes subject to the bias of authors, as they attempt to present as strong a case as possible about the hazards of sniffing (24); in substance abuse, the truth regretfully is sometimes asked to perform two functions: To inform and, with hope, to deter the susceptible.

Urinary system abnormalities have been described most often. One author encountered pyuria in 32 of 89 juvenile sniffers, most of whom had inhaled toluene (25). A smaller, but significant incidence of hematuria and proteinuria of undefined degree was also found. The study of another series of 16 glue-sniffing-youths confirmed these findings and included one instance of reduced renal clearance (6). Several other studies on a total of 74 adolescent sniffers reported normal urinalyses except for rare instances of microscopic hematuria and minimal proteinuria (2, 7).

The report on the series of 89 youths with a high percentage of urinary disturbances also noted that three-fourths of the subjects had such red blood cell abnormalities as basophilic stippling, anisocytosis, hypochromia, polychromasia, and target cells; 20 of these subjects also had anemia and 25 eosinophilia (25). Other studies, however, list no significant hematological findings except 6 cases of eosinophilia and 1 case of neutropenia (7), a finding not noted elsewhere. Another investigator performed bone marrow aspirations on 27 toluene-inhalers; in ten of these patients there were changes suggestive of disturbances in the maturation of leukocytes despite normal peripheral blood (7).

In only one of these series was hepatomegaly (1 to 2 finger breadths) described (5 of 32 boys) (7). No other physical abnormalities have been reported. Two of those with enlarged livers showed bromsulfalein retention and elevated serum levels of lactic dehydrogenase, the significance of which is open to question (7). Otherwise liver function tests were normal. Just one report exists of a child known to have sniffed glue, who also had clinical and laboratory evidence of hepatitis; a cause and effect relationship was not established (23).

Electroencephalograms on ten juvenile sniffers were found to be abnormal when taken on admission to a psychiatric ward. At this time, however, varying degrees of intoxication still existed. When repeated 1 to 2 weeks later, all tracings were normal (6). Only one case report, that of a 30-year-old male with a history of 10 years of chronic toluene sniffing, demonstrated persistent electroencephalographic changes (9). If we consider that 5 to 10% of the normal population have abnormal electroencephalograms, the significance of this single case report is open to question. In another study, cognitive functioning of a small group of youths habituated to sniffing glue for long periods of time was found not to be different from that of non-sniffing controls (8). Just one case report implicates toluene sniffing in permanent central nervous system damage: this was an adult who had permanent cerebellar damage, which was believed to be attributable to many years of toluene sniffing (26).

No deaths have been proved to be directly attributable to toluene alone, no instances of permanent brain damage, other than the one case referred to above, and no episodes of serious debilitating damage to liver, kidney, or blood-forming organs have been reported in the medical literature. Two children, known to sniff glue, were reported to the National Clearing House for Poison Control Centers to have developed hypoplastic bone marrow in one instance and aplastic anemia in the other (23); definitive cause and effect relationships have not been established. Two published case reports of deaths from suffocation in plastic bags involved youths using toluene (21, 22).

There is little published evidence to indicate that toluene-sniffing is a serious health risk. Industrial experience indicates that toluene is rapidly detoxified and excreted with no significant retention of toxic products. It appears reasonable to infer that the usual practice of glue sniffing allows for adequate periods of detoxification and clearance by the body of the inhaled solvent without production of undue and persistent organic damage. It seems illogical to emphasize those rare instances of possibly serious physical toxicity or the findings of mild hematological or urinary abnormalities as arguments against toluene-sniffing when the risk of serious and even lethal self-injury while in the acute intoxicated state is so much greater.

Halogenated Hydrocarbons

The consequences of sniffing trichloroethylene and 1,1,1-trichloroethane, the volatile solvents of many cleaning fluids including Carbona, have been infrequently studied. Presumably this is because the incidence of their use is very low compared to that of toluene. A most informative report (18) describes ten adolescent Carbona sniffers. While half were completely asymptomatic, abnormal liver function was found in the other half with elevated bilirubin, transaminase, alkaline phosphatase, and thymol turbidity, and a prolonged prothrombin time. Four became jaundiced 1 week after sniffing the spot remover, with one progressing to hepatic coma. Two of the five adolescents also had elevated blood urea nitrogen (BUN) with proteinuria; one of them developed acute renal failure requiring hemodialysis; peptic ulcer was present in one; and a hemolytic crisis secondary to glucose-6-phosphate-dehydrogenase deficiency developed in another. Two had paresthesias, tinnitus, ataxia, and headaches. All survived and recovered.

Such effects can readily be caused by carbon tetrachloride inhalation as well. As previously noted, this well-recognized hazard has resulted in the almost complete elimination of this solvent from currently available commercial products. Occasionally, either from sniffing the rare product still available containing this substance or from using an older one (dating from times when carbon tetrachloride was regularly used as a solvent, i.e., prior to the mid-1960's), poisoning by this compound can still occur. Carbon tetrachloride should be the prime suspect when evidence of pancreatitis accompanies signs of hepatic damage and renal failure following exposure to a volatile solvent.

Though animal studies on the fluorocarbons in some aerosol products give evidence of low toxicity (11, 12), no information relative to human inhalation is available in regard to the hematological, nephrotoxic, or hepatotoxic effects of these agents. Cardiac toxicity, however, does exist, with a number of deaths after their use having been reported (3) (*vide infra*). The clinical literature gives definitive evidence of a genuine lethal hazard resulting from sniffing them as solvents or propellants (27); none of them should be regarded as innocuous.

Gasoline

Since the first warning about this habit appeared in 1951 (1), there have been a number of reports on leaded gasoline inhalation (28-34). Each of these reports has described only a few patients or a single case. No abnormal physical or laboratory findings attributable to gasoline have been noted, and the hazards of pulmonary disorders and nervous system damage seen in industrial poisoning have never been detected in gasoline sniffers.

The often-anticipated risk of concomitant lead intoxication eventually figured in one recent case report (20). An adult woman sniffed leaded gasoline from a closed 1-gallon container about 1.5 hours a day for 8 mouths. This act regularly produced hallucinations and a feeling of euphoria. After a number of months, the patient began hallucinating between sniffing episodes and experienced a loss of recent memory. The diagnosis of plumbism was confirmed by the finding of elevated blood lead levels; there was a gratifying response to chelation therapy with ultimate and complete recovery.

No deaths from gasoline sniffing have been reported. Several boys, however, have been severely burned or killed by explosions, while they were indulging in this practice (35).

Naphtha

Just one report of twelve cases of lighter fluid (naphtha) inhalation appears in the medical literature (36). No major organic findings were detected, but detailed hematological, urinary, and chemical determinations were not recorded. Only one of the youths was reported to have a normal "complete blood cell count" and electroencephalogram.

Other Solvents

A few reports of the abuse of other solvents exist in the literature. Nail polish remover (acetone) sniffing has been reported, but no physical or laboratory findings were reported (4). A single, well-documented case of a 16-year-old boy who died from inhaling rubber cement containing benzene from a paper bag exists (37). The youth, found dead in his room, had cerebral and pulmonary edema plus congestion of the spleen, liver, stomach, and duodenum. Death was attributed to respiratory depression. A great variety of other substances have also been implicated in sniffing, but the true potential for organic damage of these less often abused substances is essentially unknown and can only be estimated from the toxicological and industrial studies previously described.

MORTALITY

Some 110 sudden deaths associated with solvent inhalation were reported during the 1960's, characterized by a sharp rise in incidence in the latter part of the decade (3). Most of these deaths were apparently due to trichloroethane and fluorohydrocarbon sniffing. Characteristically, the victim had been engaged in some form of physical activity or in a stressful situation such as wrestling, running to escape detection, bicycling, being caught by parents, and so on, just before or during the act of sniffing. While sniffing, the youth rather suddenly appeared startled or frightened, evidenced marked panic, and may have even dashed away a short distance before collapse and death. Autopsy findings have consistently failed to reveal a cause of death.

Many aspects of the "closed circuit" form of inhalation of volatile central nervous system depressants by sniffers resemble those obtaining during surgical anesthesia. Under the combined effects of stress, carbon dioxide retention, and increased oxygen need, epinephrine and norepinephrine are released, and myocardial sensitivity is increased. In this setting, the tendency of halogenated hydrocarbon anesthetic agents to produce ventricular fibrillation (and sometimes death) is well known. It is likely that these sudden deaths stem from a similar mechanism (3, 27). Therefore, despite the relatively innocuous nature of these substances as observed in controlled laboratory experiments or in industrial exposure, under the circumstances involved in solvent sniffing, particularly of halogenated hydrocarbons, there is a serious and significant risk of death, a risk which would not be present under other circumstances.

It is perhaps because a series of interrelated sequential events must occur to produce a sudden death that the mortality rate from sniffing is not higher and that the cause of many of these deaths has heretofore been unclear. Indeed, in the case of non-halogenated solvents, the mortality rate is still exceptionally low. Prior to the report cited above (3), only three cases of documented glue-sniffing deaths had appeared in the medical literature, two cases of plastic bag suffocation (21, 22), and the case of benzene inhalation previously described (37).

In 1964, the National Clearing House for Poison Control Centers collected nine "sniffing deaths" from newspapers, other lay media, and personal communications (23); six of these were felt to be due to plastic bag suffocation, and a seventh was thought to be probably due to plastic bag suffocation. The eighth death was that of a young man, a known glue and gasoline sniffer, who expired 24 hours after the onset of vomiting, coughing, choking, and epistaxis. Autopsy revealed only minimal intra-alveolar pulmonary hemorrhages. Toxicological studies failed to reveal traces of gasoline or toluene. The ninth death also involved a young male adult who died in a coma 3 days after developing chills and vomiting following a beer-drinking and glue-sniffing bout. Autopsy showed moderate diffuse necrosis of the liver and severe pulmonary congestion.

No estimate of the incidence of mortality or major morbidity related to violent or accidental acts commited while intoxicated is available. Though most papers reviewing the topic refer to instances of boys jumping to their deaths under the delusion of being able to fly, these events must occur with considerable rarity as accidental falls from rooftops or windows comprises but a small percentage of all accidental deaths occurring in the susceptible age group, 10 to 15 years of age.

In summary, we feel that the practice of voluntary volatile solvent inhalation bears a significant potential for mortality, even though the number of deaths seems exceedingly low relative to the number of youths who are probably involved in the practice. The halogenated hydrocarbons that appear in cleaning solutions and some aerosol sprays are the most dangerous agents. There seems to be a considerably greater safety factor when most other agents, and toluene, in particular, are used. Deaths implicating these latter substances typically entail plastic bag suffocation, rather than the toxic effects of the chemical agent itself.

REFERENCES

1. Clinger, O. W. and N. A. Johnson, Purposeful inhalation of gasoline vapors. *Psychiat Quart* 25:557, 1951
2. Press, E. and A. K. Done, Solvent sniffing, I and II. *Pediatrics* 39:451, 1967
3. Bass, M., Sudden sniffing death. *J Amer Med Assoc* 212:2075, 1970
4. Gellman, V., Glue-sniffing among Winnipeg school children. *Canad Med Assoc J* 98:411, 1968
5. Massengale, O. N., H. H. Glaser, R. E. LeLievre, J. B. Dodds, and M. E. Kook, Physical and psychological factors in glue sniffing. *New Engl J Med* 269:1340, 1963
6. Brozovsky, M. and E. G. Winkler, Glue sniffing in children and adolescents. *NY J Med* 65:1984, 1965.
7. Glaser, H. H. and O. N. Massengale, Glue sniffing in children: Deliberate inhalation of vaporized plastic cements. *J Amer Med Assoc* 181:300, 1962
8. Dodds, J. and S. Santostefano, A comparison of the cognitive functioning of glue sniffers and non-sniffers. *J Pediat* 64:565, 1964
9. Satran, R. and V. N. Dodson, Toluene habituation: Report of a case. *New Engl J Med* 268:719, 1963
10. Merry, J. and N. Zachariadis, Addiction to glue sniffing. *Brit Med J* 2:1448, 1962
11. Gleason, M. N., R. E. Gosselin, and H. C. Hodge, *Clinical Toxicology of Commercial Products*. Baltimore: Williams & Wilkins, 1957
12. Dreisbach, R. H., *Handbook of poisoning: Diagnosis and treatment,* ed. 4. Los Altos (Calif.): Lange, 1963.
13. Browning, E., *Toxicity of Industrial Solvents*. New York: Chemical Publications Co., 1953
14. Mathieu, R., State panel finds more kids addicts. *NY Daily News,* Jan. 27, 1969
15. Greenberg, H. J., Effects of exposure to toluene in industry. *J Amer Med Assoc* 118:573-578, 1942
16. Killick, E. M. and R. S. Schilling, Investigations into effects of continued exposure to vapor of volatile solvents. *J Indust Hyg Toxicol* 24:307, 1942
17. Meyer, S., Changes in blood as reflecting industrial damage. *J Indust Hyg Toxicol* 10:29-55, 1928
18. L. H., I. F. and M. I. Cohen, "Danger—vapor harmful"; Spot remover sniffing. *New Engl J Med* 281:543, 1969

19. Collins, J. M., D. M. Hennes, C. R. Holzgang, R. T. Courley, and G. A. Porter, Recovery after prolonged oliguria due to ethylene glycol intoxication. *Arch Intern Med* 125:1059, 1970

20. Law, W. R., Gasoline sniffing by an adult (lead encephalopathy). *J Amer Med Assoc* 204:1002, 1968

21. Winek, C. L., C. H. Wecht, and W. D. Collom, Toluene fatality from glue sniffing. *Penn Med* 71:81, 1968

22. Garrett, G. and S. Johnson, Plastic-bag asphyxia in a glue-sniffer. *Lancet* i:954, 1967

23. National Clearing House for Poison Control Centers. Glue Sniffing II, Washington, D.C.: U.S. Dept. H.E.W., 1964

24. Sokol, J., Glue sniffing among juveniles. *Amer J Correction* Nov-Dec, p. 18, 1965

25. Sokol, J. and J. L. Robinson, Glue sniffing. *Western Med* 4:192, 1963

26. Grabski, D. A., Toluene sniffing producing cerebellar degeneration. *Amer J Psychiat* 118:461, 1961

27. Harris, W. S., Toxic effects of aerosol propellants on the heart. *Arch Int Med* 131:162, 1973

28. Easson, W. M., Gasoline addiction in children. *Pediatrics* 29:250, 1962

29. Edwards, R. V., Case report of gasoline sniffing. *Amer J Psychiat* 117:555, 1960

30. Faucett, R. L. and R. A. Jensen, Addiction to inhalation of gasoline fumes in a child. *J Pediat* 41:364, 1952

31. Lawton, J. J. and C. P. Malmquist, Gasoline addiction in children. *Psychiat Quart* 35:555, 1961

32. Nitsche, C. J. and J. F. Robinson, Case of gasoline addiction. *Amer J Orthopsychiat* 29:417, 1959

33. Tolan, E. J. and F. A. Lingle, Model psychosis produced by inhalation of gasoline fumes. *Amer J Psychiat* 126:757, 1964

34. Kaufman, A., Gasoline sniffing among children in a Pueblo Indian village. *Pediatrics* 51:1060, 1973

35. Schmitt, R. C., H. A. Goolishian, and S. Abston, Gasoline sniffing in children leading to severe burn injury. *J Pediatrics* 80:1021, 1972

36. Ackerly, W. C. and C. Gibson, Lighter fluid "sniffing." *Amer J Psychiat* 120:1056, 1964

37. Winek, C. L., W. D. Collom, and C. H. Wecht, Fatal benzene exposure by glue-sniffing. *Lancet* i:683, 1967

Chapter 6

HALLUCINOGENS: LSD, PHENCYCLIDINE, AND OTHER AGENTS HAVING SIMILAR EFFECTS

We have found it virtually impossible to classify the substances we are about to discuss as members of a unique and discrete pharmacological group. Such compounds as LSD and DOM (STP) can, in relatively small doses, produce feelings of depersonalization and derealization and visions or illusions that the user commonly recognizes as being drug-induced. On what are often unpredictable occasions, these drugs can also produce truly psychotic hallucinatory-delusional states that may abate within days or last for many months. Other agents, belonging to well-defined drug groups, can in large doses produce similar psychotic states; hence, they are classified by some as hallucinogens. Exemplifying this type of compound are amphetamine (a central nervous system stimulant), cocaine (a local anesthetic agent), and scopolamine (an atropinic drug). Aside from these latter drugs and the various *Cannabis* preparations (to which separate chapters are devoted), we will discuss in this chapter the hallucinogenic (psychedelic, dysleptic, psychotogenic, illusinogenic) substances most commonly subject to abuse in the past decade.

In the 1960's, drug users investigated a fantastic array of substances reputedly capable of "blowing their minds," some most potent in this respect and others wholly inert. Reading newspaper reports and scientific accounts of this period one might easily get the impression that users were (and still are) offered a veritable smorgasbord of psychedelic preparations. Though such exotic compounds as psilocybin have been avail-

150

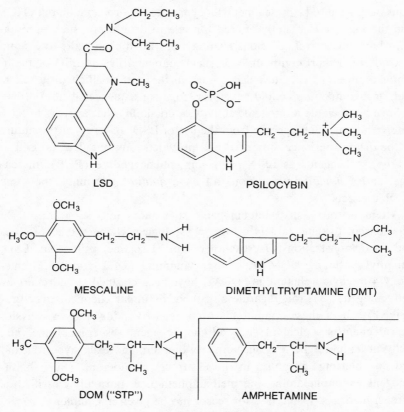

Fig. 1. *Adrenergic Hallucinogens*

Though the physiological and psychic effects of these compounds are qualitatively similar, it is difficult to find components of chemical structure common to all of them. The most potent of the adrenergic hallucinogens, LSD (lysergic acid diethylamide), has the least structural resemblance to other members of the group, and psilocybin is notable because it is a phosphorus-containing, quaternary ammonium compound.

All of these hallucinogens do contain nitrogen, and, in all but LSD, the grouping R'-C-C-N-R" occurs. The structure of a central nervous system stimulant, amphetamine, is provided to illustrate its general structural similarity with mescaline and DOM (2,5-dimethoxy-4-methyl amphetamine).

able episodically (and to the fanfare of much publicity), it is our impression that only two substances (excluding central nervous system stimulants) have been and continue to be consistently available: LSD and *Cannabis* preparations (particularly marihuana). Though preparations purported to be mescaline, psilocybin, tetrahydrocannabinol (THC), and the like are frequently offered for sale to drug users, such preparations have on several occasions been demonstrated chemically to contain instead either inert compounds or such familiar drugs as LSD or methamphetamine (1, 2). Such deceptions on the part of illicit drug sellers and/or manufacturers could have disastrous consequences if LSD proves to have appreciable teratogenic activity, a possibility that appears to have deterred many young people from the use of LSD. In terms of the nature of the drug experience, however, and provided only one drug is used at a time, such agents as LSD, psilocybin, phencyclidine (PCP), mescaline, and *Cannabis* preparations all have *qualitatively* much the same psychic effects.

Attempts to classify hallucinogenic substances into subgroups have been based, to date, largely on the physiological changes they produce and on demonstrations of cross-tolerance. Mescaline, psilocybin, LSD, dimethyltryptamine (DMT), diethyltryptamine (DET), and 2,5-dimethoxy-4-methylamphetamine (DOM) have been clasified as "adrenergic" hallucinogens (3), for, regardless of their dissimilar chemical structures (Fig. 1), all of these compounds produce, to varying degrees, physiological changes typical of such adrenergic agents as epinephrine, i.e., tachycardia and hypertension, pupillary dilation, anorexia, hyperreflexia, and an "alerting" response in the electroencephalogram. (Such hallucinogens as amphetamine and methamphetamine, normally classified as adrenergic drugs, would not, for reasons to be given in Chapter 8, necessarily fall into this subgroup.)

Though such *Cannabis* preparations as marihuana and hashish can produce many of the same psychic disturbances caused by LSD, the physiological changes produced are significantly different: blood pressure and pupillary size are commonly affected only slightly. Appetite, often manifested as a craving for sweet foods, is enhanced by *Cannabis* prepartions, and, not infrequently, a sedative or even a sleep-inducing action becomes evident. In physiological terms, *Cannabis* preparations clearly cannot be classified as adrenergic hallucinogens, though no appropriate name has gained general acceptance.

Atropinic hallucinogens (e.g., atropine and scopolamine), easily comprise a discrete subgroup whose identity derives from the characteristic physiological changes produced. The therapeutic effects of single doses of some of these drugs may persist for more than a day; their hallucinogenic effects are likewise protracted; they are described in Chapter 7.

Individuals tolerant to the effects of LSD exhibit cross-tolerance to mescaline and to psilocybin; no cross-tolerance, however, is exhibited to the effects of amphetamine or *Cannabis* preparations (1). The existence of cross-tolerance among LSD, mescaline, and psilocybin users may be interpreted as evidence that these three compounds share a common mechanism or site of action, or it might result from a common biochemical mechanism for metabolic inactivation (e.g., oxidation by hepatic microsomal enzymes), which is subject to induction upon repeated use of any one of these substances. Should this prove to be the case, cross-tolerance would stem not from pharmacodynamic but from metabolic or drug-disposition tolerance.

Users of hallucinogens frequently employ drug mixtures, either deliberately or accidently. The most commonly occurring agent in such mixtures is LSD, to which amphetamine, DOM (STP), methamphetamine, or an anticholinergic drug may be added to intensify and/or prolong the LSD experience. Mixtures of LSD and an amphetamine-type drug can produce experiences so disturbing that users have characterized them as "death trips." The great likelihood at times of purchasing such mixtures unwittingly in such areas as the Haight-Ashbury caused some users to abstain from LSD (4). Mixtures of adrenergic hallucinogens and anticholinergic agents have created special problems for user and physician alike, causing "trips" that are typically protracted (3 to 4 days is not uncommon) and exhausting, which often end in an acute panic or a psychotic episode. Treatment of adverse psychic reactions caused by these mixtures with what have become standard remedies, such as chlorpromazine (Thorazine), have resulted in cardiovascular collapse and probably, on occasion, in death (5). It is thought by some that the widespread use of large doses of methamphetamine was facilitated by the exposure of users to this drug when it was employed to intensify the effects of LSD. And, as we have commented earlier, the fairly common use of drug mixtures has made diagnosis of causative agents in adverse reactions extremely difficult, and treatment of these reactions sometimes perilous.

LSD

LSD (D-lysergic acid diethylamide, lysergide, LSD-25) is a semisynthetic compound that was first prepared by Swiss chemists searching for new drugs derived from naturally occurring constituents of ergot. Among the compounds prepared were lysergic acid hydroxybutylamide (methylergonovine, Methergine) and another molecule with oxytocic activity, a racemic mixture called lysergic acid diethylamide. The story of the accidental discovery of the hallucinogenic properties of LSD (3) is fairly common knowledge now. Only the D isomer of LSD possesses hallucinogenic activity; the monoethylamide-congener produces similar central nervous system effects, though considerably larger doses are required. The illicit supply of LSD has easily equaled demand, for amateur chemists have been able to readily procure the starting materials required for the synthesis of LSD and to accomplish the synthesis without great difficulty. The selling price of LSD, however, rarely reflects the ease of manufacture; it has been estimated that the quantity of LSD for which a user may pay $10 probably costs no more than 10¢ to make. Those who sell "acid" (LSD) often sell a variety of other drugs, such as amphetamine, marihuana, and barbiturates. Until quite recently, at least, the world of the narcotic pusher and user was distinctly separate from the world of those who sold and used hallucinogens and central nervous system stimulants (6); with the increasing incidence of heroin use in patterns of multiple drug abuse, this separation appears to be eroding.

The illicit use of LSD on a broad national scale began in the United States around 1965. A significant impetus for this development was provided by the immense publicity accorded Dr. Timothy Leary and his fulsome (and sometimes inaccurate or misunderstood) tributes to the drug's effects. Several large hospitals in Los Angeles have placed the date of the onset of the "LSD-era" as September 1965. Their psychiatric emergency services, which had previously been seeing patients with adverse reactions to LSD at the rate of about six per year, now began seeing such patients at a rate of sixty to one hundred and eighty per year and receiving, in addition, three to five telephone calls of inquiry about LSD for each patient seen (7, 8).

Psychiatrists have extensively investigated the potential therapeutic efficacy of LSD; published reports about the value of the drug in psychiatric therapy have differed sharply in their conclusions. Though the evaluation continues, the consensus at this time would deny that LSD is uniquely valuable or has any value at all, depending on the type of problem under consideration (1). These studies nonetheless have provided valuable information on the clinical effects of LSD and are the source of data for phrases such as "therapeutic doses of LSD" and "LSD given under medical supervision."

Patterns of use

Doses of LSD in excess of 35 μg are effectively hallucinogenic, and "street doses" of the drug range typically from 50 to 300 μg (2). The compound may be provided as a powder, a solution, a capsule, or a pill, the last often having a distinctive shape and color (9); in addition, drops of LSD solution quite often have been placed on sugar cubes, animal crackers (6), or pieces of blotting paper, which are then offered for sale.

Like the purchase of heroin, the buying of LSD can be a disappointing and risky business. Sellers of LSD often misrepresent the quantity of drug in their product; the actual amount of LSD obtained by the buyer usually ranges from none at all to as much as 80% of the declared content (2, 9). More serious problems arise when the buyer receives pharmacologically more than he had bargained for. On November 11, 1967, a preparation represented to be LSD and called (from the shape of the tablet and color) the "Pink Wedge," began to be sold in San Francisco. Within a 5-hour period on that day, a single clinic treated 18 Pink Wedge consumers for acute toxic psychoses (9). Advertised as 1000 μg of LSD, on analysis the Pink Wedge was found to contain 270 μg of LSD and 900 μg of DOM(STP). From time to time, users may be unable to obtain pure LSD, as, for instance, when most manufacturers are providing LSD-methamphetamine mixtures, which appear to produce many more panic reactions than do "standard doses" of pure LSD (4).

LSD is most commonly taken by mouth; only rarely is it injected subcutaneously or intravenously (6). Occasionally, tobacco is saturated with an LSD solution and then smoked, but the "high" obtained by this means is generally found to be unsatisfactory.

The schedules of LSD use do not vary significantly in form from those previously described for other drugs. Probably only a minority of drug users take LSD at short and regular intervals for sustained periods of time, i.e., once daily or once every 2 or 3 days. Those who do so have been characterized as seeking "some personal, esoteric goal" (6), which they may describe in religious or mystical terms. A very large proportion of LSD users appear to take it on a "weekend" basis, ordinarily in the company of fellow users "to relish and seek out the feelings of greater insight, inspiration and sensory stimulation and distortions which the hallucinogens may produce" and "to rouse them from their apathy, to make life more meaningful, to overcome social inhibitions and to facilitate meaningful conversations and interpersonal relationships" (6). This is a typical rationale offered by users of hallucinogenic substances; later in this chapter we will attempt to assess how well these goals have been achieved.

Patterns of multiple drug abuse in which LSD plays a major or minor role are common. When LSD is the primary drug of choice in such patterns, marihuana and amphetamine-type drugs are frequent alternative choices, and the use of heroin and generalized depressants is uncommon (7). Some users like the effects produced by the simultaneous use of two hallucinogens, such as LSD and either marihuana or mescaline (6); a smaller number of users prefer the experience of the concurrent or sequential use of LSD and a narcotic or a barbiturate. Because individual desires for and responses to multiple drug experiences vary so widely, it would be tedious, and probably not too informative, to catalogue all of the known patterns of multiple drug abuse. And ultimately, regardless of individual preferences, an individual's pattern of habitual drug usage will be determined in large part by what is offered for sale and what he can afford to buy.

According to a popular, and not wholly inaccurate, notion, the chronic user of LSD (an "acidhead") is typically a member of one of several social groups: "creative" or "arty" types, college students (or dropouts), and hippies. These stereotypes, of course, present an incomplete view of the true situation, and physicians should not exclude LSD, or other hallucinogens, from their differential diagnosis of hallucinatory-delusional states in patients who may be white or blue-collar workers. In one comparative study of regular users of LSD classified according to whether or not they had experienced psychotic episodes, the occupations of the subjects were listed. Among those who took LSD regularly, and were, in fact, members of a group devoted to its use, were plumbers, longshoremen, janitors, and tractor mechanics (8).

Effects of LSD

When taken by mouth, the effects of LSD are perceptible within 30 to 40 minutes. Users state that it may be an hour or so, however, before they are "flying," a term synonymous with maximal psychic effects. The physiological effects of LSD are most evident 1 to 3 hours after administration and are essentially absent after 6 hours (10); the psychic effects are commonly said to persist for 8 to 12 hours (4).

The physiological changes produced by hallucinogenic doses of LSD can include slight rises in blood pressure and heart rate (though occasionally bradycardia develops), marked pupillary dilation, cutaneous flushing, increased salivation and lacrimation, conjunctival injection, trembling in the extremities, hyperreflexia, leukocytosis, occasionally vomiting, and evidence of a slight ataxia (8, 10). The intensity of these changes usually appear to be dose-related. LSD has not been observed to affect respiratory rate or blood glucose levels (8). One possible consequence of the mydriasis produced is varying degrees of photophobia.

The psychic changes produced by LSD apparently vary from one individual to another; the changes we are about to describe are those likely to occur on a "trip" regarded as "good" by a user, or, minimally, as not notably "bad." The nature of bad trips will be described in a subsequent section on the adverse effects of LSD.

Among the earliest psychic effects consistently experienced by users of LSD are feelings of derealization, depersonalization, and a loss of body image; these perceptual distortions may produce considerable anxiety in the novice and trigger the onset of a bad trip. Under the influence of LSD, the self or ego appears to be divided into an uninvolved observer and a participating, involved self; the latter is sometimes visualized as an unidentified individual, whom the user may subsequently recognize as being himself. Perception of color, distance, and shape is altered so that colors appear brighter or more intense, fixed objects such as chairs or walls may change in color or shape or appear to move, and bizarre designs may be seen. Experiences associated normally with one sensory modality are translated into another; as a result of this synesthesia, colors may be "smelled," for example, and sounds may be "seen." These perceptual aberrations have been described as pseudohallucinations, illusions, or visions, since the user of LSD typically retains sufficient insight to recognize that these phenomena are drug-induced and often remembers them clearly after the trip. Under the effects of LSD, the user often loses all sense of time in a jumble of past, present, and future. Concentration sometimes is difficult, and attention can fluctuate rapidly. There is a sense of a profusion of vague ideas pressing for attention, and the user may become engrossed with "philosophical, ethical or highly egocentric issues" (1). This engrossment, coupled with impairments in judgment produced by LSD, may cause the user to believe that he has discovered new truths of fundamental philosophical importance or fresh and significant insights into himself. His descriptions of these "discoveries," however, typically seem unintelligible or nonsensical to those not under the influence of the drug (1, 9). Some users become so preoccupied with visions or thoughts as to appear catatonic or stuporous, though their attention can be gained with persistence. Conversely, though less commonly, a user's behavioral pattern may be one of apparently purposeless and disorganized hyperactivity (1). The impairments in judgment can place the user in great peril; they may lead him to believe, for instance, that he can fly or that he can ignore life-threatening situations because the death of his body is an insignificant matter, since his soul will live forever.

Less predictably, marked emotional changes may occur "ranging from ecstasy to despair" (1). Emotional lability and suggestibility may be notably enhanced (9). Great euphoria may be experienced without the user being able to explain its origin, and then small environmental changes, as the sun going behind a cloud, may quickly transform the user's mood into one of sadness or despair. Sexuality is inconsistently affected by LSD. According to users' accounts, the sexual act is considerably more pleasurable under the influence of LSD, with the orgasm being both prolonged and greatly heightened in intensity (6). More typically, perhaps, the user's preoccupation with inner experiences effectively precludes interaction with others; eroticism may remain mental with a strongly mystical flavor and may take, for example, the form of a plea for intercourse with God (11, p. 146).

A rare phenomenon is a state of chronic intoxication, produced by the daily ingestion of LSD, in which rapidly increasing tolerance to LSD has to be overcome by doubling the dose taken each day. A single case of chronic LSD intoxication has been described; the individual was ataxic, displayed decidedly impaired coordination and slurred speech, and was euphoric and expansive (12).

The mechanism underlying the psychic effects of LSD are not known. The drug is a potent antagonist of serotonin (5-hydroxytryptamine), and this fact has served as the starting point for numerous theories that purport to explain its mode of action. Since no good correlation has been observed in studies of congeners of LSD between their "hallucinogenic" potency and their ability to antagonize serotonin, the role of serotonin antagonism in the etiology of the psychic changes produced by LSD is unknown.

Absorption, fate, and excretion

LSD is colorless, tasteless, odorless, and soluble in water. Judging from the fact that its effects can be perceived within 30 to 40 minutes after oral administration, we may assume that the drug is absorbed from the gastrointestinal tract fairly rapidly; the extent of absorption is unknown. When the drug is given intravenously, the initially high plasma concentrations in human subjects fall rapidly within the first 30 minutes and decline more slowly thereafter. From these observations, it is possible to calculate that the half-life of LSD in human plasma is approximately 175 minutes (13). The plasma concentrations of LSD following intravenous injection are higher than those which should obtain if the drug were evenly distributed within the total pool of body water (13), but little else is known about the distribution of LSD in human tissue.

Likewise, little is known about the metabolism and excretion of LSD in human beings, which is the case, by and large, for all ergot alkaloids and their semisynthetic congeners. The fact that just 50 to 100 μg of LSD can exert effects that may last for 12 hours has led some to speculate that human metabolism and/or excretion of this compound occurs very slowly; others suggest that LSD may act as a "trigger," setting in motion changes that persist for hours after the drug itself has been inactivated or excreted. The latter speculation stems largely from findings in laboratory animals in which the half-life of LSD in plasma is just 7.5 minutes (13). Other animal studies have indicated that LSD is inactivated via hepatic oxidation and that little unchanged drug appears in the urine (3).

Physical dependence

No evidence has been obtained thus far to suggest the development of physical dependence on the effects of LSD regardless of the schedule of use (1).

Tolerance

Upon daily use, a great tolerance to the effects of LSD develops within 5 days (1, 14), but it will disappear after a few days of abstinence. Tolerance has been found to develop to the mydriatic effects of LSD and, according to observers' estimates and subjects' reports, to its psychic effects (15). It appears that only a few users take LSD on a daily basis, since accounts of users being obliged to increase their intake as a consequence of growing tolerance are rare.

Morbidity and mortality

It is impossible to know if all of the untoward consequences attributed to the use of LSD were indeed caused by this drug and solely by it for other drugs have been misrepresented as LSD, and what is sold as pure LSD may, in fact, be a mixture of drugs, a mixture that will perhaps induce adverse reactions more readily than LSD itself. We do not know the total incidence of untoward reactions to LSD. We do know that psychotic episodes lasting for more than 48 hours occur in clinical situations, experimental or therapeutic, at rates ranging from 0.8 to 1.8/1000 administrations of LSD (16). What the incidence of such reactions may be when LSD is taken under "street" or "psychedelic" conditions is not known; an attempt to obtain this information by a physician-questionnaire survey provided, for a variety of reasons, information that was substantially incomplete and unsatisfactory (1). The size of the lethal dose of LSD for human beings is not known. Though it has been possible to determine the lethal dose of LSD for certain animals, to the best of our knowledge no well-documented reports of human deaths attributable directly to the action of LSD exist.

ACUTE ADVERSE REACTIONS   This designation applies to untoward responses to LSD that last no more than a few days after the occasion of drug use.

1. Non-psychotic reactions. Users of LSD often refer to this type of reaction as a "bad trip" or a "bummer." In contrast to the enjoyable LSD experience in which the user relishes the perceptual aberrations, knows they are drug-induced, and does not feel threatened by them, a bad trip is commonly said to begin in the following fashion: "After taking the drug one can feel it has 'gotten away' from him; that he no longer has control of the psychologic effects he is experiencing. He wants to be taken out of this state immediately" (4). Such fear may arise from the illusion of spiders crawling over one's body or of being on the verge of falling into a black and bottomless chasm or of one's hand being purple and believing that it will always be so, and so on. The most common non-psychotic reaction to a bad trip is a state of acute panic, often accompanied by a fear of imminent insanity. Confusion or psychic depression are possible alternative components of the reaction. Precipitate flight, such as jumping through a window or the heedless rush across a busy street, represents an attempt to escape the bad trip. An unknown proportion of the non-psychotic reactions apparently end as the drug effects subside; an equally unknown proportion persist up to a few days (16).

In many discussions of the etiology of bad trips, it is said (without supporting evidence) that those most susceptible to this type of LSD experience are the naive users, for, in their reaction to the drug's effects," "they have little if any basis for comparison in everyday reality" (9), and the users with pre-existing psychiatric problems. Large doses of LSD and certain drug mixtures, such as LSD and methamphetamine, have also been cited as factors that increase the risk of a bad trip (9). Certain beliefs are prevalent among experienced users of LSD regarding the prevention of bad trips, among them that one should be free of anger before taking LSD and that the total environment (lighting, music, seating arrangements, relationships to others present, and so on) should be propitious. Yet careful analyses of a number of bad trips (8) have failed to indicate the pre-eminence of any single causative factor, and, moreover, it has been concluded that "there is no single factor that guarantees immunity from an adverse LSD reaction" (8). Psychiatrists and psychologists have been unable, on observation and testing, to discover any significant and useful criteria by which experienced users of LSD who had had bad trips could be distinguished from similarly experienced users who had never had such trips. Though the novice user may be unusually susceptible to the experience of a bad trip, it was also learned that an individual may have a bummer after 100 or more occasions of LSD use without an adverse effect (8).

2. Toxic psychoses, including suicidal and homicidal behavior. The bad trip can also be characterized by a variety of psychotic reactions, some of which disappear by and large as the effects of LSD wear off. A threatening illusion may suddenly seem real (9) and not drug-induced; the vision or pseudohallucination of a good trip becomes an often frighteningly true hallucination.

The development of such delusional states as megalomania and paranoia has led to some of the most bizarre and dramatic episodes associated with the use of LSD. The user may believe himself to be Jesus Christ and designate relatives and friends as various biblical personages. Convinced that he is weightless or that he can fly, the user may jump out a window. Convinced that he is invincible, he may stab himself (6) or stand in the midst of a busy street attempting to halt traffic (16). Though the incidence of attempted and successful suicide among users of LSD is not known, the available evidence suggests that it is "an important complication of LSD administration" (16). Suicidal behavior associated with the use of LSD may stem from several causes. Purposeful suicidal behavior can be attributed to psychic states, such as depression, that are present in patients receiving LSD for therapeutic purposes, though it cannot always be determined whether the psychic disturbance responsible for the suicidal impulse antedated exposure to LSD or was caused by it (16). When behavior that is potentially or effectively suicidal occurs in delusional states induced by LSD, it is often spoken of as "accidental," suggesting temporary insanity or the absence of a purposive attempt at suicide; it cannot be known, of course, whether the latter is indeed the case.

Bad trips may be characterized by the development of acute paranoid states that are "transient episodes not extending beyond the period of LSD activity" (12). Suspicions that others may be plotting against the user are common manifestations of this state. Physical assaults upon others have occurred, including attempted homicide (12, 16), but they appear to be relatively rare events. The number of murders known to have been committed by individuals under the influence of LSD is very small (16, 17); the accused in these cases have been variously found by juries to have been sane or insane at the time of the crime.

3. Convulsions. Seven instances of grand mal seizures presumably caused by LSD have been reported; one of the afflicted individuals was an epileptic who developed status epilepticus when the drug was administered (12). Six of the seven convulsive episodes occurred in therapeutic settings, and five of them figured in a single report on a series of 150 patients (12). These findings are somewhat mystifying. Nowhere else in the many reports on the effects of LSD, whether used illicitly or under medical supervision, have we encountered descriptions of convulsions. Considering that the report described above entailed medical usage of LSD, it seems most improbable that the convulsions could be ascribed to the action of some contaminant. Convulsions appear to be a rare and possibly toxic effect of LSD.

PERSISTENT ADVERSE REACTIONS This designation applies to untoward responses attributed to LSD that last from weeks to years after a single occasion of use or after repeated use of the drug.

1. Prolonged psychotic reactions. A variety of persistent psychotic reactions has been attributed to the use of LSD. With or without therapeutic intervention, the duration of these reactions ranges from approximately 1 week to several years. Obviously, no clear distinction can be

made between the psychotic reactions designated as acute and the shortest of the prolonged reactions.

In a few instances, the psychic effects produced by a single dose of LSD have persisted long after (3 weeks, for example) the probable period of the drug's action. Such reactions have been called "persistent hallucinosis" (12).

Schizophrenic reactions seem to be the most commonly encountered persistent psychotic response; a state resembling paranoid schizophrenia has been described most often. Disorders resembling the catatonic and schizoaffective forms of this disease have also been observed. Other psychotic disorders, such as depression, paranoia, "a confused or manic psychosis," and a "motor-excitatory" state, have been reported to be produced by LSD (12, 16).

Some of the prolonged psychotic reactions are self-limiting, but the majority require, in addition to hospitalization, the standard modes of treatment for each type of disorder. On occasion, a disorder has appeared to subside only to recur a few weeks later (16).

In any consideration of why certain LSD users develop prolonged psychotic reactions, the view is often advanced that they were unusually vulnerable to the drug's effects because of a pre-existing psychiatric disturbance. It has become a general, almost reflex explanation for any adverse psychic effect that is apparently drug-induced and that persists long after the drug has ceased to act. In our previous discussion of this type of situation in Chapter 2, we noted that retrospective studies have indicated that it is often difficult to distinguish those who develop prolonged psychotic reactions from those who do not on the basis of prior psychiatric history. In their review of untoward reactions to LSD, Smart and Bateman (16) concluded that "LSD is precipitating prolonged psychoses in many persons who cannot be diagnosed as psychotic, or who have only minor personality disturbances or none at all."

Because seriously disturbed individuals do resort to drug abuse, it has been possible to establish the existence of previous psychiatric diagnoses in some of the users who experience prolonged psychotic reactions. An intriguing corollary remains unanswered, however, namely, "how many psychotics can take LSD without a prolonged psychotic episode" (16). Evaluation of other possible etiological factors has indicated that prolonged psychotic reactions are not necessarily the result of repeated "insults" to the psyche (i.e., LSD experiences) but that, according to various surveys, 30 to 50% of the prolonged psychoses occur on the first occasion of use (16). The role of dosage, particularly on occasions of illicit use, is difficult to assess. In therapeutic settings, however, where drug purity and dosage have been known, the findings tend to suggest that prolonged psychotic episodes can follow administration of doses (0.5 to 2.0 $\mu g/kg$) that have come to be regarded as standard.

Though various factors—unfamiliarity with the effects of LSD, a history of psychopathology, high doses, and drug mixtures—have appeared to play causative roles in the development of individual episodes of prolonged psychotic responses to LSD, their lack of influence on other similar occasions of use has also been noted. In sum, we must again confess our inability to explain the etiology of a certain reaction to a drug.

2. Permanent brain damage. Speculations about the possibility that prolonged use of LSD may result in organic brain damage appear in the literature from time to time. Such indirect evidence as EEG changes, in occasional cases, has been offered in support of this view, but we are unaware of any direct evidence having been reported (9, 12).

3. Spontaneous recurrences of the LSD experience (flashbacks, flashes, splashers). Non-psychotic and, rarely, psychotic components of the LSD experience recur spontaneously in some individuals for as long as a year or more after the last use of LSD. The onset of these incidents may also be triggered by stress, fatigue, or the use of such other drugs as marihuana or a barbiturate (18). The duration of the flashbacks is difficult to ascertain, and their frequency is subject to wide individual variation; individuals experiencing as many as five to ten flashbacks a day have been described. Flashbacks appear to occur most frequently in individuals with a history of repeated use of LSD (16).

Visual images (sometimes frightening) are the commonest form of flashback, but recurrences may also involve "any sensory modality: taste, smell, touch, kinesthetics, vestibular changes and auditory images. In addition, distortions of time sense, self-image or reality sense may occur" (18). Brief episodes of catatonia and visual hallucinations have also been reported to occur more than a year after taking LSD (16). The flashbacks usually recreate experiences initially undergone during the period of LSD intoxication. Less typically, new images or other perceptual aberrations occur.

Some psychiatrists feel that flashbacks should be classified as an adverse reaction to LSD only if they trouble the user (1). For some users, flashbacks are welcome and enjoyable recreations of the LSD experience. For others, the flashback is both frightening in content and a sign of impending insanity; in these individuals, flashbacks have produced anxiety reactions, occasionally psychotic states (18), and possibly suicidal behavior.

Flashbacks may occur after the use of any major hallucinogen, including marihuana (18); they are clearly a potential consequence of hallucinogenic drug abuse and do not occur with other drugs. The etiology of these episodes remains unknown. Some believe that they can be treated by means of psychotherapy (18); no other form of treatment has proved to be effective.

4. Changes in patterns of thought and behavior (the "psychedelic" and "amotivational syndromes"). Some psychiatrists believe that permanent changes in patterns of thought and behavior develop from repeated use of LSD. Several reports have emphasized the occurrence in chronic LSD users of what Smith has called the "psychedelic" syndrome (19, 20), which is said to have two principal characteristics. The first is "a profound belief in non-violence" and a "rejection of physical aggression" so profound that vegetarianism often becomes necessary because of the association of dietary meat with killing (20). The second is a belief in magic and an intense interest in mysticism, mental telepathy, astrology, extrasensory perception, and telekinesia. Blacker *et al.* have speculated that "these beliefs may arise as learned consequences of frequent intense LSD experiences in susceptible individuals" (19). They wonder if the almost child-like personality structure does not stem in part from repeated exposure to the garishly distorted emotional experiences one can have under the influence of LSD. Hate or anger is "magnified into nightmarish proportions and experienced in an altered state of consciousness in which one is part of a world of blackness populated by horrible, primitive, cannibalistic creatures. One's anger would be turned into images of demons who attack and destroy their creator" (19). Conversely, the emotion of love may provoke images in which "tender scenes from childhood or religious themes" figure. More ecstatically, the user may perceive himself "as an inseparable part of a universe of love, 'a bag of love'" (19). Just as these experiences might condition the user to fear the consequences of anger, the "frequent subjective experience [while under the influence of LSD] of controlling the external world with one's thoughts" (19) would increase the user's belief in magic.

The "amotivational syndrome" has been described as a possible consequence of the chronic use of LSD or marihuana (see p. 212). It has been briefly characterized as consisting of "apathy, loss of effectiveness, poor frustration tolerance, non-involvement in long-term plans, etc." (1). Those reporting the existence of this syndrome make no attempt to distinguish between pre-existing personality traits and the effect of drug use.

As individuals come readily to mind who do not use drugs but who display some of the signs of one or both of these syndromes, we share the anticipated skepticism of many of our readers regarding the role of LSD in the origin of these states. In all fairness to those who describe these syndromes, it should be noted that no cause-and-effect relationship has been postulated, no claim made that chronic LSD usage inevitably produces them or that they cannot be exhibited by non-users. It is our understanding that these syndromes are, in reality, somewhat formalized statements of "clinical impressions" formulated from extensive experience with many chronic users of hallucinogens.

Our tentative conclusion is that these syndromes are possible, though not inevitable, consequences of repeated use of LSD and that their pharmacological significance is therefore unknown. Their social significance, however, may be great. Smith has conjectured that those who exhibit the "psychedelic syndrome" are not merely going through a phase to be expected in the ordinary process of psychic maturation but rather that they "will not easily be able to reenter the dominant American culture, because of a profound conflict in value systems. A person with the 'psychedelic syndrome,' committed to non-violence, will have great conflict in a society like ours where the ethic is violence and competition" (20).

Cohen regards chronic anxiety reactions, in which anxiety is accompanied by "depression, somatic symptoms and difficulty in functioning," as possibly the most common of the prolonged nonpsychotic reactions to LSD (12). Cohen also lists as possible components of this type of reaction some of the adverse effects that we have described above such as the persistence of LSD-like perceptual disturbances for weeks or months. Throughout this period, contact with and the ability to test reality remain essentially unimpaired.

Has substantive evidence been obtained in support of claims that the LSD experience enhances creativity, self-insight, and intellectual ability? Presumably objective observers have not been able to substantiate such claims (1), though Blacker *et al.* concluded that "acidheads" do "modulate and organize sensory input" in a fashion different from non-users (19). How this altered ability might change the lives of chronic users is not known.

CYTOGENETIC EFFECTS   In their review in 1968 of the effects of LSD on chromosomes, Smart and Bateman concluded that "it is difficult to reach a clear decision about the chromosomal damage caused by LSD" (21). By 1973, skepticism prevailed about the possibility of LSD-induced chromosomal damage.

Both *in vitro* and *in vivo* studies have been made of cells (commonly lymphocytes from peripheral venous blood) exposed to LSD. In some of these studies, a statistically significant increase in the incidence of cells exhibiting chromosomal damage (gaps and 1- and 2-break aberrations) has been found following exposure to LSD, and, in some of them, no such increase has been observed. Considerable dispute has arisen about the experimental designs and the interpretations of results in virtually all of these studies. We have experienced misgivings ourselves about the scientific validity of the bulk of the findings, regardless of their tenor, for reasons we will mention shortly. Indeed, we have elected not to discuss the results of the *in vitro* studies because of the great doubt in our minds about the applicability of these findings to the *in vivo* situation.

Attempting to evaluate the *in vivo* investigations of human beings, one is disconcerted at the outset to learn that no general agreement exists among investigators as to the accepted basal rate of chromosomal abnormalities to be anticipated in control subjects (21). Moreover, the fact that only lymphocytes from peripheral venous blood have been examined for chromosomal abnormalities is troubling. How representative are these cells of the susceptibility of body cells, in general, and of gametocytes, in particular, to the effects of LSD, and how indicative are changes in these cells of the teratogenic potential of LSD? Of what significance is the common finding that an LSD user has been exposed to a variety of drugs? In regard to the last question, Corey *et al.* (22) have observed that significant increases in the frequency of chromosomal breakage have almost always been made in subjects who used LSD under nonclinical conditions [though this, however, is not invariably the case (21)], whereas failures to find similar increases have occurred when the subjects had taken LSD under medical supervision, though again this is not invariably true.

The implications of this observation are several in number. Is dosage an important causative factor? Do users of illicit LSD take greater than therapeutic doses? Sometimes they do, but no relationship can be observed *in vivo* between the probable or known doses of LSD taken and the presence or absence of abnormally large numbers of broken chromosomes. Can the higher rates of chromosomal breakage encountered among users of illicit LSD be attributed to some impurity in their LSD or to the other drugs they may have taken? This seems to be a most pertinent question, but the literature on other drugs likely to be employed by LSD users, such as marihuana and amphetamine, contains no substantive information about their effects on chromosomes (21).

Great individual variability has been postulated to exist in regard to susceptibility to chromosomal breakage regardless of cause. Quite small numbers of subjects have been commonly recruited for the LSD studies (two to eight persons per group being a typical range), and variability has been prominently evident in the *in vivo* findings. The average percentage of cells with chromosomal abnormalities has ranged in "control" groups from 0 to 9.4% and, among those exposed to LSD, from 0.76 to 23.6%. Whether the differing average values for control groups should be attributed to biological variation or to differences in the selection of control subjects and in experimental designs from one study to another is an unresolved and much debated issue.

In sum, one can readily demonstrate that LSD causes chromosomal breakage under *in vitro* conditions but at concentrations so high as to cause doubt about the frequency with which equivalent concentrations are achieved in users of LSD. The *in vivo* studies have been confined to lymphocytes of human peripheral venous blood, and the significance of information obtained from studies of these cells is almost wholly unknown. Enhanced rates of chromosomal breakage have been detected in some, though not all, users of illicit LSD but rarely in individuals who have taken the drug under clinical conditions. Chromosomal gaps as well as 1- and 2-break aberrations have been observed (22). Abnormally high breakage rates have been detected as long as 12 months after the last reported occasion of LSD usage (21). As Corey *et al.* have noted: "the frequency of aberrations appears to have no relation to the dose or to the time elapsed between exposure and testing" (22).

FERTILITY, PREGNANCY, AND DEVELOPMENTAL DEFECTS Once the specter of chromosomal damage had been raised, investigators naturally initiated studies of the teratogenic effects of LSD. When LSD was given to laboratory rodents early in the course of pregnancy, an increased incidence of abortions, stillbirths, and malformed offspring was observed in some studies but not in others (21). For various reasons, there is little substantive evidence about possible teratogenic effects of LSD in human beings.

It is the "clinical impression" of some who see drug users professionally that pregnancy is *relatively* infrequent among LSD users, even though, as a group, they are typically young and often promiscuous. In one study of 100 users, only one had had a child, and only one other was pregnant (21). In addition, there is evidence to suggest that the incidence of spontaneous abortions may be unusually high among LSD users (23). If these tentative findings are subsequently supported by convincing evidence, the means by which LSD may adversely affect fertility and the viability of the conceptus will have to be investigated. Other factors, however, will also have to be evaluated: the contraceptive practices of LSD users, the frequency of legal and illegal non-spontaneous abortions in this group, and the probable fact that for a variety of reasons (malnutrition, infectious disease, multiple drug abuse, and so on) LSD users represent a high-risk obstetrical population.

The current published evidence concerning a causal relationship between the use of LSD by human beings and the subsequent birth of offspring with congenital abnormalities, including enhanced chromosomal breakage (21, 23), is generally unconvincing. No statistically significant increase in the incidence of congential abnormalities has been demonstrated to date, and the abnormalities that have been described (23) are the types one would expect to encounter routinely in obstetrical practice. One study, however, casts doubt on these conclusions.

This is the study of Berlin and Jacobson (24), which raises moderate suspicions about the teratogenic potency of LSD. These investigators observed 127 pregnancies in a group of 112 women; in each case, one and often both of the parents had taken LSD before or after conception on occasions ranging from a few to several hundred times, but variable abuse of other drugs occurred as well.

Live births occurred at term in sixty-two of the pregnancies; six infants had congenital abnormalities, and one died in the neonatal period. The remaining sixty-five pregnancies were terminated by abortion. Spontaneous abortion occurred in seven pregnancies, with abnormal fetuses in four of the cases. Many of the remaining abortions were therapeutic, commonly for psychiatric reasons; fourteen of the fetuses obtained at these abortions were examined, and four were found to be abnormal. The rate of central nervous system defects in this total group of fetuses and infants was about sixteen times greater than that in the general population.

Berlin and Jacobson had an opportunity to observe more than one pregnancy in six of the women. In these cases, the first pregnancy terminated in a normal term delivery, but abnormal fetuses were produced in four of eight subsequent pregnancies.

MORTALITY It has been possible to determine lethal doses of LSD for various animals (16). In general, they are inversely related to body size, ranging from 46 mg/kg for mice to 0.1 mg/kg for an elephant (the latter being, understandably, a single observation). Death results from respiratory failure, which in the rabbit is preceded by marked hyperthermia.

To date, LSD has not been causally related to any deaths in man, even though single doses said to be 2000 μg (and possibly more) have been employed. Louria has reported the deaths of two young men who allegedly took LSD and died shortly thereafter (11, p. 154). Since toxicological analyses failed to indicate the presence of other lethal compounds in their tissues, these two victims were said to have died from an overdose of LSD. Because no one knows what compound or compounds these men took (if indeed the deaths were drug related), the attribution of death to LSD is here little more than a suspicion.

Based on the ratios of effective to lethal doses of other drugs in animals and man, it has been *estimated* that the average lethal dose of LSD for human beings should be 200 μg/kg (16) or a dose of 14,000 μg for a 70-kg individual. This calculation also presupposes that the dose will be taken intravenously. The absence of deaths attributable to the effects of LSD may possibly reflect the fortunate circumstances that, for man, the lethal dose is considerably in excess of the effective "psychedelic" dose, and the prevalent route of administration is the oral one.

PHENCYCLIDINE

Phencyclidine (PCP, angel dust, peace pill) was synthesized in the 1950's as part of a search for general anesthetic agents with novel mechanisms of action. Marketed as Sernyl, PCP had only a brief therapeutic life. Although physicians were intrigued by the drug's effects (analgesia, apparent consciousness, nystagmus, but with muscular rigidity in place of relaxation), the postoperative effects of PCP were highly unpleasant for some patients. The mildest complaints were of graphic nightmares; some patients became delirious when the effects of PCP began to subside. By the early 1960's, Sernyl had been removed from sale, although a veterinary preparation, Sernylan, still is marketed.

PCP was first offered for illicit sale in California in the mid-1960's, but only as pills designed to be swallowed (31). The numerous reports of psychotic symptoms caused a decline in popularity of PCP. The drug reappeared in the early 1970's as a powder designed to be snorted or smoked; this time it sold well and it continues to do so. It was sold under a variety of names; only recently have we become aware that all of these names refer to one drug, PCP. It is sometimes offered for sale as LSD or THC.

The synthesis of PCP was readily mastered by amateur chemists and the inexpensive starting materials were available to anyone at general chemical supply companies. As the earliest "recipe" for PCP called for the use of flammable solvents, some of its makers were severely burnt or killed during the synthetic process; the current process is safer because it has been changed to obviate the need for the dangerous solvents (31). Supplies of PCP for users has not been a problem as amateur chemists have been able to meet the demand for this weak base.

Patterns of use

Doses of PCP of 5 mg or less are typically smoked or snorted today. Such a procedure produces the following effects in people: a sense of intoxication, slurred speech, nystagmus, a rolling gait, and feelings of numbness in the hands and feet. Muscular rigidity, sweating, apathy, and a blank stare may develop. Users report feelings of depersonalization and disordered thoughts. Drowsiness may develop as well as amnesia for the period of the drug's action. The period of PCP's effects is usually from 4 to 6 hours.

With doses in excess of 5 mg, a more pronounced analgesia is experienced. Hostile or unusual behavior, which occurs sometimes with lower doses, is more apt to be observed with the higher ones. Blood pressure is likely to be increased along with heart rate. Increased salivation may become evident, as may fever, repetitive movements, muscular rigidity, and excessive sweating.

Animals, such as monkeys, will voluntarily administer PCP to themselves, but the same is not true of LSD. PCP clearly has multiple effects on the human and animal CNS, but the underlying mechanism of its action remains unknown.

PCP is easily absorbed via all of its common routes of administration. Hydroxylated metabolites of the drug appear in the urine in the form of glucuronides; it has not yet been determined if these metabolites have any pharmacological activity. Only a small portion of PCP appears unchanged in the urine.

The half-life of the drug in the body is ordinarily around three days (31); this value can be reduced to one day if the urine is markedly acidic and continuous gastric suction is employed. The need for urinary acidification is a reflection of the fact that PCP is a weak base (see page 000) and the need for gastric suction stems from the fact that considerable amounts of PCP are secreted in the gastric juices; these two facts are relied upon heavily in the management of overdoses of PCP.

Tolerance and physical dependence

Animals exhibit tolerance to the behavioral and toxic effects of PCP. There are clinical reports that may be interpreted as indicating that people also become tolerant to the drug's effects. There are no evident withdrawal syndromes in monkeys; the situation with respect to people is less clear. Repeated users of large doses report difficulties with speech, thinking, and recent memory that persist up to one year after cessation of drug usage. There may be withdrawal from others and isolation as well as states of nervousness, anxiety, and deep psychic depression (14, 31).

PCP Toxicity; overdoses

Toxic states are characterized by problems of hostility toward others; confusional periods, accidents, and death have been attributed to overdoses, but the incidence of such effects is unknown. If coma, convulsions, or psychotic states develop, toxicity is commonly said to be severe.

Management of patients suffering from overdoses is symptomatic, but directed also toward hastening urinary excretion of the drug and its metabolites; the use of continuous gastric suction, maintaining vital functions and protecting the patient and others from the consequences of faulty judgment and hostile behavior are necessary. Two techniques are used to speed elimination of the drug from the body: acidification of the urine and continuous gastric suction. Ammonium chloride may be necessary to get urinary pH below 5.0, but on occasion, administration of cranberry juice is all that is needed. The gastric suction is needed because, as noted, significant quantities of PCP are secreted into the stomach. Suction and urinary acidification typically reduce the half-life of the drug from three days to one day (14, 31).

PCP toxicity is frequently characterized by difficult behavioral problems for which talking down is rarely a successful remedy. If drug treatment is attempted, haloperidol is preferred by many clinicians; phenothiazine are believed to augment the atropine-like actions of PCP. Additionally, such patients may require pulmonary ventilatory support of depressed respiration, treatment of fever by external means, and management of excessive salivation by suction. Convulsions may require diazepam and hypertension hydralazine.

The psychotic phase of PCP toxicity may last for several weeks after a single episode of drug usage. The psychotic state may follow or be preceded by coma and be characterized by delirium and paranoid ideation. It has been found helpful to seclude these patients from external stimuli as much as possible (14, 31).

PEYOTE AND MESCALINE

In the context of drug abuse, peyote is the commonest name given to plant preparations obtained from the mescal cactus (*Lophophora williamsii*). The dome-shaped head of this grayish-green, spineless plant is made up of one or more disks (buttons), which have the potential for flowering and contain the principal peyote hallucinogen, mescaline.

Peyote was used by the Aztecs and other Mexican Indian tribes in religious ceremonies for unnumbered centuries before the arrival of the Spaniards. Late 19th-century raids into Mexico by Indian tribes from our Great Plains area, notably the Kiowa and Comanche, resulted in the establishment of "peyote cults" in this country. The use of peyote in Indian religious ceremonies spread rapidly to our Southwest and northward even to tribes across the Canadian border. Adherents to a new faith, whose teachings and ceremonies reflect both pagan and Christian origins, formed the Native American Church in 1918. It now claims 250,000 members, each of whom may, according to recent court rulings, use peyote legally for religious purposes.

Peyote or mescal buttons are brown and hard and are only rarely available in powdered form. They are usually softened by the user's saliva before being swallowed. The buttons contain, in addition to mescaline, fifteen β-phenylethylamine and isoquinoline alkaloids. It is thought that all of these compounds are pharmacologically active, which accounts for the common finding that the effects of peyote and mescaline are not identical.

The effects of peyote are slow to develop and, initially, unpleasant. Nausea is common but rarely results in vomiting. Profuse perspiration and static tremors are also among the early effects. The initial phase, lasting 1 to 2 hours, is succeeded by the "hallucinogenic" experience in which visual hallucinations are prominent (brightly colored lights, vivid kaleidoscopic visions of geometrical forms and, sometimes, of animals and people), color and space perception may be disturbed, synesthesias are experienced, and, more rarely, auditory and tactile "hallucinations" occur (1, 25, p. 195). As with LSD, the user ordinarily retains insight, and the sensorium is otherwise undisturbed. After this phase of the peyote experience, for which mescaline appears primarily responsible, the user often falls into a deep sleep. The total experience is said to last for about 12 hours.

Mescaline was isolated from peyote buttons in 1896, and its structure was determined in 1918. Its chemical resemblance to drugs like amphetamine and DOM (Fig. 1) and to the naturally occurring adrenergic transmitter substances, epinephrine and norepinephrine, has provoked much speculation, but its significance remains unknown. This is particularly so in regard to the etiology of spontaneous psychotic disorders, where structural similarities such as these have been frequent topics of discussion and investigation.

Mescaline is usually taken by mouth in a dose of from 300 to 500 mg, indicating that it is roughly one-thousand times less potent than LSD. Occasionally it is injected. The drug offered on the illegal market is obtained either from peyote buttons or, perhaps more frequently, from the "basement" chemist. It offers the user an opportunity to achieve the "hallucinogenic" state without undergoing all of the preliminary effects of peyote, most notably the intense nausea, and to achieve it more rapidly. Because mescaline is an adrenergic (or sympathomimetic) hallucinogen, however, some of its initial effects are typical of this type of drug and are manifested whether peyote or mescaline are taken. These effects include perspiration, tremors, a sense of anxiety, and hyperreflexia. The "hallucinatory" effects of peyote and mescaline are reported not to differ markedly and, indeed, to resemble greatly the psychic effects of LSD. Those who regarded "psychedelic" experiences as potentially valuable relied primarily on peyote and mescaline before the advent of LSD. The duration of mescaline's effects, like that of peyote, is approximately 12 hours.

No physical dependence on the effects of mescaline develops regardless of the schedule of usage. Tolerance to mescaline develops, but evidence regarding its nature and magnitude is scarce; as with LSD, this drug is rarely taken on so regular a schedule as to afford an optimal opportunity for tolerance to develop. When tolerance to mescaline does develop, cross-tolerance to LSD can be demonstrated.

It might seem that reports should exist about psychotic episodes and "flash-backs" provoked by the use of mescaline, but they are not seen in the secondary literature (1, 26). Instances of extreme anxiety in schizophrenic patients who have received mescaline, however, have been reported.

At present, the demand for peyote and mescaline among drug users appears to be small. Most users of hallucinogens prefer LSD, and, as we noted earlier in this chapter, very often they receive LSD regardless of what the drug is called by the seller.

DOM (STP)

DOM is a synthetic, adrenergic hallucinogen that first came to public attention in 1967, when chemists of the FDA identified this compound as one of the active constituents of STP (26). The Synthesis of DOM was reported in the chemical literature in 1964, and it is likely that this report provided the necessary information for the "basement" chemists supplying the illegal drug trade. (Many of these chemists are known to have received postgraduate chemical training.) It is worth noting again that we now know that the original STP was, in fact, a variety of drug mixtures and that not all of them contained DOM (see Chapter 2, p. 35). Nonetheless, today STP is a common synonym for DOM.

DOM (2,5-dimethoxy-4-methyl amphetamine) bears a structural resemblance to both amphetamine and mescaline (Fig. 1). Pharmacologically, DOM, and such related compounds as DOET (2,5-dimethoxy-4-*ethyl* amphetamine), resemble amphetamine only in certain respects: they produce a sense of euphoria, and the user becomes more talkative. Unlike low doses of amphetamine, low doses of these compounds impair rather than improve the ability to concentrate, rarely cause anorexia, and provide a mild "psychedelic experience" (28). Larger doses create effects reminiscent of mescaline and, certainly, LSD.

The minimal dose of DOM that is unmistakably hallucinogenic is 5 mg for a 70-kg subject (26), which indicates that DOM is roughly fifty to one hundred times less potent than LSD. Doses of DOM of approximately 3 mg produce euphoria and "enhanced self-awareness" but only rarely preceptual distortions and "hallucinations" (27). The effects of DOM are perceptible about 1 hour after ingestion (the conventional route of administration), are maximal at 3 to 5 hours, and have largely subsided in 7 to 8 hours (26, 27). Only rarely do subjects report residual psychic effects the next day. At least 20% of the DOM administered can be found unchanged in the urine; the maximal rate of urinary excretion was found to correspond in time with the peak of the psychic effects (26).

The physiological changes produced by DOM are largely characteristic of adrenergic hallucinogens: heart rate is increased (15 to 25 beats/minute), systolic blood pressure is elevated (about 15 to 30 mm of Hg), diastolic pressure is unchanged, pupillary diameter is increased (about 15%), and body temperature rises slightly (about 1°F). Other somatic changes that may occur include paresthesias, nausea, tremors, and perspiration (26). The limited data available indicate that the intensity of these changes is a function of dose. Like epinephrine, DOM increases plasma concentrations of free fatty acids; unlike epinephrine, it provokes no significant changes in plasma glucose levels (26).

The initial psychic effects of hallucinogenic doses of DOM resemble those described above for low doses of the drug; in addition, some users may experience vivid visual imagery upon closing their eyes. As the drug effect intensifies, multiple images may be seen, objects seem to vibrate and to have distorted shapes, visual details stand out more clearly, and contrasts are enhanced. The passage of time seems to slow, the mind can be overrun with a "thousand thoughts" or occasionally be "blank," expression of thoughts can be difficult, and the user is easily distracted. Images are now seen with the eyes open. The predominant emotional tone of the experience is usually a happy one. The user retains insight throughout the experience and is able to clearly recall it later (26).

True hallucinations, paranoid ideation, anxiety, and panic reactions seem rare, even with doses of DOM as high as 14 mg (26). Only limited evidence is available, however, about the effects of pure DOM, and, judging from the experiences of users with other hallucinogens, we cannot rule out the possibility that the use of DOM may result in "bad trips" and psychotic episodes.

When DOM is taken in conjunction with chlorpromazine (200 mg by mouth), the psychedelic experience is less intense, and the user is likely to become drowsy (26). The psychic and physiological status of users of the original STP was often considerably worsened following administration of chlorpromazine (1). The combination of DOM and an atropine-like drug (probably one of the drug mixtures sold as the original STP) can produce a hallucinogenic experience lasting as long as 5 days, depending on the doses of the drugs involved.

Physical dependence probably does not develop upon repeated use of DOM, though rigorous evidence on this point is not available. Nor is much known about the development of tolerance to the effects of DOM. We would guess that, considering its chemical structure and pharmacological similarities with other hallucinogens, tolerance to at least some its effects would develop upon regular usage.

It is difficult to estimate how much DOM is being taken today. Users may buy "DOM" or "STP" and receive in fact some other drug. On the other hand, users may receive DOM instead of the drug they think they are buying or as part of a drug mixture whose composition is unknown to them.

PSILOCYBIN

Some Mexican Indians have long regarded certain mushrooms with hallucinogenic properties as sacred; naming them *teonanacatl* (flesh of the gods), the Indians reserved their use primarily for religious ceremonies. The mushrooms used were probably specimens of the genera *Conocybe, Stropharia,* and *Psilocybe* (28).

In 1958, Hofmann, a Swiss chemist, isolated from *Psilocybe mexicana* two compounds: psilocybin (O-phosphoryl-4-hydroxy-N-dimethyltryptamine, Fig. 1) and its dephosphorylated congener, psilocin. Psilocybin is the only naturally occurring hallucinogen identified thus far that contains phosphorus. Its structural resemblance to a compound of possible importance in central nervous system function, serotonin (5-hydroxytryptamine), has aroused speculation about the role of hydroxylated tryptamines in the etiology of spontaneous mental disease.

Psilocybin is commonly taken by mouth, and it is one of the most rapidly acting hallucinogens by this route of administration, with the first perceptible effects 10 to 15 minutes after ingestion of doses of 4 to 8 mg. Reactions often reach maximal intensity at about 90 minutes and do not begin to subside until 2 to 3 hours later. The effects of psilocybin usually last 5 to 6 hours in all, but doses larger than 8 mg probably prolong their duration (29).

Isbell has provided one of the most complete descriptions of the effects of psilocybin in man (29). Physiologically, psilocybin causes those changes we now regard as typical of an adrenergic hallucinogen: pulse rate, respiratory rate, and body temperature are all increased, the pupils are dilated, and systolic, though not diastolic, blood pressure is elevated. Evidence of central excitation was obtained in Isbell's study by measuring the threshold for elicitation of the patellar reflex, which was found to decrease. As with LSD, mescaline, and DOM, the absolute magnitudes of these changes are not large; when expressed as a function of the total amount of change induced by the entire psilocybin experience of some 5 to 6 hours, however, the changes are statistically significant (29).

The psychic (and physiological) reactions to psilocybin led Isbell to conclude that "LSD-25 and psilocybin are remarkably similar" (29), though, on a weight basis, LSD is one-hundred to one-hundred and fifty times more potent. The earliest subjective changes noted by subjects receiving psilocybin were that objects began to look, feel, or seem peculiar and that they experienced mild anxiety; 30 minutes after the compound had been taken, anxiety was more pronounced, being manifested as dysphoria or specifically formulated fears of impending insanity or death. Changes in mood occurred now also (commonly in the direction of elation), and, in a seeming paradox, some subjects reported the coexistence of feelings of anxiety and elation. Hearing was said to be keener, but vision was blurred. Perception of sensory stimuli was altered, and, as is typical of hallucinogens, visual distortions were most prominent. Feelings of depersonalization were common. The whole body might seem changed in size (being very large or as small as that of a child, for example) or hands and feet might not seem to be part of the body or they might take on the shape of paws; some subjects could "see" the bones and blood within a body. Remarks about difficulties in thinking and concentrating, and of being troubled by rapid, tumultuous passages of thoughts, were made frequently. Seven of Isbell's nine subjects retained insight throughout the psilocybin experience and remained oriented in regard to time, place, and person. For two of the subjects, however, the visual images gradually became true hallucinations, and, thereafter, they "felt that their experiences were caused by the experimenters controlling their minds" (29). Insight returned as the effects of psilocybin waned.

Physical dependence on the effects of psilocybin has not been reported; we would guess that it does not occur. Tolerance to psilocybin develops, and, when present, cross-tolerance to the effects of LSD and mescaline can be demonstrated (29).

As with mescaline and DOM, it is difficult to make even a rough guess as to how much psilocybin has been available to drug users. Some has been extracted from mushrooms for "street" sale, and, perhaps, some has been synthesized; it can be bought as a liquid or powder (1). As with other relatively exotic hallucinogens, the buyer of "psilocybin" may well receive some other drug or no drug at all (2). The notion of linking an hallucinogenic mushroom held sacred by ancient Indians with today's youthful drug users has taken feverish hold of many a journalistic mind, with the result that the availability and use of the "magic mushroom" has probably been greatly exaggerated.

DMT

DMT (N,N-dimethyltryptamine, Fig. 1) is representative, in its structure and pharmacological effects, of the many tryptamine derivatives that have been isolated from the "hallucinogenic snuffs" used by South American Indians (28). These snuffs are prepared from plants of the genera *Mimosa, Virola,* and *Piptadenia.* They are not active when taken orally, and one can only speculate about how the Indians discovered an effective route of administration, i.e., the dried plant material is prepared as a snuff to be inhaled or to be blown into the user's nostrils.

Aside from psilocybin, DMT and, rarely, DET (N,N-diethyltryptamine) are the only tryptamine derivatives that have been offered for sale on the illicit drug market, and then only sporadically. Compared with LSD, DMT has the principal shortcoming for the user of brevity of action; in the doses commonly available, its effects last for less than an hour and may persist for only 30 minutes (1).

DMT is either inhaled as a powder or smoked in tobacco, parsley, or marihuana soaked in a solution of DMT. Only rarely is it injected. With doses of 35 to 79 mg, the effects of DMT, both psychic and physiological, closely resemble those of LSD and other adrenergic hallucinogens (31). These effects develop quite rapidly and, as noted above, are relatively brief in duration. Some investigators feel that DMT more frequently induces disabling, though nonpsychotic, states of panic than does LSD (1). It may be that the rapid onset of DMT's effects allows the user too little time to adjust to the drug experience, and thereby a feeling of loss of control occurs more readily.

Physical dependence on the effects of DMT is not known to develop; it is not known if tolerance develops. Though DMT exhibits the properties of a typical adrenergic hallucinogen, individuals tolerant to LSD show little or no evidence of cross-tolerance to DMT (30); the apparent absence of cross-tolerance between these two compounds suggests the possibility that LSD and DMT exert their similar effects via different receptor sites.

REFERENCES

1. *Non-medical use of drugs, with particular reference to youth.* Report of the Special Committee on Drug Misuse, Council on Community Health Care, Canadian Medical Association. *Canad Med Assoc J* 101:804, 1969
2. Cheek, F. E., S. Newell, and M. Joffe, Deceptions in the illicit drug market. *Science* 167:1276, 1969
3. Pfeiffer, C. C. and H. B. Murphree, Introduction to psychotropic drugs and hallucinogenic drugs. In: DiPalma, J. A., ed., *Drill's Pharmacology in Medicine*, ed. 3. New York: McGraw-Hill, 1965, p. 321
4. Smith, D. E. and A. J. Rose, The use and abuse of LSD in Haight-Ashbury. *Clin Pediat* 7:317, 1968
5. Solursh, L. P. and W. R. Clement, Hallucinogenic drug abuse: Manifestations and management. *Canad Med Assoc J* 98:407, 1968
6. Ludwig, A. M. and J. Levine, Patterns of hallucinogenic drug abuse. *J Amer Med Assoc* 191:92, 1965
7. Ungerleider, J. T., D. D. Fisher, and M. Fuller, The dangers of LSD. *J Amer Med Assoc* 197:389, 1966
8. Ungerleider, J. T., D. D. Fisher, M. Fuller, and A. Caldwell, The "bad trip"—the etiology of the adverse LSD reaction. *Amer J Psychiat* 124: 1483, 1968
9. Smith, D. E., Use of LSD in the Haight-Ashbury. *Calif Med* 110:472, 1969
10. Forrer, G. R. and R. D. Goldner, Experimental physiological studies with lysergic acid diethylamide (LSD-25). *Arch Neurol Psychiat* 65:581, 1951
11. Louria, D. B., *The Drug Scene*. New York: McGraw-Hill, 1968
12. Cohen, S., A classification of LSD complications. *Psychosomatics* 7: 182, 1966
13. Aghajanian, G. K. and O. H. L. Bing, Persistence of lysergic acid die-

thylamide in the plasma of human subjects. *Clin Pharmacol Therap* 5: 611, 1964

14. Jaffe, J., Drug addiction and drug abuse. In: Gilman, A. G., L. Goodman and A. Gilman, eds., *The Pharmacological Basis of Therapeutics*, ed. 6. New York: Macmillan, 1980, p. 535

15. Rosenberg, D. E., A. B. Wolbach, Jr., E. J. Miner, and H. Isbell, Observations on direct and cross tolerance with LSD and D-amphetamine in man. *Psychopharmacol* 5:1, 1963

16. Smart, R. G. and K. Bateman, Unfavourable reactions to LSD: A review and analysis of the available case reports. *Canad Med Assoc J* 97:1214, 1967

17. Barter, J. T. and M. Reite, Crime and LSD: The insanity plea. *Amer J Psychiat* 126:531, 1969

18. Horowitz, M. J., Flashbacks: Recurrent intrusive images after the use of LSD. *Amer J Psychiat* 126:565, 1969

19. Blacker, K. H., R. T. Jones, G. C. Stone, and D. Pfefferbaum, Chronic users of LSD: The "acidheads." *Amer J Psychiat* 125:341, 1968

20. Medical Staff Conference, Changing drug patterns in the Haight-Ashbury. *Calif Med* 110:151, 1969

21. Smart, R. G. and K. Bateman, The chromosomal and teratogenic effects of lysergic acid diethylamide: A review of the current literature. *Canad Med Assoc J* 99:805, 1968

22. Corey, M. J., J. C. Andrews, M. J. McLeod, J. R. MacLean, and W. E. Wilby, Chrosomone studies on patients (*in vivo*) and cells (*in vitro*) with lysergic acid diethylamide. *New Engl J Med* 282:939, 1970

23. McGothlin, W. H., R. S. Sparkes, and D. O. Arnold, Effect of LSD on human pregnancy. *J. Amer Med Assoc* 212:1483, 1970

24. Berlin, C. M. and C. B. Jacobson, Psychedelic drugs—a threat to reproduction? *Fed Proc* 31:1326, 1972

25. Schultes, R. E., Hallucinogens of plant origin. *Science* 163:245, 1969

26. Snyder, S. H., L. Faillace, and L. Hollister, 2,5-Dimethoxy-4-methylamphetamine (STP): A new hallucinogenic drug. *Science* 158:669, 1967

27. Snyder, S. H., L. A. Faillace, and H. Weingartner, DOM (STP), a new hallucinogenic drug, and DOET: Effects in normal subjects. *Amer J Psychiat* 125:357, 1968

28. Farnsworth, N. R., Hallucinogenic plants. *Science* 162:1086, 1968

29. Isbell, H., Comparison of the reactions induced by psilocybin and LSD-25 in man. *Psychopharmacol* 1:29, 1959

30. Rosenberg, D. E., H. Isbell, E. J. Miner, and C. R. Logan, The effect of N,N-dimethyltryptamine in human subjects tolerant to lysergic acid diethylamide. *Psychopharmacol* 5:217, 1964

31. Petersen, R. C., and R. C. Stillman, eds., *PCP Phencyclidine Abuse: An Appraisal*. National Institute on Drug Abuse, Department of Health, Education, and Welfare Publication No. (ADM) 78-728, Washington: U.S. Government Printing Office, 1978

Chapter 7

HALLUCINOGENS: MARIHUANA, HASHISH, AND ATROPINIC DRUGS

The hemp plant (*Cannabis sativa*) grows freely in the temperate and tropical zones of the world. For more than 4 centuries, man has used this plant for numerous purposes. The most significant commercial use has been the conversion of its stalk fibers into rope, twine, and cord; hemp was, for instance, one of the important "cash crops" in colonial Kentucky, and, for more than one-hundred years thereafter, a few counties in this region met the needs of our armed forces for rope fiber. The plant's seeds have been fed to poultry and caged birds. The seeds, when crushed, yield an oil used in the manufacture of paint (to speed its drying) and soap, with the resultant solid residue being fed to cattle or used as fertilizer (1, Chapter 5).

Though physicians in the Middle and Far East have prescribed *Cannabis* preparations for various medicinal purposes for centuries, the interest of their Western colleagues was not widely aroused until the 1840's, when there ensued a moderate vogue (which lasted until roughly 1900) for the prescription of *Cannabis* extracts for a variety of indications: sedation and hypnosis, analgesia, uterine dysfunction, and such "spastic conditions" as tetanus (1, Chapter 9). These extracts continued to be listed in American pharmacopoeias in this century (though they seem not to have been prescribed frequently) until the "Marihuana Tax Act" of 1937 essentially prevented further prescription of them. Both here and abroad, physicians and literary figures (notably Baudelaire, Gautier, and

Dumas) published accounts of their personal experiences with various types of *Cannabis* preparations; these accounts were most common in the 19th century. Some of them are quite lengthy and carefully detailed (1, Chapter 6); they can be profitably read today by anyone wishing to learn about the subjective effects of *Cannabis* drugs.

The "intoxicating" (psychoactive) properties of certain portions of the hemp plant have similarily been known to mankind for centuries. The historically important routes of administration, ingestion of beverages or foods prepared with parts of the plant and inhalation of the fumes of burning hemp, remain the most prevalent routes today. Description of patterns of usage of what were probably *Cannabis* extracts, which we would designate today as "drug abuse," occur in historical accounts from some countries during the pre-Christian era; in addition, these extracts were used to enhance religious experiences in a variety of settings (group meetings, solitary meditation, and so on). The lack of historical evidence precludes any detailed description of when and by what means the concept of using *Cannabis* preparations for "recreational" purposes spread from Asia to other parts of the world and to the Western Hemisphere, in particular. The Spaniards probably initiated cultivation of the hemp plant in Chile as a source of fiber in 1545. Introduction of the "marihuana vice" to the Western Hemisphere, however, is frequently attributed to African slaves brought to Brazil in the 16th century; one commonly cited reason for this belief is the finding that identical words (*diamba* or *riamba*) are used for *Cannabis* preparations in both West Africa and Brazil (1, p. 24).

The "marihuana vice" was brought to the United States by emigrants from such countries as Mexico, Cuba, and Jamaica and by Americans who had visited these places as sailors or soldiers. Not surprisingly, the first accounts of marihuana usage as a problem worthy of public attention originated in the Gulf States and the states bordering Mexico. It is assumed that Texas was the first state into which marihuana was "smuggled," with Louisiana a close second (1, Chapter 3). Traffic in *Cannabis* preparations probably began during the first decade of this century; even rough estimates of its rate of growth thereafter cannot be made with confidence. Public alarm about marihuana usage was episodic during the 1920's, particularly in the aforementioned states. Newspapers reported the growing tally of the acres of hemp plant destroyed (not distinguishing usually between deliberately cultivated *Cannabis* and that growing wild) and also the views of some law enforcement officers that crime waves were "unquestionably . . . greatly aggravated" as a result of the marihuana habit (1, p. 31).

The recreational use of marihuana did occur during this period, of course, and it spread gradually to almost every state in the Union. The supply of alcoholic beverages in this era was prone to fluctuation, due to Prohibition, and the quality of what was offered for sale was typically problematical. It may have seemed to some users that marihuana was a more dependable and sometimes less expensive intoxicant than alcohol; in most urban areas, marihuana usage occurred in the same groups in which narcotic usage was prevalent, i.e., those in the lower socioeconomic strata, the "criminal element," jazz musicians, and other performers or artists (2, p. 13). The general public's attitude toward marihuana in the 1930's was not one of intense interest or alarm (2, p. 14); despite "exposés" of marihuana usage in the nation's schools, it seems that the average layman of this period regarded marihuana as a problem confined satisfactorily to small groups outside the mainstream of American society. The layman seems also to have accepted as fact the purported causal relationship between marihuana usage and the commission of crimes of violence (cf. Chapter 12, p. 298).

No satisfactorily comprehensive scientific study was made of the effects of marihuana during the 1930's, nor was an objective survey of the extent of marihuana usage in America undertaken. Nevertheless, by 1937, every state in the Union had banned marihuana, either by specific legislation or by inclusion of it in the state's Uniform Narcotic Drug Act, the latter being a model statute recommended by the National Conference on Uniform State Laws (2, p. 14). In 1937, Congress passed the Marihuana Tax Act, which, in effect, superimposed a federal ban on the prohibitions of the individual states. Because law enforcement officers of this period (local, state, and federal) almost uniformly regarded marihuana as a narcotic drug, the state and federal legislation closely resembled contemporary laws pertaining to narcotics.

The effort to portray marihuana as a truly dangerous drug, spearheaded by Commissioner Harry Anslinger of the Federal Bureau of Narcotics, did achieve great success in state and federal legislative halls and has probably been the main source of many of the still current public views about this substance; it did not, however, go unchallenged. A most notable dissent was registered in the report issued by the committee of physicians and public health officials appointed in 1939 by Mayor Fiorello LaGuardia of New York City; at his request, and under the auspices of the New York Academy of Medicine, the group evaluated the purported threat to public health and safety arising from marihuana usage. Information about the effects of marihuana in both "street" and laboratory settings was collected for study; particular attention was paid to the most pejorative view about marihuana then current, that marihuana smoking produces a state of supreme self-confidence and releases inhibitions against hostile impulses the result being the commission of such violent criminal acts as murder by the smoker. Virtually all of the evidence offered by Mr. Anslinger in support of this view was anecdotal. One of the gorier episodes, purportedly "culled at random" from the bureau's files, was that of a young man, one J.O., who claimed to have been under the influence of marihuana when he murdered a friend. The psychiatrist who later saw J.O., and had his past life investigated, reported in 1939 that no evidence of drug usage whatsoever had been discovered [J.O.'s story, nonetheless, reappeared in the April-June, 1966 issue of the U. N. *Bulletin on Narcotics* from an American source (3, pp. 414-416)]. Dealing, as they had to, with such dubious evidence, the LaGuardia Committee had little choice but to issue a verdict of "not proved" on this count (4). Though not denying that marihuana exerted perceptible effects, the committee's report was essentially exculpatory in regard to allegations about the profound pharmacological and behaviorial effects of marihuana. Unfortunately, the committee's report was not issued until 1944, a time when the public's receptivity to news other than that bearing on the progress of World War II and its impact on their lives was probably minimal.

The conclusions of the LaGuardia Committee, essentially that the effects of marihuana are not seriously harmful for most smokers, were an echo of two earlier studies, the *Indian Hemp Drugs Commission Report* of 1894 and the *Panama Canal Zone Military Investigations* of 1933. Subsequent studies echoed the findings of the LaGuardia Committee: the *Baroness Wootton Report* of 1968 in Great Britain, the *Interim Report of the Canadian Government's LeDain Commission* in 1970, and the report of the American *National Commission on Marihuana and Drug Abuse* in 1972 (2, 3, pp. 451-472). That a substantial segment of the public, in the face of such testimony, seemingly still believes that marihuana is actually the drug portrayed by Commissioner Anslinger strikes us as a triumph of lurid fiction over sober facts, however incomplete the latter may be at this time. Though another and more sophisticated segment of the public no longer accepts the concept of marihuana as an inciter to violence, it has nonetheless a new threat to worry about. Some psychiatrists have reported that marihuana usage leads young people to "drop out" from the mainstream of American society, exhibiting what has been called the "amotivational" syndrome. Later in this chapter, we will review the findings that have led to this conclusion.

THE MARIHUANA (HEMP) PLANT

The plant, *Cannabis sativa L.,* is a weedy annual that grows readily in the tropical and temperate zones of the world and can achieve a height of 15 (and occasionally 20) feet. Botanically, it is a close relative of the hops plant (5). The hemp plant is dioecious, i.e., both male and female forms exist. The male (staminate) plant is typically taller than the female, its flowers are borne in panicles, and it usually dies when its flowering cycle has been completed. The female (pistillate) plant is typically bushier than the male, its flowers are long catkins, and it secretes a clear, sticky resin, which covers the flowering tops and adjacent leaves. The function of the resin, it has been postulated, is to retard dehydration of the flowering elements; the hotter the climate in which the plant is grown, the greater the amount of resin usually secreted. Both forms of the plant have large leaves, palmately compound, each with five to seven linear-lanceolate leaflets, which, in turn, have serrated leaf margins. It is common in India and Brazil, for example, to regard the female plant as the only source of psychoactive compounds. Recent studies have indicated, however, that male and female plants have essentially equivalent psychoactive potency (6). The resin-covered flowering tops of the female plant and their adjacent leaves nonetheless remain the most typical components of marihuana.

Hemp has one of the longest histories of cultivation by man among all plants (5). During the past three to four thousand years, attempts have been made to identify and to cultivate "races" or "varieties" of the hemp plant for various purposes: to obtain stronger fibers, to enhance the plant's content of oil, or to increase its yield of psychoactive drugs. India is a notable example of a country in which people have for centuries cultivated varieties of the hemp plant for the specific purpose of obtaining maximal yields of psychoactive drugs.

The fact that the content of a psychoactive drug can vary widely from one "race" or variety of the plant to another must always receive consideration in any evaluation of the "marihuana problem." Exemplifying these differences were the results of a study in which hemp seeds obtained from various parts of the world were planted on a common site in Mississippi; after harvest, it was determined that the psychoactive drug content of the most "potent" plant (one of Mexican origin) was seventy times greater than that of the least potent plant (one of Swedish origin) (6). The actual difference obtaining in nature may be even larger; the Mississippi study, for example, did not include any of the plants from India that have been carefully selected and cultivated for maximal drug yields. Any crude drug preparation of plant origin that is derived from *Cannabis sativa* may be called marihuana; yet it is obvious from the foregoing that to refer to all such preparations as marihuana, with the implicit assumption that one is dealing with pharmacologically equivalent substances, could lead to confusion, and indeed it has. Experienced marihuana users would never make that mistake; they are usually able to distinguish good marihuana from bad. Marihuana of domestic origin, typically having a relatively low content of psychoactive compounds, is accordingly not prized highly; experienced users seek rather the typically more potent Mexican, Jamaican, and North African varieties. The nature of the marihuana experience, however, is not determined solely by the drug content of the mixture used; other contributory factors will be discussed later in this chapter.

Readers who consult the earlier literature on marihuana (i.e., that of 30 years ago or more) may be puzzled by references to another species of hemp plant, *Cannabis indica*. Botanists thought at one time that the hemp plant of India represented a distinct species of *Cannabis,* but they have subsequently decided that it is simply a variety of *Cannabis sativa*.

MARIHUANA AND HASHISH

The two types of *Cannabis* extracts used most frequently in the United States for their psychoactive effect are marihuana and hashish. Though the nature of these two extracts can be described in general terms, it will become evident that the names have only limited communicative value pharmacologically because the content of psychoactive drug can vary so widely from one sample of marihuana or hashish to another.

Of uncertain origin, *marihuana* may be simply a variant of the Spanish equivalent of Mary Jane (Marijuana), which was a Mexican slang word for any cheap tobacco, but which, by the end of the 19th century, referred to a *Cannabis* extract only (10, p. 5). The most potent marihuana contains just the dried flowering tops from a variety of hemp plant that is a naturally rich source of psychoactive drug; such an extract is called *ganja* in India and Jamaica (43). Marihuana may also be prepared from hemp plants containing varying amounts of psychoactive drug and may contain widely variable proportions of such other parts of the plant as leaves and stems; such preparations are called *kif* in North Africa, *dagga* in South Africa, *bhang* in India and the Middle East, and *macohna* in parts of South America (1, pp. 188-195).

Hashish, the Arabic word for "dry grass," usually refers to a *Cannabis* extract considerably richer in psychoactive drug than the marihuana preparations described above. Hashish often is an extract containing only the drug-rich resin secreted by the hemp plant, which has been obtained by boiling resin-covered parts of the plant in appropriate solvents or by some mechanical means, such as scraping these parts of the plant. In India, this type of extract has been named *charas*. In color, hashish may be brown, gray, or black. It is often sold in America in the form of small cubes. Hashish, like marihuana, is subject to considerable variation in potency from one sample to another. In comparison to the "typical" marihuana sold in America today, it is often said that on the basis of psychoactive drug content per unit weight, hashish is five to ten times as potent as marihuana (6).

Many references in the earlier literature (1, Chapter 1) to "hashish" probably do not refer to the type of preparation just described but rather to what we would call marihuana today; in some instances, it is impossible to tell which type of *Cannabis* extract the author has in mind. Moreover, in North Africa, powdered material derived only from the flowering tops is compressed into small cubes and may be called "hashish" (G. G. Nahas, personal communication).

THE CANNABINOIDS: CHEMISTRY

From specimens of *Cannabis sativa,* chemists have been able to isolate and to characterize the chemical structure of more than twenty compounds peculiar to this plant; these compounds are referred to collectively as the *cannabinoids*. Two of the cannabinoids exhibit psychoactive (hallucinogenic) activity in animals and people, several exhibit sedative or antimicrobial activity, and the remainder are biologically inert.

With the benefit of hindsight, we can now understand why the chemical investigation of *Cannabis* extracts has progressed so slowly. The cannabinoids are lipids, most of which are almost entirely insoluble in water (7); today, in their purest available form (95 to 98% pure), the psychoactive cannabinoids are dark, viscous oils. Many of the cannabinoids are very closely related in structure to one another, and it is possible to separate them only by the use of chromatographic techniques first devised in the 1950's and 1960's. Another problem chemists faced was the marked variability among *Cannabis* preparations in terms of their relative content of specific cannabinoids, which stems in part, as noted above, from the variety of the plant and in part from the conditions of its cultivation. Chemists also found that some cannabinoids are very labile compounds whose structure can change during extraction, isolation, and purification procedures; in addition they discovered that structural changes might be stimulated by certain aspects of storage (heat, length of time, and light). The conventional mode of storage of cannabinoids today in research laboratories is in a tightly sealed vessel in which atmospheric air has been replaced with nitrogen, the vessel being kept in the dark under refrigeration.

Before 1964, only one cannabinoid, cannabinol, had been isolated and structurally characterized (Fig. 3); it was found to have no hallucinogenic activity. Dr. Raphael Mechoulam and his colleagues in Israel first isolated and characterized the structure of a psychoactive cannabinoid, 1-Δ^1-3,4-*trans*-tetrahydrocannabinol (THC) in 1964. Shortly thereafter, chemists from other countries obtained the same compound from *Cannabis* extracts, but they named it Δ^9-tetrahydrocannabinol. This dual designation for the same compound, which persists to this day, originated in the common practice of naming complex organic molecules as if they were simpler organic molecules (whose structure is known to other chemists and can be indicated by a single word) to which various structural groups have been added. Mechoulam numbered the atoms in THC as if it were a monoterpene derivative (7), while others chose to regard it as a dibenz-α-pyran derivative (Fig. 2). It is important to recognize that Δ^1-THC and Δ^9-THC are the same compound (Fig. 2); we have elected to use the monoterpenoid system of numbering.

Numerous studies have indicated that THC is the most prevalent psychoactive compound in marihuana and hashish, and it is commonly assumed today that the hallucinogenic effects of such extracts are caused largely by the THC they contain. On administration to animals and to human subjects, THC faithfully mimics the physiological and psychological effects of *Cannabis* extracts (8).

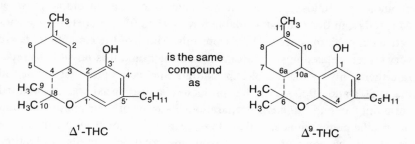

Fig. 2. *The structure of the most prevalent psychoactive compound present in Cannabis extracts, tetrahydrocannabinol (THC)*

When the nucleus is numbered as a monoterpenoid would be, the compound is designated Δ^1-THC. When the nucleus is numbered as a pyran-type compound would be, it is designated Δ^9-THC.

By weight, hashish may have a THC content of 5 to 12%. The most potent forms of marihuana have a THC content of 4 to 8% (exemplified by the *Cannabis* extract from Jamaica called *ganja,* which is more potent than the Indian preparation of the same name). Mexican marihuana typically has a THC content of less than 1% and American hemp usually less than 0.2% (2, p. 50; 7). As noted above, the resin secreted by the plant is the richest natural source of THC, followed in decreasing magnitude by the flowers and the leaves. Little THC has been found in the stems, roots, and seeds of the plant.

Chemists have also found small quantities of a psychoactive isomer of THC in most *Cannabis* extracts: 1-$\Delta^{1(6)}$-tetrahydrocannabinol ($\Delta^{1(6)}$-THC; designated Δ^8-THC in the pyran system of nomenclature). On oral and intravenous administration to human subjects, $\Delta^{1(6)}$-THC was found to produce qualitatively the same effects as Δ^1-THC; though, on a weight basis, $\Delta^{1(6)}$-THC seemed to have only two-thirds the potency of the more prevalent isomer (11). In some fresh *Cannabis* extracts, as much as 10% of the total psychoactive drug content may be in the form of the $\Delta^{1(6)}$-isomer, but, in aged samples, 1% is the common value (7). Treatment with acids easily changes THC to $\Delta^{1(6)}$-THC.

For biomedical and for legal purposes, the potency of marihuana and hashish is typically described in terms of their content of THC, the important psychoactive component. For this reason, brief mention of certain aspects of the chemistry of THC is warranted. In the presence of air, THC slowly changes spontaneously to cannabinol and perhaps to other

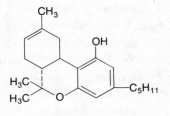

I. $\Delta^{1(6)}$-THC

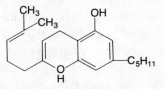

II. CANNABIGEROL

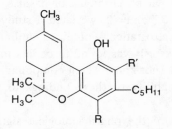

IIIa. Δ^1-THC acid A
  (R=H; R′=COOH)
IIIb. Δ^1-THC acid B
  (R=COOH; R′=H)

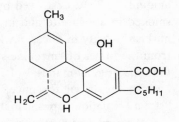

IV. CANNABIDIOLIC ACID

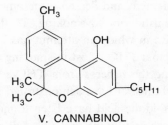

V. CANNABINOL

Fig. 3. *Various Cannabinoids*

Compound I (1-$\Delta^{1(6)}$-tetrahydrocannabinol), is a psychoactive substance, exerting effects similar to those of Δ^1-THC. Compounds II, IIIa IIIb, and IV have been postulated to be biosynthetic precursors of Δ^1-THC (7). Compound V is biologically inactive and presumably represents the oxidative degradation of Δ^1-THC.

inactive compounds. In the presence of heat of the magnitude entailed in the smoking of *Cannabis* extracts, THC is destroyed, to an apparently unpredictable extent, though heat also may merely convert THC to $\Delta^{1(6)}$-THC (7). Some maintain that the amount of THC destroyed by heat during the smoking process is very small, postulating that most of the THC in a marihuana cigarette is volatilized at a safe distance behind the burning tip (8). In this context, it is possible that comparable conditions do not obtain during the two most popular ways of smoking of *Cannabis* extracts: in a cigarette or in a pipe. The as-yet-unsmoked portion of the extract in a pipe may become hotter, because of the insulating effect of the bowl than the equivalent portion in a cigarette. There is, unfortunately, no published evidence of which we are aware comparing the amounts of THC destroyed by pyrolysis when marihuana or hashish are smoked in a cigarette and in a pipe. In Chapter 2, we cited a study of hashish toxicity in mice, in which an electrostatically obtained sublimate from the fumes of "machine-smoked" hashish was found to be less toxic than the original material (12); as we do not know which compounds in hashish are lethal for mice, the applicability of these findings to the "street" situation is problematical.

To complicate further consideration of the pharmacological significance of smoking as a route of administration for *Cannabis* extracts, it has been observed that two biologically inert cannabinoids, THC-acid A and THC-acid B (Fig. 3), are both converted to THC during the smoking process. One is left then with the confusing impression that, by different reactions, smoking can both augment and decrease the amount of THC contained in marihuana or hashish prior to smoking. To date, we are not aware of any published studies in which an attempt has been made to determine how much of the original THC is lost in smoking and how much "new" THC is derived during the process from THC-acids.

Few of the other cannabinoids isolated thus far have demonstrated biological activity. Cannabigerol and cannabidolic acid have been found to possess sedative properties; under *in vitro* conditions, both also display considerable antimicrobial activity against Gram-positive bacteria (7, 9). Some of the biologically inactive cannabinoids are thought to be either biogenetic precursors of THC or metabolites of it (7); the biological significance of the remaining cannabinoids is not at all understood.

THE CANNABINOIDS: ABSORPTION,
BIOTRANSFORMATION, AND EXCRETION

Smoking represents the most commonly used route of administration of *Cannabis* extracts in the United States. The cigarettes employed contain ordinarily 300 to 500 mg of solid material; this material may be solely marihuana (containing various amounts of THC), it may be ordinary cigarette or pipe tobacco to which varying quantities of marihuana or hashish have been added, or, for the gullible buyer, it may prove to be principally oregano, catnip, or any one of a variety of dried plant preparations other than hemp. From time to time, reports appear, usually in newspapers, of the discovery of marihuana for sale that has been adulterated with such substances as strychnine, LSD, or "rat poison." It is difficult to determine even the approximate prevalence of such practices and equally difficult to determine how many drug users have been seriously harmed by smoking such marihuana.

A marihuana cigarette containing 500 mg of *Cannabis* extract, which has a relative THC content of 1%, obviously contains 5 mg of THC. Any route of administration that permits drug-laden smoke to escape into the ambient atmosphere must be an inefficient one. In the case of the cigarette just described, research has shown that if it is smoked as completely as possible, 50% of the THC, *on the average,* will be absorbed (gain access to the smoker's bloodstream) but that differences in smoking techniques can cause the relative amount absorbed to fluctuate between 20 and 80% (8). Marihuana smoke is irritating, and many smokers dilute it with room air before inhaling it; if the smoke provokes coughing, some of it will be returned to the ambient atmosphere without having reached the lungs. The length of the interval between puffs will obviously be a factor, which is one reason why groups of marihuana or hashish smokers often pass the cigarette or pipe from one to another rapidly.

Smoking *Cannabis* extracts in a pipe, though a custom of long standing in some countries, and particularly in the Middle East, has never achieved more than mild popularity in this country, and that episodically. In America, the pipe may be filled with marihuana or with a mixture of pipe tobacco and marihuana or hashish.

As a route of administration, smoking results in a rapid onset of drug action, with effects becoming perceptible within a matter of seconds, or minutes at the most, after inhalation of the smoke. The length of the interval between inhalation and perception of the effects of THC is probably largely determined by the concentration of drug in the smoke.

The consumption of food or beverages containing THC is a popular practice in some countries, notably, India, but an infrequent one in this country. The ingestion of THC, in either the "pure" form or contained in a *Cannabis* extract which has been used to prepare a food or beverage, is followed by the onset of drug effect within 30 to 120 minutes, depending in part on the vehicle in which the THC is contained and in part on the quantity and type of food present in the stomach. It has been said that, in comparison with smoking, THC taken by mouth produces qualitatively different effects, that the effects persist for a longer period of time, and that unpleasant sequelae, such as hangovers, are more frequent (13); we do not believe that there is satisfactory experimental evidence to support the first and the third of these contentions.

In addition, it is often said that the oral route is relatively ineffective— that the amount ingested must be roughly three times larger than the amount smoked to produce an equivalent intensity of effect (8). A recently published study (14) has indicated, however, that for purposes of clinical investigations utilizing "pure" THC, both the time of onset of drug effect and the intensity of drug effect are very much a function of the vehicle in which the THC is administered. Given the physicochemical characteristics of THC and the need for a vehicle suitable for the human stomach, most investigators in the past have given THC dissolved in absolute ethanol, administering the solution in a gelatin capsule. Of all the vehicles studied in this latest investigation of the problem (14), absolute ethanol was found to be the least appropriate.

Each subject in this study received a very large dose of THC (35 mg) by mouth after an overnight fast; part of the cannabinoid was in the form of tritiated THC (50 μCi). Five vehicles were studied: sodium glycocholate (which in its acidic form is the most prevalent bile acid in human bile), sesame oil, Tween 80 (a surface-active agent), absolute ethanol, and an equal mixture of ethanol and sodium glycocholate. Blood samples were taken every 15 minutes during the first 3 hours after ingestion and at longer intervals over the next 3 days. It was found that blood concentrations of THC rose most rapidly and reached the highest level (which correlated well with the intensity of observed and reported drug effects) when sodium glycocholate was the vehicle. Blood concentrations rose most slowly and achieved the lowest peak when absolute ethanol was the vehicle; in descending order of effectiveness were sesame oil, Tween 80, and the glycocholate-ethanol mixture. In the cases of sesame oil and ethanol (unlike the other vehicles), there was an average lag of about 30 minutes before drug concentrations in blood began to rise appreciably; peak drug levels, however, were achieved at about the same time (135 to 165 minutes after administration) with all of the vehicles. Considerable individual variability was observed in the rates of absorption of THC among the subjects receiving the drug in each of the five vehicles; repeating the experiments indicated that the differences were valid in that they were reproducible: the "fast" absorbers achieved appreciable blood levels of THC relatively rapidly on each occasion tested, and the same was true of the "intermediate" and "slow" absorbers.

The peak blood concentration achieved after administration of THC emulsified in sodium glycocholate was nearly twice as large as the peak obtained after administration in ethanol. These findings indicate that the intensity of THC's effect when taken by mouth can be influenced significantly by the vehicle in which it is administered. Since this study did not contrast the effects of smoked versus ingested THC, we still do not know the relative efficacies of the two routes of administration; the study does cast doubt, however, on the quantitative significance of the bulk of the previous studies on the effects of THC by mouth, for absolute ethanol was the vehicle for drug administration.

Most molecules like THC that are not ionized and that have a high oil/water partition coefficient enter cells more readily, as a rule, than molecules of equivalent size that have either an ionic charge and/or a greater affinity for aqueous solutions. Little is known about the distribution of THC throughout the body, but, on the basis of what is known about other molecules with similar physicochemical properties, we surmise that THC enters most cells rapidly. In the study of various vehicles for oral administration cited above (14), blood concentrations of THC 12 hours after the drug had been given were found to be very high, even though, by subjective and objective criteria, the drug's effects had essentially ceased 6 hours earlier; the authors interpreted this finding as evidence of the binding of THC to plasma proteins. (Many drugs are bound to a variable extent to one or more plasma proteins; the binding is usually reversible, but, in the bound form, many drugs are biologically inactive.) Protein binding probably also accounts for the finding that THC persists in human plasma for several days after intravenous administration (15). Some of the circulating (and unbound) THC probably gains access to the fat depots of the body where it may remain for weeks (15).

When a typical marihuana cigarette is smoked (i.e., one with relative THC content of about 1%), the effects are perceived quickly, achieve peak intensity by 70 minutes, on the average (16, 17), remain at peak intensity for roughly the next hour, and decline slowly thereafter, usually disappearing 3 to 4 hours after the act of smoking (8, 16). The effects of even a high dose of THC (35 mg) by mouth persist for no more than

6 hours (14), though, with the oral route, a 1- to 2-hour allowance should be made for completion of intestinal absorption. We want to report one clinical study in which an effectively psychoactive dose (*ca.* 3 mg) of THC was given intravenously (18). The physiological and psychological effects of THC were evident almost immediately to observers and subjects at what turned out to be peak intensity. The physiological change monitored in this study (increased heart rate) lasted about 90 minutes; according to the subjects, however, the psychological effects persisted for about 5 hours. This is an uncommon finding, since it has usually been found that there is a good temporal correlation between changes in heart rate and psychic effects (8). Reports from subjects on the intensity and duration of sensations and psychic alterations are obviously an imprecise measure, under the best of circumstances; since such reports cannot be avoided in studies of psychoactive drugs, the reliability of the information obtained will be determined in no small measure by the selection criteria for subjects and the numbers of subjects studied.

Pharmacologists would classify THC as a "short-acting" drug, suggesting that THC suffers one or more of the following fates in the body: relatively rapid chemical transformation to a less active or inactive molecule, relatively rapid excretion via the urine and/or the feces, immobilization by temporary binding to plasma proteins, or sequestration within the cells of tissues presumably insensitive to the effects of THC (fat depots or skeletal muscle, for example). The available evidence, which still provides only an incomplete picture, indicates that all of the mechanisms just listed are utilized in the disposition of THC.

Regardless of whether THC is administered by the oral route, by the intravenous route, or by inhalation, the greater part of its metabolites is found in the feces and the lesser part in the urine. When the THC contained a radioactive label, one finds, for example, 35 to 65% of the dose in feces in the course of a 5-day period and 15 to 30% in the urine (14, 17). It is a usual finding that about 25% of the administered dose cannot be accounted for by radioactivity in urine or feces, even a week after the cannabinoid has been given. This percentage of the dose, it is assumed, is still in the body in the form of THC, or its metabolites, which are bound to plasma proteins or, more likely, sequestered within such tissues as fat depots (15). The cannabinoids in the feces are thought to enter the intestine as constituents of biliary secretions and subsequently, to varying degrees, to re-enter the body via absorption in a lower segment of the intestine (a process called "enterohepatic circulation") or

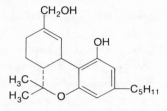

I. 7-OH-THC (11-OH-THC)   II. 6, 7-diOH-THC (8, 11-diOH-THC)

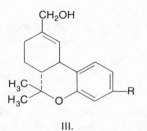

III.

In THC, R is:

$$-C^{1''}H_2-C^{2''}H_2-C^{3''}H_2-C^{4''}H_2-C^{5''}H_3$$

After metabolism in dogs or rabbits, THC is converted to 7-OH-THC and R may be:

(a) $-C^{1''}HOH-C_4H_9$

(b) $-C^{1''}H_2-C^{2''}HOH-C_3H_7$

(c) $-C^{1''}H_2-C^{2''}H_2-C^{3''}HOH-C_2H_5$

Fig. 4. *Various Metabolites of THC*

Though compound I, 7-hydroxy-Δ^1-THC, is not quantitatively an important metabolite of THC in human beings, it is of particular interest because its hallucinogenic potency, on a weight basis, is minimally equal to that of the parent compound; some investigators have postulated, moreover, that THC must be converted to 7-OH-Δ^1-THC for hallucinogenic effects to be produced. Of the known metabolites, compound II, 6,7-dihydroxy-Δ^1-THC, is the most prevalent in human beings. Compounds III a, b, and c have been isolated to date only from the urine of rabbits and dogs that have been given Δ^1-THC (19). If $\Delta^{1(6)}$-THC is given instead of Δ^1-THC (Figs. 2 and 3), the $\Delta^{1(6)}$-THC analogues of compounds I and III, a, b, and c are excreted.

to pass on unabsorbed. When THC is given by mouth, some of the fecal cannabinoids may represent unabsorbed drug metabolized by intestinal bacteria.

Of the cannabinoids excreted, roughly 50 to 70% are in non-ionized and unconjugated forms (14). Very little unchanged THC is found in either the urine or the feces. Various hydroxylated derivatives of THC have been found in the urine of animals and human subjects after administration of this cannabinoid (Fig. 4), but they account for only about one-quarter of the metabolites. When THC bearing a radioactive label of ^{3}H or ^{14}C is administered to human subjects, about three-quarters of the urinary radioactivity is associated with compounds of unknown structure (14). Of the identified urinary metabolites, 6,7-diOH-THC

(8,11-diOH-THC) is typically the most prevalent, but 7-OH-THC (11-OH-THC) is clearly of the greatest interest. In mice, 7-OH-THC has twice the pharmacological potency of THC, but, in human beings, the two compounds have roughly the same potency, judged by objective criteria. It was the consensus of the subjects in the study making this comparison, however, that THC produced a more intense "high" and one of longer duration than did 7-OH-THC (18); but, statistically, the difference between the means of the subjective reactions of the two groups of subjects was just on the threshold of significance ($p < .05$).

Upon administration of radioactive labeled THC to human subjects by inhalation or by intravenous injection, the presence of metabolites of THC (including, presumably, 7-OH-THC) can be detected within minutes; peak plasma values for the metabolites occur less than 15 minutes after the administration of THC by these two routes (17). Women should be aware that THC crosses the placental barrier. There is also some degree of temporal correlation between psychological effects and blood concentrations of the metabolites. These observations, when considered in conjunction with the many pharmacological similarities between THC and 7-OH-THC (18, 20), have led some to postulate that 7-OH-THC is the "active" form of the drug (17, 20). In their view, virtually all of the biological effects of *Cannabis* extracts are caused by 7-OH-THC. Implicit in this concept, though not so stated by its proponents, is the assumption that THC per se is biologically inactive. Though such a concept is not without precedent in pharmacology, it will be difficult to confirm.

The temporal changes in blood THC concentrations as a function of dose administered and route of administration used exemplify vividly how cautiously one should assess the medical significance of a drug's blood level at any given point in time. When relatively small doses of THC are given by mouth (17) or smoked in cigarettes (16, 17), the blood concentrations of THC reach a peak at a time determined by the route and, as expected, fall steadily thereafter. If, however, only a small dose (0.5 mg) is given, dissolved in alcohol, and injected over the course of a minute into a rapidly flowing intravenous infusion, the blood levels are maximal almost instantaneously, fall thereafter for the next 5 to 6 hours, but change very little from this point (when the concentration is roughly six to eight times greater than the peak obtained after a dose of about 20 mg by mouth) through the next 24 hours (17). This intravenous dose is so small that even experienced users have difficulty perceiving its effects (20). When appreciable blood levels of THC exist in the absence of any pharmacological effects, we assume that the THC is inactive because it is bound to plasma proteins or sequestered within unresponsive tissues. Administering even a small dose of THC in alcohol quickly by vein and thus exposing plasma proteins transiently to high concentrations of cannabinoid apparently creates conditions highly favorable to protein binding of THC. And when, in one study, a large dose of THC (35 mg) was given by mouth, a complex sequence of changes in blood levels followed (14); 90 minutes after ingestion of the drug, the mean blood concentration of THC was 7.6 ng/ml, and this was the starting point of the period during which the subjective effects were at peak intensity. But 6 hours after ingestion of the drug, the intensity of the subjective effects had waned so much as to be nearly imperceptible, yet 12 hours after ingestion, the mean blood concentration of THC had risen to 19.3 ng/ml. Pharmacokinetic studies suggest that THC in blood exhibits two half-lives, a short one of minutes and a longer one of hours. In the study described above, the authors speculate that appreciable quantities of THC were sequestered in the liver following intestinal absorption and that they gained access to the systemic circulation only after being secreted into the intestine along with the bile; some of their subjects reported experiencing a second "high" following a meal eaten 2 hours after the original high.

From the foregoing, it seems evident that meaningful research on THC concentrations in blood will have to distinguish between bound and unbound fractions. Further study of the kinetics of the binding of THC (and 7-OH-THC) to plasma proteins is also needed.

THE CANNABINOIDS: PATTERNS OF USAGE

A most systematic and informative survey of marihuana (and hashish) usage in the United States was undertaken by the National Commission on Marihuana and Drug Abuse; the results have been described in their First Report (2, Chapter 2). A later study was prepared by Abelson and coworkers (42).

Frequency, Dosage, and Duration of Usage

According to the estimates made in this report (2), 14% of adolescents between the ages of 12 and 17 and 15% of individuals over 18 have used marihuana at least once, which means that, by 1972, an estimated 24 million Americans had been exposed to the effects of *Cannabis* extracts.

Users were divided into five categories on the basis of frequency of usage:

The experimenter: A person who tries marihuana only once or uses it no more than once a month. Usually smokes a part of or no more than one cigarette on each occasion of usage.

The intermittent user: Frequency of usage ranges from two to three times per month to (no more than) once weekly. Commonly smokes part or all of just one cigarette.

The moderate user: Frequency of usage ranges from several times per week to once daily. Also usually smokes part or all of just one cigarette on each occasion of usage.

The heavy user: Uses marihuana several times daily, smoking one to (rarely) five cigarettes on each occasion.

The very heavy user: Uses *Cannabis* extracts with such frequency that he (or she) is in a state of almost constant intoxication; preference is for the more potent preparation, hashish.

In determining the incidence of users in each category, the commission supplied separate figures for the 12- to 17-year-old users surveyed and for those 18 and over. They classified 60% of the younger users and 50% of the older users as "experimenters"; the figures for "intermittent" users were 19 and 12%, respectively; 5% of the younger users and 6% of the older users fell into the "moderate" category; 4% of the younger and 2% of the older users fell into the "heavy" category. The totals fall short of 100% because not every user surveyed answered all of the questions; 12% of the younger users and 30% of the older users surveyed provided no answers about frequency of usage. The number of "very heavy" users identified was considered too small to warrant inclusion in this tally.

Any pattern of usage of less than 2 years' duration was designated "short term"; most of the users surveyed were placed in this category. Others were said to be "long-term" users because their patterns of usage extended from 2 to 10 years. "Very long term" was the designation for usage of *Cannabis* extracts for more than 10 years; very few Americans were assigned to this category.

Usage among the youth of America continued to increase from 1972 to 1977 (42). Still most prevalent in urban neighborhoods the use of marihuana has become more prevalent in rural areas.

As these categories are not yet utilized in most clinical studies, we will designate subjects only as being "naive" (those who have never been exposed to *Cannabis* extracts) or "experienced" (those whose pattern of use may range from "intermittent" to "heavy").

Patterns of Multiple Drug Usage

It has been found that multiple drug usage is very common among the users of cannabinoids (2, Chapter 2; 13); this may be inadvertent or deliberate.

It is inadvertent when the user unknowingly buys marihuana or hashish adulterated with other substances (8). Such adulterants as oregano, catnip, and a variety of dried plant preparations are by and large pharmacologically inert. Such adulterants as LSD, methamphetamine, strychnine, *stramonium* leaves (which contain an atropine-like compound), and "rat poison" may give the user an unanticipated experience, particularly if the mixture is ingested; of the substances listed, only *stramonium* leaves are known to be pharmacologically effective when smoked. The smoking of LSD is generally an unsatisfactory route of administration for this agent (see p. 154). It has been alleged that marihuana that contains heroin or cocaine is sometimes sold; since these two substances are so much more expensive than marihuana, there is good reason to doubt that such mixtures are often offered for sale (8).

The choice of a pattern of multiple drug intake is very common among users of cannabinoids; one survey indicated that the greater the frequency of marihuana (or hashish) usage, the greater the likelihood that other drugs were being used concurrently (13). There was also an excellent correlation between marihuana usage and past trials of other drugs; the past trials most often involved other hallucinogens and then (in descending order of frequency) central nervous system depressants, central nervous system stimulants, and narcotics. In terms of concurrent usage, the National Commission found that alcohol and tobacco were the two substances most commonly used in addition to marihuana; 54% of the users surveyed were concurrent cigarette smokers, and 68% of them had consumed alcohol within 10 days before they were interviewed for the survey (2, pp. 42-43).

In patterns of multiple drug abuse, it is not always possible to identify the primary drug (i.e., the one for which the user has the highest regard and would therefore prefer to use most frequently), in part because the patterns change with time and not always for reasons related to the user's desires (changes in cost, quality, and availability, for example, may be responsible for changes in a given individual's pattern of usage). If a person smokes marihuana and sniffs heroin, for instance, it is often difficult to determine if he should be classified as a marihuana user who also uses heroin or vice versa. We have broached this matter primarily because we now want to consider one of the most frequently alleged risks of marihuana usage: that it leads to the use of "harder" drugs, in particular, to the use of heroin.

It is frequently asserted that most heroin users have smoked marihuana at one time or another. We do not know how accurate this statement is, but we would not be surprised to learn that it is largely true. The young adolescent usually has little money, and so begins his early experiments in drug abuse with substances he can afford. For some it may be glue for sniffing, whereas for others it is the readily available, and usually not too expensive, "joint" of marihuana. Regardless of the age of first exposure to cannabinoids, it was the finding of the National Commission that "the overwhelming majority of marihuana users do not progress to other drugs" (2, p. 87). A few do, however, and progression to stronger drugs is particularly likely if the pattern of marihuana usage becomes "moderate," "heavy," or "very heavy." The National Commission found that the rate of progression from predominant use of marihuana to predominant use of a "stronger" drug, as well as the identity of the stronger drug, varied from one social group (or segment of the population) to another (2, p. 88). The stronger drug might be heroin, but it might also be LSD or cocaine.

It appears that only a minority of marihuana users find that with the passage of time they need a "greater thrill" and so seek a drug that will provide it. The National Commission has demonstrated satisfactorily, we feel, that "Marihuana use *per se* does not dictate whether other drugs will be used; nor does it determine the rate of progression, if and when it occurs, or which drugs might be used" (2, p. 88).

THE CANNABINOIDS: PHYSIOLOGICAL EFFECTS

The most consistently observed physiological changes produced by *Cannabis* extracts or by THC are increases in heart rate and peripheral blood flow, bronchodilation, and injection of the conjunctivae. Changes in blood pressure, respiration, and body temperature are usually minor in magnitude and variable in direction. Pupillary size is unchanged but intraocular pressure is lowered by THC. One investigative group has reported that, with the use of a finger ergograph, muscular weakness could be demonstrated (8); the degree of weakness was small, and there is no mention of this change in some descriptions of the effects of THC. With a large oral dose of THC (35 mg), "the occurrence of involuntary jerking movements of the muscles of the lower extremities, sometimes extending throughout the body and even to the facial muscles," was frequently observed (14). The jerking paralleled, in intensity and extent, the rate of rise of drug concentration in blood and the height to which it rose; these involuntary movements were invariably accompanied by complaints of dysphoric feelings, and both could be quickly alleviated by the intravenous injection of 10 mg of diazepam (Valium). Dryness of the mouth has been reported after the smoking of marihuana; it is not clear whether this dryness is caused by THC or is peculiar to the smoking situation. Moreover, though one reviewer of the effects of marihuana describes dry mouth as a "prominent" effect (6), others do not mention it (2, 8). The influence of THC on appetite is variable, ranging from none to a sharp increase, which is commonly manifested as a specific craving for sweet foods. The blood glucose concentrations of subjects who report hunger, however, are within the normal range (8).

The increase in heart rate seems to correlate fairly well with the dose of THC; this increase may range from changes of questionable significance after small doses to relative increments of nearly 100% after large doses (14, 16). Beginning with the pioneering studies of Isbell *et al.* (23) on the effects of THC in man, the view has been repeatedly expressed that one could get a satisfactory idea of the amount of THC to which a subject or patient had been exposed by the degree of tachycardia. In a laboratory setting, the agreement between dose administered and increment in heart rate is sometimes satisfactorily linear (24); at other times it is not. We wonder how good the agreement would be in other settings. Heart rate is affected by too many other influences to serve as a reliable index of the action of THC.

The temporal nature of the changes in heart rate is determined by the route of administration and the size of the dose. When tachycardia occurs, the urinary excretion of free epinephrine (though not norepinephrine) is enhanced (21). This finding suggested the possibility that THC produces tachycardia by provoking increased secretion of epinephrine, an idea that was tested with propranolol, a beta adrenergic blocking compound. Pretreatment of subjects with propranolol prevented the development of the usual tachycardia following the smoking of marihuana as well as the increase in peripheral blood flow (22, 24). These findings, however, did not support the view that the cardiovascular effects of THC are the result of enhanced epinephrine secretion. For one thing, the usual sequelae to the metabolic effects of epinephrine—increases in blood concentrations of glucose, lactate, and unesterified fatty acids—were not detected. Moreover, the vasoconstrictor effects of epinephrine are not prevented by beta adrenergic blocking drugs; enhanced epinephrine secretion in the presence of propranolol should lead to a rise in blood pressure and possibly to a decrease in peripheral blood flow, in at least some vascular beds. The investigators concluded that the cardiovascular effects of THC probably represent drug interference with certain reflexes concerned with the maintenance of cardiovascular homeostasis (22). Parenthetically, it might be noted that the smoking of cigarette tobacco does stimulate epinephrine secretion, with the expected cardiovascular and metabolic consequences (22). The significance of the enhanced urinary excretion of free epinephrine after exposure to marihuana remains to be determined.

The temporal characteristics of tachycardia and of the psychological changes produced by THC show a high correlation when the cannabinoid is given by mouth (14). When THC is inhaled, however, the peak tachycardia occurs 15 minutes later, and tachycardia has subsided by more than one-half at the time (some 45 minutes later) the subjective effects reach maximal intensity (16).

THE CANNABINOIDS: PSYCHOLOGICAL (SUBJECTIVE) EFFECTS

Many methods have been enlisted in the effort to determine the effects of THC on the human central nervous system, including informal (anecdotal) reports by experimental subjects and drug users, self-rating by subjects on questionnaires provided by investigators and objectively scored, and standardized tests of psychomotor performance, learning, retention of recently learned material, problem-solving, and the like. In addition, the electrical activity of the brain has been recorded, with electrode placement ranging from the scalp to subcortical areas.

Clinical investigations of the effects of THC are now beyond the preliminary stage. In evaluating the available evidence, it is still difficult to determine the significance both of the findings of individual studies and of discrepancies among different studies. The experimental designs of the various studies differ in immediately apparent ways and possibly in ways that will ultimately be shown to have significance. Differences in the doses of THC given are common and sometimes large. Many studies use inhalation of THC as the route of administration (a logical choice in that it simulates the most common "street" route of administration); in a smaller number, THC has been given by mouth and, in a very few, by vein. What care should be taken in the selection of subjects for experiments with THC is not clearly known. Subjects in most studies have had varying amounts of experience with the effects of marihuana and/or other psychoactive substances. The outcome of a study can probably be influenced by the attitudes, expectations, motivations, and previous drug experiences of both subjects and investigators (25). The entire setting in which an experiment is conducted is clearly of importance when the substance being studied can potentially cause lability in mood, impairment of rational judgment, and paranoid ideation. One group of investigators, for example, repeated an experiment with the same group of subjects, the first time in a "congenial" setting, the second in a "more austere" one (16); THC produced more untoward effects on the second occasion than the first.

In addition to differences due to variations in experimental design from one study to another, unexpected variability within a seemingly homogeneous study may be detected by diligent investigators. In a study in which the subjects smoked marihuana cigarettes of known and equal potency in a carefully prescribed fashion, the peak plasma levels of THC in three of the subjects were found to be 69, 37, and 21 ng/ml; utilizing these values and making certain assumptions about the metabolism of THC, the investigators estimated that these three subjects had absorbed 41, 20, and 15%, respectively, of the THC contained in the cigarettes. The frequently repeated statement that approximately 50% of the THC in a marihuana cigarette will be absorbed when it is smoked should be regarded as only a rough first approximation. Bearing in mind that the findings to be reported are subject to such limitations, we will now consider the common (and some of the less common) psychological effects of THC (2, 6, 8, 10).

Inhalation of the smoke of a marihuana cigarette is followed within minutes by feelings of well-being, relaxation, and tranquility in most people. (The individual who is notably apprehensive, depressed, or angry, however, may become more so under the influence of THC.) The user feels intoxicated but typically reports that this feeling can be much more easily suppressed voluntarily than can the equivalent effect produced by alcohol. He may feel fuzzy, dizzy, a bit sleepy, and sometimes "dreamy." He often feels more friendly toward others and finds greater pleasure in their company; a few smokers, however, become quiet and remote. The user typically reports an increased awareness of his environment: vision seems sharper and sounds become more distinct. Many things seem to be humorous, so that laughter comes easily and frequently. By the same token, misfortunes seem more tragic. Human relationships are perceived to have more significance. Not uncommonly, the user feels that he has achieved a novel profundity of thought and an extraordinary acuity of insight; it is rare for objective observers to find much merit in these insights.

Perception of the passage of time is characteristically distorted by THC, so that clock time appears to pass very slowly. Accordingly, after the actual passage of a minute, people under the influence of THC might estimate the length of the elapsed time as only 30 seconds. Feelings of depersonalization, accompanied sometimes by a perception that bodily proportions have changed, also occur, but usually only with larger doses. Colors may shimmer, and there may be visual distortions. Visual imagery occurs, though the images may sometimes only be seen when the eyes are closed. As with visions seen under the influence of LSD, the user realizes that the visual phenomena are drug-induced.

Reports of feeling "drowsy" or "sleepy" are frequently given by individuals under the influence of THC, and "dreamlike" states may occur. Such a state does not, however, obligate sleep but merely facilitates its onset for the user so inclined. Amounts of THC larger than those in the typical "joints" sold today are more profoundly hypnotic and may irresistably induce a deep sleep; this is particularly true if the user also is drinking an alcoholic beverage. Studies of the sleep patterns of subjects under the influence of THC have revealed small reductions in the amount of REM sleep in some subjects (27) but do not provide a consistent picture of sleep alteration (28). In regard to sedation and sleep, the effects of THC resemble those of ethanol, the barbiturates, and other generalized central nervous system depressant agents and represent one of the points of sharp contrast between the effects of THC and those of such an adrenergic hallucinogen as LSD.

There is no substantive evidence to indicate that sexual arousal is an inevitable, or even commonplace, consequence of THC. Stimuli that ordinarily produce sexual arousal seem to be equally effective after typical street doses of THC: Users have reported that the pleasures of sexual intercourse are enhanced by THC and that they are better sexula partners when "stoned." It is undoubtedly true that the repeated usage of THC has coincided in a very few users with the development of a behavioral pattern of sexual promiscuity (26). The infrequency of such reports suggests that it is a relatively rare occurrence; moreover, the nature of the causal relationship between THC usage and more frequent sexual activity of any kind is decidedly murky. It is worth noting also that observations on sexual behavior are frequently made in adolescents, who represent an age group in which the passage of time alone is commonly accompanied by increased sexual activity.

As with other types of hallucinogens, paranoid ideation occurs among users of THC. It is rarely reported after or verbalized during the drug experience when relatively small doses are taken, but it can become quite pronounced in some subjects or users who have taken large doses. In a study in which the subjects received 35 mg of THC by mouth in a solvent (sodium glycocholate) that permitted relatively rapid and complete absorption, any unanticipated occurrence, such as an unexpected visitor or unusually hasty movements by the investigators, provoked "intense suspicion" in the subjects, which could not be readily allayed by explanations and assurances (14). On rare occasions when the use of THC results in the development of a toxic psychosis, paranoia may be among the prominent psychotic manifestations.

The effects of THC on the intellect (mental processes and responses) and on intellectually directed motor activities (psychomotor performance) have been tested in various ways. As a first approximation, the decrements in cognitive and psychomotor performance appear to be dose-related: the larger the dose, the greater the decrement. It has been observed, however, that previous exposure to the effects of THC is also an important factor in this situation. Experienced marihuana users frequently exhibit no decrement in performance even under the influence of fairly large doses of THC, and occasionally their performance improves. The explanation for this phenomenon is yet to be discovered.

Tachycardia is approximately equivalent on these occasions for both naive and experienced users; by this measure, at least, the experienced user exhibits no tolerance. It may be, however, that selective tolerance to some of the effects of THC has developed or as Snyder suggests, that the experienced user can compensate fully for the drug's effects in these test situations (10, p. 59). Moreover, to correlate the magnitude of the decrement in performance merely with the dose is probably an oversimplification; we feel that the route of administration must also be considered. For any given concentration of a psychoactive drug in the blood, the more rapidly that concentration is achieved, the greater the intensity (albeit transiently) of the drug's effects. The maximal psychic impact of a given dose of THC will probably be greater if it is inhaled than if it is ingested.

In the milder stages of intoxication with THC, naive users exhibit no impairment on some tests, and, as a group, display variable degrees of impairment on other tests. The performance of a given subject, moreover, may vary considerably with time during the period of maximal intoxication. These findings may reflect the influence of a number of factors. We have already noted that variability among subjects has been observed in the extent to which a given dose is absorbed, whether via inhalation or ingestion, as judged by the subsequent blood concentrations of THC. In addition, intoxication with THC has been described as a state that seems to the subject to wax and wane repeatedly in a roughly cyclical fashion with the passage of time. Users' reports that the sensations of mild to moderate intoxication can usually be suppressed voluntarily has also been noted above. On tests of cognitive and psychomotor performance, subjects can obviously obtain their best possible scores only if they cooperate fully in meeting the demands of a test. Poor scores, therefore, might be obtained from subjects in a "rising phase" of their intoxication who chose not to suppress the feelings of intoxication and/or not to cooperate in the performance of the test. Conventional measures of intellectual function that depend significantly on the mood and attitude of the subject, as virtually all do, must always be regarded as potentially submaximal.

It is generally agreed that some loss of what is called "short-term" or "immediate" memory is a frequent concomitant of intoxication with THC, even for the experienced user. Users report difficulty in completing long sentences; they fear that they will forget what they have started to say so that the ending of the sentence may well be incongruous with its beginning. This specific impairment has also been demonstrated by psychological tests involving story recall, remembered digits, and the like. (Long-term memory, incidentally, is apparently unimpaired.) The result may be a "peculiarly disconnected" pattern of speech, characterized by slightly disjointed sentences and abrupt, irrelevant conversational tangents (6). Performance on tests that require both immediate memory and the keeping of a goal in mind while digits are being manipulated mentally is also impaired by THC. Some investigators feel that the impairment in immediate memory plus the altered subjective sense of time affects the user's ability to separate the past, the present, and the future and, thereby, his ability to "locate himself in the continuum of time" (10, p. 68). This, they suggest, results in the feelings of confusion and depersonalization that sometimes occur in the milder states of THC intoxication and that are more common in more deeply intoxicated subjects.

The impact of THC on an individual's ability to drive a car or fly a plane safely is a matter of widespread medicolegal interest. The pertinent evidence to date is, in part, inconclusive. The qualifying considerations of dose, previous experience with THC, and voluntary suppression of drug effects cloud interpretation of the studies reported thus far. Perhaps the first study to be made was that of Crancer and his colleagues (29), who compared the effects of marihuana and ethanol on the performance of a simulated driving test. They concluded that the subjects committed a significantly greater number of errors when under the influence of ethanol than when they were "high" on marihuana. The subjects in this study were classified as experienced users of marihuana, and their most frequent driving errors after marihuana stemmed from insufficient attention to the speedometer; otherwise, their driving was generally unimpaired. It is difficult to make much of these findings. Though the doses of ethanol were calculated to establish blood concentrations corresponding to the minimum required for conviction as a "drunk" driver (namely, 100 mg of ethanol/100 ml of blood),* too little is said in the paper about the amount of THC administered, other than the quantity of marihuana

---

* Among other criticisms that have been made of the study by Crancer *et al.* is that of Frank (13, p. 454), who contends that the dose of alcohol was seriously miscalculated. According to Frank, the dose given would have produced blood ethanol levels of 180 mg/100 ml; at this level, the average person is markedly intoxicated, and the average degree of psychomotor impairment is considerably greater than that which obtains at 100 mg/100 ml.

smoked and its relative content of THC as determined by assay at an unspecified earlier time. What one wants to know is what blood concentrations of THC obtained while the subjects were being tested, how much the subjects wanted marihuana to look "good" and ethanol "bad" in the test situation, how naive subjects would have responded under the conditions of the study, and how carefully the driving simulator imitiates the challenges faced by an actual driver. Conversely, many of the studies that demonstrated impairment of driving ability by THC have utilized only naive subjects, very large doses of the cannabinoid, ranging from 30 to 400 mg of THC, and driving simulators. It is impossible to regard such investigations as being reasonable facsimiles of what one might expect by way of driving performance from naive or experienced users after they had smoked one or two marihuana cigarettes of the potency typically available through illegal channels today. Even with the large doses of THC used in these studies, it is noteworthy that, in comparison with ethanol, which quite consistently impaired "driving skill," the response of the subjects to THC was unpredictable and individualistic (30). At the moment, we can say little more than that THC can impair the ability to drive safely but that the degree of impairment will probably vary widely among users, depending, in part, on the dose of THC used, the route of administration, the individual's previous experience with THC, and, in case of milder intoxication, his willingness to suppress the manifestations of the drug's effects.

The electrical activity of the brain, as recorded by electrodes on the scalp, changes hardly at all during intoxication with THC, though several investigators have noted small decreases in the frequency and voltage of the alpha rhythm on the electroencephalogram. With the aid of subcortically situated electrodes, it was possible to observe changes in the pattern of electrical activity from the septal region during "rushes of euphoria" in a patient intoxicated with marihuana (8, 31). By and large, however, the use of conventional neurophysiological techniques has not yet yielded information of value in any sense other than negative.

In a survey of the physiological and psychological effects of THC, activity characteristic of three types of drugs has been noted: a hallucinogen, a generalized central nervous system depressant, and a central nervous system stimulant. In some of its physiological and most of its psychological effects, THC is strongly imitative of the action of LSD and the other adrenergic hallucinogens. Physiologically, THC and LSD differ most markedly in their effects on the eye: THC does not affect pupillary size but produces "red eyes," whereas LSD causes pupillary dilation only. In terms of their effects on the user's perception of himself and the world around him, and on mood, affect, and critical judgment, the compounds are virtually indistinguishable; in terms of the dose required to produce a given effect after ingestion, LSD is clearly the more potent agent (roughly one-hundred times more potent). LSD, however, usually does not make the user feel sleepy, whereas THC does, and, in this sense, THC simulates the effects of such generalized central nervous system depressant agents as ethanol and the barbiturates. The central nervous system stimulant effects of THC are the least prominent of the three types of effect. In animals, THC enhances the stimulatory effects of amphetamine (6). Large doses of THC, as we noted previously, produced involuntary jerking movements in the musculature of the lower extremities in human subjects, which could progress upward with time until even the facial muscles were involved (14); this is the sort of disconcerting drug effect with which a "speed freak" has to cope.

THE CANNABINOIDS: PHYSICAL DEPENDENCE AND TOLERANCE

Regardless of the pattern of usage, there are no involuntary physiological disturbances that typically follow sudden cessation of THC usage; therefore, it is said that physical dependence on the effects of THC does not develop. Heavy users of THC would probably be quite unhappy if abruptly denied access to it; this reflects their psychological dependence on THC. That unhappiness could psychogenically trigger a variety of somatic complaints (e.g., headaches, stomach cramps, feelings of lassitude, and so on) that would vary in type and intensity from one user to another.

It is now felt that tolerance to the effects of THC can develop, but we have three possibilities to consider: tolerance, no tolerance, and "reverse" tolerance. It is often said that the typical American user of marihuana does not seem to develop any appreciable tolerance to the effects of THC. This conclusion is based largely on two findings: the absence of continual escalation with time in the amount of THC being used as a characteristic facet of the pattern of usage and the absence of a clear-cut demonstration that the veteran user can "withstand," on the average, doses of THC that would psychically disable (transiently) naive users. (Since THC is not known to be lethal for human beings, users can-

not inadvertently demonstrate the existence of tolerance by surviving an
ordinarily lethal dose.)

Studies with animals have indicated, however, that daily doses of THC
elicit progressively weaker effects. Human subjects given daily doses of
synhexyl (a synthetic compound related to THC both in chemical structure and pharmacological effects) requested, within 4 to 6 days, larger
doses to compensate for the gradually weakening effects (32, p. 859). In
cultures where some people have used *Cannabis* extracts daily for most,
if not all, of their adult lives, as in parts of North Africa, it is a common
belief that some degree of tolerance to the drug's effects develops. Studies
are now underway to correlate blood concentrations of THC with intensity of effects. We have already noted how well experienced users of
THC fare on some tests of cognititive function and psychomotor performance, even when fairly large doses of the cannabinoid have been
given. Does this represent tolerance or a learned ability to compensate
for the effects of THC? There is now general agreement on the answer
to this question: tolerance does develop.

Evidence that the repeated use of marihuana might lead to a state of
"reverse" or "inverse" tolerance was first obtained by Weil and his coworkers (33), who reported that experienced users seemed to be able to
get "high" on smaller quantities of marihuana than those required by
naive users. The state of being "high" was determined, in a very approximate fashion, on the basis of reports by the subjects and observations by
the investigators. There have not been any further studies of this phenomenon; we doubt that a definitive evaluation of it will be possible until
more precise definitions of various degrees of *Cannabis* intoxication have
been formulated, linking degree of intoxication with objective criteria
and blood concentrations of THC.

The evidence regarding tolerance to the effects of THC is, in part,
contradictory. We do not believe that tolerance is a problem for the
"social" users of marihuana in this country. We would not be surprised
if definitive evidence finally indicated that heavy and very heavy users
do exhibit some degree of tolerance to the effects of THC.

THE CANNABINOIDS: ADVERSE EFFECTS

For substances that seem to have been used as extensively and as frequently as the *Cannabis* extracts, remarkably few instances of untoward
effects have been reported. Of several possible explanations for this state

of affairs, the following two seem most sensible. Most users are exposed to relatively small doses of THC, which is, in comparison with LSD, a weak hallucinogen; weak psychoactive drugs cause serious untoward effects only when taken in large doses or when taken (in any amount) by individuals whose pre-existing mental and emotional status makes them peculiarly vulnerable to the drug's effects. Most of the untoward responses to THC seem to be unalarming in intensity and transient and hence do not prompt the user to consult a physician. Nonetheless, it should not be forgotten that THC is a hallucinogen, which makes its untoward effects unpredictable. As Clark and Nakashima have observed, "So with LSD, the very unpredictability of marihuana on different individuals and on the same individual at different times and under different conditions increases the risk to the user" (34).

We have chosen to divide the adverse effects of or reactions to THC into two groups: those confined to the 48 hours following inhalation or ingestion of the cannabinoid and those evident for a longer period of time.

   Acute adverse effects
Though the "good" and "bad trip" terminology associated with LSD usage has not carried over into the marihuana literature, it might well be used in this context, for the commonest adverse reaction to both hallucinogens is an acute non-psychotic panic reaction in which the user fears he is losing his mind. A variant of this panic reaction occurs most often in older (though naive) users who may interpret the THC-induced tachycardia (in the setting of the other psychic effects) as a sign that they are dying. As with the patient on a similar type of bad trip following ingestion of LSD, the technique of "talking down" is to be preferred to medication with sedatives or tranquilizers (35). Another form of non-psychotic bad trip encountered among users of THC (and, particularly, naive users) is an acute depression. Calm, authoritative assurances that the depression is drug-induced, that it will abate, and that no great harm has been or will be done to the patient's psyche elicits a favorable response in a majority of these cases. Though it is often said that the panicky and the depressed reactions occur most often in the naive user, they have also been encountered in experienced users, particularly if the setting is alien or the dose larger than expected.

The most serious of the acute reactions is a toxic psychosis. Also called an "acute brain syndrome," it has been described as very much like the delirium caused by a high fever (35), in which the patient is disoriented, confused, troubled by the true visual and auditory hallucinations, and possibly experiencing feelings of depersonalization and derealization. The patient may be prostrate during this period. By definition, toxic psychoses are self-limiting and end when the causative agent disappears (in this case, when the THC is metabolized). As a result, sleep ordinarily intervenes after 4 to 6 hours, and the patient awakes (usually the next morning) free of psychotic symptomatology.

One of the commonest endings to informal presentations of the arguments for legalization of marihuana (during which frequent comparisons are made with the legalized status of ethanol) is: "And besides, you don't get a hangover with marihuana." There is, nonetheless, frequent reference in the literature on cannabinoids to headaches and "hangover-ish" feelings. In his review of adverse reactions to marihuana, Weil notes that "Miscellaneous, mild ill-effects of marihuana (such as nausea, headache and transient paranoia) are familiar to most users . . ." (35). Weil's statement suggests that these mild adverse effects are common concomitants or sequelae to the use of marihuana, but, like most other authors in the field, he has not reported the results of a systematic survey of how people feel "the day after" the use of marihuana or hashish. The transient paranoia and the nausea (which might well stem from the feelings of dizziness experienced by many using THC) of which Weil speaks probably occur primarily during the period of intoxication, but it is not clear to what extent headache occurs during intoxication and to what extent on the morning after. The likelihood of feeling poorly the next day is correlated in individual case reports with the use of large doses and/or the development of acute adverse psychic effects (30, 35).

Persistent adverse effects

Few psychotic episodes lasting for more than 48 hours after THC consumption have been reported (2, p. 64). It is possible that some of the shorter "persistent" psychotic episodes (3 to 10 days in duration) may represent iatrogenic prolongations of either toxic psychoses or what were originally non-psychotic panic reactions (35, 36). This has been accomplished, in the view of some psychiatrists, by treating the patients as if they had presented with a full-blown psychiatric emergency, medicating them immediately and admitting them to a psychiatric ward. Repeated medication plus the surrounding presence of truly psychotic patients could serve to convince the patient, as the effects of THC wore off, that he had truly "lost his mind"; this could also slow the rate at which he regained his usual degree of contact with reality.

Reports from India and North Africa have described a fairly high incidence of chronic psychoses (usually some form of schizophrenia) in patients who were formerly daily users of large quantities of cannabinoids (32). In this country it has not been found that THC produces a specific and typical form of psychotic behavior; indeed, it is often claimed that persistent psychotic episodes are provoked by THC only in those with such serious antecedent psychopathology as ambulatory schizophrenia (35). Moreover, the incidence of psychoses linked etiologically with the use of cannabinoids is seemingly very much smaller in America than in North Africa and in the Middle and Far East. Several considerations seem to us pertinent to any attempt to explain this discrepancy. The prepsychotic patterns of usage reported for Eastern users are probably paralleled by only a small fraction of American users. How many Americans have smoked 10 to 70 pipes of marihauna daily for decades? Some psychiatrists believe that social and economic adversities can precipitate or aggravate psychiatric disorders among users of very large quantities of cannabinoids over a period of years (2, p. 86). Such socioeconomic conditions are not so prevalent in the United States as in Eastern countries. We must conclude, however, that the fundamental question of whether THC use is a significant causative factor in the onset of persistent episodes of psychosis remains unanswered. As a result, a secondary question remains unanswered: Can a chronic psychosis be precipitated by THC in anyone or only in those with serious antecedent psychopathology?

A more distressing long-term consequence of cannabinoid usage is the so-called "amotivational syndrome"; we call it more distressing because it is thought to affect a significant fraction of adolescents and young adults who use *Cannabis* extracts. The syndrome has been described by West in the following way (37): "the experienced clinician observes in many of these individuals (i.e., regular users of marihuana for 3 to 4 years) personality changes that seem to grow subtly over long periods of time: diminished drive, lessened ambition, decreased motivation, apathy, shortened attention span, distractibility, poor judgment, impaired communication skills, loss of effectiveness, introversion, magical thinking, derealization and depersonalization, diminished capacity to carry out complex plans or prepare realistically for the future, a peculiar fragmentation in the flow of thought, habit deterioration and progressive loss of insight." Some physicians feel that this syndrome is caused by THC. Investigations of the psychological and social consequences of patterns of heavy usage of THC in various countries have revealed quite different sequelae from one country to another; a heavy user in Jamaica may be a respected minor civil servant, but, in Morocco, a man with the same pattern of use may do little more than eat, sleep, and smoke *kif*. Such observations support the view that psychosocial deterioration is not an inevitable consequence of THC usage (2, pp. 64-65). Physicians who accept this view are nonetheless apprehensive that "marihuana-induced suggestibility may facilitate the rapid adoption of new values and behavior patterns, particularly when the drug is taken in a socially alienated subculture that advocates and strongly reinforces such changes" (2, pp. 86-87).

The nature of the relationship between marihuana usage and criminal behavior has been investigated by the National Commission on Marihuana and Drug Abuse. In its prefatory remarks on this subject, the commission provided a typical example of previous (and sometimes still prevalent) "cause-and-effect" reasoning: "The mere presence of the drug or the fact that an offender is a known user of marihuana is sometimes deemed sufficient to establish a causal link between the marihuana and the offense" (2, p. 70). The commission noted at the outset the many difficulties inherent in the situation where one sets out to demonstrate or deny a direct, positive, and causal relationship between the effects of marihuana and the commission of a crime.

In regard to violent crimes, the stereotyped allegation is that marihuana acts both to release the normal inhibitions against violent crimes and to embolden the individual to commit such acts. It was the finding of the commission that: "Rather than inducing violent or aggressive behavior through its purported effects of lowering inhibitions, weakening impulse control and heightening aggressive tendencies, marihuana was usually found to inhibit expression of aggressive impulses by pacifying the user, interfering with muscular coordination, reducing psychomotor activities and generally producing states of drowsiness, lethargy, timidity and passivity" (2, p. 72). The commission recognized that it could not assume that the foregoing description of the effects of marihuana applied to all users; it, therefore, investigated this situation from a diametrically opposite point of view: how many violent crimes have been committed by marihuana users, particularly offenses committed while the user was under the influence of marihuana? The commission found no evidence "to indicate that marihuana was responsible for generating or creating excessive aggressiveness or impulsivity in individuals having no prior history of impulse or personality disorder. The most that can be said is that in these rare instances, marihuana may have aggravated a pre-existing condition" (2, p. 73). Within the populations surveyed, the commission could find no significant difference in the incidence of violent criminal behavior when marihuana users were compared with non-users. The commission cited one study of young people from a disadvantaged minority group for whom "marihuana was found to play a significant role in youth's transition from a 'rowdy' to 'cool,' non-violent style" (2, p. 73), which echoes the conclusions of many authors in the 1950's about the impact of heroin usage on the street gangs of New York City.

The commission also examined the evidence bearing on the correlation between marihuana usage and delinquent behavior and non-violent crimes (shoplifting, burglary, and the like). In this context, they were interested not only in the effects of marihuana but also in antisocial acts committed in the course of drug-seeking activities. Studies of drug users with criminal records (for offenses other than violations of drug abuse laws) frequently reveal that the criminal record antedates the onset of drug abuse. In the case of marihuana, the commission concluded that "some users commit crimes more frequently than non-users not because they use marihuana but because they happen to be the kinds of people who would be expected to have a higher crime rate, wholly apart from the use of marihuana. In most cases, the differences in crime rate between the users and non-users are dependent not on marihuana use *per se* but on these other factors" (2, p. 77). The other factors referred to were *race, education, age, the use of other drugs, and having drug-using friends.* It appears again that no causal link has been demonstrated in the association of marihuana usage and antisocial behavior of a non-violent kind. It was the opinion of the commission that "the evidence suggests that sociolegal and cultural variables account for the apparent statistical correlation between marihuana use and crime or delinquency" (2, p. 76).

"Flashbacks" have been reported among users of THC as well as users of LSD (see p. 163), though the frequency seems very much lower in the former group (6, 10, p. 91, 35). Some users find the recurring drug experience to be pleasant, but others regard flashbacks as threatening and disturbing phenomena. A few who have used both LSD and THC (on separate occasions) found that smoking marihuana triggers recurrences of the LSD experiences (35).

A variety of somatic disturbances has been observed in long-term users of THC; these include conjunctivitis, chronic bronchitis, hepatic enlargement, arteritis, gastroenteritis, and poor dentition (2, p. 63, 32). Some of these observations have been made in American users. To focus on the possible causative role of THC in the development of these disturbances will require assessment of comparable populations of non-users and of non-users who are heavy smokers of tobacco. There is a report of one patient who exhibited a serious anaphylactic reaction after smoking marihuana (38). It is unlikely that the allergenic constituent of marihuana was THC because the reaction developed on the first occasion the patient smoked marihuana, and moreover she had a history of allergic responses going back 15 years.

The possibility that chronic usage of THC might lead to organic brain damage has been mentioned occasionally by physicians. Following his description of the amotivational syndrome, for example, West concluded: "There is a clinical impression or organicity in this syndrome which I simply cannot shake off or explain in any other fashion" (13). The only report linking cannabinoid usage causally with structural brain damage is that of Campbell and his colleagues (39), who demonstrated, with the technique of air encephalography, cerebral atrophy in ten young adult men who had histories of "consistent cannabis smoking" for 3 to 11 years. Differences between these patients and thirteen control subjects were most evident in the (increased) dimensions of the third and lateral ventricles, which the authors interpret as indicating that the most severely affected areas of the brain are likely to be in the region of the caudate nuclei, basal ganglia, and the structures immediately surrounding the third ventricle. (Similar changes are seen in patients with Parkinson's disease, encephalitis lethargica, and in old people suffering from arteriosclerosis.) All of the patients had histories of multiple drug abuse, with considerable individual variability in types of drugs used and patterns of abuse, though cannabinoid usage was predominant for all of them. Signs of irreversible brain damage such as these are rare in young adults, and the authors emphasize that other possible causes, such as birth damage, severe childhood infections involving the brain, and congenital syphilis, were not found in their patients. Just because this report is the only one of its kind of which we are aware and has not been confirmed by other investigators, because we must assume that an adequate number of control patients has been examined, and because air encephalography is hardly the most direct and precise means of demonstrating structural changes in the brain, we do not feel that it should be dismissed out of hand. We feel that chronic THC usage *might* lead to brain damage, though we wonder why only one report to this effect has appeared thus far, considering the widespread concern over the effects of THC and the plenitude of users theoretically available for study. Our conclusion is that this possibility is just one more facet of the "marihuana problem" about which judgment will have to be suspended until more evidence is forthcoming.

A teratogenic effect of THC or of crude resinous fractions obtained from the hemp plant has been demonstrated in rats, mice, rabbits, and hamsters; the effects on these animals' litters have ranged from resorption of the litter and stunting of the young to more specific defects such as phocomelia and encephalocele (6). Equivalent reports in humans have been largely confined to observations of highly dubious value, such as "increased incidences" of chromosomal "breaks" in leukocytes from peripheral venous blood (see p. 166).

The central depressant effects of THC are prominent with respect to the release of pituitary gonadotropins (44); a dose-related diminution of the functions of the testes and ovary has been observed.

Kolodny and his colleagues (39a) found subnormal plasma testosterone concentrations and oligospermia in young, "heterosexual" men, ranging in age from 18 to 28, during "chronic, intensive" marihuana usage. The 20 subjects selected for this study had no history of endocrine or liver disease and had never received androgens or estrogens. Moreover, in the 6 months preceding the start of study, drug abuse had had to be restricted to the smoking of marihuana (at least 4 times/week for a minimum of 6 months), though individuals with a concurrent consumption of alcohol not exceeding 415 ml/week were accepted also as subjects. An equally sized and comparably aged group of men, screened according to the criteria listed above (with the obvious exception of past and current drug abuse), constituted the controls.

Eleven of the subjects usually smoked 5 to 9 "joints" per week and nine of them smoked 10 or more weekly; 18 "joints" per week was the upper end of the range. By the criteria listed on p. 197, these men would be classified as long-term moderate or heavy users; the mean duration of marihuana usage for the entire group was 41.5 months.

Mean plasma testosterone concentration for the control group was 742 ng/100 ml. Subjects who smoked 5 to 9 joints a week had a mean concentration of 503 and those who smoked 10 joints or more weekly had a mean concentration of 309; the two means for the subjects were significantly different statistically from the controls and, also, from each other. Increases in plasma testosterone concentrations ranging from 57 to 141% were observed in the subjects after a week of abstinence from marihuana.

Examination of the semen of subjects using 5 to 9 marihuana cigarettes weekly indicated that the sperm content was essentially normal (mean: 67.9 million/ml), but the subjects using 10 or more joints a week had a subnormal mean concentration of 26.6 million spermatozoa/ml. Eighteen of the twenty subjects reported no changes in sexual function. One reported episodic impotence, which later disappeared after he stopped using marihuana; the other reported that he had been experiencing impotence and a marked reduction in libido for the preceding 6 months.

Despite continued marihuana usage, injections of human chorionic gonadotropin (4000 IU/day 1M for 4 days) produced increases in plasma testosterone concentrations ranging from 121 to 269%. These investigators concluded understandably that the suppressive action of marihuana on testicular (and ovarian) function is probably exerted primarily on the hypothalamus or the pituitary gland.

It is possible to kill animals with injections of THC, but the average lethal doses are very large: 1500 mg/kg of body weight for mice and 10,000 mg (of marihuana)/kg for dogs (13). In human beings, there have not been any documented deaths that could be attributed to any form of *Cannabis* extract (6, 13). Thorough investigations of occasional reports that a given death was caused by marihuana or hashish have invariably demonstrated a probable cause other than the use of *Cannabis* extracts. As in the case of LSD (see p. 169), if there is a lethal dose of THC for human beings, it is probably a remarkably large dose.

Potential therapeutic uses of THC

Three potential therapeutic uses of THC have received governmental sanction for preliminary investigations in human subjects. One relates to the potential value of THC as an agent capable of reducing intraocular pressure in patients with glaucoma. A second relates to the bronchodilation produced by THC and its value to asthmatic patients. And the third pertains to the ability of THC to depress the sensations of nausea and vomiting, for use with patients being treated for cancer by radiotherapy or chemotherapy (44).

ATROPINIC DRUGS

Many drugs (including adrenocortical steroids, narcotic antagonists, and bromides) and naturally occurring substances (including nutmeg and sunflower seeds) are capable of causing illusions, hallucinations, delusions, and other psychic disturbances; for most people, however, quite large doses or quantities of these agents are required to produce such disturbances. Because they are, at most, only episodically subject to abuse in the United States, we have decided to forego extensive consideration of them. There is only one other type of potentially hallucinogenic drug whose frequency of usage is such that we feel it warrants more than passing mention; this is the atropinic drug.

The principal action of atropinic drugs in therapeutic doses is to attenuate the effects of the acetylcholine that is released by postganglionic parasympathetic nerve endings and that provokes characteristic responses in tissues innervated by these nerves. The prototypical drug for this group, atropine, is a plant alkaloid produced by the deadly nightshade (*Atropa belladonna*) and also by Jimson weed (*Datura stramonium,* known also as locoweed, stinkweed, devil's apple, and thorn apple). A closely related and widely used atropinic drug is scopolamine, which is derived mainly from the shrub known as henbane (*Hyoscyamus niger*). Now available also for medical purposes are many synthetic compounds that bear little structural resemblance to atropine but are satisfactory substitutes for it in terms of their pharmacological actions.

Several aspects of the pharmacology of atropinic drugs deserve special attention in the context of drug abuse. Effective therapeutic doses of atropine or scopolamine are commonly less than 1 mg; for varying purposes, doses of 0.2, 0.5, or 0.6 mg are typical. Disturbing toxicity (rapid heart rate, blurring of near vision, headache, dry and hot skin, and so on) arises when the amount administered or used exceeds several milligrams; 10 mg of atropine has proved to be fatal for children but in adults produces the characteristic picture of poisoning by atropinic drugs: orientation is faulty, memory is uncertain, hallucinations occur, and a manic delirium may develop. At the least, the patient is excited, confused, restless, and giddy; he suffers from muscular incoordination and weakness, and speech disturbances may be prominent. His mouth is very dry, and he can swallow and talk only with great difficulty, if at all. His pupils are so dilated that the irises may be nearly invisible. His skin is hot and dry and often scarlet in color. His body temperature is definitely elevated; in children it may soar to 109° F or more. In the most severe cases, blood pressure drops and pulmonary ventilation becomes inadequate; paralysis, coma, and death from respiratory failure may follow (40). Though this syndrome has not been known to end in the deaths of many adults, it has been the cause of numerous mistaken psychiatric diagnoses, including "alcoholic delirium" or "acute schizophrenic episode."

It is also worth noting that atropine and scopolamine are absorbed rapidly into the body either by ingestion or inhalation and that these drugs are among the longest acting of any known drug. One drop of a 1% solution of atropine in the eye will cause changes in pupillary diameter and visual accommodation that persist for 7 to 12 *days* (40). When toxic doses of atropinic drugs (atropine and scopolamine, in particular) have been taken, the clinical picture described above usually persists for 2 days or more.

Preparations containing atropinic drugs as the only hallucinogenic component are only rarely employed by drug users. The most conspicuous exception has been the episodic use of a proprietary preparation named *Asthmador* (Witch's Poison), which is a powder containing 0.23 to 0.31% atropinic drugs. It is meant to be burned and its fumes inhaled by asthmatic patients; its label carries a clear caution against ingestion. Young people have found, however, that 1 to 2 teaspoons of this material, when swallowed, produces LSD-like effects. Because atropinic drugs have not been clearly identified as common objects of abuse, their sale has not been subject to special restrictions. Ethical pharmacists will not dispense most preparations of atropinic drugs without a prescription, but this fact is not an insuperable obstacle for the shrewd and determined user. Moreover, in the case of Asthmador, not even this impediment existed formerly. A relatively old proprietary preparation of unproved efficacy, whose toxic potential seemed small, it was sold "over-the-counter" just as aspirin is. After its abuse potential became apparent, its distribution was curtailed (41).

Atropinic drugs figure much more prominently as one component in a variety of drug mixtures, of which "STP" was the most widely publicized, than in their own right. By word of mouth in 1967, STP was touted as a "megahallucinogen" because of the intensity and duration (3 to 5 days) of the drug experience. Within a matter of a month or so, however, reports of extraordinarily "bad trips" and even of several deaths were being passed along the user's grapevine, and STP's period of popularity was relatively short. The exact composition of the original STP is not known; by the time samples were obtained for chemical analysis, various mixtures were being sold under the name of STP (see p. 35). Belladonna alkaloids (a term usually reserved for atropine, but which might include scopolamine as well) seemed to be a standard component of most, if not all of the mixtures. The preterminal status of users dying from STP ingestion was indistinguishable from the typical syndrome of atropine poisoning (41).

We had received personal reports that mixtures of LSD and atropine (or scopolamine) were still being sold in 1972, albeit on a relatively small scale, on the campuses of several eastern universities. Physicians must continue to remain alert to the possibility of encountering atropinic drug poisoning as the cause of a user's bad trip. The confirmatory signs (dilated pupils that are truly unresponsive to light, a hot and dry skin, dry mucous membranes, tachycardia, and fever) are readily evident, if only they are looked for and not ignored out of concern for the patient's psychiatric status. Appropriate management includes maintenance of vital signs, cautious sedation, if indicated, administration of physostigmine (other cholinergic drugs have only limited value), and a mechanical lowering of the body temperature by ice bags or alcohol sponges (40). The reasons for contraindication of the use of chlorpromazine (Thorazine) on these occasions were discussed in the previous chapter (see p. 173).

REFERENCES

1. Walton, R. P., *Marihuana. America's New Drug Problem.* Philadelphia: Lippincott, 1938
2. *Marihuana: A Signal of Misunderstanding.* First Report of the National Commission on Marihuana and Drug Abuse. Washington: U.S. Government Printing Office. 1972
3. Brecher, Edward M., *Licit and Illicit Drugs.* Mount Vernon (New York): Consumer Union. 1972
4. Mayor's Committee on Marihuana, *The Marihuana Problem in the City of New York.* Lancaster (Pa.): Jacques Cattell Press, 1944
5. Schultes, R. E., Hallucinogens of plant origin. *Science* 163:245, 1969
6. Pillard, R. C., Marihuana. *New Engl J Med* 283:294, 1970

7. Mechoulam, R., Marihuana chemistry. *Science* 168:1159, 1970
8. Hollister, L. E., Marihuana in man: Three years later. *Science* 172:21, 1971
9. Farnsworth, N. R., Hallucinogenic plants. *Science* 162:1086, 1968
10. Snyder, S. H., *Uses of Marijuana.* New York: Oxford University Press, 1971
11. Hollister, L. E. and H. K. Gillespie, Delta-8- and delta-9-tetrahydrocannabinol. *Clin Pharmacol Therap* 14:353, 1973
12. Joachimoglu, G., Natural and smoked hashish. In: Wolstenholme, G. E. W. and J. Knight, eds., *Hashish: its Chemistry and Pharmacology.* Boston: Little, Brown, 1965, p. 2
13. The Marijuana Problem. UCLA Interdepartmental Conference. *Arch Int Med* 73:449, 1970
14. Perez-Reyes, M., M. A. Lipton, M. C. Timmons, M. E. Wall, D. R. Brine, and K. H. Davis, Pharmacology of orally administered Δ9-tetrahydrocannabinol. *Clin Pharmacol Therap* 14:48, 1973
15. Kreuz, D. S. and J. Axelrod, Delta-9-tetrahydrocannabinol: Localization in body fat. *Science* 179:391, 1973
16. Galanter, M., R. J. Wyatt, L. Lemberger, H. Weingartner, T. B. Vaughan, and W. T. Roth, Effects on humans of Δ9-tetrahydrocannabinol administered by smoking. *Science* 176:934, 1972
17. Lemberger, L., J. L. Weiss, A. M. Watanabe, I. M. Galanter, R. J. Wyatt, and P. V. Cardon, Delta-9-tetrahydrocannabinol. *New Engl J Med* 286:685, 1972
18. Perez-Reyes, M., M. C. Timmons, M. A. Lipton, K. H. Davis, and M. E. Wall, Intravenous injection in man of Δ9-tetrahydrocannabinol and 11-OH-Δ9-tetrahydrocannabinol. *Science* 177:633, 1972
19. Burstein, S., J. Rosenfeld, and T. Wittstruck, Isolation and characterization of two major urinary metabolites of Δ1-tetrahycrocannabinol. *Science* 176:422, 1972
20. Lemberger, L., R. E. Crabtree, and H. M. Rowe, 11-Hydroxy-Δ9-tetrahydrocannabinol: Pharmacology, disposition and metabolism of a major metabolite of marihuana in man. *Science* 177:62, 1972
21. Weiss, J. L., A. M. Watanabe, L. Lemberger, N. R. Tamarkin, and P. V. Cardon, Cardiovascular effects of delta-9-tetrahydrocannabinol in man. *Clin Pharmacol Therap* 13:671, 1972
22. Beaconsfield, P., J. Ginsberg, and R. Rainsbury, Marihuana smoking. Cardiovascular effects in man and possible mechanisms. *New Engl J Med* 287:209, 1972
23. Isbell, H., C. W. Garodetzsky, D. Jasinski, U. Claussen, F. v. Spulak, and F. Korte, Effects of (-)Δ9-trans-tetrahycrocannabinol in man. *Psychopharmacologia* 11:184, 1967
24. Kiplinger, G. F. and J. E. Manno, Dose-response relationships to cannabis in human subjects. *Pharmacol Rev* 23:339, 1971
25. Klonoff, H., Strategy and tactics of marijuana research. *Canad Med Assoc J* 108:145, 1973

26. Kolansky, H. and W. T. Moore, Effects of marihuana on adolescents and young adults. *J Amer Med Assoc* 216:486, 1971
27. Pivik, R. T., V. Zarcone, W. C. Dement, and L. E. Hollister, Delta-9-tetrahydrocannabinol and synhexyl: Effects on human sleep patterns. *Clin Pharmacol Therap* 13:426, 1972
28. Hosko, M. J., M. S. Kochar, and R. I. H. Wang, Effects of orally administered delta-9-tetrahydrocannabinol in man. *Clin Pharmacol Therap* 14:344, 1973
29. Crancer, A., Jr., J. M. Dille, J. C. Delay, J. E. Wallace, and M. D. Haykin, Comparison of the effects of marihuana on simulated driving performance. *Science* 164:851, 1969
30. *Editorial:* Cannabis and driving skills. *Canad Med Assoc J* 107:269, 1972
31. Low, M. D., H. Klonoff, and A. Marcus, The neurophysiological basis of the marijuana experience. *Canad Med Assoc J* 108:157, 1973
32. Nahas, G. G., *Cannabis sativa.* The deceptive weed. *N Y State J Med* 72:856, 1972
33. Weil, A. T., N. E. Zinberg, and J. M. Nelson, Clinical and psychological effects of marihuana in man. *Science* 162:1234, 1968
34. Clark, L. D. and E. N. Nakashima, Experimental studies of marihuana. *Amer J Psychiat* 125:3, 1968
35. Weil, A. T. Adverse reactions to marihuana. *New Engl J Med* 282:997, 1970.
36. Negrette, J. C. Psychological adverse effects of cannabis smoking: A tentative classification. *Canad Med Assoc J* 108:195, 1973
37. West, L. J., On the marihuana problem. In: Efron, D., *Psychotomimetic Drugs.* New York: Raven Press, 1970, p. 45
38. Liskow, B., J. L. Liss, and C. W. Parker, Allergy to marihuana. *Ann Int Med* 75:571, 1971
39. Campbell, A. M. G., M. Evans, J. L. G. Thomson, and M. J. Williams, Cerebral atrophy in young cannabis smokers. *Lancet* ii:1219, 1971
39a. Kolodny, R. C., W. H. Masters, R. M. Kolodner, and G. Toro, Depression of plasma testosterone levels after chronic intensive marihuana use. *New Engl J Med* 290:872, 1974
40. Innes, I. R. and M. Nickerson, Drugs inhibiting the action of acetylcholine on structures innervated by postganglionic parasympathetic nerves (antimuscarinic or atropinic drugs). In: Goodman, L. and A. Gilman, eds., *The Pharmacological Basis of Therapeutics,* ed. 4. New York: Macmillan, 1970
41. Non-medical use of drugs, with particular reference to youth. Part of a brief presented by the Canadian Medical Association to the Government of Canada Commission of Inquiry into the Non-Medical Use of Drugs. *Canad Med Assoc J* 101:804, 1969
42. Abelson, H. I., P. M. Fishburne, and I. H. Cisin, *National survey on drug abuse: 1977. A nationwide study—youth, young adults and older adults.* Vol. I, *Main findings.* National Institute on Drug Abuse. Depart-

ment of Health, Education, and Welfare Publication No. (ADM) 78-618, Washington, D.C.: U.S. Government Printing Office, 1977

43. Rubin, V. and L. Comitas, *Ganja in Jamaica.* The Hague: Mouton, 1975
44. Jaffee, J. H., Drug addiction and drug abuse. In: A. G. Gilman, L Goodman, and A. Gilman, eds., *The Pharmacological Basis of Therapeutics,* ed. 6. New York: Macmillan, 1980

Chapter 8

CENTRAL NERVOUS SYSTEM STIMULANTS

In any layman's listing of the evils of drug abuse, one is likely to encounter the specter of the drug-crazed criminal, an individual made not only irrational by drugs but also impelled to commit vicious acts of violence. Like many bits of folklore, this concept has a foundation in fact; it seems to have arisen in the period from 1890 to 1915 and was derived most probably from accounts of behavior during the paranoid psychotic state cocaine can produce. Unfortunately, many lay people mistakenly regard violent behavior as a typical concomitant of all forms of drug abuse; yet it is a frequent consequence of the psychotoxic effects of large doses of all central nervous system stimulants.

Cocaine, a local anesthetic drug capable of producing marked central nervous system excitation, was the first agent with stimulant properties to be subjected to widespread abuse in the United States; this practice probably began in the 1890's. In the late 1930's, scattered reports began to appear about the abuse of amphetamine, a stimulant both cheaper and more readily available than cocaine. More alarming reports were published in the 1950's about the increasing magnitude of the problem of amphetamine abuse in this and other countries (most notably Japan), and, in 1958, Connell's authoritative monograph (1) on the subject of amphetamine psychosis was published. Connell emphasized that this form of toxic psychosis was not as rare as was generally supposed at that time. Until the 1960's, those who abused amphetamine typically took it by mouth; further escalation in the severity of the problem occurred in this decade with the growing popularity of intravenous amphetamine usage (2, 3). The frightening and tragic figure of the "speed freak" came clearly into focus during this period.

The abuse of amphetamine and methamphetamine will be discussed in detail in this chapter for they are the stimulants ("uppers" or "speed") most commonly used in America today; for convenience, we will hereafter refer to these two compounds as the amphetamines. The patterns and the consequences of the abuse of other analeptic drugs do not differ significantly. For various reasons, cocaine abuse will be considered separately later in the chapter.

THE AMPHETAMINES

Various explanations have been offered to account for the current prevalence of amphetamine abuse. The willingness of many physicians to prescribe stimulants for disorders in which they are essentially ineffective has been severely condemned because they expose susceptible individuals to these drugs. Edison recently reviewed the medical evidence indicating that stimulants are, at the very most, only minimally effective in the two conditions for which they are most commonly used: the management of obesity and of mild emotional depression (4). The depressant effect of amphetamines on appetite is typically transient (whereas obesity is usually a chronic problem), and numerous psychiatrists find the drugs' effects in mildly depressed individuals to be either transient or indistinguishable from those of a placebo. In 1969, the physicians of Ipswich, England, agreed to refrain from prescribing amphetamines; the results of this step were so gratifying medically that the British Medical Association adopted as official policy a similar voluntary ban the next year. The only remaining defensible indications for the use of amphetamines seem to be in the management of narcoleptics, epileptics receiving phenobarbital, and truly hyperkinetic children; the number of patients falling into these three categories is minuscule compared to the number of prescription for amphetamines in the recent past.

The American pharmaceutical industry probably has been making from 8 to 10 billion doses of stimulant drugs annually, and, as we noted in a previous chapter, the FDA estimated in 1968 that half of the yearly output was diverted into channels of illegal usage. The ease with which distributors of illicit drugs could obtain substantial quantities of stimulants in bulk or individual dosage forms by quite amateurish methods of deception (2) made possible the rapid spread of amphetamine abuse in the 1960's. Though some diversion of legally manufactured amphetamines to illicit markets may still occur, regulation of drug manufacture and sale is now most stringent. As a result, the bulk of the speed offered for sale, and particularly that in a form suitable for intravenous injection, now comes from the "basement" chemist (2).

Along with familiarity and availability, the third factor operative in the spread of amphetamine abuse has been the fact that so many people find the effects of "uppers" particularly gratifying. Adults who achieve relaxation and pleasure through the use of such "downers" as alcohol, sedatives, tranquilizers, and "sleeping pills" may find (or think they find) that an "upper" is necessary to "get going" in the morning, to function satisfactorily in certain hectic businesses, and so on. People who take no other drugs may use amphetamines as antidotes for emotional malaise or to prolong sexual pleasure. Adolescents and young adults, the groups most likely to be heavily involved in intravenous speed usage, crave action, kicks, and instant pleasure. Uncritical attempts have often been made, we feel, to explain the origins of amphetamine abuse and other drug problems on the basis of sociological situations and forces peculiar to the United States; these include the Vietnamese war and racial inequality. Though we do not feel that these attempts are wholly inappropriate, they fail to account for similar abuse in Sweden, Japan, and Great Britain. Sociological problems may exacerbate drug abuse, but we doubt very much that the origins of the amphetamine epidemic can be explained in terms of social conditions and forces. We are hard put to determine what the United States, Sweden, Japan, and Great Britain have in common sociologically, but each has experienced a noteworthy epidemic of drug abuse in the past 25 years.

Preparations used

Over the past 40 years, "amphetamine" has been manufactured in two chemical forms. It was first synthesized in 1927 as a racemic mixture; clinical use of the mixture, as a nasal decongestant and under the trade name of Benzedrine, began in the early 1930's. Its central nervous system stimulatory properties became widely known soon thereafter, and, by the end of the decade, amphetamine occupied a prominent place among the analeptic drugs.

Tests of the two isomers comprising the amphetamine racemate indicated that the dextrorotatory isomer exerted the greater pharmacological activity; as a result, dextro-amphetamine (Dexedrine) was marketed as a more potent form (on a weight basis) of amphetamine. Except for the matter of dosage, no therapeutic distinction can be made between the racemate and the dextro-isomer, for their pharmacological effects are identical. We are not aware of any chemical analyses having been performed on illicitly manufactured amphetamine to determine which form of the drug is prepared by the chemists supplying the street market.

Methamphetamine (speed, "crystal," Methedrine) is one of the many amphetamine derivatives that were synthesized by the pharmaceutical industry following the enthusiastic acceptance of amphetamine by the medical profession. It is slightly less potent than amphetamine as a pressor drug, though clearly more potent as a central nervous system stimulant. It has been marketed by many drug houses for pressor and central nervous system stimulatory purposes; contrary to the impression given by the communications media, Methedrine is a trade, not a generic, name for this drug and just one of many. Because physicians have been known to give methamphetamine unwittingly, under one of its numerous names, to combat the underlying depression present in many drug users (5), we think it would be useful to list the trade names, other than Methedrine, under which methamphetamine is sold; they include Amphedroxyn, Desoxyn, Desyphed, Dexoval, Doxyfed, Drinalfa, Efroxine, Norodin, Semoxydrine, and Syndrox.

Because many agents having pharmacological properties similar to those of amphetamine have been marketed, reports about the abuse of most of these drugs can be found. Phenmetrazine (Preludin) is a particular favorite in Sweden but is only episodically abused in this country. The "speed scene" came to Great Britain when young people there started taking what they called "Purple Hearts," which were tablets of Dexamyl or Drinamyl (a dextro-amphetamine–barbiturate mixture); there has never been a comparable vogue for Dexamyl in this country. Reports about the abuse of methylphenidate (Ritalin), pipradrol (Meratran), and mephentermine (Wyamine, and once a component of Dristan inhalers) have appeared, but again abuse appears to occur only infrequently. The popularity of amphetamine and methamphetamine relative to other central nervous system stimulants does not reflect any great pharmacological difference between these two groups of drugs, but rather the highly important factors of ready availability, low cost, and wide publicity.

Patterns of use

Relatively mild forms of amphetamine abuse were prevalent in this country from the 1930's to the early 1960's, and most users fell into two categories. In the first category were those who used an amphetamine-type of drug only on irregular occasions and usually for the specific purpose of postponing sleep: the student studying for an examination or the truck driver faced with a long trip. (Semanticists may dispute whether such patterns of usage constitute abuse; we are content merely to describe them.) Users in the second category typified a more familiar pattern of drug abuse, for their goal was purely hedonistic; they relished the euphoria and the enhanced sense of self-confidence that stimulants can produce. In this earlier period, Benzedrine inhalers (250 mg of amphetamine per inhaler) were a common source of the drug; once the inhaler was disassembled, the drug-impregnated pledget was removed and ingested, or the drug was eluted into a liquid. The abuse of Benzedrine inhalers reached such alarming proportions that, in 1949, the amphetamine in these devices was replaced by a drug with weak stimulant properties (propylhexedrine).

The incidence of amphetamine abuse increased after World War II, slowly in some countries like the United States, more rapidly in others like Japan. This increase reflected, in part, the consequences of two war-related events: millions of doses of amphetamine and methamphetamine in the guise of "energy tablets" were supplied to service personnel during the war (6), and, after the war, surplus supplies of these drugs were "dumped" onto civilian markets, most notably in Japan (3). By 1954, it was estimated that 500,000 to 1,500,000 people were involved in the abuse of amphetamines in Japan; in some cities, it was said that stimulant abuse was practiced by 5% of those in the age range of 16 to 25 years of age (5). The Japanese pattern of abuse was often one of daily use of stimulants, injected intravenously or subcutaneously; the total intake per day in some cases rose to 200 ampules, each containing 3 mg of methamphetamine (3, 6). Governmental programs of strict drug controls and public information about drug abuse have resulted in a notable decrease in the size of this problem. The Swedish problem of drug abuse, an outstanding aspect of which is the use of stimulants, will be discussed further in Chapter 11, as it entailed an experimental period of "legalized abuse."

The American speed user only infrequently progressed to a severe level of abuse prior to the 1960's. (In various times and places, *speed* has been used as a synonym for amphetamine, methamphetamine, both of these drugs, or any stimulant; in recent years, it has been used increasingly to refer only to methamphetamine. We will use the term as a synonym for the amphetamines.) Alteration of Benzedrine inhalers meant only greater utilization of the standard medicinal forms of the drug (5- and 10-mg tablets), which were obtained by illegal diversion, or, in the case of resourceful users, by deception of physicians and pharmacists (6). The drugs were almost always taken by mouth. Some users took these stimulants only on weekends in social settings, whereas others felt an almost daily need for them. In some cases, amphetamine usage replaced other forms of drug abuse (when heroin was unavailable, for example), whereas for many, amphetamine was only one drug in a pattern of multiple drug abuse. It has been used to enhance and prolong the effects of drugs like heroin and LSD. It has been used to antagonize the effects of "downers" like barbiturates. Often it has been regarded by adolescents as just "part of the scene," to be used in an unpredictably alternating pattern of multiple drug abuse that included use of marihuana and other agents (2). It is a bit surprising to us that a higher incidence of serious amphetamine abuse was not encountered before the 1960's, for factors are operative in this practice that promote the use of ever-increasing quantities of the drug; these factors will be described shortly in conjunction with intravenous patterns of abuse.

Though such mild to moderately severe patterns of oral abuse continue to be exhibited to this day by many (possibly several millions of) users of amphetamine, a new and much more pernicious pattern of abuse gained popularity in America in the 1960's: the "run" in which large doses of speed are injected intravenously at relatively short intervals for periods as long as 6 (and occasionally 12) days (2). "Speed freaks" (those who exhibit this pattern of severe abuse) may begin the use of speed during adolescence by taking "bennies" (Benzedrine tablets) or "dexies" (Dexedrine tablets) by mouth (2). The total daily intake gradually increases until eventually about 200 mg of amphetamine are being ingested. The desire for a more intense amphetamine experience (and possibly the hope for qualitatively different effects) is the typical spur to the use of the intravenous route of administration. The progression from oral to intravenous use of speed is not always an uninterrupted sequence; drug-free intervals may occur as well as periods during which other types of drugs are used primarily (2). With the change from the oral to the intravenous route, the pattern of abuse usually becomes most severe. Intravenous usage may initially entail doses of 20 to 40 mg taken three to four times a day. In most cases studied, both the dosage and frequency of use rapidly increased thereafter. Individual doses taken by speed freaks range from 100 to 300 mg and occasionally rise to 3000 mg (7); for such users, the interval between injections often falls to 2 hours or less (7). A speed freak's total daily drug intake may conceivably reach 30,000 mg or more; the equivalent total achieved by the oral route probably rarely exceeds 1000 to 2000 mg (7). Speed freaks inject both amphetamine and methamphetamine intravenously. Chemists who supply the illicit drug market commonly provide crystalline methamphetamine (hence the name "crystal" for the drug in this form), which is dissolved sparingly in water before injection; in effect, a "syrup" is injected, within which high drug concentrations are possible (2).

Four factors play a part in the rapid progression to severe patterns of abuse, once the intravenous route has been adopted. Speed freaks are commonly described as essentially hedonistic people, whose only desire is to experience the effects of speed as intensely and as continuously as possible. Some have police records and histories of heavy drinking. There is a clinical impression that, relative to their probable proportion of the general population, unusually large numbers of male homosexuals are encountered in studies of speed users (8). Unlike users of LSD, who are purportedly seeking new insights and awareness, the speed users want "action" and "kicks" (3, 9); not infrequently they are members of motorcycle gangs. Moreover, the effects of speed are so deeply gratifying to susceptible individuals that amphetamines can "hook" (create psychological dependence) a user probably as rapidly and as completely as heroin can (2, 3). In this context, it is worth noting that first experiences with speed are almost uniformly reported to be pleasurable. The third factor in the speed freak's incremental pattern of drug intake, the apparent development of tolerance to the psychic effects of amphetamines on repeated usage, provides an even more potent stimulus for increasing the amount of drug injected. And last, once a "run" ceases, the speed freak "crashes" or "falls out," i.e., he stops taking the drug and falls asleep, either spontaneously or with the aid of a "downer." It is a deep sleep from which the user ordinarily cannot be aroused. Upon awakening, the user is ravenously hungry, lethargic, and sometimes emotionally depressed. Suicidal thoughts and overt attempts at self-destruction may occur at this time. As a result, the user feels impelled to resume injecting speed to overcome the hangover from his last run. If resumption of speed administration is delayed, the hangover usually persists for several days.

The speed freak's pattern of abuse clearly leaves little time for activities unrelated to drug acquisition and use; his life style, in this respect, closely resembles that of a narcotic addict. Steady employment is impossible, and money is usually obtained by criminal means (3). The speed freak, like any user who follows a severe pattern of abuse, has obtained temporary surcease from unwelcome thoughts and worries; drugs now so dominate his life that he can think of little else.

Effects of amphetamines

The oral and intravenous amphetamine experiences are different not only because higher drug concentrations in blood are achieved by the intravenous route but also because the intravenous pattern of abuse can entail cumulative drug effects.

When amphetamines are "dropped" (taken by mouth) or inhaled as snuff would be, the user typically experiences feelings of euphoria, enhanced self-confidence, heightened alertness, greater energy, and an increased capacity for concentration. Sensations of hunger and fatigue are reduced. The user becomes more talkative and also often more irritable. He is restless and moves about frequently. Overt sexual behavior may be displayed. Physiologically, his pulse is rapid, he may experience palpitations, and his mouth is dry. His pupils are dilated, and his reflexes brisk. Fine tremors of the limbs may be exhibited. For some, the pattern of rapid speech passes into one of slurred speech. Teeth-grinding movements may occur. Ataxia can develop, and some users complain of headache and nausea (5, 7). As the drug effects wane, feelings of fatigue, "let down," and drowsiness occur; some users may be depressed emotionally, though rarely to any marked extent. Most users commonly fall asleep thereafter; the duration of the sleep is not often very abnormal. There is no hangover on awakening that can be clearly attributed to the drug experience with mild amphetamine abuse. If the pattern of oral abuse worsens, however, and, also, with the passage of time, the problem of the hangover on awakening probably will grow more severe, though it never approximates the speed freak's hangover in intensity.

The sensations experienced even before the needle is withdrawn from the vein constitute the principal appeal of the intravenous route for most speed freaks. The initial sensations (the "rush" or "flash") have been variously described by speed users as an electrical shock, being splashed with iced water, and a feeling so pleasurable that it resembles a complete body orgasm (3). The short interval between injections (less than 2 hours in some instances and probably before the effects of the previous dose have wholly waned) is prompted by the desire to recapture the transient initial sensations. A feeling of "abrupt awakening" (2) is produced by the initial sensations, which is succeeded by an extraordinary sense of omnipotence, a state described by one Australian user as "being a bit like God" (6). The user feels unusually energetic and self-confident. He sees himself as a rapid and efficient thinker with an incredible ability to make correct decisions rapidly. He wants to be sociable, for he has much to say. He is capable of great warmth but also of great anger. He is active almost continuously in some purposive fashion, often sweating a deal, without any sense of fatigue. For some, these activities will be sexual; orgasm in both men and women is said to be delayed so that sexual activities may be carried on for hours before a climax, more intense and more pleasurable than without speed, is finally achieved (2, 6). In others, however, interest in sexual activity may be unaffected, and, in a few, it may even be decreased (2, 6). In an Australian study of speed abuse, only one-third of the users reported that amphetamines enhanced sexuality (6).

Accompanying these psychic effects are the physiological effects that one would expect of adrenergic drugs like the amphetamines: a rise in blood pressure, tachycardia, pupillary dilation (and, for some, blurred vision), and anorexia. Blood glucose increases, as does blood coagulability (3). Skeletal muscle tension increases, but the musculature of the bronchi and intestines relaxes. The cardiovascular effects of these drugs may also manifest themselves in irregularities in cardiac rate and output and blanching in some vascular beds such as those of the mucous membranes. The mouth is dry (because only sparse quantities of saliva are being secreted), and swallowing is most difficult, which makes ingestion of solid food a formidable chore. Urination too becomes difficult.

Except for the initial sensations, the effects of a single dose of intravenous amphetamines differ only quantitatively from the effects of oral amphetamines. A quite different and unpleasant picture develops, however, when we consider the effects of intravenous amphetamines within a run. The reasons for the change in the nature of the intravenous amphetamine experience with this pattern of abuse are not well understood; several factors may have causative roles. The passage of time is important; the euphoria of the first day of a run is often succeeded, as the days go by, by the unhappy events to be described below. We wonder if, during a run, drug intake does not exceed the combined rates of metabolic inactivation and urinary excretion, and, therefore, owing to this cumulative effect, psychotoxic concentrations of amphetamines are achieved. The observation that untoward reactions intensify in most users as the run progresses (2) supports this speculation; alternatively, the gradually worsening psychological status of the user during a run might also reflect a temporary deterioration of "personality structure" as a result of prolonged exposure to these drugs.

For most speed freaks, time also alters their susceptibility to the amphetamine psychosis. Several observers have noted that psychotic episodes are rare in the first few months of intravenous use (3). This finding suggests that the cumulative impact of runs somehow damages the central nervous system. Whether organic brain damage is produced is not known (3). Certain persistent psychological changes have been observed in speed freaks, and they will be described below.

The first day of a run is usually a period of euphoria, full of rapid and decisive patterns of thought, enhanced self-confidence and self-esteem, and garrulous sociability; on this day, and throughout the run, users report being intensely fascinated with their own thoughts and activities, even when they are unpleasant (2). By the second day, thoughts now race through the mind so rapidly that concentration on any one of them is difficult. Abrupt changes in mood replace the unalloyed euphoria of the first day. Frightening visions (pseudohallucinations) begin to be seen by many speed freaks at this time (and, occasionally, true hallucinations occur). Shadows become people, and the user often sees his body as covered with sores and vermin. Unlike LSD and other drugs classified as hallucinogens, the amphetamines produce visions or illusions ordinarily only during the special circumstances of a run, with its prolonged exposure to large quantities of the drug. It is for this reason that the actions of amphetamines on the brain are thought not to resemble closely those of the drugs called hallucinogens, and, therefore, amphetamines are not included under the heading, hallucinogens. In addition to visual pseudoperceptions, aberrations in auditory perception occur also, especially at night; recognition that these sensory phenomena are drug-induced is commonly retained for a time at least (2).

To add to the user's unease and confusion, paranoid symptoms invariably develop during a run and gradually intensify with time; these symptoms and the disturbances in sensory perception may be related realistically to the user's awareness of the illegality of drug abuse. Trees, shadows, and parked cars may all be perceived as evidence of police surveillance. Friends may be regarded as informers, and rooms searched to locate the "bugging" equipment that the user is now sure has been installed. Strangers may be regarded as disguised policemen. Any remark, however casual and even if uttered by a close friend, may be construed as an insult or a threat. The combination of this confused, paranoid state of mind with the feeling of great energy and enhanced physical prowess can lead to explosive outbursts of violent behavior. Friends and strangers alike may be regarded as persecutors or enemies and physically assaulted. When speed users are troubled by paranoid thoughts and pseudoperceptions, they may try to quell them with opiates or occasionally barbiturates, but the desired result is rarely obtained (2). Some speed freaks, however, have learned "to live with" the paranoid symptoms; they expect the symptoms as one of the prices to be paid for speed use and view them in a wryly humorous way (2).

The desire to be sociable persists despite episodes of paranoid reaction to friends and acquaintances. Because of their reputation for aggressive behavior, however, usually only fellow speed users will tolerate speed users; hence, they tend to congregate in "splash" or "flash" houses in some cities. These houses, rented by speed vendors or the users themselves, are often crowded with people "shooting" speed (injecting it intravenously). Because of neighbors' complaints, police pressure, or failure to pay the rent, such establishments rarely remain in any one location for more than a few months at most (3).

It becomes most difficult for some users, as a run progresses, to continue to accept the visions, auditory phenomena, and paranoid ideation as reflections of drug effects, and they come to be regarded rather as reflections of reality. The amphetamine psychosis is commonly described as closely simulating paranoid schizophrenia; within a setting of clear consciousness, the individual experiences delusions of persecution plus visual, tactile, and auditory hallucinations and may exhibit repetitious compulsive behavior (1, 3, 6). The disorder usually lasts for less than a week and is a toxic psychosis, for its intensity correlates well with the rate of the drug's excretion (10). Events that occurred during the psychotic state are usually remembered clearly thereafter (3). No one knows "what proportion of users actually develop a psychosis or how many psychoses are misdiagnosed as schizophrenia" (3).

As the run progresses, and the users ability to deal effectively with the world around him deteriorates, his preoccupation with his own thoughts and behavior may manifest itself in repetitive behavior. One user, for example, strung beads for hours; another shined his shoes and his needle and syringe innumerable times (2). Examples of more inappropriate, but similarly persistent behavior have been recorded. To build a radio, one user disassembled a dozen radios; he never made appreciable progress toward his goal but remained cheerfully undaunted and could not be diverted from this activity during the course of his run. Another user, to increase the performance of his car, dismantled it and thereafter carefully examined many wildly impossible alterations, such as substituting the exhaust manifold for the carburetor (2, 3).

Eventually the run ends, and the user *crashes.* It may be an involuntary cessation of drug administration (because the supply of speed is exhausted) or a voluntary choice. Tolerance to amphetamines appears to build rapidly and, beyond the 5th day of a run, it has been estimated that no quantity of the drug produces the desired effect (2). More common reasons for ending a run appear to be exhaustion, frightening hallucinations (3), or tenseness, in both the emotional and muscular senses of the word (2). Drowsiness sets in about 3 hours after the last "fix" (instance of amphetamine usage), though some users feel they require barbiturates or opiates to fall asleep. The duration of the ensuing period of sleep, which has been reported to last as long as several days, is commonly said to be directly proportional to the duration of the run; semicomatose states spanning 4 to 5 days have been described by some users (2). The period after awakening, as described above, is one of great psychic discomfort for the user. In addition to a voracious appetite, he may be beset with anxiety, emotional depression, or irritability (3), and virtually all users feel lethargic and fatigued during this period. Such feelings may persist for weeks after a run, and new runs are often started, it is thought, to overcome these feelings (2). The emotional depression that may occur during the amphetamine hangover is understandably a vividly contrasting experience to the euphoria and sense of omnipotence the user felt during the run; the depression can be so overwhelming that suicidal thoughts and behavior ensue (3, 6).

Absorption, fate, and excretion of amphetamines

Amphetamines are absorbed adequately following ingestion, upon direct contact with mucosal surfaces and from injection sites. About one-half of a therapeutic dose is inactivated (largely in the liver) by the process of deamination; the remainder is excreted unchanged in the urine. The relative significance of the metabolic and excretory routes as means of disposing of the very large doses common in shooting speed is not known. It is known that excretion is most rapid when the urine is acidic and is relatively slow when the urine is markedly alkaline. The acidotic state resulting from the starvation that prevails during a run can in effect increase the user's drug requirements by promoting amphetamine excretion (2).

Physical dependence on amphetamines

It is conventionally said that no physical dependence on the effects of amphetamines develops, regardless of the pattern of usage. The sleep and the sensations of hunger and fatigue on awakening that follow use of amphetamines are regarded as physiological compensations to be expected after a protracted period of wakefulness, starvation, and continuous activity. Several investigators have dissented from this view, expressing the concept that the amphetamine hangover is, in effect, a withdrawal syndrome.

Kramer and his colleagues (2) feel that the length and depth (a "catatonia" in the opinion of some) of the sleep after a run and the lethargy and sense of chronic fatigue that can persist for weeks thereafter represent a withdrawal syndrome. They regard the hunger on awakening as a withdrawal symptom, for, as they point out, appetite usually wanes after the 2nd or 3rd day of starvation under other circumstances. Abnormal EEG patterns have been observed by others during the hangover; these disappeared when amphetamine was administered (3). More acutely severe symptoms do not occur, it is argued, because the amphetamines are so slowly excreted; an analogy is clearly being made here to the narcotic drug methadone, whose withdrawal syndrome is mild because, it is believed, its rate of bodily disposition is relatively slow.

At this time, reasonably good arguments can be mustered in defense of either point of view. We know little about the true nature of physical dependence, and much of our meager knowledge is derived from studies of narcotic addiction. There is no logical reason, however, to insist that physical dependence on amphetamines and the subsequent withdrawal syndrome, if indeed they exist, conform in pharmacodynamic principle and pattern with the situation that obtains in narcotic addiction.

Tolerance to amphetamines

Though it is usually said that tolerance develops to (some of) the effects of amphetamines, this phenomenon has never been systematically investigated. Because there is relatively little certain knowledge about amphetamine toxicity, and particularly the quantitative aspects, it is difficult to cite doses tolerated by users that would harm an ordinary person. We will therefore simply report the observations that seem to bear on the matter of tolerance to amphetamines.

Tolerance appears to develop to the euphoric and other "desirable" psychic effects of amphetamines (11). This may be inferred from the observations that dosage size increases considerably as a run progresses (2). A tendency to increase the amount of drug used over a matter of weeks and months in patterns of oral and intravenous abuse has also been noted (2, 7). It is difficult to say, however, whether these observations reflect the development of tolerance, the desire for a more intense amphetamine experience, or a combination of the two factors. Tolerance to the cardiovascular effects of the amphetamines, and, more specifically, to their vasoconstrictor actions, is strongly suggested by the fact that speed freaks can survive single intravenous doses of 1000 mg or more with only an occasional untoward physiological effect. The risk of a cardiovascular disturbance would be high, in our opinion, if a non-user were similarly exposed to amphetamines. Though mention is sometimes made of cerebrovascular accidents caused by intravenous speed (7), specific instances have yet to be documented (3).

Our ignorance of the quantitative aspects of amphetamine toxicity precludes even rough estimates of the degree of probable tolerance that speed users develop. Tolerance to the euphoric effects of these drugs may become absolute for, as we noted above, some believe that after the 5th day of a run, no dose of amphetamines produces the desired effect, regardless of its size (2). This must be regarded as a tentative conclusion, however, based in large part on reports made by speed freaks.

No tolerance seems to develop to the "awakening" or "anti-sleep" actions of these drugs. The undiminished effectiveness of amphetamine in the treatment of narcolepsy (11), and the state of persistent wakefulness during a run lend support to this view.

When tolerance develops, we have no clear idea of how long it persists once drug administration has stopped. According to Bell (6), tolerance is retained "long after" the last dose of amphetamines has been wholly excreted.

Acute amphetamine toxicity

Violent behavior and the onset of a psychotic state are the two most common untoward events that can occur during the course of amphetamine's action.

When paranoid suspicions arise in an individual who has a falsely inflated view of his own intellectual and physical prowess, who can exhibit dogged perseverance in the achievement of a goal, and who has an essentially clear state of consciousness, this individual's capacity for effective antisocial behavior can be readily appreciated. He is not hobbled by neuromuscular incoordination, as the belligerent drunkard may be, nor is he distracted by the vivid visual pseudoperceptions that may divert an acidhead before he can act on the paranoid thoughts that can arise during LSD use. The speed user can take the steps he feels necessary to exact retribution or to protect himself from persecutors in an effective manner and with great singleness of purpose. Whether a speed user reacts to his paranoid pattern of ideation with overt acts of violence appears to depend in part on his personality and the norms of the society in which he lives. Louria (12, p. 175) has noted that considerably less violence has been associated with the "speed scene" in Sweden than it has in the United States. When abuse of speed was rife in Japan, authorities in that country found that many criminals had histories of speed usage, and, for one 2-month period of study, 31 of the 60 murderers convicted in this period had a history of amphetamine abuse (6).

There is no evidence whatsoever that would enable one to determine to what extent known crimes of violence in the United States can be attributed to the effects of amphetamines. Many such crimes, moreover, may occur in splash houses and not be reported. Even when criminal behavior is linked with amphetamine abuse, establishing a cause-and-effect relationship (i.e., determining whether a crime was committed while under the influence of amphetamines) can understandably be a formidable assignment.

The amphetamine psychosis is a toxic paranoid psychotic state that can develop after the ingestion or the injection of what are usually large doses of these drugs. On very rare occasions, a psychotic state has been precipitated by therapeutic doses only. Regardless of dosage size, however, it rarely occurs in individuals who have no history of amphetamine abuse (6). In a way not at all understood, repeated amphetamine abuse increases a user's susceptibility to the psychotogenic effects of these agents. Even non-psychotic paranoid ideation, in fact, is rarely encountered in the absence of an antecedent period of heavy speed abuse lasting for several months or more (3). For most users, the psychosis subsides completely within a week after drug usage has stopped.

Many psychiatrists feel that the amphetamine psychosis, of all drug-induced psychotic states, most closely mimics endogenous paranoid schizophrenia; others doubt that this view is wholly accurate, and the differences between the two opinions remain unresolved (10). There is general agreement that delusions of persecution occur during the psychotic state in a setting of clear consciousness. It is not at all known whether the violent behavior stemming from paranoid thoughts occurs both prior to and during the psychotic state or during the latter only; given the circumstances in which these aggressive outbursts occur, it is an understandable gap in our knowledge. Ideas of reference and repetitious patterns of compulsive behavior are also distinguishing features of the amphetamine psychosis (3). Visual, auditory, and tactile hallucinations have been reported to be present by some observers, whereas others have denied the occurrence of one or more of these perceptual aberrations (10). The hallucinations, regardless of their nature, tend to disappear within 1 to 2 days. The rate of disappearance of the delusions (about one-half that of the hallucinations) closely parallels the rate of urinary excretion of amphetamines (10). Behaviorial patterns have usually returned to normal before delusional thinking subsides.

In our discussion of the amphetamine psychosis in Chapter 2, as a model of the drug-induced toxic psychosis, we noted that two facets of this phenomenon remained in dispute. First, the significance of the observation that some, but not all, speed users develop an amphetamine psychosis. (This is *apparently* true, even if consideration is limited to users with long histories of speed abuse.) Second, about 5 to 15% of the users who develop an amphetamine psychosis fail to recover completely; they continue to exhibit psychotic disturbances for months or years after the last episode of drug abuse. In each case, the dispute has centered about the question of whether a peculiar antecedent vulnerability existed in those who succumbed to the psychosis and in those who failed to recover from it completely. For a more extensive discussion of these matters, the reader is referred to Chapter 2.

Marked tremors and pains in muscles and joints can develop after several days of a run; these disturbances are probably consequences of prolonged exposure to large doses of amphetamines. The user may attempt to combat them with narcotics or barbiturates or may accept them as a warning that the run should be ended.

In their review of speed abuse, Cox and Smart (3) tried to ascertain if the commonly heard phrase, "Speed kills!," was a statement of literal fact. They concluded that "it is not certain that speed itself is a lethal drug." Deaths have occurred in individuals, other than speed users, with oral amphetamine doses of about 150 mg (3, 6), but others have survived 400 or 500 mg. There appears to be considerable individual variability in reactions to the amphetamines. Among speed freaks, who take enormous quantities of central nervous system stimulants by vein, convulsions are unknown (2) and prolonged, serious cardiovascular reactions rare. The "overdose" phenomenon in the world of speed has been described as a severe chest pain, followed within minutes by several hours of unconsciousness (2). This sequence of events is not known to end in death. To explain the absence of speed-induced deaths, we can only fall back on the commonly offered, though unsubstantiated, explanation that, in the course of speed abuse, considerable tolerance to the central nervous system stimulatory and cardiovascular effects of the amphetamines develops.

Chronic amphetamine toxicity

Certain physical stigmata may mark the chronic speed user. Weight loss (20 to 30 lb or more) is a common finding; this reflects the fact that each run is effectively a period of total starvation. Nonhealing ulcers, abscesses, and brittle fingernails develop, possibly as secondary consequences of malnutrition (2). Bruxism occurs frequently during runs and often can be controlled only by a strong conscious effort; evidence of this tooth grinding, possibly in conjunction with abraded and ulcerative areas of the oral mucosa, can be detected on appropriate examination.

Speed users who inject their drugs via a parenteral route (most typically the intravenous one) are no more careful of antisepsis than their counterparts in the world of narcotic addiction. As a result, they are subject to the same spectrum of infectious diseases (hepatitis, endocarditis, and so on) as the heroin addict; this was discussed in detail in Chapter 2.

In addition to a psychotic state that persists for months or years, other and more subtle chronic psychological changes have been observed in speed users. Some of these changes may reflect attitudes and behavioral patterns learned during amphetamine experiences. Some chronic users frequently exhibit intense or "hypomanic" absorption in activities, whereas others display extreme suspicion toward everyone, even after many drug-free months (2). More ominous are the reports of a reduced ability to concentrate and an impairment of memory, particularly for very recent events (2, 3). These disorders, plus reported difficulties in making mental connections, are manifestations of what has been called the "scrambled brains" syndrome of the speed user or characteristics of the "burnt-out" speed freak. It is not known whether these disorders represent organic or functional brain changes (2, 3).

COCAINE

Cocaine ("snow," "coke") has figured prominently in the folklore of drug abuse from the late 1800's onward; to this day some users regard it as the "king of drugs." Always expensive and often not available regularly, cocaine represents, in terms of its psychic effects, the first form of speed to be used in the United States. Though it does not conform to our definition of a narcotic, cocaine and its usage were restricted by the Harrison Narcotic Act in 1914 in the same ways opium and its derivatives were. Since that time, and in a seemingly inexplicable fashion, the incidence of cocaine abuse has waxed and waned.

Cocaine is an alkaloid present in the leaves of *Erythroxylon coca,* which has been described as a "tree" (13, p. 361) or a "greenish-brown shrub" (14); indigenous to Western South America, abundant quantities of this plant, in the wild state, can be found in Peru, Colombia, Ecuador, and Bolivia. At this time, *E. coca* is being grown commercially in South America and in Malaysia to provide the cocaine-free coca extracts used as flavoring agents in a number of soft drinks. The coca leaf bears no pharmacological relationship to the cacao (cocoa or chocolate) bean or to the kola nut; even in the medical literature, however, one may encounter authors who confuse cocoa extracts with these other plant products having somewhat similar names.

When the Spanish invaded Peru, they encountered the practice of chewing coca leaves, which was reserved for those of high station in the Incan civilization, primarily in conjunction with religious ceremonies. Though they themselves remained in superstitious fear of the leaves, the Spanish did encourage the widespread utilization of coca leaves by the Indians to minimize discontent (14), and, to this day, coca leaf-chewing is prevalent among Andean Indians. In 1858, cocaine was isolated from coca extracts, and the first account of its local anethetic properties was published in 1862. Following the report of Karl Koller in 1884 of the use of cocaine as a local anesthetic agent in the eye, the drug rapidly gained widespread medical attention. In addition to being the first local anesthetic drug physicians ever possessed, cocaine was tried in a variety of disorders, including asthma and colic. Because its psychic effects were known, it was for a time recommended for problems such as asthenia, irritability, and inadequate sexual drive; as many potential or actual drug users may be found in any population of patients presenting with such problems, we assume that these early attempts to use cocaine as a psychotherapeutic agent exposed susceptible individuals to its effects and probably facilitated the growth of cocaine abuse (14).

The patterns of abuse of cocaine closely resemble those of the amphetamines. The two most widely used routes of administration in the United States are nasal inhalation ("sniffing") and intravenous injection. The common unit of commerce in the illicit market is a "spoon" (or 1 gm) of "cocaine." The user commonly receives cocaine diluted with other substances to about the same extent as the heroin sold today, i.e., the cocaine has been diluted twenty to thirty or more times. A user may consume his entire current supply of cocaine in the course of a "spree," which is like a run with speed but usually shorter. The drug is injected intravenously in a regularly repetitious pattern. Because cocaine is inactivated relatively rapidly, the interval between injections may be 20 minutes or less, and the spree may last no longer than an evening. The other patterns of cocaine abuse also closely resemble those already described for speed. Cocaine and speed both figure in patterns of multiple drug abuse. In their 1968 report on certain aspects of legalized heroin addiction in Great Britain, Bewlay and his colleagues noted that the typical addict in their study took over 100 mg of cocaine daily in addition to 260 mg of heroin (15).

Recently, much attention has been accorded to a technique for the administration of cocaine called "free basing"; strictly speaking, more than an administration technique is involved for the user must first rid the cocaine of all adulterants and convert it to the free molecule. This is accomplished by boiling "street" cocaine in (diethyl) ether to dissolve the free drug as the heat liberates it from salts of the parent compound (hydrochloride or sulfate). When cocaine so prepared is mainlined or snorted, a powerful stimulant effect is experienced almost instantaneously, the "flash" or "rush" that the chronic user desires. Described as highly pleasurable and akin to a sexual orgasm, the user who has experienced the "rush" after intravenous heroin has no problem in distinguishing between the two sensations.

Free basing cocaine leads eventually to the development of tolerance and to the use of very large doses that make cocaine toxicity inevitable. Moreover, it is a perilous technique because ether is highly flammable, or when confined within an enclosed space, highly explosive.

When cocaine and speed are compared with respect to cost, certainty of supply, and duration of effect, speed is clearly the more satisfactory agent for purposes of stimulant abuse. Moreover, even experienced users cannot distinguish between the initial sensations produced by intravenous injections of cocaine and of speed; only with time (cocaine's effects wane more rapidly) can the two drugs be identified (2). Why cocaine is bought when speed is available we do not know. The power of word-of-mouth advertising in the world of drug abuse should not be underestimated, and cocaine most certainly has a powerful reputation. It would surely be unwise to also assume that many stimulant users are aware of all of the pharmacological comparisons that we have just made.

Cocaine's behaviorial effects do not differ significantly from those produced by the amphetamines; they simply persist for a shorter period of time. The cocaine user therefore is subject to the same visions and paranoid thoughts as the speed user, and the same unpredictable outbursts of violent behavior; the same behavior, we suspect, makes cocaine an appealing drug for professional players of contact sports, such as football. (Older descriptions of the attitudes and activities of cocaine users could also be readily used to describe a psychopathic criminal.) The users may be stimulated sexually; though cocaine has had the reputation for decades of being a potent aphrodisiac, its effects on sexuality are probably no more predictable than the effects of the amphetamines. The abuse of cocaine can produce a psychotic state similar to the amphetamine psychosis, characterized by delusions of persecution and hallucinations. This, too, is a toxic psychosis, which usually clears within several days.

Cocaine readily penetrates mucous membranes, such as those of the oral or nasal mucosa. Cocaine is sometimes injected subcutaneously; subcutaneous users typically exhibit scars and abscesses at the injection sites. These lesions are the consequence of the user's disregard for sterile precautions, the presence of irritant or contaminated diluents in the material injected, and the protracted ischemia at the injection site caused by the vasoconstrictor action of cocaine. Cocaine is largely subject to metabolic inactivation in the liver, though small amounts of the unchanged drug may appear in the urine (13, p. 363).

No physical dependence on the effects of cocaine is said to develop, though depression and apathy are typical aftermaths of a cocaine spree (11). Therefore, the possibility that these sequelae represent withdrawal symptoms is as applicable to cocaine "addiction" as it is, in accord with our previous discussion of "physical dependence" on speed, to amphetamine "addiction."

Some authors believe that tolerance to the euphoric effects of cocaine develops (13, p. 363) and describe daily intakes of cocaine as high as 10,000 mg without serious harm to the user. Others deny that any tolerance to cocaine develops (7). Obviously, this phenomenon has not yet been studied definitively.

Though cocaine is sometimes said to be the most potent of all stimulants subject to abuse, no satisfactory evidence in support of this view has been presented (11). Deaths from acute cocaine poisoning have occurred with the medical use of this drug, in which delirium, convulsions, and Cheyne-Stokes breathing precede unconsciousness and respiratory arrest (13, p. 363). Though convulsions are thought to occur occasionally during sprees, the incidence of drug-induced deaths among cocaine users, if indeed any occur, is not known. By and large, the cocaine user is exposed to the same spectrum of acute and chronic toxic effects as that already described for the amphetamine user.

REFERENCES

1. Connell, P. H., *Amphetamine Psychosis* (Maudsley Monographs, No. 5). London: Oxford University Press, 1958
2. Kramer, J. C., V. S. Fischman, and D. C. Littlefield, Amphetamine abuse. *J Amer Med Assoc* 201:305, 1967
3. Cox, C. and R. G. Smart, The nature and extent of speed use in North America. *Canad Med Assoc J* 102:724, 1970
4. Edison, G. R., Amphetamines: A dangerous illusion. *Ann Int Med* 74: 605, 1971
5. Connell, P. H., Clinical manifestations and treatment of amphetamine type of dependence. *J Amer Med Assoc* 196:718, 1966
6. Bell, D. S., Addiction to stimulants. *Med J Austral* 1:41, 1967

7. *Non-medical use of drugs, with particular reference to youth.* Report of the Special Committee on Drug Misuse, Council on Community Health Care, Canadian Medical Association. *Canad Med Assoc J* 101:804, 1969

8. Black, J., The "speed" that kills—or worse. *NY Times Magazine* June 21, 1970, p. 14

9. Medical Staff Conference, Changing Drug Patterns in the Haight-Ashbury. *Calif Med* 110:151, 1969

10. Angrist, B. M., J. Schweitzer, A. J. Friedhoff, S. Gershon, L. J. Hekimian, and A. Floyd, The clinical symptomatology of amphetamine psychosis and its relationship to amphetamine levels in urine. *Int Pharmocopsychiat* 2:125, 1969

11. Kosman, M. E. and K. R. Unna, Effects of chronic administration of the amphetamines and other stimulants on behavior. *Clin Pharmacol Therap* 9:240, 1968

12. Louria, D. B., *The Drug Scene.* New York: McGraw-Hill, 1968

13. Goodman, L. and A. Gilman, *The Pharmacological Basis of Therapeutics,* ed. 2. New York: Macmillan, 1955

14. Blejer-Prieto, H., Coca leaf and cocaine addiction—some historical notes. *Canad Med Assoc J* 93:700, 1965

15. Bewley, T. H., and O. Ben-Arie, Morbidity and mortality from heroin dependence. 2. Study of 100 consecutive inpatients. *Brit Med J* 1:727, 1968

Chapter 9

THE MEDICAL DIAGNOSIS
OF DRUG ABUSE

The possibility of making a medical diagnosis of illicit drug usage and the contributions that a physical examination can make in determining whether a drug has been used (and if so what drug) depend on a variety of factors: the specific substance or substances employed, the frequency with which they have been employed and the resultant degree of physical dependence and/or tolerance, the time and size of the last dose, the method of administration, and the occurrence of any persisting secondary complications.

An individual may come under medical scrutiny as a result of drug abuse in a variety of ways: as a comatose or psychotic patient brought into a hospital emergency room, as an individual who is or has been convulsing, as a reckless driver apprehended by the police, as an inattentive drowsy youngster from a classroom, as a patient with hepatitis or some other infectious disease, or as an individual, who though in contact with reality, is manifesting changes in his usual pattern of behavior. Thus, the physician has to consider the possibility of illicit drug use in a number of differing situations. He should also be alert to this possibility in his routine medical evaluation of all older children, adolescents, and adults for whom he provides care of any nature. And all too frequently today he may be asked to examine a reluctant youth brought for detection of drug abuse by a suspicious parent, school official, or law enforcement agent.

Even if the patient freely states he has used illicit drugs the problem still may not be entirely clear. As noted in earlier chapters, "street" pills

249

of underground manufacture may include a multiplicity of substances un-known to the user, and they may frequently be misrepresented to the user. For instance, a youth, thinking he is buying mescaline, may indeed be getting LSD (1). Additionally, the narcotic addict, amphetamine user, or alcoholic may readily discuss his abuse of these substances but may withhold the information that he also uses barbiturates to the point of dual addiction. The youth experimenting with marihuana may openly admit its use yet keep hidden the fact that he has frequently taken heroin.

Nor can cultural patterns of use be depended upon to provide informa-tion as perhaps they could in years past. Drug abuse occurs at all social levels, and specific drugs do not have any fixed racial or economic bound-aries. It probably remains true that, excepting alcoholism, which has no age-specific patterns, drug abuse and addiction is largely a problem among adolescents and young adults. Drug abuse problems, however, do occur outside this age range with some frequency.

Obtaining information about drug usage through interviewing requires tact and diplomacy as well as a non-judgmental attitude; for instance, to bluntly ask an individual reluctant to divulge sensitive information for which he fears serious punishment Do you use drugs? almost compels a negative answer. A more accepting and encouraging situation can be cre-ated by stating: Many people are using drugs today. What drugs have you used? Do you have any worries about drug abuse? If a high index of suspicion exists that a patient does indeed use illicit substances, and is likely to deny it, it may be best to defer questioning in this area until the physical examination when self-concern and worry about body integrity and potential discovery is maximal; at this time, an opportunity for the patient to discuss his problem honestly may arise. In any event a false negative answer in the first patient-physician contact may well be re-versed subsequently as trust and confidence in the physician grow as well as assurance about the privileged nature of the patient's communications. A freely given confidence is the desirable goal, rather than forced admis-sion by confrontational evidence, as the former initiates the open and non-coercive relationship essential for rehabilitation.

It must, however, be recognized that a large proportion of drug users will remain undetected even under the most benevolent questioning and careful examination. In the absence of frank intoxication, definitive with-drawal symptoms, or specific physical signs in the patient who denies drug abuse, the physician has little choice but to accept the patient's statement while maintaining an open mind.

Laboratory tests may be useful, but they indicate only whether the substance looked for was present in the blood or urine at the single moment in time the biological sample was obtained. They do not provide data on how frequently the subject has used the drug, nor do they often detect the user who has abstained for a few days. Moreover, false positive tests or sample mix-ups can occur.

We reject as impractical, meaningless, and invasive of personal rights involuntary mass urine-screening tests of large groups of individuals as, for example, all public school students and teachers. Aside from the moral and ethical aspects of such procedures, the true addict, and other drug users concerned about detection, can be depended upon to find methods of substituting innocent urine specimens. A system of supervised sample collection is appalling to contemplate. Nor can such mass screening be viewed in the same light as, for instance, mass screening for tuberculosis; it will not uncover a previously hidden disease, since the drug user knows what he is doing.

HISTORY

The history from the patient himself may or may not be revealing. A spouse, parent, teacher, or other individual who has had occasion to observe the patient's behavior may offer more significant information. Of course the discovery of drugs or administering apparatus (the "paraphernalia" or "works") among the patient's possessions, usually hidden, is virtually pathognomonic. Small glassine bags or other similar containers containing a whitish powder (which may or may not have a bitter taste), unidentified pills or capsules of any color, small packets, vials or unlabeled cigarettes containing dried plant material, unexplained tubes of model plane cement, other volatile solvent-containing products, or aerosols are other indications of possible drug abuse. The discovery of a hidden hypodermic needle and syringe or eye dropper usually reveals heroin or stimulant use. Discarded paper or plastic bags, balloons, or rags containing hardened glue, aerosol products, and so on indicate the possibility of solvent inhalation.

Personality changes with shifting friendships from known reliable companions to unknown individuals whom the adolescent will not bring to his home, deteriorating schoolwork or progressively poorer job performance, increasingly prolonged absences from home, changing styles of clothing, increasing demands for money, and a breakdown in interfamily communication all suggest a troubled person who *may* be resorting to drugs. Suspicions, particularly of adolescents, should not be formed hastily, however, for all youths inevitably experience emotional struggle. The above behavioral changes may only be a part of normal adolescent anxiety, turmoil, and confusion, and drug abuse may in fact play no part in their lives.

PHYSICAL EXAMINATION

Appearance

In general there is little by way of appearance that sets the drug user apart from the rest of the population. Various characteristics have been attributed to users of given substances. The passive, peace-loving follower of meditative religions or astrology has been associated with the use of LSD and other strong hallucinogens. The young, emotionally disturbed runaway is frequently suspected of multiple, indiscriminate drug abuse, readily taking anything offered him that promises a new, different, and exciting "high." The inner-city school dropout or unemployed, unskilled young adult in an urban ghetto is often said to be the most likely candidate for narcotic addiction. High school and college students are believed to be occasional or regular users of marihuana. These stereotypes have limited validity, but it is probably fair to make one generalization, that the majority of alienated, homeless adolescents living in such urban retreats as the Haight-Ashbury in San Francisco or New York's East Village or in rural communes do use a wide variety of illicit drugs with varying degrees of frequency as do many of the somewhat older young adults who also populate these areas.

There is perhaps only one mode of dress that indicates a high likelihood of a specific form of drug abuse. The narcotic addict, in an effort to hide puncture marks, may wear long sleeves in exceedingly hot weather.

Nutritional status generally offers little in the way of information except for the individual who has been heavily "into" drugs for some period of time. Either intent upon getting his "fix" or anorexic under the influence of the drug, he may fail to meet minimal needs and gradually become malnourished.

Sensorium

Generally it can be expected that the non-addicted drug abuser will arrange his schedule of drug administration so that his anticipated arrival at the doctor's office or clinic will not coincide with evident drug effects. Therefore dulling of affect, drowsiness, nodding, slurred speech, agitation, uneven gait, and so on will rarely be present. Occasionally a provocative, "acting out" adolescent may have just smoked marihuana or taken a barbituate or an amphetamine prior to being seen and will demonstrate the appropriate pharmacological consequences. Such a youth, however, is likely to boast openly of his use of drugs, so that his altered level of awareness is readily explained.

In the intermittent drug user, only hallucinogens may cause uncontrolled, prolonged, or recurrent psychic changes in the absence of significant blood levels of drug. These are "flashback" phenomenona and will evidence themselves as persistent or intermittent disordered thought processes. Flashback phenomena can occur in the apparently emotionally healthy individuals, but for some youths, major underlying emotional disturbances may manifest themselves by similar disturbances. The two causes cannot be easily differentiated.

The narcotic addict may well be seen while under the influence of a drug. Requiring regular injections, he loses volitional control over his habit and may have had to take a "fix" shortly before seeing the physician and will show varying degrees of drug effect depending on the amount of time that has elapsed since "shooting up." He may have the typical nodding, drowsy, withdrawn appearance and entirely detached attitude plus pinpoint pupils or milder forms of these symptoms in which he may relate to the situation at hand but demonstrates a diminished attention span and difficulty in verbalizing consecutive coherent thoughts. Nonetheless, it is not unsual to find the narcotic addict in a state of equilibrium ("straight"), apparently alert and quite normal. Alternatively, the addict who has been unable to get his usual dose on time may display agitation, irritability, anxiety, sweating, lacrimation, some degree of mydriasis, and a desire to conclude the examination as quickly as possible because he anticipates or is actually experiencing early symptoms of withdrawal.

The alcoholic may also reveal his situation by giving evidence of some degree of intoxication, for he is chronically dependent upon alcohol to cope with the stresses in his life. Symptoms include slurred speech, inappropriate affect, diminished attention span, and similar evidence of central nervous system depression. If such depression exists, the patient's breath probably will have the characteristic odor of alcohol. Indeed, only with alcohol and paraldehyde ingestion and volatile solvent inhalation will the breath have a significant odor. Should the long-term alcoholic present with the cerebral changes that occur in Wernike's encephalopathy or Korsakoff's psychosis, his condition will be manifested mentally and neurologically, even in the absence of recent alcohol intake.

In summary, though most casual or intermittent drug users will not demonstrate alterations in their sensorium or level of consciousness when examined, a few users of hallucinogens and a few chronic alcoholics may give evidence of psychotic changes in the absence of recent drug ingestion. One should keep in mind that these changes can easily be confused with those seen in the many individuals who develop psychoses unrelated to drug abuse. On any occasion, the particular drug effects observed are of course direct manifestations of the particular drug, the dosage, the route of administration, the amount of time that has elapsed since administration, and the individual's own level of tolerance.

VITAL AND OTHER SIGNS

The circumstances attending a visit to a doctor's office and a physical examination are in themselves anxiety producing for some patients. This anxiety alone can easily produce mild to moderate tachycardia, tachypnea, and/or hypertension in susceptible individuals. Therefore possible physiological responses to psychic stress should be taken into consideration when evaluating abnormalities in vital signs as possible indications of drug abuse.

Blood pressure
It has been reported that experimental narcotic addiction results in slightly elevated systolic and diastolic blood pressures, but the levels are not above acceptable normal limits (2). Greater, but transient, elevations of 15 to 30 mm of Hg are seen during acute heroin withdrawal. Amphetamine ingestion may also result in mild to moderate hypertension at the time of intoxication and for variable periods thereafter. With barbiturates, tranquilizers, and volatile solvents, blood pressure changes roughly parallel the degree of central nervous system depression that exists but to a lesser and more variable degree than respiratory changes. No major alterations in blood pressure have been reported to result from hallucinogen usage except for those systolic and diastolic elevations that would be compatible with the psychic stress engendered during a "bad trip" or panic state (3).

Pulmonary ventilation

For narcotics, sedatives, hypnotics, and volatile solvents, as with all central nervous system depressants, depression of pulmonary ventilation is a prime pharmacological manifestation and is directly related to the degree of drug intoxication present at any given moment. Amphetamine ingestion readily produces tachypnea. No characteristic alterations of respiration occur with hallucinogen use.

There is no evidence to suggest that ventilatory changes continue after a drug has been detoxified either completely or to a blood level compatible with an individual's level of tolerance.

Pulse rate

Alterations in pulse rate most readily identify amphetamine abuse, which results in a tachycardia directly proportional to the degree of over-all toxicity experienced. Some narcotic addicts also demonstrate slight increases in pulse rate, which are often further increased during acute withdrawal. Users of hallucinogens, and marihuana, in particular, readily demonstrate pulse rates up to 150. Since pulse rate is highly variable, except under basal conditions, and can be most sensitive to emotional factors that produce psychogenic tachycardia, the finding of an elevated pulse rate is essentially meaningless in the diagnosis of drug abuse (3).

Though bradycardia may well be a manifestation of an overdosage of depressant drugs, it is doubtful that blood levels of narcotics, barbiturates, tranquilizers, and so on in a given patient compatible with his being able to accomplish an ambulatory visit to a doctor's office would result in any significant slowing of the pulse rate.

Temperature

Temperature elevations do not occur in uncomplicated drug abuse, with the sole exception of toxic doses of atropinic drugs. When a known or suspected drug user is febrile, he must be evaluated for possible related infections or such foreign body reactions as hepatitis, tetanus, septicemia, endocarditis, sterile or infected abscesses, and thrombophlebitis. Atropine poisoning must also be considered (4). It is also possible that some of the adulterants used to "cut" drugs are pyrogenic.

Integument

Of all the signs of drug abuse, the most widely noted signs, which are often considered pathognomonic, are the various manifestations and complications of skin puncture. Formerly held to be characteristic of narcotic addiction and still largely manifest by this group, they may also result from the injection of any drug administered by the parenteral route.

Heroin purchased on the street, as noted in Chapter 3, is generally "cut" with such adulterants as talc, quinine, and lactose. Capsules or tablets of commercially prepared drugs intended for oral use, including amphetamines and barbiturates, as well as drugs of "underground" manufacture, also contain inert and often irritant binders. Aseptic techniques are rarely observed in the preparation of underground drugs. Only minimal attention, if any, is paid to antiseptic conditions by the injector. Filtration of insoluble material is incompletely accomplished, if at all, by passing the dissolved material through a wad of cotton or gauze. When the drug is injected, therefore, both chemically irritant materials and infecting agents may enter the body, causing local abscesses, thromboses, and scarring. Most pure drugs when properly prepared for injection, appropriately diluted, and administered under sterile conditions do not usually produce skin lesions.

The lesions caused by "skin popping," or subcutaneous injection of narcotics, are often located in such readily accessible areas as the arm and thigh. They may occur anywhere on the body, however, even in sites out of the patient's reach, the drug having been injected by a companion in such instances. To avoid detection some "skin poppers" have resorted to less frequently revealed areas such as the lower abdomen and even the vaginal wall. This latter phenomenon is revealed by a palpable thickening of the vaginal wall on pelvic examination.

In examining a person who regularly uses the subcutaneous route for drug administration, one may find a great variety of lesions. There will be the puncture mark itself, either fresh or healing, and with or without underlying tissue involvement. In the early stages of an untoward local reaction there can be heat, swelling, and erythema of varying degrees progressing, in some instances, to outright abscess formation, rupture, and drainage. When the reaction progresses beyond a mild local inflammatory stage, and possibly even when sepsis does not occur, the local tissues may be sufficiently injured to result in permanent scarring manifested by two types of lesions: first, a hyperpigmented, flat, round, or ovoid macular area with indiscrete margins ranging in size from 1 to 3 cm or more and, second, a round or ovoid "punched-out" depression with well-defined borders 1 to 5 cm in diameter. In the latter lesion, the skin often appears atrophic and shiny and may be depigmented as well (2).

The "mainliner," or intravenous user of drugs, also develops progressive signs at the site of the veins used, with the added complication of venous thromboses. The sites selected are generally those of the antecubital fossa and forearm. Additionally, a desperate addict in search of a patent vein or trying to hide his habit may resort to any area of the body he can reach, including abdomen, legs and feet. Even the external jugular vein, the sublingual veins, and the dorsal vein of the penis have been utilized.

The mildest cutaneous signs of intravenous injection are fresh, healing, or healed puncture marks frequently resulting in minimal but distinct hyperpigmentation over the vein after multiple venipunctures throughout an extended period of time. It is unlikely that a casual, intermittent, non-addicted "mainliner" would demonstrate these permanent changes in pigmentation, though recent injection sites may well be evident.

The most prominent signs of chronic intravenous drug abuse are frequently referred to as "railroad tracks." Resulting from repeated puncture of the skin overlying a vein, this lesion may extend over the course of the vein from 2 to 20 cm in length appearing as an atrophic, flat, sometimes pigmented scar transversed by multiple fine cross marks. In the long-term addict, such lesions often provide a detailed anatomical survey of the accessible superficial venous system (2, 5).

Acute lesions, such as local abscesses and acute thrombophlebitis, also occur and may prompt the user to seek medical help. It is safe to say that if an adolescent or a young adult presents with an acute subcutaneous infection, abscess, or thrombophlebitis in regions accessible to self-injection, and if recent systemic medical treatment can be ruled out, drug abuse must be suspected as a prime cause (4).

There is a type of skin lesion that is sometimes considered pathognomonic of heroin addiction: the "rosette" of cigarette burns consisting of some 10 to 20 circular or linear scars on the anterior chest wall. Such burns occur when the addict "goes on the nod" with a cigarette dangling from his mouth, which, as the head droops down, makes contact with the skin. The analgesia induced by the drug blunts pain reception and reflex withdrawal (2). Cigarette burns between the fingers may be seen in alcoholics and narcotic or barbiturate addicts as well as users of other generalized depressant drugs.

A variety of tattoos have been noted on drug addicts, varying from those designed to hide tell-tale venous scars to those that serve as an "identification card" to fellow users. The latter tattoos appear to be less popular today, but still may be seen on some younger and a number of older addicts, appearing as a few dots or small cross often in the "snuff box" area between thumb and forefinger (2).

Since some plastic surgeons have begun advocating surgical removal of "railroad track" scars to assist the rehabilitation of the ex-addict, the presence of surgical scars in the antecubital fossae or on the forearms may become a more common finding in individuals with a history of intravenous drug abuse than heretofore (5).

Last, it has been reported that accidental and suicidal ingestion of barbiturates has been accompanied, on occasion, by vesicle and subepidermal bullae formation. As the blister fluid has been found to contain significant concentrations of the drug in question, it is believed that this phenomenon is a direct manifestation of drug toxicity. Though such findings appear to be limited to those taking lethal and near-lethal doses, we conjecture that blisters could be an infrequent occurrence in any individual taking large amounts of barbiturates (6).

Lymph nodes

Regional adenopathy related to the site of injection is commonly encountered. Many addicts and habitual drug users employing systemic routes of administration demonstrate small, firm, discrete, non-tender, palpable axillary and/or epitrochlear nodes or even inguinal nodes if the lower extremities are a frequent site of injection. The most likely cause of the adenopathy is a regional reaction to the contaminants commonly present in illicit substances. Autopsies performed on addicts have revealed a 75% incidence of generalized glandular enlargement particularly in the area of the pancreas, liver, and duodenum (2). The meaning of this finding is not clear.

Eyes

Miosis is generally one of the physical signs characteristic of heroin intoxication. The failure of a contracted pupil (miosis) to dilate in a darkened room when vision is fixed on a far object is highly suggestive of recent opiate intake. Pinhole pupils will be seen in the individual who has not developed significant tolerance only during the time of intoxication; normal pupillary size and responsiveness gradually returns as the drug becomes detoxified and excreted. In the heroin addict who has developed tolerance, however, lesser degrees of miosis will be seen; therefore, eye signs can be a less sensitive indicator than is generally believed. Miosis induced by opiate usage can be reversed by the administration of such narcotic antagonists as N-allylnormorphine (Naline). Dilation of the pupil (mydriasis) is an early sign of withdrawal in the addict (3).

Mydriasis occurs with hallucinogen intoxication (excepting marihuana) and is a predictable pharmacological action of such sympathomimetic and atropinic drugs as amphetamines, atropine (Asthmador cigarette smoking or ingestion), and scopolamine (a not uncommon component of mixed street pills). It is a common finding in the individual acutely intoxicated with these drugs, but it is uncommon in the ambulatory patient who does not demonstrate other features characteristic of these drugs. Individuals experiencing mydriasis and a resultant intense photophobia may wear dark glasses indoors. One should, however, make sure that such a patient has not received medically induced mydriasis as in the treatment of glaucoma or iritis and is not either wearing prescription lenses or following a costume fad in wearing tinted glasses. Pupillary changes do not occur with the use of barbiturates, marihuana, alcohol, and most solvents.

Sustained nystagmus on lateral gaze will occur during intoxication by such generalized central nervous system depressants as barbiturates. This phenomenon has not been reported to occur with drugs in other categories commonly implicated in abuse.

Scleral injection occurs during marihuana smoking and has been reported to persist for up to 2 years thereafter without further drug usage. Since scleral injection is a common finding during physical examination of many patients for a variety of reasons (from vernal conjuctivitis to exposure to smog), it cannot be considered an informative abnormality per se in the diagnosis of drug abuse.

Scleral icterus in the previously healthy adolescent and young adult can be considered as highly indicative of infectious or serum hepatitis. Since serum hepatitis is a frequent, and at times nearly epidemic, complication of the use of contaminated needles, drug abuse must be considered a leading cause in such individuals. In addition, scleral icterus may also be a sign of toxic hepatitis due to inhalation of volatile solvents containing chlorinated hydrocarbons.

Nose

The finding of a perforated or severely ulcerated nasal septum can be considered almost pathognomonic of persistent cocaine sniffing. The vasoconstricting effect of this drug upon the mucous membranes can, with chronic application, result in tissue ischemia, necrosis, and, ultimately, septal perforation. This lesion has also been reported among some heroin sniffers but not users who inhale volatile solvents.

Glue, heroin, or Methedrine sniffing may produce a reactive rhinitis manifested by a nasal discharge and reddened mucosae. (Increased nasal secretions also occur on narcotics withdrawal.) The physical signs, however, would not differ from those caused by an upper respiratory tract infection or allergic rhinitis.

Mouth and throat

Many addicts or chronically habituated drug users pay little attention to oral hygiene and have rampant dental decay. But since a far larger segment of economically deprived individuals than just the addict population receive unsatisfactory dental care, the finding of major neglect is probably more suggestive of poverty than drug abuse.

Some amphetamine users have been reported to experience uncontrolled bruxism. If clinically noted or historically reported by others to occur during waking hours, such an observation should lead to the consideration of abuse of this class of drugs. Grinding of the teeth during sleep, however, is a common event for many individuals, users or nonusers, and cannot be considered significant in the diagnosis of drug abuse (7).

Neck

Other than cutaneous evidence of the use of the jugular vein as an injection site (usually found only in those who have no other accessible patent veins), there are no significant findings referrable to the neck, cervical lymph nodes, or thyroid gland.

Chest

Though percussion, auscultation, and X-ray of the chest in both the casual and chronic drug abuser generally will be unremarkable, pulmonary function studies in chronic heroin addicts may demonstrate decreased lung volume and decreased diffusing capacity (2). Such insoluble binders of tablets and adulterants of heroin as talc and starch can, when injected intravenously, embolize to the lungs to produce multiple pulmonary thromboses and/or granulomas. With repeated body insults of this nature, diminished pulmonary function, and, ultimately, pulmonary hypertension may result. We doubt that such findings would be demonstrable in the intermittent and casual drug user (4).

Pulmonary infection may also be an indicator of drug abuse. Injection of microorganisms present in contaminated and unsterile material can produce either localized pulmonary abscesses or more diffuse pneumonic processes. Such an infection is particularly apt to be staphylococcal, though a variety of other organisms including fungi may be implicated. In the heroin "mainliner" who becomes acutely ill with pulmonary disease, the edema of overdosage must be differentiated from pneumonitis of bacterial origin (2, 8).

Heart

Alterations in cardiac rate are as discussed above under vital signs. Bacterial endocarditis, either right or left sided, is a not uncommon finding in the addict and should be considered in any individual suspected of even casual parenteral drug abuse who presents with a fever of unknown etiology. Conversely, the diagnosis of bacterial endocarditis in an individual with no prior evidence of heart disease, valvular lesions, or congenital anomaly should at least raise the suspicion of illicit drug injection. Of course bacteremias and even septicemias occur frequently with injection of contaminated material without the development of endocarditis.

Right-sided endocarditis has been found to involve the tricuspid valve only. Often silent, without clinically detectable abnormalities, this condition may not make itself known until embolization produces septic pulmonary infarcts. Left-sided disease may involve both the mitral and aortic valves, and generally produces classical symptoms of valvular disease and systemic emboli (2, 8).

Though elevated S-T segments have been noted in the electrocardiogram of a significant number of narcotic addicts, and multiple premature atrial/ventricular beats have been noted in some amphetamine users, these findings are not sufficiently specific to warrant their addition to the diagnostic armamentarium of drug abuse. Periarteritis has been detected in a few heavy amphetamine users; whether a causal relationship exists is unclear (9).

Abdomen

An enlarged liver and/or abnormal liver function tests (with or without clinical jaundice) should raise the suspicion of viral hepatitis. As previously noted, the occurrence of this disease in the adolescent or young adult should make one suspect "mainlining" or "skin popping" in the absence of known contact, ingestion of contaminated foods, or a possible iatrogenic source. For the most part, hepatitis transmitted via contaminated needles and blood products is of the "serum" variety. One may be able to detect the presence of the Australia antigen if the test is performed early in the course of the disease or if the patient is a carrier. The "infectious" type, however, may also be transmitted by needles, as well as by the fecal-oral route. Thus, though the incubation period and laboratory data may point to one viral agent or the other, both must be considered as possibly being secondary to contaminated needle usage.

In urban areas frequented by alienated youths and young adults, hepatitis incurred through the use of contaminated needles is endemic if not epidemic and is seen far more frequently than that contracted by the fecal-oral route. Such considerations must be applied to urban and suburban middle class populations as well. We suspect that some cases of hepatitis are due to unrecognized drug abuse but are erroneously attributed to other causes. Many individuals develop hepatitis, of course, without an evident source and without being drug users.

In addition to the overt forms of liver disease, it has been reported that approximately one-third of narcotic addicts present with an enlarged liver, elevated transaminase levels, and/or abnormal flocculation tests even in the absence of a clinical history of hepatitis or jaundice. These findings have been variably interpreted as indicative of a chronic or intermittent anicteric hepatitis or of the chronic hepatotoxic effects of one of the adulterants used in diluting heroin. Experiments with pure morphine have not reproduced these chronic liver findings, and narcotics are not believed to exert a specific toxic effect on the liver (2).

Kidney

Though uncommon, a number of instances of focal or generalized glomerular sclerosis have been reported in association with heroin addiction (10). The precise genesis of these lesions, however, is unclear. In the vast majority of addicts, there are no specific renal findings. But the incidence of proteinuria and a nephrotic syndrome is sufficiently higher in heroin users than in the general population as to suggest a significant relationship.

Various clinical pictures have been observed ranging from a relatively stable mild proteinuria to relatively rapid and progressive disease. Most characteristic is a nephrotic syndrome with proteinuria, edema, hypoalbuminemia, and hypercholesterolemia. A high percentage of these individuals develop renal failure and die. Biopsy findings tend to relate membranoproliferative glomerulonephritis with the milder forms of disease and focal and segmental glomerular sclerosis with the nephrotic picture.

Endocrine system

Except for the alterations in the pituitary-gonadal axis referred to below, there are no significant and constant findings related to the endocrine system of the drug user.

Genito-urinary system

There are no major physical signs in the genito-urinary tract specifically referable to drug abuse, except when the dorsal vein of the penis or the vaginal wall is used as an injection site and shows appropriate cutaneous or mucosal signs. Girls and women either addicted or chronically habituated to drugs, and particularly heroin, often experience menstrual irregularity, sometimes to the point of secondary amenorrhea. Fertility is also reduced along with viability of the conceptus; these disturbances are manifested in subnormal rates of conception and elevated rates of spontaneous abortion, stillbirth, premature birth, and "small-for-date" babies. The role of poor nutrition and casual, if not frankly neglectful, life style of the typical chronic drug user as well as the effects of the drugs themselves are undoubtedly both contributory (11).

Since menstrual irregularity is common among adolescent girls and not uncommon among young women in general, it cannot be taken as a specific indication of drug abuse.

Nervous system

Neurological findings that would contribute to the diagnosis of drug abuse are, with several exceptions, those referable to the specific central nervous system effects of the drug involved and the degree of intoxication or withdrawal that may exist at the time examined. In the alert, oriented non-intoxicated individual, there are usually no suggestive neurological abnormalities. Exceptions are the persistent neuropathy that has been reported to occur following glutethimide administration, the neuropathy associated with alcoholism, and the tremors that may continue for variable periods following amphetamine intoxication.

Summary

The critical factors that point toward or confirm the diagnosis of drug abuse are: a positive or highly suspicious history by the patient or concerned observers, the finding of drugs or apparatus for administering drugs on the patient or among his belongings, the presence of intoxication at the time of examination with concomitant disturbances in thought processes characteristic of the drug or drugs involved, the discovery of typical skin lesions, and the detection of drugs or metabolites of drugs in blood or urine. Other physical findings, as described, may collectively lead clearly to a diagnosis of drug abuse but, taken singly, will be of little assistance.

Though one or more of the findings listed above are generally present in the examination of an addicted or chronically habituated patient, the casual drug user more often than not will not present with historical or physical findings that will establish a firm diagnosis. Thus, we again emphasize that establishing a relationship of mutual trust and confidence between physician and patient can be most constructive in creating at atmosphere in which the actual facts of an individual's drug use may come freely into the open. We strongly recommend that the information offered herein not be applied to the patient in the form of a "lie detector" test coupled with punitive, coercive attitudes. Little can be accomplished by such an approach if one hopes to move from diagnosis to rehabilitation.

LABORATORY DETECTION

Routine procedures

There are no specific findings regarding hemoglobin values, red blood cell indices, or white blood cell counts that are specifically characteristic of drug abuse. Red blood cell basophilia, reticulocytosis, burr cells, and even nucleated red blood cells have been noted on occasion to follow nutmeg ingestion. Diminished serum iron, when present in a habituated or addicted drug user, most probably reflects poor nutrition and/or anemia due to the frequent sale of blood for money to buy drugs. In experimental human addiction, an absolute lymphocytosis with a high percentage of atypical cells has been noted. Hematological parameters are otherwise within normal ranges in uncomplicated drug addiction, habituation, or experimentation (2).

Conventional urinalyses do not show any abnormalities referable to drug abuse.

Detection of drugs in blood or urine

Techniques are available for detecting most of the drugs or their major metabolites that are widely subject to abuse today in blood or urine specimens from the suspected user. General screening procedures for narcotics, barbiturates, and amphetamines as well as analyses for specific drugs are available today on a routine basis in most laboratories. Methods for the detection of LSD and the tetrahydrocannabinols of marihuana in blood and urine exist, but their application is still confined to research laboratories.

REFERENCES

1. Cheek, F. E. and S. Newell, Deceptions in the illicit drug market. *Science* 167:1276, 1970
2. Sapira, J. D., The narcotic addict as a medical patient. *Amer J Med* 45: 555, 1968
3. Dimijian, G. D. and F. A. Radelat, Evaluation and treatment of the suspected drug user in the emergency room. *Arch Intern Med* 125:162, 1970
4. Louria, D. B., T. Hensle, and J. Rose, The major medical complications of heroin addiction. *Ann Intern Med* 67:1, 1967
5. Shuster, M. M. and M. L. Lewin, New York: Needle tracks in narcotics addicts. *NY J Med* 68:3129, 1968
6. Groschel, D., A. R. Gerstein, and J. M. Rosenbaum, Skin lesions as a diagnostic aid in barbiturate poisoning. *New Eng J Med* 283:409, 1970
7. Cox, C. and R. G. Smart, The nature and extent of speed use in North America. *Canad Med Assoc J* 102:724, 1970
8. Cherubin, C. E., B. Baden, F. Kavaler, S. Lerner, and W. Cline, Infective endocarditis in narcotic addicts. *Ann Intern Med* 69:1091, 1968
9. Citron, B. P., M. Halpern, M. McCarron, G. D. Lundberg, R. McCormick, I. J. Pincus, D. Tatter, and B. J. Haverback, Necrotizing angiitis associated with drug abuse. *New Engl J Med* 283:1003, 1970
10. Rao, T. K. S., A. D. Nicastri, and E. A. Friedman, Natural history of heroin-associated nephropathy, *New Engl J Med* 290:19, 1974
11. Gaulden, E. C., D. C. Littlefield, O. E. Putoff, and A. L. Seivert, Menstrual abnormalities associated with heroin addiction. *Amer J Obstet Gynecol* 90:155, 1964

12. Fujimoto, J. M. and R. I. Wang, A method of identifying narcotic analgesics in human urine after therapeutic doses. *Toxicol Appl Pharmacol* 16:186, 1970

13. Bloomer, H. A., R. K. Maddock, Jr., and S. B. Sheehe, Rapid diagnosis of sedative intoxication by gas chromatography. *Ann Int Med* 72:223, 1970

14. Curry, A. S., Rapid method of screening for barbiturates. *Brit Med J* 2: 1040, 1963

Chapter 10

MANAGEMENT OF SELECTED CLINICAL PROBLEMS: PHARMACOLOGICAL ASPECTS

Some of the clinical problems encountered in drug users, including acute drug intoxication or withdrawal symptoms, are direct consequences of drug abuse, whereas others are not uniquely related to abuse and reflect the practices of some drug users. These include the infectious diseases that are the result of unsterile injection techniques. We have chosen to discuss the management of some of the problems in the first category, in which the use of a certain type of drug is indicated; these problems are concerned largely with acute drug intoxication and the supervised withdrawal (detoxification) of addicted patients, plus the use of drugs as adjuncts in rehabilitative programs for drug users.

NARCOTIC ADDICTION

The heroin or methadone overdose
Narcotic antagonists of the conventional type, such as nalorphine (Nalline) and levallorphan (Lorfan), are useful only in cases of narcotic overdosage. Some of these agents possess an inherent (though limited) ability to produce respiratory depression, and pulmonary ventilation may be impaired further if they are administered to patients who have taken toxic amounts of compounds like the barbiturates or alcohol. Unfortunately, there is no infallible sign of narcotic poisoning. If the patient is still able to respond to questions, he can occasionally provide

267

useful information, but usually, he knows only the name given the drug by the seller. Friends or relatives who may have brought the patient to the physician can usually offer only hearsay evidence. A fresh needle puncture just suggests the possibility of narcotic usage, for users are injecting various types of drugs and drug mixtures today. [Nor, alternatively, is a fresh puncture mark required for diagnosis; the "overdose" syndrome has developed after the "sniffing" of heroin (1).] Various patterns of pulmonary ventilation may be present when the patient with a narcotic overdose is first seen: tachypnea or dyspnea may be observed as well as varying degrees of ventilatory depression, including apnea; if the patient is seen in the early stages, respiration may still be essentially normal. The pulmonary pathology typical of narcotic overdose, pulmonary edema and congestion, can be manifested by râles, frothy sputum, and, radiologically, as a diffuse bilateral infiltrate; it may be detectable when the patient is first seen, its onset can be delayed for as long as 24 hours after that time, and, in some patients, it may never develop to an observable degree (1, 2). Pulmonary function may also be compromised by the aspiration of secretions or gastric contents (1). Pupillary miosis, when present in conjunction with other significant findings, is perhaps the most reliable sign of narcotic overdose; in severely hypoxic individuals, however, the pupils will probably be dilated.

Treatment often must be initiated, because of the gravity of the situation, before there can be significant resolution of questions pertaining to differential diagnosis; it is important, therefore, to be aware of the various possible sequelae to the use of narcotic antagonists and to make provision for them. Apparatus for facilitating pulmonary ventilation should be available, including an endotracheal tube and equipment to provide positive pressure ventilation with oxygen. It is highly desirable to have the continued assistance of an anesthesiologist in coping with the more severe degrees of central nervous system depression.

The initial dose of nalorphine is customarily 3 to 5 mg by vein. If a response is to be obtained from this first dose, it will be evident within several minutes thereafter at most. The goal of nalorphine therapy is not to restore pulmonary ventilation to a safe level; it should not be given until full consciousness is recovered, for reasons to be discussed shortly. Wholly satisfactory responses to the *initial* dose of nalorphine occur only infrequently, and, over a period of 20 to 25 minutes, the initial dose may be repeated several times, if necessary, until the patient has received a total of 20 mg of the drug. If no favorable effect has been produced by this cumulative dose, the possibility of narcotic overdose can be regarded as highly doubtful. Conversely, if nalorphine produces further depression of respiration, one can be fairly certain that the patient has not taken an overdose of a narcotic. To prevent this development (i.e., the further depression of respiration), a narcotic antagonist such as naloxone (Narcan), should be used (5, p. 522). Unlike nalorphine and levallorphan, naloxone is a "pure" narcotic antagonist; it lacks the "narcotomimetic" (agonist) properties of nalorphine and levallorphan and cannot produce respiratory depression under any circumstances. The initial intravenous dose of naloxone to be used in cases of suspected narcotic poisoning is 0.4 to 0.8 mg.

If pulmonary ventilation is improved by nalorphine, a tentative diagnosis of narcotic overdose can now be made. In such instances, however, three untoward developments may yet occur. The duration of action of the antagonist is usually shorter than that of the narcotic; thus, unless the patient is carefully watched, and the antagonist given again when necessary, the patient's status can, within several hours, revert to that present initially. The etiology of the pulmonary edema and congestion of narcotic overdose remains unknown (see Chapter 3); they impede oxygenation of the blood and are not reversed by narcotic antagonists. Moreover, a pneumonia from aspiration or other causes may develop shortly after admission or within the next several days. The action of a narcotic antagonist in regard to respiration is probably largely, if not wholly, a central one, restoring the sensitivity of the medullary respiratory center to carbon dioxide. Airway problems and those pertaining to the diffusion of gases across the pulmonary capillaries remain and require appropriate attention. And last, most victims of heroin or methadone overdose are narcotic addicts. Narcotic antagonists can precipitate withdrawal symptoms rapidly. Once evoked by a narcotic antagonist, the withdrawal symptoms cannot be easily alleviated; probably because their onset is so abrupt, they are commonly severe and may include convulsions. The indiscriminate use of narcotic antagonists in a narcotic addict can produce a withdrawal syndrome so severe that it poses more of a threat to life than does the heroin overdose (5, p. 523). Though it is true that the dose of antagonist required to improve pulmonary ventilation may also elicit some withdrawal symptoms, they will, in most cases, be relatively mild and preliminary manifestations of withdrawal. (It is a curious facet of the pharmacology of the antagonists that the greater the degree of physical dependence on narcotics, the smaller the dose of antagonist required to elicit a full-blown withdrawal syndrome.) If withdrawal symptoms appear, it would then be prudent to attempt to achieve satisfactory pulmonary ventilation by mechanical means rather than by further doses of the antagonist. The finding that, today, many heroin addicts have just a limited degree of physical dependence owing to the grossly diluted drug they receive (see Chapter 3) probably accounts for the fact that there are relatively few reports in the literature about heroin overdose that describe the development of severe, antagonist-induced withdrawal syndromes during treatment. If the patient is a participant in a methadone maintenance program, he will have a high degree of physical dependence on narcotics for he has been receiving 80 to 120 mg of pure methadone daily. Injudiciously large doses of narcotic antagonists will provoke intense manifestations of withdrawal in such patients.

Management of the infant born to an addicted mother

To the degree that a pregnant woman is physically dependent on narcotics so too will her unborn child be, for such drugs readily cross the placenta. There is a low fertility rate among female addicts; when pregnancy does go to term, the infants born to such women comprise a significant percentage of the "high risk" newborns seen today in hospitals serving low income populations in urban areas. Though little evidence exists to suggest that infants born to addicted mothers are at a greater risk for congenital anomalies than those born without the history of prenatal narcotics exposure, there is a greater likelihood of low birthweight (under 2500 gm) in these infants, who have, as a result, higher rates of morbidity and mortality. Additionally, unless gradual maternal detoxification has occurred well in advance of delivery, the infant, when born in a state of physical dependence, will exhibit the withdrawal syndrome. Indeed, withdrawal symptoms have even been postulated to occur *in utero* for it has been noted that an increase in fetal activity often develops at the same time the mother herself feels the need for a "fix" (6).

The phenomenon of neonatal narcotic withdrawal was regarded as little more than a medical curiosity until the late 1940's and early 1950's (6). Increasing numbers of cases then began appearing in the literature, and, today, most pediatricians readily consider the diagnosis of possible withdrawal syndrome on being confronted with an irritable, tremulous newborn.

It has been reported that anywhere from 50 to 90% of infants born to addicted mothers will undergo withdrawal and that of the affected infants, 80 to 90% will demonstrate their symptoms within 24 hours after birth. Approximately one-half of them will exhibit moderate to severe symptoms, and the remainder will have only a relatively mild illness (7, 8). The broad variation in the numbers of infants involved and the variability in their symptoms reflect the differences that existed in the daily amounts of drug that had been taken by the mothers.

The typical narcotic withdrawal syndrome in the dependent infant consists of tremors, irritability, restlessness, watery stools, and a shrill cry. These symptoms may also be accompanied by vomiting, poor food intake, fever, and, less frequently, twitching, yawning, sneezing, nasal congestion, lacrimation, and hyperhidrosis. Severely dependent infants may progress to convulsions, depressed respiration, apnea, and cyanosis. Marked respiratory difficulty and peripheral vascular collapse can ensue and may result in death.

Symptomatology is directly proportional to the amount of narcotic the mother had regularly taken. It has been estimated that a daily maternal dose of 6 mg of heroin produces only quite mild symptoms in the infant whereas 12 mg/day will result in moderate to marked difficulty (6). It is usually impossible, of course, to determine in advance the magnitude of physical dependence involved, and the physician should be prepared to cope with many eventualities in any baby born to an addicted mother, ranging from no symptoms at all to convulsions and peripheral vascular collapse. Most infants, however, exhibit variable degrees of irritability and tremulousness.

Other factors may also confuse the issue. Mixed drug abuse is not uncommon, and the presence of intoxicating levels of barbiturates, amphetamines, or hallucinogens in the newborn can complicate the picture immeasurably. The drug-dependent infant, having tolerance to narcotics, is usually born without signs of major central nervous system depression; if an unusually large dose of narcotic has been taken by the mother just prior to delivery, depression may be evident. In the latter case, hospital-administered analgesics and anesthetics, which cross the placenta readily, may add further to this depression.

The complexities of the situation are well illustrated by considering the arrival of an unanticipated mother at term, whose state of addiction is neither known nor recognized. She may have taken a sizable "fix" just before entering the hospital, but because of her labor pains she may not be "on the nod" but have an appropriate sensorium for the situation. The usual obstetrical premedication and anesthesia may have an unexpectedly profound depressant effect on the infant depending on whether its tolerance had been exceeded by the "fix." The true state of affairs generally does not become clear until the postpartum mother begins her own withdrawal and her infant does likewise. These two events may occur simultaneously or within a few hours of each other, the infant trailing the mother because of his less mature drug detoxifying systems. The absence of withdrawal symptoms in a mother despite suggestive findings in her infant may be testimony only to the efficiency with which she is continuing to be supplied with illicit drugs in the hospital.

The infant's withdrawal syndrome generally becomes evident within the first 24 hours of life, reaches a peak at 48 to 72 hours, and then gradually wanes over the succeeding days. The duration of symptoms is, as are so many aspects of this syndrome, highly variable; symptoms have been reported to clear in as short a time as 4 days or to last, on rare occasions, as long as 40 days. It is difficult to conceive how withdrawal from narcotics could be the cause of symptomatology that lasts for very long periods of time. We suggest that the infant with signs persistent beyond 14 days be carefully re-examined for other possible causative conditions.

Morbidity and mortality figures differ widely from earlier to later reports. Data from the 1950's indicated an over-all mortality rate of 34% and a 93% death rate in those untreated (6). Later evaluations offer a more encouraging picture with mortality rates ranging from 0 to 17% (7, 8, 9). The usually smaller dose of heroin in today's average "bag," and thus the lower degree of physical dependence that exists for both mother and child combined with more effective neonatal care for "high risk" babies seem to account for this improved outlook rather than significantly better withdrawal techniques alone. Specific anti-addiction therapy today appears to be less heroic than before, and the average symptomatology is much less severe in current descriptions than in those of 25 years ago (6, 8).

Nonetheless, even today narcotic addiction and withdrawal present a significant hazard to the dependent infant when compared to normal infants. Perlmutter (7) found, in a study of 22 addicted mothers, a low birthweight in 56.5% of their infants (average weight of 2296 gm) as compared to 13.7% for the hospital as a whole and a perinatal mortality rate from all causes of 17.4% in the study group, compared with a rate of 2.2% for normal infants. Zelson *et al.* (8), in a considerably larger study, had an even lower mortality rate of just under 4%. In any event it appears that neonatal deaths attributable to complications of the withdrawal syndrome are quite rare in current experience and that most deaths in such infants are due to problems engendered by their low birthweight and other less well defined factors inherent in the suboptimal prenatal care and nutrition that their mothers have had.

No concise agreement on the optimal therapeutic regimen exists among authors. The wide divergence of opinions and the highly variable clinical pictures can be confusing; we conclude that most infants experiencing heroin withdrawal today probably have only a mild to moderate illness and that most do well, regardless of the therapeutic agent chosen for detoxification. Many may do well with no therapy at all, though it is reasonable and worthwhile to treat all infants of addicted mothers who become even mildly symptomatic. Such treatment is simple and relatively safe and may well avert progression to more serious manifestations of withdrawal. The duration of therapy is a highly individual matter, but current trends suggest that the initially effective dose, that which controls symptoms without undue sedation, be maintained for 4 days with subsequent tapering in dose and/or frequency of administration. The total treatment time is from 7 to 40 days (the average being 10 to 14 days) depending on the individual infant's needs.

Paregoric (7), methadone (6), barbiturates (9), chlorpromazine (8, 9), and, recently, diazepam (Dr. Judith Frank, private communication) are all agents currently being used. Other strong narcotic preparations and barbiturates are generally less favored as being no better than those listed above.

Chlorpromazine (Thorazine) has been the most widely used drug, with satisfactory results being obtained in a dose of 0.7 mg/kg every 6 hours, either orally or intramuscularly; it appears to be the agent of choice. Paregoric in a dose of 4 to 5 drops every 3 to 4 hours orally has also been found to be of value. More recently diazepam (Valium), 1 to 2 mg orally or intramuscularly every 6 to 8 hours, is being successfully used in some institutions with a high degree of effectiveness. Phenobarbital, 2 mg/kg every 6 hours, has also been reported to be useful, but because of its central nervous system depressant effects on an infant in possible risk of compromised respiration, plus the possibility of paradoxical excitation from barbiturates that occurs in this age group, it should be used with caution. Methadone, 0.5 mg every 4 to 6 hours, has also been given with beneficial results, but, since it is relatively long acting and no more effective than non-addicting agents in most situations, it may well have a role only in the severely dependent baby if even then. Obviously the recommended doses are only approximate, and adjustment must be made according to a particular patient's needs.

Babies born to mothers on methadone-maintenance therapy have the same problems as those born to mothers on heroin. Though an early report (4) suggested that there were few if any untoward consequences, more recent data (11, 12) show that not only do methadone infants experience withdrawal but that it may be more severe and more prolonged than that with heroin. In Zelson's experience (12), 91% of such infants will be symptomatic, with the onset of difficulties at roughly the same time as with heroin addiction (i.e., within the first 4 days of life), but with a much later peak intensity, at 7 to 14 days.

It should be appreciated that these findings are to be expected, pharmacologically. Both methadone and heroin are narcotics, and both readily cross the placenta. The methadone-maintenance mother receives a controlled, "addicting" dose of drug of around 100 mg/day. In contrast, the daily heroin intake of the street addict is both much lower and more unpredictable. An average, 10-bag-a-day habit may provide little drug, or as much as 30 mg of heroin. Since both drugs are approximately equipotent, milligram for milligram, the baby born to a methadone-maintenance mother is commonly more severely "addicted" (physically dependent) than one born to an illicit heroin user; and its withdrawal closely duplicates the experiences with neonatal withdrawal of the 1950's and early 1960's.

The treatment of a newborn's withdrawal symptoms from methadone is the same as that for heroin but must be continued for a longer period of time. Results will usually be highly satisfactory, with a low morbidity and mortality rate. The good prognosis, in this instance, as contrasted to the early heroin experiences, may be due in part to the excellent prenatal care the mothers have been given, along with usually satisfactory maternal cooperation.

Methadone babies, however, still have low birth weights as compared to the norm, though less so than heroin-addicted infants, and they are more subject to hyperbilirubinemia than either heroin-addicted or normal newborns (12).

Only meager data are available on the long-term effects of methadone on growth and development. Preliminary studies at Beth Israel Hospital in New York City (Dr. Saul Blatman, private communication) have indicated that such children up to 5 years of age, at least, show no detectable differences from non-addicted infants. Moreover, all methadone-maintenance mothers came regularly for ongoing baby care, in contrast to heroin addicts all of whom immediately stopped coming.

Despite the addiction potential of barbituates, reports of infants suffering from withdrawal from these drugs have been few. Desmond et al. (13) described a group of 15 infants subjected to barbiturates *in utero* all of whom experienced hyperirritability, restlessness, voracious appetite, frequent regurgitation, and a number of other symptoms similar to those of postnatal narcotic withdrawal. For the most part, these problems were late in both onset after birth (63 hours to 7 days) and peak intensity (2 to 6 weeks). Only four of the mothers of these babies were classified as addicts. The remainder were on medically prescribed phenobarbital in dosages of 90 to 120 mg/day. Five were also receiving Dilantin and/or Mysoline. Withdrawal was effected with paregoric, phenobarbital, or Thorazine, each with equally good results. We would also recommend the use of diazepam (Valium), particularly for those babies whose symptoms are prolonged.

In regard to infants born to alcoholics, Shirkey states, "Despite long and frequent human experience with this drug, there are no known definite, direct, deleterious effects [on the fetus or newborn]" (14); this view is no longer tenable (cf. p. 104).

There appears to be no acute neonatal problems comparable to those seen in the narcotic dependent infant occasioned by even heavy maternal use of non-addicting drugs. Though hallucinogens and central nervous system stimulants do pass through the placenta, it must be anticipated that a mother who delivers while intoxicated will also produce an intoxicated infant. Treatment in such circumstances is purely supportive and symptomatic.

The use of methadone in the detoxification and maintenance
 of narcotic addicts

Methadone, first synthesized in Germany, was introduced into general medical use as a narcotic analgesic in the late 1940's. Though the chemical structure of this drug differs substantially from that of morphine, their actions are qualitatively identical, and cross-tolerance and cross-physical dependence between these two drugs and other narcotic analgesic drugs can exist. Quantitatively, approximately 2 mg of methadone can be substituted for 2 mg of heroin or 4 mg of morphine. The minimum lethal dose in a non-tolerant adult is estimated to be about 75 mg of methadone hydrochloride (5, 16).

Methadone has been studied as a heroin substitute by being administered parenterally to known addicts. Behavior and subjective sensations are reported to be very similar to that produced by morphine. From the pharmacological point of view, methadone must be considered as virtually identical with most other chemical classes of narcotic analgesics, including heroin, with two significant exceptions; it is effective orally (with an effect approximately equivalent to 45% of that of an intramuscular dose), and it acts for longer periods of time than heroin or morphine (5).

It is these latter two qualities combined with the phenomena of cross-tolerance and physical dependence that makes methadone the current drug of choice for the detoxification (medically supervised withdrawal) of addicts and that led to its use in the long-term management of narcotic addiction. Indeed, today, the mere word *methadone* is often mistakenly held to be synonymous with *methadone maintenance*. It is important to keep in mind that there are a variety of uses of this drug, each with differing legal implications for the physician.

First, methadone is a useful narcotic analgesic drug and as such can be used for the alleviation of pain. Second, as noted earlier, a schedule of tapering doses of methadone is the method of choice for withdrawal of an addicted individual. In most states, a physician may use methadone legally for this purpose. Additionally, in selected cases, methadone may also be administered daily in such doses as are necessary to keep the patient comfortable for a limited period of time preparatory to withdrawal, while concomitant efforts to establish motivation for rehabilitation are undertaken or while awaiting entry into a rehabilitation program for which there is a substantial waiting period. State laws governing the use of narcotics in these latter two categories do vary and should be consulted. Last, methadone is used for the indefinite maintenance of the narcotic addict. Federal drug regulations still classify use of the drug for maintenance as experimental and require that it be undertaken only in duly authorized research programs.

Methadone has played an insignificant role in street drug abuse until recently. But with increasing numbers of maintenance programs coming into being (by the end of 1971 it was estimated that some 10,000 addicts were under treatment in the cities of New York and Washington alone), with dispensation of the drug in tablet form in many instances, and with the concomitant laxity in control that inevitably accompanies rapid expansion, diversion of the drug into illicit channels is becoming more frequent. Illicit methadone is used for two purposes: for self-imposed withdrawal to lose tolerance to heroin and thereby to reduce daily heroin requirements or for "mainlining" or oral usage to produce a "high." Deaths from overdoses of this drug have occurred on a number of occasions.

METHADONE WITHDRAWAL   Withdrawal from narcotics in the physically dependent individual (detoxification) is generally best managed with the patient in hospital, though, increasingly, ambulatory programs are being established for this purpose. Persons with a small "habit" of two to three bags of heroin a day can often be easily withdrawn without recourse to narcotic substitution; diazepam is a useful agent in such instances. Substantial degrees of addiction, however, warrant alleviation of the withdrawal syndrome with methadone substitution, whereby detoxification is virtually symptomless.

The patient is observed after the intake of narcotics stops, and, if significant symptoms appear, an initial dose of 15 to 20 mg of methadone is given orally (or intramuscularly if vomiting occurs). Additional doses of 10 to 15 mg every 4 to 6 hours can be given if symptoms are not suppressed or if they recur. After 24 to 36 hours, the daily methadone requirements can easily be calculated by adding up the total number of milligrams given. Immediately thereafter, this dose (given in two divided doses) is reduced by 20% each day, and this schedule is usually well tolerated. Most patients can be detoxified in less than 10 days and generally feel well thereafter or experience only very mild withdrawal symptoms for a few additional days (16).

SHORT-TERM METHADONE STABILIZATION   Short-term maintenance is usually employed as an ambulatory procedure in carefully selected cases where multidisciplinary services providing evaluation and motivation are available or where a well-motivated patient is awaiting entry into a rehabilitation project. A stabilizing, single daily dose is determined on the basis of the patient's symptoms, starting with 20 mg of methadone/day. The patient must come to the doctor daily, should receive his drug in liquid form, and should be observed drinking it to avoid diversion of the drug to others.

METHADONE MAINTENANCE   In 1965 Dole and Nyswander first reported their success with the use of methadone "blockade" (17). In subsequent years "methadone maintenance" programs based on their experience and protocol have become widespread. Currently this approach appears to be gaining acceptance progressively (though not without criticism) as the method with the highest potential of all known therapeutic modalities for alleviation of drug-related crime and for restoration of the confirmed narcotic addict to an economically productive life.

Dole and Nyswander based their approach on the observation that psychiatric treatment following detoxification had consistently failed to be effective in all but a relatively few instances, with craving for narcotics and resumption of abuse occurring in most. These investigators, while not rejecting psychological determinants, also postulate that the persistent craving has a metabolic basis, stemming from a biologically altered response to narcotics in susceptible individuals (18). They felt that some medication that would "block the abnormal reaction of addicts to heroin" (i.e., their drug hunger) would allow the individual to return to a constructive life. Methadone fit their requirements of a drug that would "eliminate" the euphoric appeal of heroin and the withdrawal symptoms that draw addicts back to drug use; be sufficiently free from toxic or dysphoric effects that patients would continue with treatment; and be orally effective, long-acting, medically safe, and compatible with normal daily activity (19). The fundamental principles of methadone maintenance depend on the drug's oral efficacy, its long duration of action, and its pharmacological kinship with heroin that results in the production of "sufficient tolerance to methadone to block the euphoric effect of an average illegal dose of diacetyl morphine" (19). When so used, they view methadone as an "antinarcotic agent" and differentiate between its use as a blocking agent and the distribution of heroin on demand, which simply substitutes legal heroin for that obtained illegally and which maintains the addict's status quo (20, 21).

Regardless of the confusion that may arise from the terminology applied to methadone maintenance, it should be kept in mind that it is a form of highly controlled rehabilitative therapy, based on the mechanism of cross-tolerance and the substitution of one narcotic agent for another. It should not be confused with the use of such true narcotic antagonists as naloxone whereby the narcotic is "neutralized," i.e., is actively prevented from exerting its effects. Given intravenously, methadone can produce a "high" even in a markedly tolerant individual if given in sufficiently large doses, and abrupt cessation of daily therapy will result in withdrawal symptoms though of slower onset, lesser intensity, and longer duration than those seen for equivalent degrees of heroin dependence.

The prototype of most programs, that of Nyswander and Dole (22), currently requires that candidates be 18 years of age or older, have 2 years or more of heroin abuse, have a history of several relapses after withdrawal, have failed at other efforts at rehabilitation, have no major medical complications, and have the wish to enter the program voluntarily. The patient is first brought to maintenance over approximately a 6-week period either in a hospital or while under closely supervised ambulation (23). Methadone is given by mouth initially in small divided doses of approximately 10 mg twice a day, the dose being titrated so as to be high enough to alleviate withdrawal symptoms and low enough to avoid oversedation and excessive urinary retention or constipation. The dose is increased gradually over 4 to 6 weeks to a maintenance level of 80 to 120 mg/day in a single dose. With such doses, patients have been found to function normally, have minimal side effects, generally experience no craving for heroin, and are refractory to the usual street dose of heroin whose concentration is nearly always well below the patient's current level of narcotic tolerance.

The second phase is a long-term ambulatory period of approximately 1 year. The patient returns to the clinic daily, receives his drug diluted in fruit juice, is observed to drink it; his urine is tested to ascertain whether he has been using any drugs illicitly. Those individuals who evidence sufficient responsibility are given several days' supply of methadone diluted in juice to take home, diminishing the frequency of clinic visits and thus enabling some to take jobs or return to school. Generally such a step has proven satisfactory with the drug being in an inappropriate vehicle and too dilute for intravenous injection.

The third and last phase currently is an indefinite period of time when the patient has been stabilized as a productive member of society. Medically, treatment resembles that in the second phase; at least one dose of medication must be taken in the clinic per week, and one urine specimen is checked.

In all phases, supportive services are readily available and are related to the needs of the individual patient. Only a few have been found to need little more than medical supervision. Most need substantial support, guidance, and assistance in developing job skills and in resolving personal problems.

Dole and Nyswander think that methadone maintenance will prove to be necessary for indefinite periods of time. In reviewing 350 patients withdrawn from methadone and returned to a narcotic-free state, they reported that most felt a return of their former craving for heroin, even when an excellent adjustment had led the patient to feel that he could live without drugs. Most sought readmission to the program and, if not taken back, did, in fact, start taking heroin again. These investigators conclude that their experience "definitely does not support the traditional assumption that drug hunger is a symptom of social and psychological problems" (24).

The regimen appears medically quite safe with few complications. The most troublesome side effect has been persistent constipation, which is generally managed satisfactorily with hydrophilic colloids or other laxatives and occasional enemas. Reduction of libido also occurs. Amenorrheic women have usually experienced an eventual return of normal menses, and a number have conceived and delivered normal infants while on methadone maintenance (10, 25).

Perhaps the greatest hazard, and a potentially lethal one, exists for the children of parents on maintenance when the juice-diluted drug is stored at home in the refrigerator. Severe narcotic poisoning, and even death, has resulted from consumption of these solutions by an unknowing child (26). As one remedy for this problem, Jaffe has demonstrated that acetylmethadol, a synthetic congener of methadone hydrochloride, is a useful substitute. Its effects persist for 72 to 96 hours and can satisfactorily be given in the clinic three times a week, which obviates the necessity of sending medication home with the patient as an alternative to daily visits (27).

One cannot yet fully evaluate the effectiveness and impact of methadone maintenance upon narcotic addiction. Dole and Nyswander report that 80% of all patients who enter the program remain for at least 2 years, that of those who had previously been involved in crimes, 90% have ended such activity, and that 75% of all patients retained in the program have returned to productive lives (28, 29). No other therapeutic modality used today can even approach these claims.

Critics of methadone maintenance generally fall into three categories: first are those who condemn the perpetuation of the addicted state and the long-term use of a narcotic agent for moral, sociological, and/or psychological reasons (30, 31, 32). Others accept maintenance as valid therapy under highly controlled circumstances but fear that the easing of restrictions on distribution to reach more addicts may result in illicit diversion of methadone on a large scale and the addition thereby of another narcotic to illegal street traffic (33, 34). A third group perceives weaknesses within the program protocol (35). Scrutiny of the Dole-Nyswander program indicates that approximately 20% of those on methadone maintenance have resorted to the use of such other agents as alcohol, barbiturates, or central nervous system stimulants and that 14% have had to be discharged as a consequence of psychotic, delinquent, or other provocative or disruptive forms of behavior. Maintenance (in its present form) does not appear to be a valid method for treating addicts with such traits (36). Connor and Kremen concluded that there should be a much more structured program of ongoing therapy and a wider range of supportive services, after evaluating a group of patients on methadone and finding that they suffered from moodiness, loneliness, poor self-image, and conflict in sex-identification, despite outward social productivity (37).

External review committees will need to examine long-term results of methadone maintenance from the point of view of both the return of an individual to a rewarding and meaningful life and the relief of society from the burden of the addict and the addict's attendant crime. It appears that methadone maintenance has won a place in the therapeutic armamentarium for management of the narcotic addict who has failed or has been unresponsive to other forms of treatment (38, 39, 40). Certainly programs are developing throughout the country at a rapid pace (38, 39). We do not see methadone maintenance as the panacea to the problem of addiction, but rather as one of a number of approaches, each of which has its rightful place in further investigations but none of which can reach a substantial number of the "hard-core" addict population or answer the question of how to prevent individuals from becoming users of narcotics.

The use of narcotic antagonists in rehabilitative programs for addicts

The search for *the* most effective method for the treatment of narcotic addicts seems to be an incorrect and inappropriate goal. Narcotic addicts are not a homogeneous group. Though they are all dependent on narcotics to some degree, they differ in other and probably significant respects, such as chronological age, degree of social and emotional maturity, pattern of narcotic usage, duration of drug usage, and socioeconomic background. The different programs of rehabilitation currently being tried vary considerably in their requirements for success, which means, in part, the demands made on the addict and the safeguards provided against the consequences of resuming narcotic usage.

Methadone maintenance is, relatively, the least demanding program of rehabilitation. The patient takes a drug daily, so his "drug craving" may continue to be satisfied, if only symbolically. Because his daily dose of methadone confers sufficient cross-tolerance to narcotics, he is safe from the temptation to resume taking drugs regularly that a subsequent episode of gratifying heroin usage might provoke. It is not a satisfactory program though for the user who wants to be "out of the drug scene" entirely. The various forms of psychotherapy, ranging from conventional personal treatment to taking up residence in a "therapeutic community," are drugless and highly demanding programs with respect to the patient's motivation and "will power"; the patient must cope with the reality of himself and the world around him without the "crutch" of drugs. The incidence of therapeutic failures is high in this form of rehabilitation; bereft of pharmacological safeguards, a single episode of heroin usage can trigger resumption of the previous pattern of narcotic intake. Rehabilitative programs in which narcotic antagonists are used fall in a "middle ground." Rehabilitation depends largely on the efforts of psychiatrists, vocational counselors, social workers, and the like (as in many of the psychotherapeutic programs), yet the patient receives a safeguard (the antagonist) against the consequences of using heroin again. Such programs now are still receiving experimental evaluation, and the preliminary results available would probably not encourage an objective observer to predict that they will prove helpful in the rehabilitation of substantive numbers of narcotic addicts; we nonetheless feel, consonant with the view expressed above, that they should be given full consideration and should not be "written off" simply because their probable incidence of "cures" falls short of the expectations and hopes of some people.

The rationale for the use of antagonists derives from the following clinical observations: Narcotic antagonists can abolish or greatly attenuate all the effects of heroin addicts find pleasurable. Moreover, even if an addict's pattern of usage of heroin or any other narcotic drug is so regular that physical dependence on the narcotic would ordinarily develop, such dependence will not develop if the addict receives concurrently adequate doses of narcotic antagonists. Thus, while he is receiving an antagonist, the addict's craving for narcotics cannot for all practical purposes be periodically reinforced by the "pleasures" of the drug experience, nor can fear of the withdrawal syndrome provoke drug usage.

In actual practice, the use of narcotic antagonists poses a number of problems. All of them exhibit one or more of the following undesirable properties: the duration of action is relatively brief, a matter of hours in the case of nalorphine (Nalline), for example. They are only weakly active when given by mouth, unless the oral dose is greatly increased; this has been a problem particularly with naloxone (Narcan). They are psychoactive compounds capable of producing dysphoria and, in some patients, hallucinations. One of the antagonists, cyclazocine, has been found, however, to mimic many of the effects of the antidepressant drug, imipramine (Tofranil), in emotionally depressed patients who were not drug users (41). The antagonists with prominent "narcotomimetic" (agonistic) properties produce physical dependence on regular usage, and a (relatively mild) withdrawal syndrome develops if intake is stopped abruptly or markedly decreased.

As pharmacological adjuncts in the rehabilitation of narcotic users, naloxone and cyclazocine among the antagonists have been the most extensively investigated. Naloxone (Narcan) seems to exemplify the purest type of antagonist available, in that it exerts no perceptible or measurable pharmacological effects other than to block many of the effects of heroin and all of the other narcotic drugs. Given to a subject who is not under the influence of narcotic drugs, it has essentially no action; given to a subject under the influence of a narcotic drug, naloxone abolishes the narcotic effects in a way identical to that already described for nalorphine. A single intravenous dose of naloxone is effective for about 3 hours. In addition to its short duration of effect, naloxone is not readily effective when given by mouth, and this, too, is an obstacle to its acceptance in rehabilitative programs. The continued participation of ex-drug users in rehabilitative programs will obviously not be facilitated if they must visit the clinic daily (which, at present, can mean for some a fairly long trip each day). To overcome the limited efficacy of naloxone by mouth, quite large doses of it (3 gm) are being used; such a dose confers protection for the following 24 hours. It is far from the ideal solution to the problem because naloxone is a fairly expensive drug. (Injections of naloxone pamoate are currently receiving experimental consideration as one means of solving the problem of how to give the drug. A single intramuscular injection of naloxone pamoate has been shown, in the face of heroin "challenges," to confer protection for 48 to 60 hours (M. Fink, personal communication).

Fink and his colleagues have described their experiences with naloxone by mouth in seven hospitalized male narcotic addicts (10), whose mean age was 31 and whose mean period of prior narcotic usage was 11 years. All of the subjects represented voluntary admissions, and each had chosen to participate in the naloxone program, after having been offered a choice of several types of rehabilitative programs. The optimal medication schedule was determined by "challenging" the narcotic blockade with intravenous doses of heroin (20 or 40 mg) at various times after different doses of the antagonist. It was found that 100-mg doses of naloxone at 8 A.M. and 7 P.M. protected the subjects against essentially all of the effects of 20 mg of heroin; 40 mg of heroin given 5 hours after the morning dose of naloxone produced no objective signs or subjective sensations immediately, but 2 to 3 hours later the subjects experienced anything from a mild to the customarily intense reaction to this dose of the narcotic.

During the study, naloxone administration was stopped in one subject when thrombocytopenia developed; two weeks after the discontinuance of medication, the platelet count had returned to normal. Another subject withdrew from the program for unspecified reasons. The other five subjects received naloxone daily for 3 months, at which point the study was abruptly concluded because of an unanticipated shortage of naloxone.

Currently, Fink's group is supplying former addicts with daily oral doses of 3000 mg of naloxone routinely, which provides a satisfactory degree of blockade for 24 hours (M. Fink, personal communication). As a first approximation, naloxone is clearly capable of doing what has been asked of it: produce a satisfactory narcotic blockade, and it does this without causing any other significant pharmacological effects. Its relatively short duration of action, its relative ineffectiveness when taken by mouth, and its relatively high cost all prevent it from being an ideal narcotic antagonist for use in rehabilitative programs.

One of the earliest reported pilot studies with cyclazocine was conducted by Martin and his colleagues (3) in the United States Public Health Service Hospital in Lexington, Kentucky. The subjects were male prisoners who had violated federal narcotic laws. They were adjudged to be in good health and displayed no signs of major psychiatric pathology. The efficacy of the narcotic blockade (when challenged by morphine or heroin) was measured with the aid of three criteria: photographic records of changes in pupillary diameter, obtained under carefully controlled conditions; and, in a double-blind study, reports of subjective effects by the subjects and notations of objective effects by experienced observers. The daily oral dose of cyclazocine investigated most extensively was 4 mg per subject, given as 2-mg doses in the morning and evening; this dosage level was not instituted immediately but achieved by progressively increasing doses with time beginning with 0.1 mg twice a day until the subject was "stabilized" on cyclazocine (i.e., until tolerance had developed to such possible untoward effects of cyclazocine as sedation, sleeplessness, and visual imagery, which occasionally was truly hallucinatory). Among six subjects, the cyclazocine blockade was maintained for from 13 to 33 days, and it was challenged in two ways. In addition to cyclazocine, the subjects received rapidly increasing doses of morphine subcutaneously, until a daily dose of 240 mg was achieved (60 mg every 6 hours). The effects of morphine during this period were found to be equal to or less than the effects of 10 mg of morphine given subcutaneously in the absence of cyclazocine. Abrupt discontinuance of the morphine (but continued administration of the antagonist) produced a withdrawal syndrome so mild that some of the subjects did not recognize it as such. The blockade was challenged also by single doses of heroin or morphine given subcutaneously or intravenously. The only observed and reported effects of 60 mg of heroin by vein were a prominent flush and a sensation of "pins and needles." Fink has noted that naloxone-treated subjects experience a similar sensation when given heroin by vein, though not when given morphine (M. Fink, personal communication). When cyclazocine administration was abruptly stopped, a recognizable, though mild, withdrawal syndrome developed. As one might infer from the dosage schedule selected, these investigators found that 2 mg of this antagonist by mouth produced a satisfactory degree of blockade for approximately 12 hours.

Of the two antagonists, naloxone and cyclazocine, which is to be preferred for rehabilitative programs? Cyclazocine is the more effective drug by mouth but, unlike naloxone, it may produce unpleasant effects (dysphoria, hallucinations, irritability, sleeplessness, etc.), especially during the initial period of use. Though tolerance to these effects develops in virtually all patients, it may take from 2 to 6 weeks to "stabilize" a patient on cyclazocine (3); this process could erode seriously a drug user's motivation to become rehabilitated and his confidence in the physician.

There is not enough evidence yet available to make even a rough estimate of the severity of this problem; among the small group of six subjects studied by Martin et al. (3), five had only relatively minor complaints during stabilization, including headache, constipation, and sedation.

A meaningful assessment of the probable value of rehabilitation programs in which narcotic antagonists are used will require considerably more data than are available now. Clearly we need information about larger groups of patients and longer periods of time (i.e., years, not weeks or months of treatment). And even these numbers will probably be of limited value only; as Martin et al. point out in reference to cyclazocine (3): "Since this method of treatment controls only the pharmacological factors responsible for drug-seeking behavior, its effectiveness will be directly related to the importance of the pharmacological factors in the disease." The initial enthusiasm for naltrexone, an antagonist related chemically to naloxone, needs now to be supported by greater experience with its use before a more definitive judgment can be made (5, p. 575). Because we believe that psychic factors are probably of much greater importance in the majority of patients than are pharmacological ones, we feel that the success of narcotic antagonist programs will be determined largely by the nature of the "ancillary" services offered the patients and by how competently these services are rendered. It is a curious adjective to use, in our opinion, for such services as various forms of psychotherapy and vocational counseling that probably play a substantive role, and possibly a pre-eminent one, in determining the degree to which a drug user can be induced to give up his psychological dependence on drugs.

GENERALIZED CENTRAL NERVOUS SYSTEM DEPRESSANT DRUGS

Supervised withdrawal

When a patient presents with a pattern of usage of these drugs such that it seems probable that physical dependence on them has developed, the physician should initiate a program of withdrawal so that this dependence can be lost. (The criteria by which one judges whether physical dependence has developed have been described in Chapter 4.) The pharmacological principle (cross-physical dependence) underlying withdrawal from generalized depressant drugs is identical to that used in narcotic addiction. With the aid of an appropriate drug, a dosage schedule is instituted in which the daily dose steadily decreases with time until drug intake falls to zero; at this point, as with narcotic withdrawal, physical dependence on and tolerance to the effects of this group of drugs should be essentially absent.

Within this category of drugs, the physician's candidate for withdrawal today is most likely to be either an alcoholic or a barbiturate addict; the incidence of addiction to nonbarbiturate hypnotic drugs and the so-called "minor tranquilizers" appears to be relatively small. There is no general agreement about the drug to be used for supervised withdrawal. Many compounds could be used, and many have, in fact, been tried. Pharmacologically, the only critical requirement is that cross-physical dependence exist between the agent of addiction and the one given during withdrawal. (This holds true, we feel, despite the occasional favorable reports about the use of drugs not in this group, such as the phenothiazine tranquilizers, for the purpose of effecting withdrawal.) Many physicians choose a barbiturate for this purpose; it is a suitable drug with an adequate duration of effect and margin of safety. Alcohol could be used but rarely is; its duration of action is relatively short, the range between effective and dangerous doses can be uncomfortably small, and it intensifies the gastritis so commonly present in alcoholics. Recently, reports about the successful use of such pharmacologically suitable drugs as chlordiazepoxide (Librium) and diazepam (Valium) have appeared. More experience with the use of these "minor tranquilizers" is needed before claims for the unique value of these drugs (because of their psychotropic properties) can be evaluated; at the least, they should, in proper doses, be as useful as barbiturates (16).

Withdrawal should be undertaken in hospitalized patients, for only in such a setting can possible untoward developments be coped with optimally. Whenever possible, a medical history should first be obtained and a physical examination performed to learn if the usual schedule of withdrawal should be modified or perhaps even deferred temporarily. A history of seizures, not related to drug abuse, for example, would suggest the desirability of slowing the standard pace of withdrawal and the need for particularly careful observation of the patient during the process. Severe, untreated organic disease, such as congestive heart failure, identifies a patient for whom this potentially hazardous procedure poses an additional and substantive risk; in situations such as this, physicians should consult an appropriate local agency or the Drug Enforcement Agency in the Department of Justice to learn what latitude the current regulations afford them in terms of maintenance of the addiction by the physician while treatment for the organic disorder is being instituted.

One of the purposes of supervised withdrawal is to prevent the emergence of serious withdrawal symptoms, most notably convulsions and/or delirium. To this end, the physician begins the procedure by obtaining his own measure of the patient's degree of physical dependence on generalized depressant drugs; this is accomplished by determining how much of the drug (i.e., the one to be used during withdrawal) is required to produce a state of mild intoxication, as evidenced by nystagmus on lateral gaze, slurred speech, slight ataxia, and possibly drowsiness. Blachly recommends 200-mg doses of pentobarbital (Nembutal) by mouth, repeated at 6-hour intervals, until intoxication is evident (42). The total quantity of barbiturate required to produce intoxication should be given daily (in divided doses) for the following 24 to 48 hours; this quantity produces what has been designated the "stablization level" (21), and, if it has been estimated correctly, the patient should be essentially free of irritability, tremulousness, and insomnia while under its influence. Most patients can tolerate without marked discomfort a decrease thereafter of 100 mg/day in the initial stabilization dose. Withdrawal can be completed in most patients in 10 to 21 days; on rare occasions, however, withdrawal may require as long as 2 months for completion.

The more severely addicted individuals will not become intoxicated by 200 mg of pentobarbital every 6 hours. For such patients, Blachly recommends that, on the 2nd day, the dose be increased to 300 mg (the interval between doses remaining constant) and, if that fails, to increase the size of the dose to 400 mg on the 3rd day. Occasionally patients have been encountered who did not exhibit sufficient signs of intoxication until the quantity of barbiturate being ingested in a 24-hour period approached 2500 mg (16).

During withdrawal, the physician should be alert to the possibility that his patient may have a mixed addiction, i.e., he is physically dependent concurrently on a narcotic and a generalized depressant drug. Such a possibility would be strongly indicated if the patient exhibited the autonomic disturbances characteristic of narcotic withdrawal. Though simultaneous withdrawal from the two types of drugs is possible, it is an undertaking we would recommend only for physicians with considerable experience in this area. A less demanding approach involves suppression of the more serious manifestations of narcotic withdrawal with methadone until withdrawal from the generalized depressant has been completed, after which a tapering of the daily dose of methadone can be started.

Not all addicts will tolerate the withdrawal schedule described above. In some instances, the premonitory signs will be relatively mild, consisting of tremulousness, orthostatic hypotension, and insomnia; when such signs appear, it is prudent to maintain the patient on his current dosage for an additional 24 to 48 hours. If the signs have abated at the end of this period, the withdrawal schedule may be resumed. An occasional patient may exhibit only a short period of tremulousness, which is then followed by one or more frank convulsions, usually of the grand mal type. One extra dose of 200 mg of pentobarbital may be all that is needed to prevent further convulsions; little success has attended the use of such conventional anti-epileptic agents as diphenylhydantoin (Dilantin) in this type of situation. If convulsions persist, despite the extra dose of pentobarbital, the physician should initiate standard anticonvulsant regimens of intravenously administered pentobarbital or diazepam. Depending on the patient's response to these measures, the physician will decide when, within the next several days, the withdrawal schedule can be continued.

An agitated psychotic state (often called the "delirium") can develop during supervised withdrawal as well as following abrupt cessation of, or a sharp reduction in, drug intake; it is equally difficult to suppress in either situation. If delirium develops during supervised withdrawal, the physician should anticipate that even though he increases temporarily the patient's daily intake of barbiturate, the psychotic state may not subside completely for several days.

To conclude our discussion of this general topic, we will touch briefly on several matters. It is worthy of note that a number of European physicians think that abrupt withdrawal of all drugs is the preferable approach to individuals addicted to generalized depressants (16); supportive medication of the type described above is given only if delirium develops or if the patient experiences more than one convulsion. We feel that the technique of supervised withdrawal probably errs on the conservative side medically for a number of patients. The best information now available suggests that less than one-half (and perhaps even less than one-quarter) of the patients undergoing abrupt withdrawal experience convulsions; reliable data about the incidence of the delirium are not available, nor do we have useful information about the variability to be expected in the duration and intensity of the psychotic state. Short of status epilepticus, the convulsions do not pose as much of a threat to the patient's life as does the possibility of exhaustion and cardiovascular collapse developing during the delirium. Though the delirium may arise during supervised withdrawal, we would like to think that its intensity is attenuated under these circumstances, but we really do not know. The patient undergoing supervised withdrawal, moreover, probably presents fewer problems in management for the physician and the supporting staff than does one experiencing abrupt withdrawal. We do not know either if the two types of withdrawal have any influence on the receptivity of patients to subsequent attempts at rehabilitation. Though supervised withdrawal has gained fairly general acceptance in America today, its advantages, qualitatively and quantitatively, over abrupt withdrawal have not yet been defined.

Many of the arguments over which drug to use in supervised withdrawal serve no useful purpose, in our opinion. Though we have elected to describe the use of a barbiturate in supervised withdrawal, we would not be disturbed, for example, if those clinicians who have already expressed a strong preference for the use of paraldehyde in the withdrawal of alcoholics continued to exhibit this preference. Paraldehyde is a suitable drug for the purpose; the alleged advantages of one generalized central nervous system depressant for withdrawal purposes over the others are usually hard to document in a convincing way. We would disagree only with those who advocate the use of pharmacologically unsuitable drugs for supervised withdrawal. Phenothiazine tranquilizers, such as chlorpromazine (Thorazine), are quite distinct pharmacologically from generalized depressants. They exhibit no clinically useful anticonvulsant activity nor can they, as psychotropic drugs, prevent the development of delirium during withdrawal. In the withdrawal of patients *severely* addicted to generalized depressants, a significantly higher mortality rate has been recorded among patients receiving phenothiazines than among those given generalized depressants (16). A relatively uneventful withdrawal period associated with the use of phenothiazines occurs most often, we would guess, in patients who have only a mild to moderate degree of physical dependence; one valid means of evaluating the efficacy of the phenothiazines would entail, we feel, a comparison of the results of tranquilizer usage with those of the European physicians who effect withdrawal by the abrupt discontinuance of all drugs.

It would not be consonant with the goals of this section to discuss all of the medical problems that may require the physician's attention when he initiates withdrawal in an addict. The alcoholic, for example, may present with disturbances resulting from altered fluid balance, gastritis, vitamin deficiences, and the like. The experienced physician will be aware of the possible existence of such problems and, when indicated, will institute remedial measures concurrently with the withdrawal program.

The use of such agents as disulfiram (Antabuse) in the rehabilitation of alcoholics

Virtually all patients in rehabilitation programs relapse into drug usage one or more times during treatment. Among the possible remedies proposed for this common problem has been the concept of a drug that would somehow "punish" the patient for resuming drug usage; this type of drug is now available only for use in the rehabilitation of the chronic alcoholic.

The conventional dose (0.5 gm/day) of disulfiram (tetraethylthiuram disulfide; Antabuse) produces remarkably few effects in patients who refrain from alcohol. Some may complain of a peculiar taste (metallic or garlic-like) in their mouths and some of mild gastrointestinal upsets. A few will experience dermatological disturbances (urticaria, allergic dermatitis, or acneform eruptions). Complaints of headache, tremor, fatigue, dizziness, lassitude, restlessness, and reduced sexual potency have been associated with the use of disulfiram as they have with the use of a great many drugs; in almost all such instances, establishing a causal relationship between drug and complaint has proved to be most difficult.

If patients receiving disulfiram ingest alcohol, the purported ability of this drug to inhibit the activities of certain enzymes, most notably aldehyde dehydrogenase, becomes evident within 5 to 15 minutes. The initial sensation is one of heat in the face. Bodywide vasodilation follows facial flushing and is accompanied by an intense throbbing sensation in the head and neck and a pulsating headache. Sweating increases, and nausea may be followed by recurrent vomiting. Respiratory difficulties may be accompanied by blurred vision, vertigo, weakness, anxiety, and confusion. Hypotension develops accompanied by chest pains and postural syncope. At this time, blood acetaldehyde concentrations are five to ten times greater than normal, and the above clinical picture is sometimes designated the "acetaldehyde syndrome" (43).

The intensity of the acetaldehyde syndrome on any occasion seems to be the resultant of three factors: the body concentration of disulfiram, the quantity of alcohol ingested, and the patient's individual degree of sensitivity to acetaldehyde. The last factor has not been well defined as yet but is invoked to account for the finding that a mild version of the syndrome has appeared after consumption of only 7 ml of alcohol. (The disulfiram patient known to be sensitive to acetaldehyde must even be warned against exposure to alcohol on the skin; though aftershave lotions and rubbing alcohol, for example, may contain methanol rather than ethanol, disulfiram can arrest to a substantial degree, the oxidative metabolism of methanol at the stage of formaldehyde formation.) In its milder forms, the acetaldehyde syndrome lasts for about 30 minutes and, in its more severe forms, for several hours. The exhausted patient usually sleeps for several hours after subsidence of the syndrome and awakes thereafter free of significant physiological sequelae (43).

A frightening array of severe disturbances has occurred during the period of this syndrome, involving principally the cardiovascular and the central nervous systems. Cardiac arrhythmias, acute congestive heart failure, myocardial infarction, and cardiovascular collapse have been observed as well as marked respiratory depression, convulsions, and the loss of consciousness. In addition to fatalities preceded by some of the untoward events just mentioned, deaths have occurred for which no cause could be found. The risk of endangering a patient's life by the use of disulfiram has prompted some physicians to use instead, citrated calcium carbimide (Temposil). The newer agent seems to possess the same mechanism of action as disulfiram. Effects of the carbimide drug last from 8 to 12 hours, and, if a patient is exposed to alcohol during this period, the resulting acetaldehyde syndrome seems to be characterized less frequently by severe cardiovascular disturbances (43).

The acetaldehyde syndrome is usually attributed to partial inhibition of the enzyme, aldehyde dehydrogenase, by disulfiram; as a result, when ethanol is metabolized to acetaldehyde as the first step in its biodegradation, the activity of the enzyme required for the second step (aldehyde to acid) is inadequate to catalyze the reaction at its usually rapid pace, and acetaldehyde levels in the body begin to rise. Disulfiram has been shown to inhibit the activities of other enzymes as well; these include xanthine oxidase, dopamine-β-oxidase, succinoxidase, and hepatic catalase. It is not known whether the results of these enzymatic blockades contribute to the disturbances that characterize the acetaldehyde syndrome.

From the foregoing, it is quite clear that disulfiram is indeed a drug capable of "punishing" an alcoholic when he "falls off the wagon." And because the effects of disulfiram persist for at least 3 to 4 days after the last dose, an alcoholic cannot act immediately on any decision to resume drinking without peril. The drug should be used of course only with the full cooperation of the patient and with his complete awareness of what will happen if he drinks while taking disulfiram. Patients should be hospitalized for the start of disulfiram therapy, and, during this period, some physicians advocate giving them a preview of what may happen by means of a "test drink," i.e., one just large enough to provoke a mild form of the acetaldehyde syndrome; as the dosage of disulfiram is usually standardized (0.5 gm/day), as is the size of the test drink, the intensity of the syndrome evoked provides a rough estimate of the patient's sensitivity to acetaldehyde.

The alcoholic willing to take disulfiram as a part of his program of rehabilitation must be a patient willing not only to take a drug daily but to accept the fact that by taking it, the consequences of "just one drink" will be decidedly unpleasant. He must be willing to accept also the need for constant vigilance against unexpected sources of alcohol such as the sauces on some foods, such medicinal fluids as cough syrups, and the like. It is a critical test of an alcoholic's desire for rehabilitation for him to accept disulfiram therapy and, more importantly, for him to continue taking the drug. Even when allowance is made for patients in whom this drug is relatively contraindicated because of their response to its allergenic effects, their exquisite sensitivity to acetaldehyde, or the presence of serious cardiovascular or pulmonary disease that would increase the probability of a fatal outcome from the acetaldehyde syndrome, one is left with a group of alcoholics on disulfiram that represents an unknown fraction of the total population under treatment but one that is often referred to "selected," a euphemism indicating a minority, we suspect.

REFERENCES

1. Steinberg, A. D. and J. Karliner, The clinical spectrum of heroin pulmonary edema. *Arch Int Med* 122:122, 1968
2. Louria, D. B., T. Hensle, and J. Rose, The major complications of heroin addiction. *Ann Int Med* 67:1, 1967

3. Martin, W. R., C. Gorodetzky, and T. McClane, An experimental study in the treatment of narcotic addicts with cyclazocine. *Clin Pharmacol Therap* 7:455, 1966
4. Wallach, R. C., E. Jerez, and G. Blinick, Pregnancy and menstrual function in narcotics addicts treated with methadone. *Amer J Obstet Gynecol* 105:1226, 1969
5. Jaffe, J. H. Opioid Analgesics and Antagonists. In: Gilman, A. G., L. Goodman, and A. Gilman, eds., *The Pharmacological Basis of Therapeutics,* ed. 6. New York: Macmillan, 1980, p. 494
6. Hill, R. M. and M. Desmond, Management of the withdrawal syndrome in the neonate. *Pediat Clin N Amer* 10:67, 1963
7. Perlmutter, J. F., Drug addiction in pregnant women. *Amer J Obstet Gynecol* 99:569, 1967
8. Zelson, C., Heroin withdrawal syndrome. *J Pediat* 76:483, 1970
9. Kahn, E. J., L. Neumann, and G. Polk, The course of the heroin withdrawal syndrome in newborn infants treated with phenobarbital or chlorpromazine. *J Pediat* 75:495, 1969
10. Fink, M. A. Zaks, R. Sharoff, A. Mora, A. Bruner, S. Levit, and A. Freedman, Naloxone in heroin dependence. *Clin Pharmacol Therap* 9: 568, 1968
11. Rajegowda, B. K., L. Glass, H. E. Evans, G. Maso, D. D. Swartz, and W. Leblanc, Methadone withdrawal in newborn infants. *J Pediatrics* 81: 530, 1972
12. Zelsun, C., Infant of the addicted mother. *N Engl J Med* 288:1393, 1973
13. Desmond, M. M., R. P. Schwaneche, G. S. Wilson, S. Yasunaga, and I. Burgdorff, Maternal barbiturate utilization and neonatal withdrawal symptomatology. *J. Pediatrics* 80:190, 1972
14. Shirkey, H. C., ed., *Pediatric Therapy,* ed. 3, St. Louis: C. V. Mosby, 1968, p. 161
15. Neumann, L. L., Drug abuse in pregnancy. In: Harms, E., ed., *Drugs and Youth: the Challenge of Today.* New York: Pergamon Press, 1973
16. Jaffe, J. H., Drug addiction and drug abuse. In: Gilman, A. G., L. Goodman, and A. Gilman, eds., *The Pharmacological Basis of Therapeutics,* ed. 6. New York: Macmillan, 1980, p. 535
17. Dole, V. P. and M. Nyswander, A medical treatment for diacetylmorphine (heroin) addiction. *J Amer Med Assoc* 193:646, 1965
18. Dole, V. P. and M. Nyswander, Heroin addiction. A metabolic disease. *Arch Int Med* 120:19, 1967
19. Dole, V. P., M. Nyswander, and M. J. Kreek, Narcotic blockade. *Arch Int Med* 118:304, 1966
20. Dole, V. P. and M. Nyswander, The use of methadone for narcotic blockade. *Brit J Addict* 63:55, 1968
21. Nyswander, M. E., The methadone treatment of heroin addiction. *Hosp Pract* 2:27, 1967

22. Dole, V. P., M. Nyswander, and A. Warner, Successful treatment of 750 criminal addicts. *J Amer Med Assoc* 206:2708, 1968
23. Nicholas, A. W. and P. Torrens, Outpatient induction to methadone maintenance treatment for heroin addiction. *Arch Int Med* 127:903, 1971
24. Dole, V. P., Research on methadone maintenance treatment. *Int J Addict* 5:359, 1970
25. Blatman, S. and P. Lipsitz, Infants born to heroin addicts maintained on methadone: Neonatal observations and follow-up. In: *Proceedings of the Third National Conference on Methadone Treatment* (National Institute of Mental Health). Washington, 1970
26. Blatman, S., Methadone and children. *Pediatrics* 48:173, 1971
27. Jaffe, J. H., C. Shuster, B. Smith, and P. Blachly, Comparison of acetyl-methadol and methadone in the treatment of long-term heroin users. *J Amer Med Assoc* 211:1834, 1970
28. Dole, V. P., Methadone maintenance treatment for 25,000 heroin addicts. *J Amer Med Assoc* 215:1131, 1971
29. Dole, V. P., W. Robinson, J. Orraca, E. Towns, P. Searey, and E. Caine, Methadone treatment of randomly selected criminal addicts. *N Engl J Med* 280:1372, 1969
30. Faigel, H., Methadone maintenance for treatment of addiction. *J. Amer Med Assoc* 215:299, 1971
31. Jonas, S., Methadone treatment of addicts. *New Engl J Med* 281:391, 1969
32. Myerson, D. J., Methadone treatment of addicts. *New Engl J Med* 281:390, 1969
33. Brill, H., Methadone maintenance: A problem in delivery of services. *J Amer Med Assoc* 215:1148, 1971
34. Methadone: Cracks in the panacea. *Sci News* 97:366, 1970
35. Walsh, J., Methadone and heroin addiction: Rehabilitation without a "cure." *Science* 168:684, 1970
36. Perkins, M. E. and H. Block, Survey of a methadone maintenance treatment program. *Amer J Psychiat* 126:33, 1970
37. Connor, T. and E. Kremen, Methadone maintenance. Is it enough? *Brit J Addict* 66:53, 1971
38. DuPont, R. L. and R. Katon, Development of a heroin-addiction treatment program. *J Amer Med Assoc* 216:1320, 1971
39. Jaffe, J. H., M. Zaks, and E. Washington, Experience with the use of methadone in a multi-modality program for the treatment of narcotics users. *Brit J Addict* 4:481, 1969
40. Ranzal, E., Mayor seeks $92 million for methadone. *NY Times,* March 5, 1971
41. Fink, M., J. Simeon, T. Itil, and A. Freedman, Clinical antidepressant activity of cyclazocine—a narcotic antagonist. *Clin Pharmacol Therap* 11:41, 1970

42. Blachly, P. H. Procedure for withdrawal of barbiturates. *Amer J Psychiat* 120:894, 1964
43. Ritchie, J. M., The aliphatic alcohols. In: Gilman, A. G., L. Goodman, and A. Gilman, eds., *The Pharmacological Basis of Therapeutics,* ed. 6. New York: Macmillan, 1980, p. 376

Chapter 11

DRUG ABUSE AND THE LAW

Conventional legislative restraints on drug abuse have taken the form of restrictions on importation and manufacture and stipulations about the conditions of legal possession of drugs. The penalties for violations, fines and/or imprisonment, have been typically harsher for sellers than users. (Because some sellers today are also users, the distinction between them is becoming increasingly difficult to make and sometimes turns only on the quantity of drug found in a violator's possession.) Contrary to common belief, it is not an offense under American federal law to be a drug user nor is the act of self-administration of a drug an offense; certain state and local laws vary, however.

Laws have been most effective when drug abuse has been relatively unpopular, but they have largely failed at times when the demand for illicit drugs has been high. The incentive to violate drug abuse laws is high because truly enormous profits can be realized in the illicit drug trade; this is particularly true for the importers and "wholesale distributors." Even the lowly pusher can make what is for him a most gratifying profit. Of all the forces acting to perpetuate drug abuse today, the magnitude of the sellers' profits is among the most important. Because of psychological dependence on drugs (often designated "drug craving"), a user may almost involuntarily violate drug control laws; so great is the intensity of craving in some users, they are virtually incapable of being deterred from drug abuse by restrictive laws, regardless of the penalty.

297

DRUG ABUSE AND AMERICAN FEDERAL LAW

The history of American federal laws pertaining to drug abuse is not pleasant for us to recount. For about the first 65 years of this century, the voice of law enforcement agencies was loud in regard to drug abuse; that of the medical profession was essentially inaudible. Federal enforcement officials saw the drug user only as a criminal: the ultimate recipient of illicit drugs and the person for whom elaborate arrangements for drug smuggling had been created. Local law enforcement officials also regarded the drug user as a criminal: someone apprehended, or sought, for crimes of theft designed to provide money for drugs and, less frequently, a person responsible for crimes of violence. If these officials ever also detected tragedy and misery as part of a drug user's lot, they did not let such observations temper their unvarying public posture that drug users were criminals who belonged "behind bars."

Throughout most of this period, the position of the American medical profession did not differ substantially from that of the law enforcement officials. The typical physician knew little about drug users. In medical school and later from his older colleagues, he learned that people "enslaved" by drugs were moral degenerates and, of course, criminals. (The 1918 edition of a once-popular textbook of pharmacology, Cushny's, refers repeatedly to narcotic addicts, for example, as "morphinomaniacs.") He was told that they were uncooperative, unreliable patients whom he would be well-advised to avoid, for the outcome of any attempt at rehabilitation was likely to be a failure, and, moreover, by dealing with drug users, a physician might well end up involved with the police or federal agents. In addition, drug users belonged to a special, morally stigmatized group of patients, which included sexual perverts, and any physician who attempted to study or to help such patients did so at the risk of having many of his colleagues regard him as a man with unnatural or morbid interests. Though the record of this period is studded with many valiant individual attempts to portray drug abuse as a disease and to help drug users, the majority of practitioners were content to ignore the problem, and they commonly refused to accept the user as a patient. Exceptions were made only in cases of alcoholism, the most socially acceptable form of drug abuse, though even alcoholics were grudgingly accepted as patients.

We can see justification for the positions of both groups. Drug users *are* criminals: technically, for possessing illegally certain substances and, in more easily recognizable ways, because they often steal or rob to get money for drugs and occasionally commit more serious crimes. They remain to this day most difficult patients. They are typically uncooperative, irresponsible, and immature people, many of whom resist rehabilitation apparently because they prefer drug abuse to the "straight" life. They frustrate physicians and often threaten the feeling of therapeutic competence that all practitioners must have.

Though we can understand the basis for the prevalent views of law enforcement officials and physicians in the earlier decades of this century, we do not by the same token condone them. We feel that physicians were particularly remiss in this period for their failure to study drug abuse more thoroughly; with but individual exceptions, the profession, as a group, "turned its back" on a difficult unpleasant problem. As a result, we think two particularly undesirable consequences ensued. First, very little progress was made in understanding the fundamental nature of drug abuse and in evaluating various rehabilitation programs for drug users. And second, the only voice molding and reinforcing the views of the general public and legislative bodies about drug users was that of the law enforcement agencies. From the "lawman's" view, transmuted by sensational journalists into scenes of gory violence and of broadly hinted at sexual debauchery, emerged the prevailing lay image of the drug user as a "cunning, cringing, malicious, degenerate criminal."

The present century did not begin with the two groups so aligned. Federal law enforcement agencies were relatively weak at this time; their budgets were very small, and the only laws relating remotely to drug abuse were revenue acts, some 50 years old, that levied an import tax on opium. For its part, the American Medical Association was taking a strong public stand against worthless patent remedies and the addiction liability of narcotic drugs, heroin in particular. The first Pure Food and Drug Act was passed in 1906, but its provisions were of little avail in stemming the drug abuse rampant at the time. In this period, it has been estimated, there were from 150,000 to 300,000 morphine addicts in this country; both on an absolute basis and as a fraction of the total population, it is probable that the narcotic problem was more severe then than it is now. Narcotic drugs were as freely available then as are aspirin today, and the Harrison Narcotic Act of 1914, which restricted use of these drugs to "legitimate medical purposes" and legal possession of opium and its derivatives to those who had been duly licensed, seems today to have been one logical step that should have been taken to reduce the high incidence of drug abuse prevalent at that time. It is a curious fact of American history, however, that the important reason for the passage of this famous act was that the United States, as an adherent to the Hague Convention of 1912, was required to regulate domestic production of and traffic in narcotic drugs. (In 1914, cocaine was considered a narcotic and accordingly possession and use of it were regulated by the act.)

One can only speculate why Congress, in face of a serious domestic epidemic of drug abuse, regulated that abuse largely as the result of an international commitment. Would there have been no Harrison Act without a Hague Convention? Were "decent people" thought to be unaffected by drug abuse, and therefore was there no strong domestic impetus for a regulatory law? In implementing the Harrison Act, Congress did give birth later to a law enforcement agency that strongly influenced American attitudes and activities about drug abuse until that agency's dissolution in 1968. Since the Harrison Act was nominally a revenue measure, enforcement of it was vested in the Department of the Treasury. Here a relatively small group of zealous officials and agents were assembled; they attacked the "traffic in drugs" with skill, diligence, and an almost religious fervor. They regarded anyone who dealt in narcotic drugs—importer, distributor, street vendor, and user—as criminals, and they regarded physicians as dangerously "soft" on drug users and felt that, unless carefully policed, they would coddle addicts. In 1930, these men were subsumed administratively by a new unit designated the Bureau of Narcotics.

The bureau was never a large organization. Even in 1964 when public concern over drug abuse was high, and the government, in response, had made one of its standard promises to wage an "all-out war" on this problem, the bureau had a budget of only 5.5 million dollars and just 290 agents in the field to conduct its extensive domestic and foreign activities (1). Though small in size, the bureau's influence was great. In matters pertaining to drug abuse, the bureau's voice prevailed in Congress, in part because its technically accurate, but incomplete views of the drug user stood unchallenged by the medical profession as a group.

In the 1920's, the law was enforced with particular vigor against physicians. After successful prosecution of several physicians who had actually been trafficking illegally in narcotic prescriptions, treasury agents arrested a number of physicians, notably in New York City, who had been experimenting with heroin maintenance as one aspect of a rehabilitation program for narcotic addicts. These arrests were made despite the fact that federal law (the Harrison Act and subsequent amendments) permitted physicians to prescribe narcotics for "legitimate medical purposes" and in the face of a Supreme Court ruling in 1925 that physicians could administer moderate amounts of drugs "in order to relieve conditions incident to addiction." In the absence of effective opposition from the medical profession, the Treasury Department, utilizing certain earlier and more restrictive interpretations of the act by the Supreme Court, promulgated the following regulation: *"An order purporting to be a prescription issued to an addict or habitual user of narcotics, not in the course of professional treatment but for the purpose of providing the user with narcotics sufficient to keep him comfortable by maintaining his customary use, is not a prescription within the meaning and intent of the act; and the person filling such an order, as well as the person issuing it, may be charged with violation of the law."* Because no recognized medical group was able or willing to provide authoritative definitions of what "legitimate medical purposes" or appropriate "professional treatment" might be in cases of drug abuse, this regulation effectively limited a practitioner's options in the management of a narcotic addict; he could not, for example, evaluate the efficacy of psychotherapy combined with narcotic maintenance. The bureau rigorously enforced this regulation and obtained convictions for a number of physicians (2). Officials of the bureau reacted vehemently to any attempts at management of addicts on an ambulatory basis, for they felt that such attempts were not rehabilitative but served only to maintain an addiction (1). During this period, it apparently did not seem incongruous to either officials of the bureau or to most physicians for law enforcement officials to usurp the practitioner's role of determining what modalities of treatment might be most efficacious in a particular medical disorder.

In the case of marihuana, the ability of the Federal Bureau of Narcotics to influence public and congressional opinion was strikingly demonstrated. In the mid-1930's marihuana came to be brought into this country in significant quantities, particularly by sailors entering ports on the Gulf of Mexico. This was a period when the exploits of gangsters, particularly bank robbers, were reported regularly on radio and on the front pages of the nation's newspapers. The country was said to be in the grip of an unprecedented "crime wave." Once the prevalence of the "marijuana vice" among lawbreakers was established, it was concluded by law enforcement agencies that many of the crimes were committed by "criminals who relied on the drug to give them a false courage and freedom from restraint" (3, p. 31). Law enforcement agencies, among which the bureau was prominent, issued much misinformation about marihuana, particularly in regard to its supposed ability to provoke criminal behavior. The campaign was successful in that a number of states enacted laws in 1935 and 1936 making possession of marihuana a legal offense (3, p. 37). The bureau persuaded Congress to enact the Federal Marihuana Act or Marihuana Tax Act in 1937. Ostensibly a revenue measure, the act imposed a tax on marihuana sales; in actuality, its definitions of those who might legally sell or possess marihuana precluded almost all licit commerce in *Cannabis* products and enabled agents of the bureau to arrest anyone possessing marihuana or hashish, which was, from the outset, the bureau's probable goal. The United States has since paid dearly for the zeal and lack of biomedical knowledge the bureau exhibited on this occasion. The untruths that the bureau disseminated about the effects of marihuana, particularly the ones likely to capture public interest and create concern, such as the supposed provocation of criminal behavior and the arousal of sexuality, have persisted to this day. As a result, the current American view of the marihuana problem is seriously distorted. *Most* people do not assault, rape, or kill others as a result of using marihuana, they do not become psychotic as a result of its effects, and it is not a potent aphrodisiac. Because these lurid and largely unrealistic fears have been implanted in the public mind, and still continue to be, a rational evaluation of the magnitude of the threat posed by marihuana abuse is most difficult to achieve.

The Bureau of Narcotics has pointed with pride to the marked drop in the incidence of narcotic addiction in America that occurred between the two world wars. They cite, by way of example, the fact that, whereas one in every 1500 draftees in World War I was rejected for military service for reasons of narcotic addiction, only one in 10,000 draftees was rejected on these grounds in World War II. Though we believe that vigorous enforcement of anti-narcotic laws by the bureau accounted in part for the decline in this period, we wonder if other factors did not also play important roles. Prohibition (the Volstead Act) was in force throughout much of this period; this law was similar in format to the Harrison Act, and both were enforced by agents of the Treasury Department (in insufficient numbers for the national need in both instances). Prohibition was a conspicuous failure. The supply of illicit alcoholic beverages was plentiful through the efforts of large numbers of bootleggers and smugglers, and public disrespect for the law was widespread. There appears not to have been a comparably large number of people attempting to smuggle narcotics into this country during the 1920's and early 1930's, and the public, in general, seemed to have no desire to violate the Harrison Act. The demand for narcotics was confined to a relatively small group of devoted users who were not satisfied solely with other readily available drugs, such as barbiturates, or who did not get enough of a thrill breaking the law by becoming intoxicated in a speakeasy. It is our view that the Harrison Act was not seriously tested in this period. When organized crime began the smuggling of narcotics into this country on a large scale after World War II, the inability of the bureau to stop illicit drug traffic of this magnitude quickly became evident as the incidence of heroin addiction increased sharply. The bureau's inability to be an effective deterrent at this time and subsequently is understandable. We have already noted that it possessed only 290 agents with which to wage the federal "war" against opiates, cocaine, marihuana; utilizing its operatives both domestically and in the foreign countries where opium poppies or *Cannabis* were grown or processed, it clearly lacked the manpower to combat large-scale smuggling.

Throughout the postwar period, the attitude of the Bureau of Narcotics remained uncompromisingly punitive. It sought a "massive deterrent" from Congress and received it in the Boggs Act of 1952, which made imprisonment mandatory for narcotics convictions; when this measure failed to stem the growing incidence of narcotic addiction, the only congressional response was to amend the act in 1956 to make the penalties harsher (1). The bureau praised the act for making "the risks commensurate with the profits." Though the bureau has obtained the evidence needed to convict many importers and sellers of narcotics, critics have noted that the bureau has also seemed to make little distinction between the criminals who supplied the drugs and those who used them; the few physicians who decried this attitude in the 1950's gained little public support from the profession in general.

As the incidence of drug abuse in America increased significantly in the 1950's and accelerated even more rapidly in the 1960's, the attitude of the medical profession toward this problem slowly changed. Physicians who championed the view that drug abuse was not a discrete clinical entity but merely a symptom of an underlying psychological disorder now gained a more sympathetic hearing from their colleagues. The view that hospitalization was more appropriate for drug users than imprisonment likewise gained advocates within the profession. When Dr. Vincent Dole gained federal permission to evaluate methadone maintenance as adjunct to programs of rehabilitation for narcotic addicts, the profession regained some of its lost initiative in regard to determining the most efficacious means for the management of drug users. The social stigma attached to drug abuse waned appreciably in this period; this development was probably inevitable, for, throughout this period, the number of users from middle and upper socioeconomic groups grew steadily larger. Physicians moreover became better acquainted with the little known facts about the psychopathology of drug abuse.

Under the impact of almost daily reports in the 1960's from the communications media about the growing incidence of drug abuse, particularly among adolescents and young adults, the attitude of many members of the general public changed also in the direction of conceding that perhaps rehabilitation had a place in the fight against drug abuse. This shift in public opinion was reflected in 1966 by the passage of the Narcotic Addict Rehabilitation Act by Congress, the first federal legislation to designate narcotic addiction a disease rather than a crime (4). It would be gratifying to be able to say that America had adopted an enlightened attitude about drug abuse in the decade from the harshly punitive amendments to the Boggs Act in 1956 to the Rehabilitation Act of 1966, but we feel that such a conclusion would be substantially false. The acceptance of rehabilitation programs for drug users stemmed, we think, largely from feelings of desperation and fear, even panic, about the spread of drug abuse to young people of the "middle classes." We do not think that the public has an appreciably better understanding of the phenomenon of drug abuse today than it had 25 years ago. We think that the public has concluded that, since threats of fines and imprisonment have been seemingly ineffective, it is time to try a new remedy. Though the stigma, but not the fear, attached to marihuana usage has waned, there is still an appreciable stigma in the public mind attached to other forms of drug abuse; today the drug user is envisioned as a young, irresponsible, unclean, sexually promiscuous person who despises all of the values and aspirations of "middle America." It is an accurate portrait of some drug users.

In 1968, Congress coped with the disarray existing among the various federal agencies responsible for enforcement of drug abuse laws. Up to this time, the Bureau of Narcotics dealt with offenses involving narcotics and marihuana; its agents could not, however, impound LSD, barbiturates, or amphetamines. Offenses involving these drugs fell under the provisions of the Drug Abuse Control Amendments of 1965, which were enforced by agents of the Food and Drug Administration (FDA) within the Department of Health, Education and Welfare; the responsible unit within the FDA was the Bureau of Drug Abuse Control (BDAC). As patterns of mixed drug abuse became more prevalent, and a given seller might, for example, have both LSD and marihuana in his possession, the problems of law enforcement grew more complex. To resolve the problem, Congress merged the Bureau of Narcotics and the BDAC into the Bureau of Narcotics and Dangerous Drugs (BNDD), which, for a variety of reasons, was lodged within the Department of Justice (4). Subsequently, the BNDD was replaced by the Drug Enforcement Administration (DEA); in the face of the flood of drugs coming into this country from South America, the DEA appears to be no more effective than its predecessors.

It would be premature to attempt a definitive judgment of the efficacy of the DEA at this time, but, to date at least, it does not seem to have had an appreciably greater deterrent effect on drug abuse than the separate bureaus prior to 1968 had. Expectations for an improved performance on the part of the DEA in the near future must be tempered by the following considerations. It is our impression that the DEA lacks sufficient manpower to enforce drug abuse laws effectively. When it was formed, the DEA had 600 agents, and Congress authorized employment of some 200 more; for domestic needs and foreign intelligence operations, this total strikes us as being most inadequate. In a broader view, we wonder if such laws as the Harrison Act and the Drug Abuse Control Amendments can truly be enforced in this country today at a price that is acceptable. Given the present incidence of drug abuse in America and the favorable attitude toward drug usage exhibited by what is a minority of our population but what is, in absolute numbers, a sizable group, we feel that strict enforcement of these laws could be achieved only by converting this country into a "police state." Though we do not favor repeal of the laws, our expectations are not high that enforcement of them will substantially ameliorate the problem of drug abuse.

In summary, we feel that four periods or phases have occurred in American attitudes and laws pertaining to drug abuse during the first 80 years of this century. The first period, from 1900 to 1914, was one in which no effective legal restraints were imposed on drug abuse. The problem of narcotic addiction was perhaps greater in this period than it has been at any other time in our national history. The second period began in 1914 with the passage of the Harrison Narcotic Act and lasted until about 1950. The law enforcement officer's view of the drug user as a particularly odious type of criminal deserving only punishment prevailed throughout this period. The available evidence suggests that the incidence of drug abuse in America fell sharply during this time. We feel that much of this decline should be attributed to an inexplicable falling off of interest in drug abuse and does not reflect, to any substantial degree, the activities of law enforcement. The dates of the third period cannot be set definitively; they range from a starting date of approximately 1950 until the late 1960's. The period began when organized crime started marketing grossly diluted heroin via an extensive and well-supplied network of pushers. The incidence of heroin addiction began to rise, and the law enforcement apparatus that *seemed* to have controlled drug abuse so effectively in the 1920's and 1930's was unable to quell the new epidemic. Harsher and harsher criminal penalties were legislated for drug abuse throughout the 1950's but to no avail. In the 1960's, the era of "hippies and hallucinogens" began; formerly a problem primarily of urban ghettoes, drug abuse now appeared on college campuses and in urban and suburban high schools. The public image of the drug user slowly shifted from that of a criminal pure and simple to the more complex view of a disturbed individual whose drug usage reflected deeper problems; rehabilitation rather than imprisonment was now viewed as possibly the more appropriate treatment for drug users. With this view ascendent, the third period ended, and the fourth and present one began; in this period we shall see whether further research, education of the public, and various types of rehabilitation can effect a significant decrease in the present incidence of drug abuse. As with so many diseases, attempts at prevention will probably be more rewarding in the foreseeable future than attempts at a cure.

Legalistically, the United States has experimented, deliberately or not, with several approaches to drug abuse in this century. The period of no restraints yielded a record crop of drug users. The periods of strict restraints were characterized by a decline in drug abuse when interest in this phenomenon waned and an epidemic of drug abuse later when drug popularity ballooned once again. Ironically, now that public opinion favors at least a trial of rehabilitation for drug users, the medical profession, after decades of apathy toward the problem, finds that it understands the underlying nature of drug abuse only poorly and has as yet little to offer by way of truly effective treatment.

Though we have expressed our pessimism about the prospects of controlling drug abuse by means of restrictive laws, we do not advocate repeal of the laws for several reasons. Sanctions against importers, distributors, and "street" vendors of illicit drugs will always be necessary in our opinion. More importantly, we feel that a substantial segment of the public now firmly believes that there is a "pill" (or "chemical solution") for every malady. As the drugs subject to abuse temporarily ameliorate very common maladies of the "mind and spirit," repeal of the drug abuse laws, we fear, would lead to the use of these agents on a scale even greater than exists now. A very large proportion of our population is already psychologically dependent on drugs prescribed for them by physicians; given legal access to the now-"forbidden" drugs, we are afraid that these same patients, and others, would abuse them on a scale that would be truly detrimental to the well-being of this country.

THE ENGLISH "SYSTEMS"

During the 1950's, the contrast between the incidence of narcotic addiction in America and in Great Britain was truly striking; we had a population of addicts numbered in the tens of thousands, and it seemed to be growing daily, while Britain had a relative handful of addicts, and their numbers were stable. It seemed as if the British had an almost magical technique for coping with narcotic addiction. American physicians and politicians spoke glowingly of the English "system" and advocated its adoption by this country.

No one was more surprised than the British to hear that they had a "system" for coping with narcotic addiction. In truth, the British "system" consisted of nothing more than the right of physicians to supply narcotics legally to addicts for the purpose of maintaining their addiction, providing certain stipulations were met. In the words of the Rolleston Report of 1926, addicts for whom morphine or heroin could be prescribed included "Persons for whom, after every effort has been made for the cure of addiction, the drug cannot be completely withdrawn, either because: (1) complete withdrawal produces serious symptoms which cannot be satisfactorily treated under the ordinary condition of private (general) practice; or (2) the patient, while capable of leading a useful and fairly normal life so long as he takes a certain non-progressive quantity, usually small, of the drug of addiction, ceases to be able to do so when the regular allowance is withdrawn." The report also recommended that narcotic maintenance should not be undertaken by a physician without the concurring opinion of a colleague. No physician was required to inform any governmental agency of the existence of addicts in his practice, but it was a legal offense for an addict to obtain narcotics from more than one physician. The addict population was identified and counted, however, by means of routine governmental examination of pharmacists' records.

From the 1920's until well into the 1950's, Britain never had at any one time more than a few hundred addicts; many were middle-aged, a large fraction was from the medical and paramedical professions, and most were classified as "therapeutic" addicts, i.e., they had been exposed to narcotics first in the course of medical treatment (5). Few English physicians accepted addicts as patients, and they typically did little for their patients but provide the necessary prescriptions. Most British physicians who accepted addicts as patients exhibited no more interest in or concern about the welfare of narcotic addicts than did American physicians. Some urged hospitalization on their addicted patients with a "cure" as the goal, but one, when an "addict" had returned to him after months of hospitalization for rehabilitative purposes, unhesitatingly gave that patient his usual narcotic prescription (5). Another physician prescribed 9000 mg of heroin for an addict; three days later, to replace pills "lost in an accident," he prescribed an additional 600 mg of heroin for the same patient (6, p. 66). Though the English newspapers spoke often of addicts being "under treatment," it is evident that British physicians, by and large, accorded their addicted patients little "treatment"; they were inert conduits through which the addict received his supply of narcotics.

The "dam broke" on narcotic addiction in England in the mid-1960's, as the number of new addicts identified rose from 56 in 1961 to 259 in 1965. And in 1966, 522 new addicts became known, a number greater than the total of all new addicts identified throughout the period 1945 to 1964. More alarming still were the findings that the new addicts were quite young, many were in their twenties and some in their teens, and that a high percentage of the newcomers had become addicted through illicit channels (7). Some English physicians held that the British "system," at least as manifested by the activities of some practitioners, contributed both to the spread and the persistence of heroin addiction. Physicians who laxly prescribed greater quantities of narcotics than required by addicts gave heroin addiction, according to these critics, the character of an infectious disease. Glatt observed "of the many youngsters taking hemp or amphetamines, the more adventurous begin to experiment with heroin obtained from 'registered' addicts. They become addicted and introduce a fresh circle of acquaintance to the habit." And Bewley concluded, "The chief source of illicit heroin and cocaine in this country is the sale of these drugs by addicts who have more than they need prescribed for them . . ." (7). The easy availability of narcotics from the few physicians known as "easy marks" to the addicts also impeded rehabilitation; Glatt noted that "Relapse is the more probable because of the ease with which recognised addicts can lawfully obtain drugs from their doctor" (5).

In their advocacy of the British "system," some Americans have maintained that our problems of death from overdoses and the various infectious diseases that typically plague American heroin addicts would essentially disappear if our addicts were granted legal access to pure heroin and professional equipment for injection. This argument was refuted when Bewley and his colleagues published the results of a survey of mortality and morbidity among British heroin addicts in 1968. They found that, though addicts were supplied with sterile, disposable needle-and-syringe units designed to be used only once, many addicts used the same syringe repeatedly, until it no longer functioned. Many carried the syringes loosely in coat pockets, and, though there would appear to be no need to do so, many shared their syringes with fellow addicts. The survey noted that there had been a minor epidemic of hepatitis among addicts in London in 1966. When frantic for a "fix," addicts used the nearest source of water, which might be a public toilet bowl. Most disturbing were the mortality figures. Bewley et al. calculated the mortality rate among British heroin addicts as 27 to 28 deaths per 1000 addicts per year; though no reliable rate can be computed for American addicts, Bewley's estimate is nearly twice as high as the highest estimate we have encountered for narcotic addiction mortality in this country (8). An English observer concluded, "It is certain that the British practice of prescribing maintenance doses for addicts, so that the patient knows how much he is taking (and that it is pure), has not made heroin taking safer" (9).

The findings of Bewley's group cast doubt on the validity of two common assertions about drug abuse. When narcotic addicts are asked about their preference for heroin, many reply that heroin fulfills their needs in a way that no other drug does. When an American narcotic addict adopts a pattern of multiple drug abuse, addicts and supporters of "legalized heroin" often explain that such a pattern would not be necessary if American addicts could obtain reasonably potent heroin at a nominal price and in reliable supply. The typical addict in Bewley's study, however, took 260 mg of heroin and 110 mg of cocaine daily; for 63% of the addicts, dependence on cocaine began *after* dependence on heroin had been established. Moreover, in addition to being heavy smokers, 88% of Bewley's addicted subjects used two or more additional drugs rather regularly; in addition to the cocaine already mentioned, *Cannabis* preparations, amphetamines (by mouth), and barbiturates were popular drugs of abuse.

The original British "system," which was terminated in 1968, seems to us to have suffered from flaws both in theory and practice. The "enabling act" of the British "system," the previously described Rolleston Report of 1926, stipulated that maintenance be conducted with a "nonprogressive quantity" of narcotic. If strictly adhered to, such a prescribing pattern would mean that, within weeks or several months at most, the addict would experience only weak and transient drug effects because tolerance to heroin had developed. We suspect that few addicts would remain content for long under these conditions; young addicts, in particular, would supplement the legal heroin with illegal narcotics, supplement the legal heroin with other drugs, or adopt both practices. Many British addicts, as Bewley's group discovered, did resort to a combination of legal and illegal drugs.

In practice, the British "system" failed in part because British physicians, by and large, had no greater concern about drug users than their American counterparts had. As in America, many physicians in Great Britain declined to accept drug users as patients; and those who did accept addicts, often treated their addicted patients in what appears to have been a negligent fashion. It seems that many did not even describe the technique of sterile injection to their patients (8). Most seemed to regard drug addiction as an essentially incurable condition and confined their "therapeutic" efforts to the issuing of prescriptions for narcotics. A few (probably less than ten in number) became widely known among London drug users for the liberality of their narcotic prescriptions; by providing the excess narcotics that would be sold by addicts to susceptible, non-addicted individuals, these physicians most probably contributed significantly to the spread of heroin addiction in England.

In 1968, the original British "system" was revised so that only physicians attached to addiction treatment centers or clinics could prescribe narcotics for the maintenance of addiction. Physicians who saw addicts for maintenance were required to have a special governmental license, according to The Dangerous Drug Acts of 1967, which established the regulations of the revised "system," and identity of each addict under treatment was to be reported to the Home Office. In this revised "system," a greater attempt is being made to rehabilitate the patient, though the usual problem of motivating an addict to cooperate in rehabilitative measures remains an important impediment. Some heroin addicts have been switched to maintenance on methadone, and, thus, the revised British "system" is not unlike the methadone maintenance programs currently in effect in the United States.

THE SWEDISH EXPERIMENT

The Swedish trial of legalized drug abuse was small in scale and short-lived. The intravenous abuse of central nervous system stimulants was growing in that country in the early 1960's at a rate calculated to double the population of users within 20 years and so became a matter of national concern. Lax customs regulations permitted smugglers to provide the two stimulants in greatest demand: phenmetrazine (Preludin), which was the overwhelming favorite, and methylphenidate (Ritalin). These two compounds had the reputation among Swedish users of being the most potent aphrodisiacs of all the central nervous system stimulants. In 1964, a prominent journalist decided that drug abuse was essentially a psychological disorder, which manifested itself as a craving for drugs. He concluded that the government should treat drug users as medical patients and provide the drugs they needed. He felt that it was particularly inhumane that "sick people" should have to behave like criminals purchasing smuggled drugs on a "black market"; in doing so, of course, they became legitimate targets of the police who, the journalist claimed, treated them in a harshly punitive manner. The typical attitude of the Swedish police and courts toward drug users was, contrary to the journalist's assertions, rather lenient. To promote his cause, the journalist formed the National Organization for the Help of Addicts and Abusers, and, through his access to the communications media, mounted a campaign designed to pressure the government into providing maintenance therapy for drug users. In 1965, the body governing medical practice in Sweden, the National Medical Board, succumbed to this pressure and authorized a trial of maintenance therapy. Established hastily, it was a poorly conceived trial. No funds were provided for appropriate facilities or for rehabilitation. More importantly, though the experiment was in essence modeled on the original British "system," it apparently did not occur to anyone in authority that maintenance with central nervous system stimulants is quite different from maintenance with narcotics. Though the narcotic addict can remain essentially stable with a regular supply of heroin or methadone, the psychic and physical status of most intravenous stimulant users steadily deteriorates with continued use of large doses of these drugs (6, Chap. 5).

Later in 1965, the government, in a move hardly designed to clarify its over-all position in regard to drug abuse, banned the prescription of Preludin for any purpose whatsoever.

Three physicians participated in the drug maintenance trial initially, but two withdrew shortly after its inception, in part because they were reasonably certain that a portion of the drugs they provided their patients were being given or sold to others. The remaining physician was an enthusiastic participant in the trial, to say the least. It was his belief that drug abuse could be likened to a craving for candy; give the users all the drugs they want, he said, in effect, and they will in time tire of them (6, p. 87). In the furtherance of his view, he permitted central nervous system stimulant users to write their own prescriptions, which he then signed; narcotic users were similarly accommodated with large quantities of morphine and essentially unlimited amounts of stimulants. Though the conditions of the trial limited the number of users this physician could accept as patients at any one time, he circumvented this restriction easily by providing prescriptions, on request of his patients, for their relatives, wives, and friends, though he apparently never saw any of these individuals. These so-called "satellite" patients in turn provided drugs for still other individuals. The population of drug users in Sweden doubled in the period 1965 through 1967, and it has been estimated that, during this time, about 25% of all Swedish drug users received all or a part of the drugs they used from this physician, either directly or indirectly (6, p. 88). By compiling a record of his prescriptions, critics of this physician arrived at astounding totals: in the course of a year, seeing an average of 75 users monthly, this physician had prescribed about 325 *gallons* of stimulant solutions (for intravenous use), 240,000 tablets of Ritalin, and 165,000 tablets of methamphetamine. Some narcotic addicts received prescriptions for 30,000 mg of morphine *monthly*. Nor were the participants in the trial any less criminal in their behavior; many had police records prior to the onset of drug abuse, and, during the period of the experiment, one-third of the users receiving drugs lgeally were arrested for various criminal offenses (6, p. 88).

Though the Swedish users participating in the trial received their own needles and syringes, they, like their British counterparts, ignored sterile precautions and often shared their syringes with other users. Some of them developed hepatitis presumably as a result. It was the Swedish experience that central nervous system stimulant users hospitalized for hepatitis became, in part because of drug craving, significant disciplinary problems. Some were discharged or discharged themselves and, thereafter, had to be treated on an ambulatory basis.

As the experiment progressed, criticism of it grew in volume and vehemence; the journalist and his adherents rebuffed these critics, dubbing them inhumane reactionaries bent only on the punishment of drug users. Though the National Medical Board was unhappy and apprehensive about the course the experiment was taking, it was reluctant to intervene; to do so would incur the nationally publicized wrath of the journalist and other members of the press. To establish a convincing defense of its position, the government would be obliged to present a rather detailed account of just how the experiment had progressed. Moreover, to admit defeat openly would sap public confidence in the board and perhaps impede subsequent projects for the rehabilitation of drug users. Early in 1967, however, a girl died of an overdose of narcotics. When an investigation revealed that she had obtained her morphine from one of the patients participating in the experiment, the board promptly and quietly revoked the privilege of prescribing drugs for the maintenance of users from the lone physician participating in the experiment. His patients were referred to more conservative practitioners for further treatment of drug abuse (6, pp. 93-94).

One does not need the advantage of hindsight to identify the defects in the Swedish experiment, for many of the shortcomings of the original British "system" had been publicized by 1965. Like the British, the Swedes found that merely granting users legal access to drugs via a physician does not per se substantially ameliorate the problem, and, if the participating physician has a permissive attitude toward drug abuse, a legalized drug supply can lead to an increased incidence of drug abuse. The connection between drug abuse and crime has been imperfectly analyzed by advocates of legalized maintenance; as some users have demonstrated a criminal (or antisocial) tendency prior to the abuse of drugs, it is unlikely that an official supply of drugs will subdue this tendency, and particularly so when the drugs supplied are central nervous system stimulants. No one should be surprised that the users tried to get a larger supply of drugs than they needed or that the excess was sold under conditions that, in effect, recruited new users. Many adolescents and young adults relish opportunities to "rip off the Establishment," and many are eager to share their way of life and their goals and values with the uninitiated. Any maintenance program for drug users that does not provide strict controls for drug supplies, physicians genuinely interested in the long-term welfare of the drug user, and a fully implemented rehabilitative program is, in our opinion, doomed to repeat the British and Swedish experiences.

ON THE LEGALIZATION OF MARIHUANA

"If adults can get 'high' on alcohol legally, why can't we do the same with marihuana?," a number of young people have asked. "After all, a marihuana 'high' is no worse than the effects of a couple of drinks." This is perhaps the most often-heard argument in favor of legalization of the sale and possession of marihuana: that the marihuana drug experience is no more harmful than the alcohol drug experience. This being the case, advocates of legalized marihuana ask, "How can you justify the fact that alcohol is legal and marihuana illegal?" They point out too that the illegality of marihuana leads to undesirable consequences. Because so many young people are now using marihuana, we will soon have a population of young adults quite accustomed to breaking the law and with only a cynical regard for "law and order." Repeated contact with sellers of marihuana will, in some cases, they say, expose young people to frequent invitations to try a little speed or a little heroin; this exposure, it is argued, facilitates the transition from the use of marihuana to more serious forms of drug abuse by susceptible individuals. Legalized marihuana, it is said, will also protect the user from the extremes in potency that are now encountered with "street" marihuana: on the one hand, from "marihuana" that is really catnip and on the other, from extremely potent *Cannabis* preparations or marihuana impregnated with other potent drugs. It would also eliminate the small, but known, risk of getting marihuana adulterated with rat poisons or other toxic substances.

Opponents of legalized marihuana reply that it remains to be demonstrated that the effects of marihuana are, for most people, no worse than those of alcohol. Even if this proves to be the case, they say, it is a weak argument for legalization of marihuana. It is a bit like defending murder on the grounds that capital punishment exists, for neither is desirable in the eyes of many people. America is already paying a stiff price for the legalization of alcohol, they point out; it is paid in the carnage on our streets and highways caused by drunken drivers, in the Monday absenteeism that plagues many industries, in broken homes, in the wreckage of lives, and in many other ways. If the legalization of marihuana means that the country will acquire another public health problem of the dimensions of alcoholism, opponents say, we find the prospect pretty unappealing. Other opponents ask what is going to be legalized. What is marihuana? Would you include hashish? Tetrahydrocannabinols? If not the stronger *Cannabis* preparations, how would you determine acceptable limits of potency?

A part of our position in this matter is that one of the first questions to be answered is to determine *if* marihuana can be legalized. The analogy between alcohol and marihuana, if not drawn on too extensively, can provide a useful basis for this discussion because we believe that laws legalizing the sale and regulating the use of these two substances would be similar in nature. The potency of an alcoholic beverage is determined by its content of alcohol, which can be readily measured. The potency of marihuana, according to current concepts, reflects its content of certain tetrahydrocannabinols (THC); THC can be determined, though no rapid method of analysis yet exists. In sealed containers, the potency of most alcoholic beverages remains unchanged and probably would remain so for centuries. We have no comparable assurance about the potency of marihuana; rather there is evidence to suggest that potency might decrease under certain conditions of storage. It is a matter that requires more thorough study. After decades of investigations involving thousands of subjects, there is now a known correlation between various blood concentrations of alcohol and the average degree of psychomotor impairment present. We know also how the concentration of alcohol in expired air and in urine varies as a function of blood concentrations. We possess fairly simple but acceptably accurate instruments such as the "Breathometer," which trained laymen can use to measure the alcohol in exhaled air and obtain thereby an indirect but legally acceptable determination of blood alcohol concentrations. In sum, we can define legally impermissible states of alcoholic intoxication on the basis of the probable degree of psychomotor impairment present at given concentrations of alcohol in blood. These laws can be enforced because police personnel can obtain a measure of alcohol in blood relatively rapidly and simply.

It is possible now to measure the concentrations of the active principles of marihuana (or metabolites of them) in blood only with the resources of a modern research laboratory. There is some evidence to suggest that the effects of marihuana are dose-related (see Chapter 7), but it is scanty, and observations in at least several thousand more subjects will have to be made before we can predict with reasonable assurance the possible effects of marihuana of given potency and quantity in an average subject. The relatively small amount of evidence now available suggests that most people can smoke one or two marihuana cigarettes of the range in potency typically available in America today without being profoundly disturbed, in either a non-psychotic or psychotic fashion. The degree of impairment in psychomotor performance present under these circumstances is currently being evaluated in a variety of ways, and the results of these studies should enable us to determine whether certain activities, such as driving an automobile, would be contraindicated. Many authorities suspect, on the basis of what is known now, that the degree of psychomotor impairment and incidence of such disruptive drug experiences as states of depression, panic reactions, and psychotic episodes increase as a function of the doses of THC. We would expect, for example, that users of hashish or the "stronger" marihuana cigarettes should experience on the average a more profound degree of *"Cannabis* intoxication." A preparation's potency is not the only factor to be considered, of course; equivalent doses of drug could be received if one individual used a small quantity of a relatively potent preparation and another used, within a short period of time, a suitably larger quantity of a weaker preparation.

If the sale and possession of marihuana are to be legalized, it seems to us that our legislators must be able to answer the following questions before appropriate enabling legislation can be written. What is to be legalized? Can "marihuana" be described in regard to its composition and pharmacological potency with sufficient accuracy to enable representatives of the FDA and law enforcement officers to determine when the law has been violated? What will be the potency of "legal" marihuana? To protect the consumer, will any stipulations about packaging have to be made to prevent appreciable changes in potency under usual conditions of storage? What degree of marihuana (*Cannabis*) intoxication is both safe and likely to be acceptable to the public? Can this state be described with sufficient precision so that law enforcement officials and physicians can readily identify individuals who exhibit legally impermissible degrees of intoxication?

Because the foregoing questions cannot be answered at this time, and because we feel that satisfactory legalization requires that they be answered, it is premature in our opinion to consider legalization of marihuana. Whether it would be desirable to legalize marihuana is, of course, another matter and one about which we have mixed feelings. Just as many people consume alcoholic beverages in moderation and with no harmful effects so, we suspect, do many people use marihuana. Judging by what is now known about *Cannabis* drug experiences, legal sanction against moderate marihuana smokers, it seems to us, are unnecessary. Moreover, undiscriminating enforcement of these sanctions has entailed unjustifiably harsh penalties and stigmatization of some young people, a number of whom seem to have been just moderate users. Conversely, we know that many Americans—five million of them or more—cannot restrict their intake of alcohol to a pattern of moderate use and do much damage to themselves and to others. Given access to legal marihuana, we are confident that a number of users would eventually develop severe patterns of abuse. No one can know whether the number of marihuana users exhibiting severe patterns of abuse would approximate the number of "heavy drinkers" in America today, but the possibility troubles us. In the balance, we feel that the legalization of marihuana might well do more harm than good. We can think of no practical mechanism that would ensure only moderate use of marihuana and doubt that one can be devised. (We have failed dismally to regulate the consumption of alcohol, and comparable problems would arise in the restriction of marihuana utilization.) And last, we would note that, though the FDA permits new drugs to be prescribed before their long-term effects are fully known so that presumably useful agents can be utilized without undue delay, it would be desirable, conditions permitting, to know something about the long-term effects of any agent liable to be used repeatedly over a period of years before it receives a governmental stamp of approval. The relatively recent finding of oligospermia and subnormal plasma testosterone concentrations in long-term, heavy users of marihuana (see p. 219) should remind us that much remains to be learned about the consequences of various patterns of cannabinoid usage. Probably in reaction to the repeated unfounded allegations about the behavioral effects of marihuana, there has been a strenuous effort on the part of some people to give this substance a "clean bill of health" as quickly as possible. Since marihuana has no demonstrated therapeutic effects, we think it would be highly desirable to know more about the consequences of chronic exposure to marihuana before any final decision on legalization is made. On purely medical grounds, we can think of no good reason for a hurried decision.

REFERENCES

1. Walsh, J., Narcotic and drug abuse: Report of advisory commission prescribes for old problems, new dangers. *Science* 143:662, 1964
2. Jaffe, J. H., Drug addiction and drug abuse. In: A. G. Gilman, L. Goodman, and A. Gilman, eds., *The Pharmacological Basis of Therapeutics,* ed. 6. New York: Macmillan, 1980, p. 535
3. Walton, R. P., *Marihuana. America's New Drug Problem*. Philadelphia: Lippincott, 1938
4. Walsh, J., Narcotics and drug abuse: The federal response. *Science* 162:1254, 1968
5. Glatt, M. M., Reflections on heroin and cocaine addiction. *Lancet* ii:171, 1965
6. Louria, D. B., *The Drug Scene*. New York: McGraw-Hill, 1968
7. Bewley, T., Heroin addiction in the United Kingdom (1954-1964). *Brit Med J* 2:1284, 1965
8. Bewley, T. H., O. Ben-Arie, and I. P. James, Morbidity and mortality from heroin dependence. *Brit Med J* 1:725, 1968
9. Gilder, S. S. B., The London letter: Heroin morbidity and mortality. *Canad Med Assoc J* 98:1018, 1968

INDEX

319